LAND OF MY FATHERS

D0507910

MAXIM WLETIC

Magnus Maximus — Macsen Wledig

Copyright *Gwasg y Brython and Palais Des Beaux Arts, Lyo*

LAND OF MY FATHERS

FATHERS

2000 years of Welsh history

GWYNFOR EVANS

Original hardback edition, first impression: 1974
Second impression: 1976
Third impression: 1978
Fourth impression: 1981
Fifth impression: 1984

This paperback edition produced with the kind permission
of John Penry Press, Swansea
First impression: St David's Day, 1992
Seventh impession: 2008

Cover design and back cover photograph: Y Lolfa
Front cover photograph by Anthony Griffiths

ISBN: 0 86243 265 0

Printed, published and bound in Wales
using acid-free and partly recycled paper
by Y Lolfa Cyf., Talybont, Ceredigion SY24 5AP
e-mail ylolfa@ylolfa.com
internet http://www.ylolfa.com/
tel (01970) 832 304
fax 832 782

Cyflwynedig i
FFRED FFRANSIS
ymladdwr glew dros Gymru

Translated from the Welsh

Contents

Page

CHAPTER 1. CELTIC WALES

Section

   I   The Celtic Legacy   15
  II   Background of first century Wales   19

Chapter 2. ROMAN WALES

    I   The Roman Invasion   23
   II   The Welsh Defence   24
  III   The Druids   28
  IV   Nature of the Roman Occupation   30
   V   The Military and Defence System   34
  VI   Magnus Maximus (Macsen Wledig) and
      the Roman Heritage   37

Chapter 3 WELSH WALES

    I   The Irish   42
   II   Cunedda   44
  III   Renaissance   47
  IV   Creation of Brittany   49
   V   From Brythonic to Welsh — Taliesin
      and Aneirin   51

Chapter 4 INDEPENDENT WALES

    I   A Country of Small States   56
   II   Vortigern (Gwrtheyrn)   59
  III   Myth of English Expulsion of the Welsh   63
  IV   Arthur   68
   V   Toughness of the States   69
  VI   Maelgwn Gwynedd   72
  VII   Men of the Old North   75

page

Chapter 5 CHRISTIAN WALES

I	From Elen to Cadog	81
II	Illtud and Education	86
III	Dewi (David) in the Surge	90
IV	Steeping Gwynedd and Powys in the Gospel	96
V	The Celtic Christian Community of Nations	99
VI	The Unbroken Continuity of the Tradition	103
VII	Consequences of the Christian Revolution	106

Chapter 6 FACING THE ENGLISH

I	The Saints of Bangor-on-Dee and Augustine	109
II	Cadwallon and the Welsh Defence	114
III	The End of Rheged and Gododdin	117
IV	Age of Cadwaladr	117
V	The Church of the Welsh	120
VI	Golden Age of Ireland	123
VII	Offa's Dyke and Beyond	124
VIII	The Grip of the States	126
IX	Art, Literature and Learning	128
X	Merfyn Frych	131
XI	Rhodri Mawr	136
XII	Anarawd	138
XIII	Hywel Dda	141
XLV	Age of Maredudd ab Owain	147
XV	Gruffudd ap Llywelyn	152

Chapter 7 FACING THE NORMANS

I	The Normans' Powerful Incursion	160
II	Rhys ap Tewdwr	164
III	Gruffudd ap Cynan	166
IV	Revival of National Strength	175

CONTENTS (*continued*)

		page
V	Owain Gwynedd	179
VI	The Lord Rhys	187
VII	Court Poets and Story-tellers of the Mabinogion	198
VIII	Giraldus Cambrensis and the Church Struggle	204
IX	Llywelyn Fawr (Llywelyn I)	208
X	Llywelyn ap Gruffudd (Llywelyn II)	218

Chapter 8 THE CENTURIES OF GLYNDWR AND THE UCHELWYR (NOBILITY)

I	Government by English Officials	237
II	Wars of Madog and Llywelyn Bren	240
III	Scottish Revival under William Wallace	242
IV	The Glory of the Uchelwyr (Nobility)	242
V	Dafydd ap Gwilym	246
VI	Owain Lawgoch and the Expectation of a Deliverer	250
VII	The Great Effort to Restore Freedom	252
VIII	Welsh Feuds between English Parties	271
IX	Pyrrhic Victory of the Welsh	281
X	The Great Century	286
XI	Colonialist Interlude	290

Chapter 9 "FOR EVER AND HENCEFORTH INCORPORATED AND ANNEXED   294

Chapter 10 FACING THE BRITISH

I	Treachery of the Nobility	304
II	The Loyal Remnant	309
III	The Coming of Britishness	316
IV	More Feuds between English Parties	320
V	Upholders of the Tradition	322
VI	Griffith Jones and Welsh Education	326
VII	Howel Harris and the Spiritual Revival	330
VIII	Pantycelyn	335

CONTENTS—*(continued)*

		page
IX	New Growth from Old Roots	339
X	Merthyr Insurrection: Chartists: Beca	348
XI	Treason of the Blue Books	366
XII	The Glory of the Gwerin	374
XIII	Bourgeois Victory	387
XIV	Establishing the English System	395
XV	Michael D. Jones and the National Awakening	399
XVI	Decay	416

Chapter 11 WALES ENDURES 443

INDEX 454

Illustrations

	Page
Magnus Maximus	*Frontispiece*
Moridunwm — Roman Carmarthen	16
A Roman Villa at Llanilltud Fawr (Llanwit Major); Voteporex Stone; The Nevern Cross	17
Pentre Ifan Cromlech; The Dying Gaul; The Trawsfynydd Tankard	24
Celtic Head; Tal-y-llyn Copper Plaque; Silver Brooch from Pont-y-saer, Anglesey; Llangenau hand bell	25
Bednoc Stone, Margam Mountain; Cross of Enniaun Plaque from Llyn Bach, Anglesey; Dog and Beast relief from Caerleon	32
Penally Cross, Pembrokeshire; Conbelin's Cross, Margam; The Cross of Grutne, Margam	33
Saint David by John Petts	80
Page from the Book of Kells	81
Saint David's Cathedral	96
David the Waterman Pray for Wales — by David Jones	97
The Wales of "The Heptarchy"	160
The Lord Rhys	161
Page from the Chronicle of the Princes	176
Carreg Cennen Castle; Coins minted by Hywel Dda; Owain Glyndwr's Great Seal	177
Page from Black Book of Carmarthen	192
Giraldus Cambrensis	193
Strata Florida	208
Dolbadarn Castle; Dynevor Castle	208
Llywelyn II	209
Harlech Castle; Wales 1267: The Montgomery Treaty Carrying the head of Llywelyn II through London Owain Glyndwr's Parliament House, Machynlleth	224
Llywelyn II Memorial Stone at Cilmeri	225
Owain Glyndwr War 1400-1403; Owain Glyndwr War 1404-1409; William Wallace	240

ILLUSTRATIONS (*continued*)

	page
Owain Glyndwr	241
Snowdon in Winter — by Kyffin Williams	256
Caernarvon Castle and Town, 1750	257
The Screen, Llananno Church, Radnorshire	288
Wales 1500: Crown Lands	289
"The Act of Union", 1536	304
Frontispiece of the 1588 Bible	305
Griffith Jones	320
James Davies' School, Grosmont, Gwent, 1815-48	321
Williams Pantycelyn; Merthyr Tydfil, 1830; Pontypridd — built by William Edwards in 1755; Penillion Singing near Conway—by J. C. Ibbetson	336
Chartist Attack on Newport, 1839	337
Three Chartist Leaders	352
Rebecca attacking a toll-gate	353
Welsh living room	368
Merthyr Tydfil about 1840	369
Composer's ms. of National Anthem of Wales; Lliwedd; Welsh Not; Nantgarw Procelain Plate	384
Salmon Leap on the Rhondda c. 1815	385
Wattstown, Rhondda in the 1920's	385
Michael D. Jones; Thomas Gee	400
David Lloyd George — by Augustus John	416
Wales 1916: recruiting cartoon	417
O. M. Edwards; Wales 1927: unemployed miners marching to London; Aneurin Bevan	432
Saunders Lewis	433
Wales 1947: Protest against War Office seizure of Land in Welsh-speaking Wales; Wales 1971: incident in language campaign; Capel Garmon fire-dog from first century; Part of Cardiff Civic Centre	452
20th century scene on Carmarthenshire Black Mountain—Freedom	453

Preface

I WROTE this personal view of Welsh history to fill a gap. The story of the Welsh past has not been narrated in one volume since Sir O. M. Edwards's *Wales* was published in the *Story of the Nations* series in 1901. Since then we have had the fruit of work of a growing body of historians in valuable and sometimes splendid studies of periods, persons or themes. These scholars have placed Wales deeply in their debt. I have relied completely on their research, although sometimes I have departed from their interpretation of the facts.

The history of Cymru has an astonishing continuity and unity. Its unity derives from the persistence through the centuries of a unique civilisation, and from the effort made in every generation to defend and transmit it. In the heroic periods the whole community seems to be involved in this effort. At other times the loyal remnant were as few as they were in the lean days of ancient Israel, whose history has been far better known to the Welsh people than that of their own nation. But no generation has been without men and women of deep commitment who strove to secure the conditions in which the national civilisation could endure.

I called the original book *Aros Mae* (It Endures), because Wales still lives. Her civilisation is in ruin in much of the land today, it is true. The policy of assimilation which inspired the Act of Union, 1536, has had much (though incomplete) success in destroying the language which is the main vehicle of the traditional culture. Television may yet complete its success. Only in faith can one assert that *Hen wlad fy nhadau* (the old land of my fathers) will have a national future. Yet when one considers the immensity of the power of the psychological and structural pressures directed against this vulnerable little nation, and the sad apostasy of so many of her own people, the survival of any measure of her traditional life is something of a miracle.

The lyric by Ceiriog of which *Aros Mae* are the first two words sings of "new shepherds on these old mountains". Numbers of this new generation are responding to the challenge of the task of rebuilding on the ancient foundations. They seek to create in Wales the conditions of a community of hope — a fair society that shall be both Welsh and free.

I am deeply grateful to the friends who have made the publication of this English version possible. It was on the field of the National Eisteddfod at Bangor in August 1971 that Mr. and Mrs. Raymond Garlick generously offered to undertake the arduous work of translation, Mrs. Garlick to make the actual translation and Mr. Garlick to edit it. Mrs. Garlick has translated the whole, but when pressure of academic work prevented Mr. Garlick from continuing his editorship the able help of Miss Jennifer Thomas was enlisted. Between them the three have completed the heavy task as a labour of love. Professor Gwyn Williams of Trefenter has beautifully translated the poetry in the book.

Mr. Tegwyn Jones has not only helped again with the photographs, but has undertaken once more the onerous task of compiling the index.

Mrs. Margaret Davies and the late Professor Alun Davies, whose untimely death was such a severe loss to Welsh society and historical scholarship, most generously read through, and made corrections in, the manuscript.

Celtic Wales

I. THE CELTIC LEGACY

HOWEVER tenuous traditions may appear to be, they often reveal more tenacity than political institutions which seem to be strong enough to last for ever. When the Roman Empire was at the height of its power the Celts of Gaul were taking delight in the arts of public speaking and poetry. Nora Chadwick tells us:

> 'Gaulish oratory was the most highly prized in the empire . . . Love of poetry is perhaps the characteristic of the ancient Gauls which impressed itself most deeply on the Romans; and of course native Gaulish poetry was purely oral.'

According to Lucian in the second century A.D. the Celts believed that the power of eloquence was stronger than physical force. Seven hundred years after the disappearance of the temporal western empire of Rome, Giraldus Cambrensis could note in the twelfth century the Welshman's gift of speech:

> 'Nature gave them all without distinction, from the poorest of the poor to the greatest men, boldness of speech and confidence when answering in the presence of princes and noblemen, in every vicissitude.'

Like other customs among the Celts of two thousand years ago, that capacity to enjoy poetry and public speaking still characterizes the life of Wales today.

Scholars now can discuss the Celts as one people and discover that they have much in common, in character and culture, no matter which country they come from — Brittany or Scotland, Wales or Ireland. These common characteristics are revealed in their history and their religion, their literature and their art, their virtues and their weaknesses. It was from the Greeks who had settled in the south of France that the Celts of the middle of the continent derived many of the best characteristics of their culture. They brought these with them when they crossed — often through Brittany and Devon — to Wales. The last wave came as a result of the attacks of the Teutonic tribes on Gaul a little before Julius Caesar came to Britain.

The culture of Wales is Celtic, although the Iberians — the neolithic people who were a much larger element in the population at the beginning of our history — left the stamp of their character upon it. Like the Cornish and the Bretons, the Welsh are Brythonic Celts: the Irish, the Scots and the Manxmen are Goidelic Celts. The Celts are people who shared a common language and culture, and we have seen how in their early culture language held a central position. In modern times Welsh culture has been nowhere more radiant than in its poetry, and its great preachers and statesmen are proof enough that rhetoric has not disappeared from our land. Down the ages the arts which received the most careful attention of the Welsh were those based on language. To a greater degree than in most other countries, the history of Wales is the history of its language.

The Celts were religious people and respected education, but very little is known of either their education or their religion. They believed that they were surrounded by supernatural beings, and these they worshipped in the open air, in groves and glades rather than temples: one might almost say they were nature worshippers. Rivers and mountains were sacred to them. The enchantment of legend has preserved the names of some of their gods, like Lleu and Nudd: Nudd was worshipped in the pagan temple built by the Irish in Caer-ludd (Lydney) in the fourth century A.D.

One important element in this pre-Christian religion was the mother-cult, to which the enduring name Moel Famau still bears witness. This reflects the honour in which women were held. The Celts believed in reincarnation — which was in keeping with their belief in the immortality of the soul — and to women was accorded the august role of mediating in the rebirth of the souls of the dead. Women were sufficiently

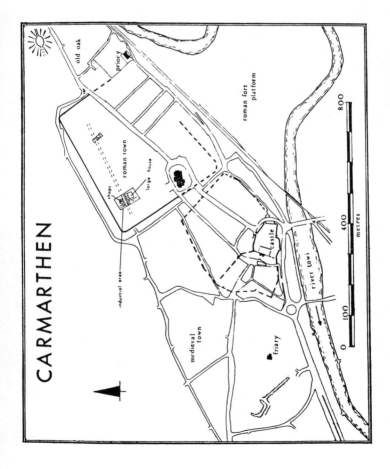

Moridunum—
Roman Carmarthen

A Roman Villa at Llanilltud Fawr (Llantwit Major)

Imaginative reconstruction by Alan Sorrell Copyright National Museum of Wales

The Nevern Cross

Voteporex stone at Carmarthen Museum

respected to get the highest possible education in the days of
the Roman Empire. This is reflected in Nora Chadwick's
observations about women letter-writers:

> 'Some of the most interesting letter writers of the time are women —
> Hedibia, the last of the line of the druids of Armorica (Britanny) whose
> name has come down to us, and who corresponded from her home in
> Bordeaux with St. Jerome in Bethlehem; St Paula writing from
> Bethlehem to Marcella in Rome; Bassula writing from Trêves to
> Sulpicius Severus in Aquitania; Palladia, the wife of Salvian, from
> whom we have the first intimate domestic letter of the period, writing
> apparently from Marseilles to her parents in the North. Therasia, the
> Spanish wife of St Paulinus of Nola, signs eleven of her husband's
> letters jointly with him — some of them to the most important
> ecclesiastics of the day, St Augustine among them . . . These Gaulish
> women were in all respects as well educated and as intelligent as the
> men.'

Some of the Celts accepted Christianity early enough to
have a place in the New Testament such as the Galatians whom
Paul addressed. Three centuries after the time of Paul, Jerome
referred to the fact that the Celts had a language other than
Greek and that this language resembled one spoken on the
banks of the Moselle, which flows into the Rhine. This
language was probably related to Brythonic. Some might see
in the Epistle which Paul wrote to the Galatians a resemblance
between the latter and the modern Welsh. Paul's words
suggest that they lacked stamina and the ability to persevere.
'I am astonished,' he says, 'at the promptness with which you
have turned away from the one who called you and have
decided to follow a different version of the Good News.' He
was afraid that they had turned their backs not only on the
religion he had given them but on their great friendship for
him personally, and that he who had been so beloved by them
was now regarded as an enemy. 'You would even have gone
so far as to pluck out your eyes and give them to me,' he says
of their relationship in the past. What impelled Paul to write
to these Celts was their instability. This is reminiscent of the
remarks of Giraldus Cambrensis about the Welsh of the
twelfth century:

'It is a nation which is called back from an intention or action already begun with the same ease as it is sent to undertake any adventure.'

More than one writer of antiquity gives a vivid description of the character of these people. We gather that the Celts were fond of going to war, that they were brave and lively of spirit. There was nothing devious in their nature: on the contrary, they were a very direct and proud people, and childishly boastful — even bombastic. Strabo says that this pride made them unbearable in victory and totally disheartened when they had lost. They loved decoration and bright colours. They were concerned for their appearance, keeping their hair long — at least among the chiefs, and shaving their beards, leaving a moustache to grow over their lips. They had quick minds and according to Diodorus they learnt easily, having great respect for their philosophers, theologians and poets. They are said to have been sociable people, fond of feasting and extremely hospitable. Most of these characteristics are given in Giraldus's description of the Welsh of the Middle Ages.

For two centuries these were the most powerful people in Europe, and their power stretched from Galatia across the middle of the continent to Gaul and Galicia in Spain and these islands. In 390 B.C. the Celts heavily defeated the Romans in the battle of the Allius and in 389 sacked Rome. 'About 300 B.C.,' says Grenier, 'Celtic power is found at its zenith, as their inexhaustible energy and their population indicate.' They were too scattered a people, unable to concentrate their strength, and under pressure from Rome on the one hand and the Teutonic tribes on the other they lost their power and their freedom. Their power on the continent finally came to an end when Gaul was conquered by Rome in 58 B.C. Only six Celtic peoples remain now, those of Brittany, Ireland, Cornwall, the Isle of Man, Scotland and Wales. Of these only two are in possession of any national freedom, and the continuation of the national life of all of them is in the balance, with Ireland in a stronger position than the others.

II. THE BACKGROUND OF FIRST CENTURY WALES

WALES was Celtic in language and culture and form of government, although part of the population belonged to the different and more primitive race that lived in the country before the coming of the Celts. Signs of their life remain in stone, in bronze and bone, in pottery and racial memories. The oldest human artifact found in Wales is the stone axe used near Cardiff about two hundred thousand years ago, and no one lived here permanently at that time nor for thousands of years after. In the Traeth Lafar and Cantre'r Gwaelod legends there are vague memories which suggest that the coastal outline of Wales was different from that of today. It is to the Neolithic or late Stone Age that the strongest early settlements belong, especially in Anglesey, the Llŷn peninsula and Pembrokeshire. We can gather from the many graves and remains of dwellings found on the coast of the Irish Sea that it was over the sea that these settlers came. For that matter, it was from across the sea that most people came to settle in Wales: the sea has almost as important a part in our history as the mountains. The sea kept Wales in touch with Ireland and Brittany and Spain. There was much more communication between Wales and Europe before it became incorporated into England than in the centuries after this event.

Graves in the form of a ship have been found, again suggesting that the sea had an important place in the mind or subconscious of the people who made them. To those who came here over the sea, Wales was the land of the far west, looking towards the setting sun. Perhaps an abiding memory of this gave rise to the appearance, a millennium or two later, of the idea commonly found in Welsh and Irish legend of an Island of the Blest across the sea — like the Avalon to which Arthur was so tenderly conveyed.

Yn y fro ddedwydd mae hen freuddwydion
A fu'n esmwytho ofn oesau meithion;
Byw yno byth mae pob hen obeithion,
Yno, mae cynnydd uchel amcanion;
  Ni ddaw fyth i ddeifio hon golli ffydd,
Na thro cywilydd, na thorri calon.

In that happy region there are old dreams
that soothed the fears of lengthy aeons;
there live for ever all the old hopes,
there is success for all high intentions;
  no loss of faith will cause its blighting,
  no shameful turn, and no heart breaking.

These earliest inhabitants were rather short, slight, dark people who came from the region of the Mediterranean — less muscular than those who followed them during the first and second Bronze Ages. The physical characteristics of these Neolithic people are still prevalent in the land. The newcomers depended mainly on rearing stock, as did the Celts after them, and as Welsh farmers do to this day. It was from animals that they got the raw materials of their domestic crafts — leather, wool and bone, and probably their small industries. The axe factory found on the slopes of Penmaen-mawr shows that they were not short of industrial and commercial skill on quite a large scale.

The most striking remains of the Stone Age are the cromlechs, of which there are about seventy to be found in all parts except mid-Wales. These are the graves of the chiefs, the great of their day. We know nothing about any of these people, about their exploits or their ideas, their triumphs or their sufferings, nothing about their language; but the siting of their graves suggests that a primitive culture had spread over Wales by about 2000 B.C. Standing in silence today, they testify to one thing about their builders: life must have had great value in their eyes for them to have bestowed such solemnity upon death.

Man's attempt to find completeness of meaning and a

purpose in life accounts also for the principal characteristics of
the early Bronze Age. By now people were living on
1,800   the higher ground, and on some of the hills there are
1,000   still to be seen stone circles that had a religious purpose
B.C.   long before Iolo Morganwg borrowed the idea for his
Gorsedd of Bards of the Isle of Britain. The people of
this period showed their engineering ability by moving large
blocks of blue stone from Pembrokeshire to Stonehenge. They
showed a still stranger skill in the astronomy which was the
basis of their calendar. At the top of the Black Mountain, not
far from Llyn y Fan, stands a line of spaced stones placed there
in that age in such a way as to be used for making complicated
calculations in scientific study of the movements of the moon.
In a review of *Megalithic Lunar Observations* by A. Thom,
Richard Atkinson writes:

'The degree of correspondence between the deduced ancient values
and those of today is far too great to admit the hypothesis of chance. . .
We are accustomed to the idea that observational astronomy began
with the Babylonians in the first millenium B.C. and that they recorded
their sightings of eclipses and the like in a rather tiresome form of
reed-impressed script on clay tablets. What are we to make of the idea
that a thousand years earlier the barbarians of Bronze Age Britain
were recording and preserving astronomical data of much greater
accuracy and refinement without any recorded script at all? How were
they doing it? The answer, presumably, is that they were doing it by
word of mouth, and that they were capable of, and accustomed to
reducing the tables of the Nautical Almanack or the astronomical
Ephemeris to something that approximated to the epic form.'

The earliest Celts probably arrived here about 1000 B.C., the
first of several waves who came between then and the Roman
conquest. These centuries saw great technical advances,
1,000   particularly in the working of metal to make food
B.C.   implements as well as military weapons. They learnt
to make iron, and the story of the maiden of Llyn y
Fan embodies a reminder in legend of the dangerous magic
which was attributed to iron by the people of an earlier culture.
Among the bronze and iron objects of this period which show
craft and artistic talent there are two particularly rich collections

found in two lakes, one in Anglesey and the other in Glamorgan. The Llyn Cerrig Bach hoard was found during the construction of an aerodrome for the R.A.F., and it was when they were adapting Llyn Fawr, near Rhigos, to make a reservoir for the Rhondda that workmen found the objects there. It used to be stated dogmatically that these things were never made in Wales — or in Ireland either — and that they came from England. This belief has now been shattered: first it was proved that the Irish did make them and then, with the positive proof of Tal-y-llyn, Merioneth, and of many other sites, came evidence that in Wales too there were talented metal workers at least two or three centuries before Christ. These craftsmen used to travel from one patron to another, as the poets did later on, carrying the tools of their craft with them.

The chiefs and the soldiers, the bards and the craftsmen: it was these people who constituted the Establishment, as we call it today. Government was in their hands. They were Celts, and government was Celtic, although the majority of the people of Wales came from a different race. It was the Establishment, which included the government — the chief or the king and his officials and councillors — who decided the language and culture of the people; and so Celtic language and culture were supreme. Frequently in the history of Wales, and of all the Celtic peoples, a similar situation has arisen in which it is the character of the Establishment that decides the language and culture of the people.

Roman Wales

I. THE ROMAN CONQUEST

SUCH were the people who were living in the land we call Wales when Julius Caesar invaded Britain in 55 and 55 and 54 B.C. Although they were out on the fringes of the Celtic world and completely outside the Roman 54 Empire, the Brythons of Britain and the Celts of B.C. Ireland were in touch with Gaul, and it was this relationship which lay behind Caesar's decision to attack. On his second attempt he succeeded in getting as far as the valley of the Thames, but nearly a century went by before anything was heard of Wales. Wales entered 43 the light of history when the Emperor Claudius A.D. decided to overrun Britain and make it part of his empire.

Four legions, composed of perhaps fifty thousand soldiers, crossed the Channel in 46 A.D. In less than a decade 46 the country east of the Severn and south of the A.D. Humber and Trent was occupied, leaving the legions the task of conquering Wales, where the hill people lived a simpler pastoral life.

As the Irish and the Danes, the English and the Normans learnt after them, the Romans found the task of subduing Wales an extremely difficult one. The Welsh had obvious advantages when fighting to defend their country. They were helped by its mountainous nature, and they built many strong forts on the tops of hills. Because they lived scattered over a countryside without any towns, or even large farms and barns, they could move easily and take their possessions with them. To these advantages was added the tight society of a community that valued its independence highly, and had the spirit to defend it to the end. What Giraldus said of the Welsh of the twelfth century may be applied to the people of Wales of the first century:

> 'They aim at defending their country and their freedom; they battle for their country, they labour for freedom: for these it seems sweet not only to fight with the sword but also to give their lives.'

It is the moral factor which decides the fate of nations: man's spirit can prove greater than the power of leviathan. A nation is swiftly overcome if its spirit is weak; but with unyielding determination it can vanquish powers that appear to be utterly invincible. So much is learnt from the history of Wales.

II. THE WELSH DEFENCE

DURING the four centuries before the Romans came, the laborious and skilful work of the Welsh in building hilltop forts is remarkable. Lasting down to our own time, they are more numerous in Wales than in any other part of Britain, the most important remains we have of pre-Roman Welsh life. By 1960 five hundred and eighty of them had been discovered; of these three hundred and forty are more than an acre in area, and sixteen are over twenty acres. Long before it was the land of the castles Wales was the land of hill forts. Since so little archaeological work was done in Wales in the past, they are still coming to light. For example, in the west and south-west of Carmarthenshire, in a region which makes up one-fifth of the county, 74 hill forts and enclosures have already been found. It can be gathered from this that the population of Wales was probably larger in pre-Roman times than in the Middle Ages, and probably heavier than the population of mid and east England — where there were more bogs and forests — an important factor to remember when considering the fate of the Brythonic language in England. Some of them

Pentre Ifan Cromlech near Preselau Hills

Copyright *Alewyn Evans*

The Dying Gaul

The Trawsfynydd Tankard

Celtic Head from the Roman Town of Caer-went

Tal-y-llyn Copper Plaque

Silver Brooch from Pont-y-saer,
Anglesey

show extraordinary building ability. The small forts, mainly in the west, have been compared with castles; and the bigger ones with fortified towns or villages. Where there are remains of circular stone houses, the number of people living in them can be estimated. For example it is calculated that about 1,400 people lived in the big 28-acre fort of Garn Boduan; for a fort of seven acres on Conwy mountain the estimate is between 150 and 300. Only a very few of these great monuments of the Iron Age have been excavated yet, but enough has been done to show that there was trade between these pre-Roman Welsh and people living around the Mediterranean.

Because of these advantages Wales was better equipped for self-defence than the rest of the region south of Scotland. This remained true throughout the millennium that followed. When the Romans left, three and a half centuries later, Wales again was to be most successful in defending itself. Since the Roman conquest of England had not diminished the independent and militant spirit of the Welsh, under Ostorius the Romans decided that their safety demanded the conquest of Wales. Its population at that time consisted of five peoples, who were distributed roughly in this way: Silurians in Monmouth, Glamorgan and Breconshire; Ordovicians in mid-Wales; Deceangles in Flint and north Denbighshire; Venodotians in north-west Wales (Venodotia is the Latin form of Gwynedd); and Demetians in Cardigan, Pembroke and Carmarthenshire. The economic regions correspond remarkably closely to the territories of these peoples.

Another striking fact to be remembered is that the eastern border, which is the only land border Wales has, was close to the line later taken by Offa's Dyke and the edge of modern Wales. Of very few nations can it be said, as it can be said of the Welsh, that their territory has remained the same for most of the last three millennia. The probable result of this unusual Welsh situation is that it can be claimed that the majority of the Welsh of this generation are descended from the people who inhabited the country when Ostorius and his legions came here in 47 A.D.

Recorded Welsh history begins about fifteen years after the crucifixion of Christ with the attack of Ostorius upon the Silurians and the Ordovicians. These were strong and stubborn people, led by Caradog (Caratacus) the first national hero of the Welsh and the first figure in our history whom we can (thanks to Tacitus) see clearly. Although Caradog was not from the land that would be known as Cymru (Wales) he spoke the Brythonic tongue, and in identifying himself with the defenders of the threatened parts of Wales he took his place in Welsh history. The family of Caradog came to England from Gaul some time after the invasions of Julius Caesar, and his father, Cynfelyn (Cunobelinus, Shakespeare's Cymbeline) — the strongest of the Brythonic kings in England — created a large kingdom in the south of that country. After its swift conquest Caradog spent three years among the Welsh, who were already being driven together by the Roman threat, preparing their resistance by his leadership of the Silurians and also the Ordovicians.

47- 52 A.D.

The only part of the fight against the people of east Wales which has been recorded is the last great battle — which was fought somewhere in the north-east, perhaps near the upper Severn. Caradog went there, according to Tacitus, because he could not hope to make an earlier stand, 'with his smaller number of soldiers against a well disciplined army'. During centuries of fighting the Welsh later learnt to avoid pitched battles, and had Caradog stuck to the guerilla tactics which proved so effective afterwards, up to the days of Glyndŵr, no doubt the Romans would have had even greater difficulty in conquering the Welsh. However, he decided to stand and fight on the field of battle, and gathered behind him (says Tacitus) 'everyone who considered peace with Rome another name for servility'. This is how Tacitus describes the first recorded battle between the Welsh and their foes:

'He (Caradog) chose a spot protected by high, rocky hills, and in the place where the hills were less steep he built a rampart of large

stones piled on top of each other; a river flowed through the plain,
its fords and shallows of uncertain depth. Ostorius was very surprised
by the fearless attitude of the Brythons and the spirit which permeated
the whole army. He saw a river to cross, a fence of stakes to throw
down, a high slope to climb, and every part defended by a great
number, but the Roman soldiers were impatient to attack. The sign
was given. The river was crossed without much difficulty. The struggle
by the fence of stakes was stubborn, but the Brythons had to yield at
last and they fled to the tops of the hills. They were followed eagerly by
the Romans. The legionaries and not only the light military pushed
their way to the top of the hill after firing a shower of spears. Since the
Brythons had neither breastplates nor helmets, they could not continue
to fight. The legions carried all before them. The victory was decisive.'

Caradog managed to escape to the Brigantes, who inhabited
what is now Lancashire and Yorkshire, but there he was
betrayed to the Romans. With his wife, his daughter and his
brother, he was taken as a prisoner to Rome, and marched in
chains in a victory procession through the streets of the
capital. Tacitus describes his brave and dignified behaviour.
When he came before the tribunal he spoke thus:

'To you the situation is full of glory; to me full of shame. I had
arms and soldiers and horses; I had sufficient wealth. Do you wonder
that I am reluctant to lose them? Ambitious Rome aims at conquering
the world: does the whole human race therefore have to bend to the
yoke? For years I resisted successfully: I am now in your hands. If
vengeance is your intention, proceed: the scene of bloodshed will
soon be over, and Caradog's name will fall into oblivion. If you spare
my life, I shall be an eternal memorial to the mercy of Rome.'

His words and his demeanour made such a deep impression on
the Emperor Claudius that a full pardon was bestowed upon
this first Brython of whom we have a proper picture.

Although the men of the south and the centre of Wales had
lost this great battle, and also their leader, the war was not
over. The defence continued. Ostorius built a permanent
station at Caerleon-on-Usk, which developed within a
generation into the great legionary fortress whose remains we
can see today; nearby the town of Caer-went was built. He
died when the war was only half-way through. Before his
successor Allus Gallus arrived, the Welsh attacked fiercely,
causing heavy losses to the second legion, and the Romans did

not succeed in progressing far under Gallus, nor Veranius who came after him. It was Suetonius Paulinus who left the greatest mark on Wales to this date. It was in the direction of Gwynedd that he moved first. He aimed at Anglesey in particular, overcoming a number of Welsh forts on the way, and rebuilding at Caerhun and Caernarfon. He hoped, said Tacitus, 'by subduing the warlike spirit of the Brythons to emulate the brilliant success of Corbulo in Armenia'.

59–
61
A.D.

III. THE DRUIDS

WHY did Suetonius hope to subdue the spirit of the Welsh by attacking Anglesey? What was there in Anglesey that gave them strength? These apposite questions find an answer in Tacitus. He says that the people of the island were warlike and gave sanctuary to others of like temper. Although he does not refer to the natural mineral resources, their presence may have been an additional reason for trying to conquer the island. Tacitus mentions the druids there in particular. It was they who sustained the spirit of resistance among the Brythons.

Who were these druids who played such an important part in the life of the Celts? In the past people have been inclined to accept uncritically the picture of them given by Julius Caesar and other hostile witnesses from the Roman world, who considered them to be dangerous nationalists. Political considerations coloured their opinions. These explain the emphasis upon the supposedly evil customs of these opponents, and lie behind the savage mockery which has succeeded in creating an image of the druids as cruel and uncivilised beings. It must be said that the fictions of Iolo Morganwg and the extreme romanticism of his followers have done nothing to restore their reputation in Wales. According to this view they were priests in whose religious cult, human sacrifice in forest groves played a part. Without denying that practices of this kind were found among the Celts, scholars now doubt whether the druids had any part in them. In her book *The Druids*,

Nora Chadwick comes to the conclusion that they were the
intelligentsia of the Celts, their teachers, philosophers and
judges, entrusted with the education of the young. Everything
in early education was delivered by word of mouth, without
putting a single note upon parchment, without anything being
read or written. Their education was committed to memory
in courses that could last for many years, and by summarizing
it in poetry which was easier to remember than prose. 'It is
said' (Julius Caesar observed of their education) 'that they
learn there a great number of verses (*versuum*). And some
remain in this discipline for twenty years.' It was this custom
of keeping everything in the memory and not writing
anything down which caused the fame of the druids of Gaul
to retreat before Latin culture. In Mrs. Chadwick's view,

> 'Druids were the native intellectual class of the early Celtic peoples
> of Gaul, the earliest teachers and philosophers in Europe known to us
> outside the classical world. Their interests were lofty and concerned
> with contemplation of the natural universe, and they, perhaps first of
> the spiritual teachers of Europe, declared souls to be immortal . . . We
> cannot fail to be impressed by their preoccupation with spiritual and
> intellectual matters. It is, in part, this deep concern with spiritual and
> intellectual matters which constitutes the chief lasting claim of the
> druids on our attention. Education was in their hands, and rarely has
> it been carried on with more sustained and prolonged assiduity.
> Rarely has it been devoted to matters less utilitarian or more majestic.
> Their central subjects were nature and the universe; their leading
> doctrine, the immortality of the soul . . . That they were philosophers
> rather than priests there can, in my mind, be no doubt . . .
>
> 'They were held in high honour, both as judges and as essential
> officials in matters pertaining to ritual and were exempt from all
> military responsibility . . .
>
> 'There can be no doubt that the druids were the most enlightened and
> civilising spiritual influence in prehistoric Europe.'

If this is true it is not too much to see in the druids the
predecessors of the Christian saints, offering 'a path to the
chancel from the glade'. Certainly they were looked upon as
the guardians of the spirit and traditions of the Welsh. It was
they who inspired the defence of Wales. They were the
nationalist intelligentsia of their day, and Anglesey was their
main centre. If Paulinus could destroy them, the subduing of

the whole country would then be comparatively easy. So the
legions tramped from Chester, through the beauty of the Vale
of Dyfrdwy (Dee), to launch a well-organised assault on
Anglesey, conquering the island and annihilating the druids —
the most astonishing happening in the early history of Wales.
About five and a half centuries later Aethelfrith, king of
Mercia, was to massacre the monks of Bangor-Is-
615 coed for the same reason — that they were giving
moral support to the Welsh cause.

Immediately after the conquest of Anglesey Buddug
(Boadicea) rose in rebellion and Paulinus was obliged to go
there to quell the disorder, leaving a part of the twentieth
legion in Chester. Before long the second legion would be in
Caerleon. For two centuries the Romans maintained two of
their three legions on the border of Wales, evidence of the
vigour of the Welsh and their Irish cousins. In spite of the
importance of the victories over Caradog and Anglesey
Wales was not yet wholly conquered. The two able Romans
who completed the conquest were Frontinus and Agricola.
From the fortress which had just been built in Caerleon in
about 60 B.C. Frontinus campaigned vigorously in south
Wales for three or four years, finally subduing it after an
attack in which the Roman soldiers sailed up the river
valleys of Wysg (Usk) and Taf, Nedd (Neath) and Tywi
(Towy). In mid-Wales the Welsh had just annihilated a
regiment of cavalry, and this led Agricola to organise a strong
army to invade the heart of the country successfully, and then
to aim again at Anglesey in order to finish the work of Paulinus
there. After a generation of costly military effort the Romans
had finally conquered Wales.

IV: THE NATURE OF THE ROMAN
OCCUPATION

FOR three centuries after the conquest Wales was a region of
the Roman Empire. It was organised as a military region for
some time without indigenous political institutions. Today,

fifteen centuries after the fall of Rome, and after the disappearance of other proud empires, including the British Empire, Wales still remains a nation, and still a region without its own political institutions.

Ostorius laid the foundations of three centuries of comparative peace, and during this time the Welsh developed in accord with their own talents and assimilated some of the higher civilisation of Rome. Although the country and its population were small, the Romans had learnt to respect their military prowess. The two legions which they kept in Chester and Caerleon each had five or six thousand men. The third was stationed in York. As J. E. Lloyd has observed, two legions were not kept on the borders of Wales without very good military reasons. To these were added, shortly after the conquest, thirty forts in Wales itself — with as many as a thousand infantrymen in the biggest ones when fully garrisoned. The country between Caerleon and Caerfyrddin (Carmarthen) and between Caer (Chester) and Caernarfon constituted the five thousand square miles of Roman Wales. Generations followed each other there as soldiers and over-seers of mines, although it was the natives who laboured at digging out the coal, iron, lead, copper and gold. Dolau Cothi, in the middle of Cantref Mawr, the chief natural bastion of the Lord Rhys a thousand years later, was the only place in Britain where gold was constantly mined, beginning in about 75 A.D. The remains can still be seen near the road between Cwrt-y-cadno and Pumsaint in the parish of Caeo. A considerable numbers of miners worked there under Roman overseers and engineers. The remains of stone buildings from that period were found there recently, among them the strong walls of the treasury in which the gold was stored, a cavalry station and remains of what may have been a Romano-Celtic temple. Of the water-system there Barry-Jones who has organised the excavations at Pumsaint, says:

'The gold-mining site at Dolaucothi is now recognised to be of European importance in the history of prehistoric and Roman tech-nology . . . The two major aqueducts represent the highest and lowest of at least seven hydraulic systems.'

By now nine systems have been found there. Other metals were mined. The copper of Anglesey extracted from Mynydd Paris, was almost as important as coal was to a later age. The relationship of the Romans with Anglesey was characteristic of their relationship with the whole of Wales. If they came to destroy, they stayed to develop.

As only a comparatively small amount of archaeological work was done in Wales until very recently, it was believed that the Roman occupation was wholly military, and that there was scarcely any civil and civic Roman life outside Caerwent. This view has had to be revised. The remains of about an acre and a half of substantial buildings have been found at Llanilltud Fawr (Llanwit Major). These large houses and non-military buildings were still lived in throughout the age of the saints, and bearing in mind the history of Llanilltud Fawr as an educational centre at that time, this is significant. It used to be held that Roman influence was strong in Glamorgan and Monmouth but not in the west and north. About five years ago the remains of a large Roman farmhouse were found in Dyffryn Ceidrych, one of the most beautiful valleys running into the Vale of Tywi in Carmarthenshire. The name of the farm in whose orchard these remains were found is Llys Brychan — again significant. Llys Brychan lies at the foot of Garn Goch, one of the most notable hill forts in the country. Y Garn Goch may have had a population rising into two to four thousand. Perhaps it was the main political centre of the Demetian Welsh before the establishment of Carmarthen. From the top of the enormous walls of this fort can be seen Dinefwr and Dryslwyn across the meandering Tywi. The summits of the Preselau rise on the western horizon, and Mynydd Myddfai to the east. Standing there above such a beautiful, orderly and historic landscape, one cannot help wondering why all Welshmen are not ardent nationalists.

In the town of Carmarthen Barry-Jones and J. H. Little have made the most remarkable discoveries, which have completely shattered the belief that Caerwent was the only Roman town in Wales. Their excavations have shown that there was a town of some importance at Moridunum as well

Bodvoc Stone, Margam Mountain (top)
Copyright National Museum of Wales

Cross of Enniaun (left)
Copyright National Museum of Wales

Plaque from Llyn Cerrig Bach, Anglesey
(first right)
Copyright National Museum of Wales

Conbelin's Cross, Margam
Copyright National Museum of Wales

The Cross of Grutne,
Margam
Copyright National Museum of Wales

Cross Penally, Pembrokeshire
Copyright National Museum of Wales

as at Chester, and that it may have been bigger than Caerwent. It was built in about 70 A.D., the year that Jerusalem was razed in the east of the Empire.

In that same year, within a generation of the crucifixion of Christ, far away to the west Carmarthen was rising. While the nation of Israel was being scattered and dispersed over the face of the earth by the flail of the Empire, the Welsh nation was being formed in its cradle. Nearly two thousand years later the children of Israel would be gathered together again in their ancient fatherland; by then it was the Welsh nation that was being scattered and dispersed.

It appears that the Roman soldiers left Carmarthen before the end of the first century, but the town remained. The biggest building yet found was built in the fourth century — a sort of town villa, 130 feet long, perhaps the residence of the governor. It was the capital city of the Demetian Welsh, and its inhabitants included few immigrants. The size of Carmarthen, which served an agricultural region, suggests that the population of Dyfed in the days of the Romans was larger than in the Middle Ages. There were seats in the amphitheatre, the centre of social life, for five or six thousand people. Its drainage system works effectively to this day. The remains of rows of shops and an industrial site were also found. The language of the people who lived their sophisticated lives in Carmarthen during the Roman centuries was Old Welsh or Brythonic. By the days of Macsen Wledig no doubt the language had become similar to the Welsh of Aneirin and Taliesin.

The discoveries at Carmarthen lend support to the view that there may be a strong historical foundation for some of *The Dream of Macsen Wledig*. It is said there of Elen, whom Macsen took as wife:

'The next day in the morning, the damsel asked for her maiden portion . . . And she asked to have the Island of Britain for her father . . . and to have three chief castles made for her, in whatever places she might choose in the Island of Britain. And she chose to have the highest castle made at Arfon . . . After that two other castles were made for her, which were Caerleon and Carmarthen.

'And one day the emperor went to hunt at Carmarthen, and he came as far as the top of Y Frenni Fawr, and there the emperor pitched his tent. And that encamping place is called Cadair Facsen, even to this day ...'

This suggests that the 'Island of Britain' was Wales, and that the storyteller had mistaken the meaning of Britannia. It can also be assumed that there was a Roman town in Caernarfon, but unless and until this is confirmed Carmarthen can share with Caerleon the claim to be the oldest town in Wales.

There were also small settlements around the other forts where the soldiers, who were very rich compared with the Welsh, used to buy their products and handiwork. No doubt there were substantial buildings in these little towns, similar to those whose foundations were uncovered in the vicinity of Y Gaer, near Brecon. Perhaps these towns declined when Agricola moved many of his soldiers from Wales, before the end of the first century, to help him in his wars in Scotland. It is not improbable, however, that there was just as much town life in Wales in the second century as there was in the seventeenth. There can be no doubt that future archaeological discoveries will change a good deal of the picture that used to be given of the Roman and pre-Roman periods.

V. THE MILITARY AND DEFENCE SYSTEM

BETWEEN the dozens of forts ran the roads, at least 800 miles of them — about nineteen on average between one fort and the next. Had the Romans done nothing else but build these roads they would have changed the nature of the society substantially, and for the better, by bringing people from different parts into communication with each other and making Wales into more of a community. Apart from the road from Caerleon to Chester, which ran for the most part near the subsequent border, there were probably two other roads running through Wales from south to north — one from Cardiff to the fort near Brecon, and on past Caersws to Chester; and the other from Carmarthen through Llanio and

Pennal to Caernarfon. There were in addition roads across the country, including the recently discovered one that ran from Carmarthen to the west past Meidrim. In the second half of the twentieth century we know that good roads are the key to economic development: transport communications have always been of vital importance. Wales would have to wait for eighteen hundred years to get roads as good as those of the second century. But for these, it would have been much harder for the saints to travel on their mission of peace in the fifth and sixth centuries; and no doubt the bards of the Middle Ages had reason to be thankful for the lengths that remained clear in their day. The roads made a great contribution towards making Wales one, from Flint to St. David's, from Holyhead to Chepstow.

The third century saw an increase in the attacks of a people Wales was to hear much about and see much of, in fine weather and foul: the Irish, who were called Scots. Like the Welsh, the Irish were of Celtic stock. Like the Welsh they spoke a Celtic language. Sometimes they are referred to as Q Celts, and the Welsh as P Celts: Q or C in Irish (like Mac and Cenarth) has a P or B in Welsh (Map or ap, and Penarth). With the passage of time the presence of the Irish was to strengthen the Celtic element in the life of Wales, but although some of them settled peaceably there were other invasions which were bitter and destructive. Their attacks lasted for more than two centuries, endangering the language and the quality of Welsh life more than the Romans did after the initial slaughter of the druids. They attacked along the western seaboard from Scotland down to Cornwall. They sailed up the mouth of the Severn in sufficient strength to force the Romans to move their chief fort from Caerleon to Cardiff; for the same reason a strong fort was built at Holyhead, to be used by the Roman navy, together with Caernarfon, to defend the copper works of Anglesey.

These attacks taxed to the limit the defensive power of the Romans and the Welsh; and in England they were faced with fierce attacks from Scotland by the Picts, and from across the Channel by the mixture of Teutonic tribes whom the Romans

called Saxones — a word which was Cymricised to give
Saeson. The Count of the Saxon Shore was killed and the
Duke of the Britains captured by the invaders. Both these
men, the highest Roman officers in Britain, were Teutonic.
It was thought that the barbarian antagonists had managed to
make an agreement with each other to attack from
367   three sides at once in 367 A.D. These dangerous assaults
must have developed the ability of the Welsh to defend
themselves. Like other inhabitants of the Empire, they became
Roman citizens in 212 A.D. by the edict of the Emperor
Caracalla, and in the time of Macsen Wledig they seem to
have been completely responsible for defending, under Roman
supervision, this corner of Roman civilisation.

England became more and more familiar with Teutonic
people throughout the Roman period, and perhaps even
earlier, as colonists in the eastern parts. Sometimes they were
called in as foederati by the Romans to assist with defence, as
it is possible the Irish were invited into Pembrokeshire. Their
presence was accepted. The Saxons lived peacefully side by
side with the Brythons of England, and with the Irish too, for
some of them had also settled there — there was a colony of
them at Silchester in Hampshire. Britanni was the general
name given to them all, Brythons, Irish and Saxons, and by
the end of the Roman period it is possible that the Saxons
were in control of the centres of power of the large area of
England to the east of a line running from York to the Isle
of Wight. In the third and fourth centuries the Teutons
probably formed the majority of Roman soldiers in England,
and they were not confined to the military forts: there is quite
a lot of evidence to show their presence in the cities, after
their defences had been strengthened. No doubt many of this
prestigious military class had also retired to urban civilian
life at the end of their military service. The soldiers
contributed to the deterioration of the cities in the
first half of the fourth century, and increasingly to their
Saxonising in the second half. The custom of paying in land
and goods had made it easier for them to settle there. But for
the fact that the Wales of that time was in control of its own

defence, doubtless many districts there too would have been Teutonised or Anglicised by the Roman soldiers in the same way. It is nonsense to believe that the English occupied and populated England in a short series of bloody attacks after the middle of the fifth century: this myth was effectively disposed of by Wade-Evans.

VI. MACSEN WLEDIG AND THE ROMAN INHERITANCE

AFTER 47 A.D., 383 A.D. is the next most notable date in our history, for in that year Macsen Wledig (Magnus

383   Maximus) departed from the island where he had made a great name for himself as an honest and able man who fought with brilliant success against the Picts and the Irish. This Spaniard was named Emperor by his army, which we hear of a few years later in Illyria on the shores of the Adriatic. It is said that he marched towards the continent from Caernarfon, perhaps with the Red Dragon, an imperial ensign, to the fore. For the next five years Macsen was recognised as co-emperor with Theodosius and Valentinian II; from Trier

in Gaul he ruled over five western provinces of the

388   Empire. He attacked Italy and was executed on 28th July, 388, after being defeated by Theodosius.

Our tradition gives a prominent place to Macsen and to Elen, reputed to be the daughter of Eudwy of Gwynedd, his wife. Some Welsh royal families, among them the kings of Dyfed and Powys, claimed descent from him through a daughter of his who married Gwrtheyrn (Vortigern). This is inscribed on the column of Eliseg near Llangollen, which records in ninth century script that Macsen, through his daughter Sevira, the wife of Gwrtheyrn, was the ancestor of the kings of Powys. It must be admitted that another tradition traces their lineage back to a less exalted source: a slave. Macsen was a Christian who won the praise of the Pope and Saint Martin of Tours, who was to have a great influence on Wales later on, and his monastic family is closely connected with the beginning of Christianity in Wales. Sulpicius Severus records the frequent visits of the monk Saint Martin to the Emperor in Trier, and says that his wife, who was a fervent Christian, was often present during their conversations.

Probably Macsen's greatest achievement for the Welsh, and the one which made the deepest impression on them, was the formal transference to them of the responsibility for defending their own country. Thus the people of the states of Wales were now recognised as responsible people within the Empire, in effect dependent solely upon themselves, with no Roman soldiers on their soil. The legions at Chester and Caerleon had moved nearer to eastern England to strengthen the defence against the attacks being made there. Perhaps the other forts in Wales had seen no Roman soldiers for a long time, though England was to remain under Roman rule for a generation after Macsen left. After three centuries of Roman oversight the Welsh were once again — as they had been for centuries before the Caesars — completely responsible for their own existence, the first people within the Empire to become self-governing.

The impression which three centuries of Roman rule had made on the Welsh was deepened by Macsen and made wholly indelible. *Romanitas* became an integral and valuable part of the Welsh tradition; the spiritual and intellectual life of the people was leavened by Roman civility. It secured a continuation of what was best in the education and learning of the druids, and there is a continuous line of great Welsh scholars from the days of Illtud to the fourteenth century. Although no remains of stone churches are left standing — apart from the one in Caerwent — it was in the Roman period that Christianity began to spread throughout the country. Ernest Renan described the Welsh as the Teutons of the Celts because they had, in his opinion, such a gift for organisation. Perhaps it is not too fanciful to see here again the mark of the Romans on those Celts who came most profoundly under their influence. Apart from the moral and cultural legacy which the Romans left, they also brought with them improvements in agriculture and building, houses and costume; and of course they built the roads. Many of the most important aspects of the life of the Welsh were enriched in this way.

On consideration, even if the occupation had been of a purely military character, it would have been impossible for thousands of Roman soldiers to have lived and had children in Wales or its borders for generations, with merchants, craftsmen and servants around them, without leaving a deep impression upon its life. It is the Welsh language which shows most clearly the extent of their influence. One of their bequests was the alphabet. Although Latin had not become the language of the people as it had in the English towns, about a thousand Latin words came into the Welsh language during this period, including words for simple daily things that Brythonic must have had a word for. For example, there must have been words for *pont* (bridge) and *mur* (wall), *fflam* (flame) and *cyllell* (knife), *pysgod* (fish) and *dysgl* (dish)*i* and for *corff* (body) and parts of the body like *coes* (leg), *braich* (arm), and *boch* (cheek). Latin was firmly enough established as a literary language in Wales for most of the Ogham stones of the Irish from the 5th and the 6th centuries to carry inscriptions in Latin as well as Irish.

Attention must be drawn here to a very significant fact. In spite of all that was borrowed from Latin, and although Latin was the language of government and law and political order, the political and legal terms borrowed from Latin are few. Such words as *gwlad* (country), *brenin* (king), *cenedl* (nation), *tref* (town), *bradwr* (traitor), *aillt* (subject) and *mab aillt* (bondman) are Welsh not Latin. This suggests that there had evolved a political and legal order already established in Wales before the Romans came. The political expertise of the continental Celts is suggested by the fact that Germanic languages have borrowed Celtic political terms. For example the German word *Reich* and the Welsh word *rhi* (lord) both come from the Celtic *rigion*.

The word 'Welsh' itself reminds us of our Roman background, for this was the word the English used for all the inhabitants of Britain, Brythons, English and even Irish who

were Roman citizens, living peacefully within the Roman
order. It is the word the Germans used for Romans everywhere. To the English 'Welsh' was the same as 'Roman';
to be Roman was to be Welsh. The meaning of the Welsh
word for a Welshman, *Cymro*, is a man from one district;
Cymry meant fellow-countrymen. Thus the English citizens of
the island were also 'Welsh' at that time, but later the word
became confined to the Welsh as we know them today, the
people who were remembered as having been under the rule
of Rome and who adhered most closely to the Roman
tradition.

The influence of the Roman Empire on Wales was massive,
but in spite of this the native tradition remained unbroken. It
received much from Rome without losing its Celtic character.
This was enriched and not supplanted. In his *History of Europe*,
H. A. L. Fisher has observed:

> 'It was part of the Roman strength to mingle diplomacy with force,
> to make no more disturbance of local customs than was necessary, to
> attack only such forms of religious belief as, like the worship of the
> Druids, were political in their object, and to preserve old laws and
> institutions where . . . they adjudged them to be good . . . Local
> languages — Punic, Lycaonian, Celtic — (were) permitted to co-exist
> with the *lingua franca* of the Empire which was Latin.'

When writing developed as a common usage, under the
Christian Church (the earlier tradition was oral), it was the
native law and the history of kings and important events in
Wales which were recorded, and Welsh literature which was
written down. Writing Welsh remained habitual within a few
miles of the centres of the power and military glory of the
Romans at Chester and Caerleon for centuries to come.
Fifteen centuries later, the most important Welsh novelist and
the chief poet of the nineteenth century would be living and
writing in the neighbourhood of those two great fortresses.
Twelve hundred years after the departure of Macsen, Wales
found itself a part of another empire. The influence of the two
on the Welsh tradition was very different — the one shaping
it and the other shattering it. What is the fate of the Welsh

language on the native heaths of Islwyn and Daniel Owen today? In spite of the amount of gold and copper taken from Wales to strengthen the Roman Empire, it contributed more to our life than it took out: the British Empire took much more out than it put in. It came close to taking all. Considering the constructive contribution of Rome, however, the Welshman of the fourth century had reason to be as proud as Paul when he said of his Roman citizenship: 'But I was born a citizen.'

Welsh Wales

I. THE IRISH

THE great achievement of the Welsh after the departure of the Romans was the successful defence of their inheritance. In this they were alone amongst the peoples of the Western Empire. This is the most impressive fact in the early history of Wales, that of all the nations of the Roman Empire the Welsh alone repulsed the barbarians and transmitted their civilisation intact to future generations in the confused period which followed the fall of Rome. In continental Europe the barbarians from the outside destroyed the whole of the Western Empire. For a generation a reasonable degree of order was maintained in the life of England, but by the middle of the fifth century the Celtic and Roman and Christian tradition there was overwhelmed in most of the country by the barbarian inundation. Wales remained the principal if not the sole heir of *Romanitas* on the island.

Yet it was not without effort or opposition that the tradition of the Welsh developed. Their Celtic cousins, the Irish, were the greatest threat. Their settlement in Dyfed from the third century, perhaps in a peaceful fashion as allies, has already been noted. They lived as peaceably amongst the Welsh as the Normans, Flemings and English who settled there eight hundred years later; and their descendants are there today. The stones which carry inscriptions in Ogham, the Irish alphabet, show that they were dominant there. Even in the eighth century the Irish of the Cork community claimed that Tewdos ap Rhain, the king of Dyfed at the time, was descended from one of their chiefs, Eochaid Allmuir. Perhaps the English of the sixth century referred to Pembrokeshire as 'Little Ireland beyond Wales'. This does not mean that the majority of the population were Irish, but the ruling class was. The belief that Welsh was the language of the majority and that only a small minority spoke Irish is supported by the fact that, of the five hundred or more saints few were not Welsh-speaking Welshmen. No doubt linguistic difficulties explain the rarity of Irish saints in Wales and Welsh saints in Ireland. We know that Saint David, who lived in a very Irish area, was a Welsh-speaking Welshman, although no doubt he also spoke Irish. Their gravestones and the Latin inscriptions on many of them prove that the Irish element had not been untouched by the Christianity and Roman civilisation which had left a deep impression on Welsh culture.

By the seventh and eighth centuries civilisation in Ireland was reaching greater heights than anywhere else in Europe, and Welsh culture too benefited from contact with it, especially in legend and folk literature. A strong Irish element runs through the *Mabinogi*. Near the beginning of the story of Pwyll Prince of Dyfed comes the sentence, 'After the first sitting Pwyll arose to take a walk, and made for the top of a mound which was above the court and was called Gorsedd Arberth'. There, near Narberth, was the principal court of the Irish kings, not far from the place where the monument of Voteporix — a king of Irish lineage — was found.

No doubt this established Irish community was as concerned as the Welsh to defend the country from destructive attacks from Ireland — just as the English were as anxious as the Brythons in England to preserve that country from Teutonic attacks from across the sea. Between these periods of danger, trade and peaceful relations with Ireland were resumed. But the attacks increased in the fourth and fifth centuries and, as Patrick's story shows, one of their unpleasant motives was to steal people as slaves.

They would sail towards the mouth of the Severn, settling in the regions of Cydweli and Gower and, higher up, on both sides of the estuary — in Monmouthshire and Somerset. An old Irish manuscript refers to this, as well as to a kingdom which united lands on both sides of the Severn Sea. It was probably the Irish who built the pagan temple inside the hill fort at Lydney in the fourth century. This is near the banks of the Severn, but they penetrated more deeply into the country in Breconshire and Carmarthenshire. The name of a prince of Irish lineage,

Brychan Brycheiniog, gave Sir Frycheiniog (Breconshire) its
name. Brychan was said to be the son of Marchell, the daughter
of Tewdrig, chief of Brycheiniog, who married — in Ireland
— Amlech, son of the Irish king Coronac, who followed
Tewdrig in the kingdom of Brycheiniog. Amlech would
have come to Brycheiniog from Ireland along the Roman
road which the Christian saints followed shortly after him,
the same route that Marchell took when she was carried on the
coffin of her father to her wedding in Ireland, through Cwm
Wysg in Breconshire, past Mynydd Myddfai, Llansefin and
Llangadog. This Irish-Welsh wedding and the journeying to
and fro suggest a peaceful country and a close and friendly
relationship between Irishman and Welshman.

In Llyn Safaddan (Llangorse Lake) in Breconshire can be
seen the remains of the one Irish lake-dwelling in Wales,
although there is a reflection of the same way of life to be seen
in the legend of the maiden of Llyn y Fan, which lies below
the cliff of Cadair Arthur. The Irish were numerous enough
in north Carmarthenshire for a few of their names to cling to
streams and mountains, such as Mihartach and Mihertach —
streams which run into the Sawdde in Llanddeusant — and
Mynydd Mallaen above Cil-y-cwm: Mall-ân is how it is
pronounced, in the Irish way.

The west of Gwynedd was the other large area where the
Irish had settled in strength about the same time as in Dyfed,
and where their language was perhaps heard in some districts
until as late as the eleventh century. The words Llŷn and
Portin-llaen (with the accent on the last syllable) suggest that
they had come from a more northern part of Ireland than their
fellow countrymen in Dyfed—from Leinster (Laigni in Irish).

II. CUNEDDA

IT may have been because of the danger that the Irish might
take over the country that Cunedda moved down
400   from Manaw Gododdin, near Stirling in Scotland;
perhaps indeed he was directed to Wales for this
purpose as one of the Dukes of Britain. The experience of

Scotland itself showed that this danger was not imaginary, for the Irish gave their own name, Scots, to the country which became to a large extent Irish Gaelic in language. Cunedda and his army probably came by sea, for it was very difficult to travel through Lancashire with its bogs, forests and large rivers. He was not the first to come to Wales from Scotland. People came from there to Wales two thousand years before the time of Cunedda, in the late Bronze Age, and after him saints, soldiers and craftsmen journeyed to and fro. Although the territory of England separated Wales from Scotland, they were united at this time by the sea. Centuries later the sea ceased to unite them, though England continued to separate them. According to the history given by Nennius, it was the coming of Cunedda with his eight sons and grandson at the turn of the fourth century which was the most important event in the formation of Wales since the first century. Assuming that Nennius was correct, it is the memory of the sons — including Ceredig and Edern, and the grandson Meirion — which still lives in the names of districts; but the only place where Cunedda's own name is found is in Allt Cunedda near Cydweli. The control of the wide area of country between the Teifi and the Dyfrdwy (Dee) came into his hands. He shared it among his family in the same way as small states were shared seven centuries later by William the Conqueror among his barons, and it was to him that homage was paid by the princedoms between Ceredigion and Edeirnion. Just as some royal families had claimed that they were descended from Macsen Wledig, so others claimed Cunedda as an ancestor — a somewhat lesser lineage than that of the royal families of England, who in the seventh century all claimed to be descended from Woden. Many of these families had very long histories, as much as five centuries and more. The family of Gwynedd, the principal royal line of Wales, claimed descent from Cunedda through Maelgwn Gwynedd, his great grandson, down to Prince Dafydd who was executed in Shrewsbury in 1283 — a pedigree of more than seven centuries. Although Wales had the image of a wild and turbulent country, the long history of these families suggests a comparatively peaceful and civilised situation which had been freer than usual from the civil and foreign wars which so often shorten the lives of kings and princes. At all events, Cunedda Wledig at the beginning of the fifth century, like Macsen Wledig at the end of the fourth, must be considered among the founding-fathers of the Welsh nation.

The victories of Cunedda, though aimed at preventing their rule, did not by any means annihilate the Irish; they and their language remained to enrich life in some parts of Wales for centuries after this. However, the Welsh element in the life of Wales became stronger and secured an overall mastery. Most important of all, the Welsh language, which remained until this time in its old Brythonic form, was safeguarded through this. But for Cunedda it is possible that Wales would have developed as a Gaelic-speaking country; but with the support of Welsh government the Welsh language took over in all parts. Even this early it is apparent that the language of the ruling class of society, if it is numerous enough, determines the language of the whole country. A large part of eastern England was turning to English as its language at this time for precisely the same reason. It is possible that the Brythons were in the majority in these parts but that the English were dominant. By the end of the century the Brythons seem to disappear, and there is no further mention of them in this region nor in the middle or south of England. They had not been killed. They had been turned into Englishmen; and what turned Brythons into Englishmen was the English language. Thus too in Wales the Irish disappeared because the Welsh language made them into Welshmen.

It is Cunedda Wledig, a Brython of Pictish descent, who came to Wales from Scotland, who is mainly responsible for the Welshness of Wales. His family had been important in Scotland for generations: his father's name was Edern, his grandfather was Padarn Peisrudd, and his great-grandfather Tegid. The Latin forms of the names — Eternus, Paternus, Tacitus — suggest Roman associations, and this is made clearer by the word Peisrudd in the grandfather's name, the *pais rudd* or red cloak showing Roman office. Cunedda gave his sons Latin names. It is possible that he was called upon to defend Wales by Macsen or by the able Roman 399-401 general Stilicho, who was reorganising the defence of England about this time. A similar task was fulfilled in Ystrad Clud (Strathclyde) by Ceredig Wledig, to whose soldiers Patrick addressed his epistle; and it is on a sixth century stone inscription (in Castell Dwyran, Carmarthenshire) that Voteporix, of Irish descent, is referred to as 'Protector'— a continuation of a Roman office like that held by Cunedda Wledig and Ceredig Wledig, and later by Emrys Wledig, precursor of Arthur. Taliesin and other poets show the high significance of the title *Gwledig* when they speak of God as *Gwledig Nef*, the ruler of heaven.

Like their father, two of Cunedda's sons and his grandson had Christian names. It can reasonably be deduced from this that Cunedda was a Christian. This could have been an additional inducement for sending him to Wales where his coming marks the opening of the early Middle Ages. He must have been an able soldier and leader to have been able to organise a successful invasion and settlement from so far away, and to establish foundations which remained strong for so many centuries. '*Kaletach wrth elyn nac asgwrn*' said Taliesin of him as a soldier — 'He was harder than a bone to his enemies'; but he was much more than a soldier. Only a statesman could have accomplished what he did.

III. RENAISSANCE

SINCE a certain amount of centralised authority was characteristic of the Roman order, and since it was in southeast England, and London for the most part, that that authority was centred, the life of Wales during the Roman occupation was to some extent directed towards the east. It is almost a natural law that the peripheral districts of a country take second place, and that the regions near the centre of government enjoy precedence. When Roman rule came to an end the Welsh ceased to look eastwards; they turned rather towards Scotland and Brittany, and still more towards Ireland. When the Welsh became self-governing, London ceased to have any place in their lives. The country did not become more insular as a result of its separateness; on the contrary, it came into a closer relationship with other countries and more open to their influence. The self-governing Welsh turned their eyes towards the route along which so many of their forefathers had journeyed to Wales — the seaways.

As a result, a rich Celtic civilisation developed around the Irish Sea in the fifth century, and each of the six Celtic countries had a fruitful influence upon the culture, the religion and the economy of the others, thus preparing the way for the notable Celtic renaissance which reached its brilliant climax in Ireland.

The Irish Sea became a Celtic lake. The Western sea-routes had been vigorous in megalithic times and the immediate pre-Roman period. Their importance tended to diminish with the Roman occupation but their revival in the fifth century was encouraged by the perils of the eastern land routes. It was not only soldiers and pirates who traversed the Irish Sea, but saints and missionaries, evangelists and merchants, artists and craftsmen. The metal workers travelled over it as freely as the pioneers of the Church — up to the Isle of Man and Scotland, down to Cornwall and Brittany, as well as between Wales and Ireland. They brought new ways of working bronze and iron; they brought new values and ideas; they even brought to some parts, as will be seen, a new language.

Moreover it was not only between the Celtic countries that this relationship flourished. Archaeologists are discovering more and more evidence that trade with countries of the Mediterranean was on the increase. It was the capture of Gibraltar by the Arabs at the end of the seventh century that brought this trade with the Mediterranean to an end, just as the terrifying presence of the Black Pagans later decimated peaceful traffic over the Irish Sea. Before then, however, the horizons of Wales grew wider and its life opened into flower.

IV. THE CREATION OF BRITTANY

IT is against this background that the colonising of Brittany by the Welsh and Cornish in the fourth and fifth centuries must be seen. The Brython still lives in the Breton's name as the name of the Brythonic tongue lives in Brezonneg which is his word for his language. Nora Chadwick, the main authority in this field, has shown that there is no foundation for the old belief that it was Brythons who were forced out of Britain by the English who then colonised Brittany. She observes:

'A consideration of these early traditions would seem to me to dispose of the contention that the Britons migrated under pressure from the Saxons. Tradition and language alike lead us to believe that the Breton immigrants came almost wholly from Wales and the Devon-Cornish peninsula, as yet untouched by Saxon threats.'

If they were driven out at all, the pressure of the Irish rather than the English is more likely to have been responsible for this. It is unlikely that the English drove anyone out of England — neither to the west nor to the south, neither to Wales nor to Brittany. As the Irish settled in Wales, so the Welsh and Cornish settled in Brittany. And as the Brythons of England were Anglicised so the natives of Brittany were Brythonised — their Latin being supplanted by a new language, resembling Welsh and Cornish, which were developing from Brythonic at this time. It was during the long centuries of separation that the main differences developed between the three languages.

It is possible that some fled to Brittany to escape the terrible yellow plague which struck Wales about the middle of the sixth century and killed Maelgwn Gwynedd. In the life of St. Teilo we are told that he and his followers led a 547 group that stayed for a time in Brittany to escape the plague. He travelled through Devon and Cornwall, visiting Geraint the prince of Devon on the way there and on the way back. Samson, one of Illtud's pupils at Llanilltud Fawr (Llantwit Major), took the same route and he also is mentioned as having escaped the plague. There is a host of similar examples of communication between Wales, Cornwall

and Brittany during these centuries. To quote one more, it was
from Brittany along the Roman road which the saints has
followed, according to E. G. Bowen, that Brynach the Irishman
— friend and chaplain of Brychan Brycheiniog — came to
Brecon (by way of Milford Haven); he established many
churches in Wales, particularly in Pembrokeshire where his
fellow Irish were so strong. It is surprising to us, who know so
little about the other Celtic nations, that the Celtic peoples of
the fifth and sixth centuries mixed with each other so much
and in such a creative way. Christianity came to Ireland
mainly from Wales; the Scots came to Scotland from Ireland;
Cunedda and our early literature came to Wales from Scotland;
and the Bretons came to Brittany from Wales and Cornwall.

The saints had much to do with the colonisation of Brittany,
and most of this splendid company came from Wales. Their
biographies are the main source of information for the origins
of the Breton nation; Brittany is a notable example of the
importance of the Christian Church in the forming of the
Celtic nations. There, even more than in Wales, Christian
foundations are reflected in local place names. Because the
newcomers inherited the order established in the Roman
period, the Church there developed very early upon a more
orderly system than in Wales, yet it was notably decentralist.
The saints who went there from Wales included able leaders
and organisers ,men of business and diplomats. It is significant
that they were often members of royal houses, reared to lead
and to accept responsibility. In their story no unhealthy
separation between Christianity and society can be detected.
The Christian saints were political leaders, like the prophets of
Israel long before them. This is a marked characteristic of
Welsh life. Since they considered that the establishing of a
Christian society in Wales was an essential part of their office,
it is not surprising that they led and organised the creation of a
Christian community on a large scale in Brittany. In Wales at
this time there was another sort of Christianity, a more pietist
religion uninvolved in politics and social life in all its aspects.
This, too, had its necessary place: it is not possible to measure
the value of the segregated life of those who devoted themselves

to prayer and meditation. Yet it appears that the pattern of the founders of the Breton nation was the more common. These spiritual leaders were not men of the world, but they did not turn their backs on the world either. Their function as they saw it was to lead the world, in it though not of it.

It is from Brittany itself that we get most of the biographies of the saints, which are such an important historical source in spite of their many incredible anecdotes. The earliest were written at least two centuries before anything of the sort is found in Wales. It is a very rare thing in these biographies for mention to be made of anyone coming from either Scotland or Ireland to Brittany, or even from Devon and Cornwall, and no one at all from the south-east of England. They are almost all associated with Wales; Welsh culture was supreme there. Still more unexpectedly, a number of the leaders of the migration came from mid-Wales, still further emphasising the Welshness of its character. Brittany is in a sense the first Welsh colony, and by far the most successful.

V. FROM BRYTHONIC TO THE WELSH OF TALIESIN AND ANEIRIN

DURING the two centuries after the departure of Macsen Wledig and the coming of Cunedda, when the foundations of Brittany were being laid by the Welsh, a great change occurred in the language they spoke. Brythonic became Welsh. So big a language change must have taken centuries — the centuries before Taliesin and Aneirin. Why this great change took place is a mystery, and how it occurred in such a rapid and ubiquitous manner throughout the Brythonic west, in Scotland, Wales and Cornwall, despite the five hundred miles between their extremities. Perhaps the change had begun earlier than scholars believe, but before it could happen at all over such a widespread and dispersed territory there must have been close communication among the Brythons. Some important instances of this have already been indicated. It is significant that the change occurred at the same time as the growth of the

Christian Church, when it was at its most vigorous, and it is reasonable to suppose that the evangelists were one of the main agents of the transformation, since they moved about so much in Wales itself and in the other Brythonic countries. This change strengthened linguistic unity, but it did not create it. For centuries before the coming of the Romans Wales had been a cultural unit — not homogeneous, of course — with one language. It remained a cultural unit with one language; where Brythonic had previously been spoken, Welsh was spoken now. Welsh is a result of an internal development within Brythonic, not a language which has come into Wales from outside. There was never a complete break in the tradition.

Very little is known about Brythonic since the Welsh and the Brythons had only an oral tradition, and Latin was the literary language in the time of the Romans. Personal and place names show that from the point of view of development it was in a similar state to Latin, with its case declensions and compound words. It is the absence of these characteristics from Welsh which makes it so different from Brythonic. The final syllables of the Brythonic words disappeared, as well as the linking vowels in the compound words, and new mutations developed. For example, the name of Caradog's father was Cynobelinos: the *os* disappeared at the end and the *o* in the middle, and *b* was mutated into *f*, making Cynfelin in Welsh. The Brythonic form of Caradog was Caratacos: the *os* has disappeared, and the *t* has mutated into *d*. Some will hold that this is not changing one language for another but only a development within the original language, and the Brythonic should be called Old Welsh.

If the way in which Brythonic disappeared is a provoking mystery, what happened to the language of the people of England while this great change was taking place in the Welsh language is a greater mystery still. For most of England the silence is deafening. There is no record of communication between the Welsh and the other Brythons of the island, apart from the contacts with the kingdoms of the north and the south-west. In the period immediately after the coming of the Romans there is barely a mention of any other Brythonic kingdom or social organisation between Elfed, in the west of Yorkshire, and Devon; there are few references anywhere in the fifth century, after the departure of the Romans, to any political system apart from cities. The first known kingdoms, which emerge about the end of the sixth century, are Saxon ones whose rulers came from different parts of Germany during the preceding centuries. It is reasonably certain that no Welsh was spoken in mid and southern England, apart from the small part of the old Powys now in England, and the country to the west of Gloucester: it is possible that Somerset and Devon spoke the language. Pockets of Brythonic probably survived elsewhere.

Most of the south of Scotland was Welsh-speaking, as well as parts of north-west England. It is a surprising fact that the earliest Welsh literature comes from Scotland, where Aneirin and Taliesin lived.

> 'Gwŷr a aeth Gatraeth oedd ffraeth eu llu,
> Glasfedd eu hancwyn, a gwenwyn fu,
> Trichant trwy beiriant yn catáu—
> A gwedi elwch tawelwch fu.'

> The men who went to Catraeth were a speedy band,
> fresh mead their sustenance, it became poison.
> Three hundred were in order embattled
> and after rejoicing there came silence.

These are well known lines from the *Gododdin*, the great poem composed by Aneirin in the second half of the sixth century when he was a bard at the court of Mynyddog Mwynfawr, chief of the land that stretched southwards from the Firth of Forth and which included Manaw Gododdin, the home of Cunedda about a century and a half earlier. The court of Mynyddog, where Aneirin made his poem, was in Edinburgh, his capital city.

According to Ifor Williams, on whose scholarship we depend so completely in this whole field, Taliesin, who addressed his poems to Prince Urien and his sons before Aneirin composed the *Gododdin*, was a contemporary of Aneirin;

but in contrast to Aneirin, who came from Scotland, he was probably a Welshman from Powys. A eulogy of Cynan Garwyn, king of Powys, is attributed to him, and he celebrated Cynan's victories in Anglesey and Dyfed, and even in Cornwall. This prince was a very warlike person, but there is no mention of his fighting against the English. Taliesin describes the court, where the bard, as he says himself, was appreciated as he deserved. It is recorded in *Hanes Taliesin* that he also addressed poems to Maelgwn Gwynedd, who was descended from Cunedda. If this is true then he flourished in the first half of the sixth century. This is quite possible, for when he addresses Urien he describes himself as an old man with white hair. Taliesin refers in his poems to visits to other courts in Wales as well as to Scotland and the north of England. The journeys of the poets between Wales and Scotland deepened the effect of the Christian relationship (as Anthony Conran says, 'In Welsh, Christianity seems to have been taken for granted from the start') and expedited the dissemination of the linguistic changes. Although the two countries were geographically so far apart, they were culturally very close. An indestructible link between Wales and Scotland is the fact that so much early Welsh literature came from there, as did Cunedda whose deeds preserved the Welshness of Wales. If there was a threat to the Welsh tradition from the direction of Ireland, the support from Scotland was strong.

circa 515-590

If it were not for a solitary manuscript, there would be no record of the work of Taliesin — any more than there is of the work of Talhaearn Tad Awen, Myrddin and Arofan and other early poets whose work has been completely lost, so that nothing remains but their names. The quality of the work which does exist shows that this was not a new tradition but that centuries of culture lay behind it. For a thousand years the Celts had been accustomed to chant the praises of their leaders, and thus to unite, inspire and sustain the standards of the people. Since this was being done orally, in declamations to the music of the harp or some other instrument, the *Hengerdd* ('Old Songs') consist of poetry which appeals to the ear. It is fine, dignified poetry, economic and polished, with developed metres and brilliant images. Taliesin, for example, describes the dead legions of English soldiers after a battle thus:

Cysgid Lloegr llydan nifer	The English sleep, a wide host,
A lleufer yn eu llygaid.	with daylight in their eyes.

If it was a primitive society which produced this work, it was also a cultured one. This is one of the great wonders of our history — that the Welsh language was the medium of such beauty and civility in such an uncivilised age; that a radiance streamed through it when the lights of Christian Europe had been extinguished. When Gaul and Spain and Italy were in the grip of the barbarians, and the western frontier of the Roman Empire was in the Balkans; when the darkness over England was so profound that only a few fragments are known about its condition and its history; a century and a half after the pitiful cry of the Brythons to Agitius — 'the last of the Romans' — for succour; a generation before Mahomet fled to Medina: nearly a millennium before Columbus sailed for the West, this is when a superb and shimmering stream of Welsh literature began upon its course down fourteen hundred years.

Independent Wales

I. A COUNTRY OF SMALL STATES

In the fifth century, if not before, Wales assumed the political form that was to persist more or less for eight hundred years, namely a nation without a centralist state system, but rather a number of small states continuing in part perhaps from the pre-Roman period. The cantons of Switzerland were in this sort of situation before they formed a weak state which would unite them without sacrificing more of the political freedom of the single canton than effective self-defence demanded. Wales may have been moving towards that sort of system in the thirteenth century when its strength was shattered by the government of England.

The decentralised system of Wales has had a very bad press. If Wales itself was not united yesterday, Welsh historians today are almost unanimous in condemning it, sometimes with scorn. 'Wales in the Middle Ages was the Balkans on a small scale, a conglomeration of pilfering little kingdoms', is how one of them burst out. Could Mussolini have spoken differently about the little states of Italy in the Renaissance period? Although it is the standpoint of power politics rather than the welfare politics which the historians take — the conventional British standpoint — some sympathy is due to them: it is natural to lose patience with a system which makes a clear, simple and smooth narrative impossible.

Though these states were so small, they were nevertheless effective, as their longevity demonstrates. The fact which testifies to their effectiveness is that of all the countries which had been a part of the Roman Empire, Wales alone succeeded in defending its cultural and political heritage. On the continent, as in England, Teutonic states displaced the Empire. Thanks to the toughness of the Welsh states the Christian civilisation of Wales was transmitted without a break in continuity through the centuries that followed the Roman withdrawal. They had their civil institutions, their political systems, their laws and patterns of defence. It is possible to argue that this sort of system is preferable from every point of view save defence to having one state only for the whole of Wales. Instead of centralising political and cultural activities, it meant that there were a number of royal courts, each with its officers and lawyers, its poets and musicians. Socially and culturally the country had the same kind of advantages as the Germans had in the eighteenth century, when Germany was made up of a collection of small states, each with its own political and cultural centre. its opera house, its writers, artists and scholars. If civilised life is more important than military glory, this decentralised Germany excelled the strong and united Germany of Bismarck and Hitler. It is because they speak thoughtlessly that many speak scornfully of the Wales of the small states. The tragedy eight hundred years later was that a disunited Wales could not prevent itself being overthrown by the huge imperialist state of England. By the thirteenth century a measure of political unity, but no uniformity, was necessary to defend the nation, although even a united Wales was too small and accessible to withstand successfully the might of the powerful Norman empire. Certainly the weakness of the Welsh states was not that they were too small to foster a rich economic and cultural life, any more than Iceland is too small today. The trouble was helplessness in the face of the imperialist power of huge adjacent England. It is the good fortune of Iceland that no England, Spain or France has been able to devour it — as the Welsh and the Bretons, the Basques and the Catalans have been swallowed up.

No doubt it is necessary to stress that a nation is not the same as a state. They are forever being confused. British politicians of the twentieth century are continually talking of 'the nation' as if there were only one nation in Britain. There is one state here, the British state, but there are four nations. In the Wales of the Middle Ages there was one nation, but a number of states. The state should function as a servant; it is a political system, whose function is to serve society. The great tragedy of Wales is that the state which was beginning to develop in order to perform this service for the nation as a whole was shattered in the thirteenth century.

In political life the state was the most important institution, but socially the *cenedl* was the basic entity in Wales. The meaning of *cenedl* has changed. Its current meaning is 'nation', but in the early Middle Ages it meant a 'relationship' which could be a family relationship inside a people. Most of the members had a common ancestry and were related to the ninth degree. Strangers could come to belong to this community through conquest or because they lived in the same part of the country. Apart from being a cluster of states, Wales was also a community of communities. The tight texture of the community of the 'cenedl' was the hidden strength of the Welsh. This is what made them so difficult to conquer. Since the people were rooted in a land and belonged to each other and were aware of their relationship, a consciousness of their duty to preserve and protect their land and society was fostered in them. Faithfulness and loyalty to their community were bred in them. This made Wales invincible.

The most important political institution in the state was the monarchy. Each state had its king and around his person the whole social and political life of the kingdom was woven. Two kingdoms which remained independent until the end of the eleventh century were established among the Silurians, but neither bore their name. The first royal name we hear in Morgannwg is that of Glywys, father of Gwynllwg and grandfather of Cadog; and the kingdom was called by his name for three centuries, until the time of Morgan Mwynfawr when Glywysing was supplanted by Morgannwg. It was Venta (Caer-went), the chief town, that gave its name to Gwent and also to its people and its dialect, Gwenhwyson and Gwenhwyseg. Caradog Freichfras, who was born at about the time of the departure of Macsen Wledig, was its first king, and no doubt his name shows that his family retained a vivid memory of that other Caradog who performed heroic deeds there more than three centuries earlier. Shortly afterwards the name Cynfelin appears in the family — the Welsh form of Cynobelinos, the father of the early Caradog; but the desire to continue the Roman tradition was revealed in the name of Caradog's son, Honorius (Ynyr).

When the Roman soldiers left England in 410 there were organised states, some of them established for one or 410 more generations, spreading over the whole of Wales, from Môn to Mynwy (Anglesey to Monmouthshire); but to the east of the Welsh border there were none which are known to us.

The main development in the fifth century in the history of the western states from Anglesey to Pembroke was the subjection and assimilation of the Irish. This was done peaceably in Dyfed, but it was not brought about in Gwynedd without bloodshed. The victory of Cadwallon Lawhir, circa the grandson of Cunedda over the Irish at Cerrig y 470 Gwyddel near Trefdraeth, Anglesey, was final.

II. GWRTHEYRN (VORTIGERN)

THERE was great energy in Powys. Indeed, for periods during the following five centuries Powys was to be the most vigorous of the Welsh states, and there is reason to believe that its population did most to strengthen the Welshness of other parts of Wales in the early period. The Ordovician pattern had no doubt continued there throughout the Roman centuries. The strong man who ruled there at the beginning of the century, when Cunedda came to Wales, was Gwrtheyrn (Vortigern), the son-in-law of Macsen Wledig. Perhaps the name Gwrtheyrn is a title, since it means chief lord, suggesting that his authority stretched outside his own kingdom. He kept his court in Gwrtheyrnion, Radnorshire, and he acquired Dinas Emrys in Caernarvonshire, the property of his mother-in-law Elen. Nennius, the fountain of information about him, records that Craig Gwrtheyrn on the southern banks of the Teifi was his property; this remains at Llanfihangel ar Arth and is one of the finest hill forts in the south. Quite a lot of Welsh history revolves around him, and if we are to believe all that Bede and Nennius (who gives eighteen chapters to him) say, he left his mark on England too. The name of this 'proud tyrant', as Gildas calls him, is the most frequent in the politics of the Brythons of this period.

Two important things are said about Vortigern: first that he was anti-Roman, and second that it was he who was responsible for bringing the English to England. According to the legend, he invited Hengist and Horsa to Kent; after they came they turned against the Brythons and, with the assistance of more shiploads of English, killed and destroyed them, forcing the survivors to flee to the mountains of Wales. These fugitives are the original Welsh. This is the story most frequently read in history books: the Welsh are alleged to be a flock of refugees who had lost their country. There is not a jot of truth in this story of an overwhelming English conquest, unless it refers to the attack of the Jutes on the south-east of England in the sixth century, and the fighting for generations between them and the natives, when England was already a largely under English control. The forefathers of the Welsh had been living in Wales for thousands of years before this legend was created. The famous historian Gweirydd ap Rhys saw the foolishness of the story a century ago. In 1870, in the first of the great volumes *Hanes y Brytaniaid a'r Cymry*, he observed:

'We have to try here to remove one mistaken idea which is disseminated by many Welsh and English historians, namely that it was the Saxons who forced the Brythons out of England and into the mountains of Wales, and this as recently as the sixth century! It is perfectly clear, once our attention has been awakened to it . . . that Wales like every other part of this land, according to the testimony of Caesar, had plenty of inhabitants, and this since before the Romans, let alone the English, ever set foot on the Island of Britain . . . The work of the Silurians, one tribe of the province, successfully withstood the whole might of the Romans in the island, and this over four centuries before the attack of the Saxons on England, i.e. in the age of Claudius Caesar (A.D. 50), an absolute proof that this Principality was full of inhabitants even then.'

Here speaks the voice of commonsense, but in spite of the lack of convincing evidence some historians still give credence to the legend that the English conquered England in a series of bloody attacks of short duration, pushing the Brythons who were not killed into the west.

Although we must decline to blame Vortigern for Anglicising England, it can be accepted that he was anti-Roman, even though he was brought up in a family, that used Latin. No doubt there was a general reaction against Romans and *Romanitas* at the beginning of the fifth century, a time when Rome was failing to defend the Brythons effectively against attacks from the north, the west and the east. Salvian describes the situation on the Continent a few years later:

> 'What better proof is there of the injustice of Rome than that renowned leaders, whose Roman status should have been a great spur to their glory and honour, were being driven so hard by the unjust cruelty of Rome that they no longer wished to be Roman? . . . What cities are there, or even towns or villages, where there are not as many oppressors as there are officers? What place is there where the daily bread of widows and children is not being stolen by the country's leaders? . . . To these people the enemy is kinder than the tax gatherers.'

It would be natural for an intelligent and ambitious man with a strong kingdom behind him to place himself in the forefront of the anti-Roman movement outside the borders of his territory, and indeed to come into contact in the process with groups of Englishmen in England who were pagans. At all events, Vortigern got the reputation among orthodox monks of being anti-Christian; perhaps because he was a supporter of the heretic Pelagius who was also a brilliant Brython. After Pelagianism had been condemned by the Church it seems to have become an expression of anti-Romanism in the countries of Britain and a way of asserting their independence. But in the eyes of the orthodox being a Pelagian was almost as bad as being a pagan:

> 'A sweet accord existed between Christ, the head, and the members,' observes Gildas, 'until the Arian agnosticism (Pelagianism), fierce as a serpent, and vomiting on us its foreign poison, caused a destructive split between brethren who lived in harmony.'

To oppose the growth of this heresy Saint Garmon came on his first visit to the island in 428. Like so many of
428 the saints, he too was a political leader, and no doubt as well as a religious mission he had a political one on this occasion, on behalf of representatives of the Empire. He succeeded in giving order to the political life of many parts of England. The two aspects of his work brought him into conflict with the now ageing Vortigern. Accompanied by a legion of priests, Garmon met him in Caernarfon and again in Gwrtheyrnion when the king fled there. Vortigern must have been demoralised by losing the support of his people, or he was terribly guilty of some sin — perhaps his marriage with his own daughter — for he fled again, to his fort in Dyfed this time. Today, however, he is remembered as a Welshman who created a strong kingdom, as one who strengthened the Welsh people and who evinced the supremacy of their states in this island fifteen hundred years ago. He died in
430 A.D. 430, near the banks of the Teifi, perhaps at Craig Gwrtheyrn (Vortigern's Rock).

The struggle for and against Roman values, in which Vortigern was a main protagonist, was a fateful one for Wales and England. In Wales *Romanitas* won: in England it lost. The great native opponent of Vortigern in this contest was Emrys Wledig (Ambrosius Aurelianus), whom Geoffrey of Monmouth calls a son of Cystennin (Constantine) and grandson of Macsen Wledig (Magnus Maximus), and who is called by Nennius two and a half centuries later, 'king amongst all the kings of the nation of the Brythons'. It appears that Emrys was the chief supporter of the Roman tradition, and it was his military success which saved it in Wales and Cornwall. In England it vanished completely under the wave of English barbarism. If Cunedda Wledig did most to guarantee the Welshness of Wales, it was Emrys Wledig who protected the spiritual heritage of Rome.

III. THE MYTH OF THE EXPULSION OF
THE BRYTHONS

It is a striking fact that although a few Brythonic kings are named in the Anglo-Saxon chronicles, no strong and integrated state is known to have been founded to the east of the Welsh border during the hundred years after the departure of the Romans. In Wales there were many effective states, which between them ruled the whole country; in England not one whose name is known to us between the Brythonic kingdoms in the north and Cornwall and Devon. The name of neither kingdom nor principality descends to us from this time; only unbroken silence. The explanation generally given for this is that hosts of English invaders have overwhelmed the country, extinguished its culture and its Christianity, destroyed its cities and killed all the Brythons who were not chased away to inhabit the mountains of Wales. As previously indicated, there is no foundation at all for this belief. Nor is there acceptable evidence for any cataclysmic conquests whatsoever; the notion is wholly derived from a misunderstanding on the part of the author of a book entitled *De excidio Brittanniae*. He was writing at the beginning of the eighth century, but his work was attributed — first by Bede and then by Nennius — to Gildas, who was writing in the sixth century. This completely confused the account of the history of the period.

To say this does not, of course, mean that there were no attacks and colonising activities by the English in England in the fifth and sixth centuries nor that parts of the south-east were not occupied by fresh invaders, led perhaps in Kent by Hengist and Horsa. Here no doubt the English like the Picts and Irish continued to attack and, still more, to colonise as they had done for centuries. They probably multiplied their incursions and continued to mix with the Brythons as they had long done. The Teutonic people who had settled over the generations included Angles, Saxons, Jutes, Suevi, Franks from the Rhineland and, perhaps most numerous of all,

Friesians, whose language is nearest that which became dominant in England. It is here that Arthur takes his place, as the military leader of the Brythons against the increasing pressure of the Germanic population and against the Picts. But there was never an 'adventus Saxonus' as Bede conceived it.

Until the middle of the fifth century England succeeded in sustaining its life fairly well, at least as well as Gaul, where the continued presence of Roman soldiers gave an advantage. It was an extremely difficult period: the cities, many of which had been occupied by Germanic soldiers, were becoming empty, the economy and culture were languishing. This happened, however, throughout the Western Empire: England was no exception. Civilised life continued there for some time in the midst of the deterioration, as the letters of Patrick (who died in 461) bear witness. He refers to the time of his father, a Christian and a Brython who held an important office, possibly in the Vale of Severn, as if it were still serene and undisturbed and rich in its Latin culture. The same impression is left by the descriptions of visits by Garmon in 429 and 440.

In an entry for about 442-3 in the Gaulish Chronicle 452, to whose significance Wade-Evans drew attention, 442-3 there is contemporary evidence that the situation was changing for the worse, and changing quickly The note reads: 'The Britains until this time ripped apart by various tragedies and misfortunes, placed under the rule of the English'. No reference is made here to an English invasion from outside; rather is it suggested that someone who held some authority in Gaul — Agitius perhaps — had conveyed the responsibility for government in England to the English element in the life of the country. Since it was only in the cities that there was any form of government, the authority would be there. By the middle of the fifth century the effective part of the establishment in England seems to have been Teutonic. It may be that the Brythonic tongue had long been superseded by Latin in the towns. Latin in its turn was superseded by a Teutonic language which spread through the thinly populated rural areas because those who spoke it were in control. It is not necessary to assume that their control was achieved by violent conquest in which the Brythons were slaughtered wholesale. Where the establishment is numerous enough there is always a tendency for subordinate people to adopt its language.

The situation continued to worsen, and in 446 the Brythons sent a famous letter of fervent appeal for help to
446   Agitius, 'the last of the Romans':

> 'The barbarians are driving us towards the sea,' says the letter, 'and the sea is driving us towards the barbarians. Between these two kinds of death we shall either be slaughtered or drowned.'

Once again we notice that there is no mention of the English as invaders. It is more likely that it was the Picts or the Irish, who had caused so much destruction before, who were 'driving towards the sea'; unless they were all co-operating with the English pirates as they had done in the great attacks in A.D. 388 which had caused the return of Stilicho. On top of this Wade-Evans notes another very significant fact: in the letter the name Agitius is spelt in the English way. This suggests that the letter, which was an appeal on behalf of all the Britannic citizens, derived from the English element to whom authority had been transferred three years earlier.

Unfortunately, coincident with these rending assaults a fundamental and more dangerous change was taking place in the country's economy and in the minds and wills of the people. Perhaps the cruel pressure of taxes and the tyranny of officials had choked their spirit and caused uprisings as well as harming the economy; but whatever the reason, the civic and economic life of England languished grievously. It is possible that before the end of the fourth century a money economy had ceased. Since the cities ruled wide territories around them, many more people suffered than their own citizens. At the same time, the will to maintain the Roman way of life wilted and died, and the country lapsed into anarchy. No doubt Teutonic attacks added much to the chaos, but it is this inner failure which did most to destroy the society of both Brythons and English; this, rather than a great English invasion, ruined the country.

L F—E

It is strange how completely order was destroyed in England, even within a few miles of the Welsh border. Wroxeter (Caerwrygon), for example, was once a city of substantial size, about four times as large as Caer-went. For some years, up until A.D. 66, it was the fort of the fourteenth legion, and for centuries it was the rich capital of the Cornovicians. Because of its fortunate position — not far from Shrewsbury (Amwythig) where Pengwern, the principal court of old Powys, remained for many centuries yet — it was safer than much of England from the attacks of the Picts, the Irish and the English. The city disappeared completely. It was not killed: it died of lack of will to live. The process of dying had been going on since the beginning of the fourth century. By the middle of the fifth the city was uninhabited. By the middle of the seventh century no doubt Brythonic in the district was as mute as its Latin, and the English tongue alone was heard amid the ruins:

> Drain ac ysgall mall a'i medd,
> Mieri lle bu mawredd.

> Thorns and the blight of thistles own it,
> briars where once was grandeur.

Wroxeter is an image of the greater part of England. The people slipped into the twilight of barbarism like a sword into the sheath, and in this twilight was born the English nation. The old tradition died, not so much through a treacherous conspiracy from outside as from a spiritual failure within. The will to live was wanting. Perhaps the Roman order in the period of decline had contributed towards this by destroying the spirit of self-dependence on the one hand, and on the other by depriving the people of a great cause for which to live and die. The words of Seignobos on the effect of the last century of the Empire on the continent of Europe are appropriate here:

'Since the inhabitants of the Empire were disarmed for generations, and subjected to a remote government which refused to allow them a part in public affairs, they stopped feeling part and parcel of a society which could inspire them with love and self-sacrifice. They became subjects, ready to obey the Government and unable to resist it, but without any feeling of patriotism for the Empire they felt to be an exploiter.'

If selfish apathy was reigning in England, there was a healthier spirit in the hills of Wales, where the people were aware of their membership of their society and responsibility towards it. Their culture may have been rougher: their loyalty was stronger. They possessed more self-confidence, and perhaps they were inclined to look down on the people of the lowlands as the softer people of the plains and their cities were scorned by the Israelites of the hills. Their leaders could depend on their readiness to make even the supreme sacrifice to defend their heritage. That is why there is such a remarkable difference between the sustaining of an unbroken tradition in Welsh society and the great collapse in England, and indeed the destruction in every other part of Europe. In few countries has the native way of life continued unbroken from the time before Christ until our own day. The most important succession for a country is the cultural succession; the absolutely essential continuity for civilisation is the continuity of tradition. The splendour of the history of Wales is that the tradition of the nation has persisted through thousands of years.

Not far from Wroxeter, Llywarch Hen would be in anguish centuries later after losing each of his twenty-four sons, with Gwên, the youngest, killed guarding the ford:

> Gwên wrth Lawen a wyliodd neithiwr;
> Dan bwysau nid ildiodd
> Am Ryd Forlas, oer adrodd.
>
> Pedwar mab ar hugain imi a fu,
> Eurdorchog, tywysogion cad:
> Gwên oedd y gorau gan ei dad.
>
> Gwên near the Llawen watched last night,
> under pressure didn't yield:
> a cold tale about Morlas Ford is told.
>
> Once I had twenty-four sons,
> gold-torqued, leaders in combat:
> Gwên was his father's favourite.

Much cold water has been thrown over the standard of the heroic age, but were it not for the heroism the heritage of Wales would not have been passed on. The Welsh nation would be as dead today as Wroxeter.

IV. ARTHUR

It was the Arthur called king who became in the thought of future generations the most perfect embodiment of this heroic spirit. Although so many world famous legends have been woven around him, he must be accepted as a historical figure who, like Caradog four centuries earlier, made a notable contribution to the endeavour which ensured the continuation of the Welsh tradition. Through this he won a special place among the great in the gallery of the defenders of Wales. He is surrounded by colourful mystery. No one knows his place of birth or burial, where he lived or, with one exception, where he fought the twelve battles listed by Nennius. He is referred to in the *Gododdin*, which was composed in Scotland at the end of the sixth century, as we have seen; and he is named in other early Welsh poetry, and in triads, and in some of the lives of the saints.

Nennius, a Welshman from the south-east of Wales, is the chief source of our knowledge about him: he was writing at the end of the eighth century or the beginning of the ninth. It is he who says that Arthur was a prince of battles (*dux bellorum*), and that he fought 'among the kings of the Brythons', who were confined to the west. He it is who lists the battles, and these could have been copied by him *circa* from an old poem. The only one which can be located 470- definitely was fought in Scotland. His most famous 510 victory was at Mount Badon about 490. The dates of his life are uncertain, but he probably died at the end of the first decade of the sixth century, at the battle of Camlan, the last of his battles, where he fought in civil strife against Medrod and his own people. He was mortally wounded and disappeared from the sight of man — 'Anoeth byd bedd i Arthur' ('The grave of Arthur is a mystery') says the old triad. These battles were fought in the second half of the fifth century after the futile appeal to Agitius, and they were fought against the Picts of the north and the Irish of the west as well as against the English. Arthur co-operated with the Welsh and Brythonic kings as a general and a cavalry leader, going to the places where he was most needed. It is possible that he received a commission from Agitius.

He was a Brython from the west who spoke the language of the Welsh. Geoffrey of Monmouth, the Welshman of Breton descent who developed legends about him in such an attractive manner, says that he was the son of Uthr Pendragon (the meaning of *dragon*, according to Ifor Williams, is Chieftain, leader) whose name still remains in the Welsh tradition. His court was said to be Gelli-wig, Cornwall; *Culhwch and Olwen* and *The Dream of Rhonabwy* are Welsh tales which record the same. All the Celts from Scotland to Brittany lay claim to Arthur; he lived when they were in close contact with each other, and he remains through the centuries a link between them.

It is Wales, however, which is most indebted to him — the Welsh-speaking hero who was not a Welshman. It was his dedication as a leader, and his heroism and military skill, which won the series of brilliant victories against the enemy who could perhaps have overwhelmed Wales were it not for him. This is what has won for him his position amongst the greatest benefactors of our nation, but his most illustrious place is in her legends. Of all the great men who defended and enriched our tradition, he is the most colouful and the most mysterious. It is about him that most has been written. As with Glyndŵr a thousand years later, no one wanted to believe that he was dead. The Welsh kept his name alive. What of his spirit?

V. THE TENACITY OF THE STATES

AN outstanding characteristic of the Welsh states is their stability, and the longevity of their royal families. This is rarely appreciated. It is an image of a quarrelsome, warloving nation perpetually at one another's throats, which English historians have made of Wales. After being thrust back into the mountains, they say, the Welsh could not live in agreement with each other; they were wholly disunited — 'a race of quarrelsome nightingales'. This is the picture of themselves that the Welsh have accepted, to the detriment of their self-respect and confidence. Could it not be that all this is more true of our powerful neighbours in England? The English failed to unite England. It was their Danish conquerors who did that for them. It was Canute, after the second Danish conquest, who was responsible for the unity of England; and the feat was possible because the English combined with the Danes against their other conquerors, the Vikings. Canute ruled England as part of his Danish Empire. The English loved Canute who issued 'the last and most comprehensive Code' of English law before the Norman conquest. He treated them with respect and handled their laws and traditions in a civilised manner, giving the English language parity with Danish, so different from the treatment which was to be meted out to the language and laws of Wales.

The first English king to rule a united England was Edward the Confessor, who ascended the throne in 1042. He owed his accession to the fact that his family, the family of Alfred, was the sole survivor of a royal family in England. In striking contrast to the situation in Wales, all English royal families save the dynasty of Wessex had become extinct. F. M. Stenton, a leading English historian, observes that 'English history between the sixth and ninth century is the record of incessant wars', and this before the two Danish conquests and the Viking and Norman conquests. According to Stenton, English history begins at the end of the sixth century, with the landing of Saint Augustine in Kent in 597, when the tradition of Wales was already old. And if Edward the Confessor was the first Englishman to rule the whole of England, he was also until recently the last.

Some Welsh royal dynasties continued to rule their little states without a break between 597 and 1066, and some of them had been there, as we have seen, over a long period before 597. The histories of the royal families of Gwynedd, Dyfed, Morganwg, Gwent and Powys, began two centuries and more before that. This reflects more peace and civilisation in Wales than some people wish to admit. We should remember that the centuries we are now discussing, the fifth and the sixth, were the age of the saints and the age of the development of the Welsh language; the age which saw the spiritual revolution, and the age of the greatest intellectual energy experienced in Welsh history. This was made possible by the quality of the leaders and the order which they sustained; Political success depended on the standard of civilisation of the society. By now this society was very old, its roots stretching down to the early Celts and further than that. Wales had been its motherland for close on two thousand years.

In the first half of the sixth century Gildas scourges five kings, two of them belonging to the peninsula to the south of the Severn Sea, and three to Wales. The monument of one of the three, Votiporix, is in the museum at Carmarthen today, and his name is carved on it in Roman capitals as well as in Ogham letters. They all lived in the part of Britain that Gildas called Britannia, an early example of the limitation of this term to the Welsh West.

Gildas was a monk who had been a disciple of Saint Cadog, and it was in the great monastery of Cadog in Llancarfan, as a confessor of the saints, that he is last heard of. He was a Pict, whose family came to live on the banks of the Clyde in the county of Lanark (Llannerch), where Cadog established a monastery at Cambuslang — the church there remains dedicated to him. This was therefore Gildas Albanus, and not the author of *De Excidio Brittanniae* which is a much later work, and which has been wrongly attributed to him. He wrote his letter chastising the five kings in the manner of Jeremiah, in order to convince the lords of the land of their sin. But the men he chastises are sure of their position, with no suggestion of danger from within or without. The society reflected in his writing is a settled one — an orderly society living under a law firmly administered. Gildas took the virtues of that order established by leaders in whom he saw no personal

virtues. He fails to name one good man, but the worst of all
the bad ones he believes to be Maelgwn Gwynedd, 'The
Dragon of the Island' as he was called — a reference to the
foundation of his strength in Anglesey, where his father
Cadwallon Lawhir had vanquished the Irish.

VI. MAELGWN GWYNEDD

MAELGWN Gwynedd was the great-grandson of Cunedda.
He therefore represented the most important Welsh royal
dynasty who were to some extent overlords of all the other
kings. It can be presumed that he ascended the throne at the
end of the fifth century, before the death of Arthur. He was a
big man — big in body (he was called Maelgwn Hir, Maelgwn
the Tall), big in his natural ability, his generosity and in
his crimes. Though perhaps exaggerated, the crimes attributed
to him by Gildas are frightful; indeed, he is as fierce in his
rebukes to him as Elijah was to Ahab and Jezebel. Maelgwn
is said to have murdered his wife, the sister of Brochwel
Ysgithrog king of Powys, and his nephew in order to marry
the nephew's wife. Whether or not this springs from Gildas's
malicious imagination, it is obvious that he was a short-
tempered, undisciplined man. The fact that he was on bad
terms with the saints — the evangelical monks — is reflected in
their biographies centuries later. They show that he had
quarrelled with a number of the greatest Christian leaders,
including Cybi in Anglesey, Tydecho in Powys, Padarn in
Ceredigion, Beynach in Dyfed, and Cadog in Gwynllwg,
the last of whom used fasting as a weapon against him. He is
portrayed as a cruel tyrant, but a stronger man even than
Arthur who also had his troubles with the saints according
to their *Lives*.

Saint and prince used to come into headlong collision with
each other because they were, like Thomas â Becket and Henry
II in England, struggling for authority. The Roman Empire
knew this quarrel well: 'Christians are counted as public
enemies,' said Tertullian, 'because they do not attribute vain,

false and foolish honours to the Emperor'. The history of
Vortigern and Maelgwn Gwynedd shows that the great
question of the relationship between Church and State was a
very old one in Wales. There was a great principle at stake in
this struggle, namely the nature of the supreme authority
in society: governmental and military authority, or moral
and intellectual authority? No doubt the confidence with
which the Welsh church leaders withstood the secular power
owed something to the royal descent of some of them. Socially
they were the equals of the princes. Perhaps the conflict went
back much further even than the age of the saints, back to the
pre-Christian period, to the Druids. In *Rhwng Chwedl a
Chredo*, Pennar Davies notes:

> 'It is difficult to evade the conclusion that the belief that the military
> and political leaders of society should take their lead from the wisest
> and best informed was part of the principle of Druidism . . . To the
> 'Celts' of old there was — in the intellect the spirit, the muse—a
> higher authority than the strength of the arm and the club. On the
> basis of this principle the learned and gifted class advised and chastised
> the leaders and the warmongers and reconciled them when necessary.'

In mid career Maelgwn did something which shows what
an extraordinary man he was. For a time he gave up his throne
when at the peak of his power; he turned his back on the
world and became a monk, a course subsequently followed by
princes in other Celtic countries. The saints were not pleased,
however, when he returned to his royal function, although he
helped the Church generously, bestowing lands and special
rights upon it; for example, he is said to have given Cybi the
Roman fort at Caergybi (Holyhead) in order to build a church
there. His period as a monk throws light on the relationship
between politics and the Church, and more is shed by his early
education. Gildas says that the young prince from Gwynedd
received his education from, 'the chosen master of almost
the whole of Britain'. He must have been referring to Illtud
or Cadog who both presided over great and illustrious
institutions in Bro Morgannwg (the Vale of Glamorgan). The
fact that the heir to the throne of Gwynedd should be educated
near the banks of the Severn Sea tells us much about the unity

and homogeneity of the Welsh society and about its stability and the state of its civilisation within a generation of the despairing appeal which was sent from England to Agitius.

Gildas was angered by the 'ciwed gnafaidd' — the knavish rabble — of poets and singers who sang the praises of Maelgwn Gwynedd, and he contrasted their compositions with the Church's sweet hymns of praise. 'The stories and plays of men of the outside world' also came in for criticism. Eight hundred years later the monks still feel much the same towards Dafydd ap Gwilym and his fellow-poets. Our response is different from that of the puritanical monk to this testimony that the royal courts of Aberffro and Dyganwy were patronising poets, conteurs and singers so soon after the departure of the Romans, and that there were twenty-four poets around the king on important occasions. In his anger Gildas testifies to the fact that there was a vivid life in Wales, varied and creative, a life which had been wonderfully enriched by the great Christian revolution which was afoot at the time.

The role of the poets and their songs of praise was to remain for a thousand years after this a fundamentally important element in Welsh life and tradition. According to D. Myrddin Lloyd:

'The poems of praise were an old tradition among the Celts long before the establishment of the Welsh nation . . . Between the days of Gildas and the time of Einion Offeiriad a Welsh Christian mind had worked on this poetic tradition, and had seen it in a very different light. The praise-poem was a way of holding a mirror up to society, and especially to the leader, and — through this picture of what it and he should be — inflaming their love for that image. Wales was proud of its legal system and its rights; but in the crisis that presented itself to each generation in its turn, the maintaining of law and rights — all the benefits of society—depended on patience, on courage, on the *character* of the leader and on loyalty to him. If he were unwise — open to vainglory, perhaps, or cowardice—he could easily bring his people under the foot of the enemy. "*A braint, diffaith y weithion*" ("And dignity—now it is destroyed") said Cynddelw Brydydd Mawr, after the death of Madog ab Meredudd and his son in the same year. All the passion of the period before 1282 is in the praise-poems. It was not ceremony or flattery, and society held that the status and vocation of the poet had to be protected.'

In spite of the gravity of the crimes which Maelgwn Gwynedd is accused of by Gildas, he was a great leader of men, who made a heavy impress on his contemporaries and a positive contribution to his generation. The order of Gwynedd was strengthened in a way that enabled it to become a strong structure for Welsh nationhood for more than seven centuries after his day. He nurtured the language and culture of his kingdom, and he helped the Church, leaving the Welsh and Christian tradition of his country stronger because of his rule. When he died in 547 of the yellow plague which 547 ravaged the countries of Europe, the greatest Celtic leader of his generation and century was laid to rest at Llanrhos.

VII. THE MEN OF THE OLD NORTH

THE successor of Maelgwn Gwynedd was his son Rhun, whose strengths and weaknesses had no Gildas or saint's biographer to record them. In spite of this his leadership is recognised among the Welsh kings of his period, and he was notable enough to find a place in *The Dream of Rhonabwy* by virtue of his wisdom. He is referred to in the Gwynedd version of the laws of Hywel Dda, strangely enough because of the part he played in an attack on Scotland. According to the story told there, an army came from the north to punish the men of Gwynedd for killing Elidr Hael, a chieftain from Scotland, in Arfon; and Rhun ap Maelgwn Gwynedd led the counter-attack as far as the river Forth.

These attacks to and fro between Wales and Scotland testify to two things: first, that there was close communication between Wales, the Brythonic kingdoms in Scotland and the north of England — the territory of the 'Men of the North'; and second, that the enemies of the Welsh and the northern Brythons were very mobile, and could travel hundreds of miles into enemy territory. As we have seen, Taliesin refers to a military assault on Cornwall by Cynan Garwyn of Powys.

There is no mention of military buildings slowing down the movements; the fort and the castle had ceased to play an important part in military operations. This suggests that it would have been quite possible for Arthur's army to fight in different battles very far apart within a short space of time. It is noticeable that there is no mention of fighting against the

550-
570

English in Rhun's time, although a hundred and fifty years had gone by since the departure of the Romans from England. On the other hand, there is mention in Welsh tradition of the relationship of another Rhun — Rhun the son of Urien Rheged — with Englishmen, and it is not warring but evangelising that is mentioned. It is said that it was Rhun the son of Urien who converted Edwin, king of the English kingdom of Deifr, to Christianity.

A little later, before the end of the century, there are quite a lot of stories of fighting between the Men of the Old North and

572-
592

the English kingdoms in the north-east of England, between the Humber and the country of the Gododdin, namely Deifr (Deira) and Brynaich (Bernicia) — possibly the first of all stable English kingdoms. Nothing is known of a Brythonic kingdom in these parts. The Brythons did however unite in an alliance to march against the English, and did so under four leaders: Urien Rheged, Gwallog, Morgan and Rhydderch from Strathclyde. Aneirin and Taliesin are our chief sources of information about this decisive campaign, and although there was no military alliance between the Welsh and the Men of the Old North there was great pride in Wales on account of the heroism of their Brythonic brethren. It was here amongst the Cymry that their history and literature were treasured, greatly nourishing Welsh patriotism. The half century or so of uneasy peace which had been secured by Arthur's victories

577

had ended both in the south and in the north. An English victory at Deorham to the south of Gloucester is recorded in 577 but the Welsh seem to have had no part in the battle. Some have contended that Deorham isolated Wales from the Brythons of the south, but there is no record of communication between the peoples during the preceding century, and in any case the sea-routes were still open. The fighting in the north had more effect.

There were three strong Welsh kingdoms in the north. Two of them lay wholly within Scotland. Ystrad Clud (Strathclyde) was in the mid south-west with its capital at Dumbarton, and its ecclesiastical centre at Glasgow, where the Welsh Brython Cyndeyrn (Kentigern) established a church; the principal church there bears his name to this day. This is the kingdom of Ceredig Wledig with whose soldiers Patrick corresponded; it comprised Aeron (Ayr). Caeredin (Edinburgh), where Aneirin lived, was the capital of Gododdin, which stretched southwards from the river Forth. Rheged, with its capital at Caer Lliwelydd (Carlisle), contained the most south-westerly parts of Scotland, around Merin Rheged (Solway Firth). We hear too of Elfed in the west of Yorkshire, a very small kingdom which was perhaps established there by Gwallog in the sixth century, but was lost again in the following century when Ceredig was driven from the area by Edwin of Northumberland. It would be a mistake to think that it was only Brythons who inhabited these countries. English of Friesian origin came there early on. Aber Gweryd (the Firth of Forth) was called the Friesian Sea, and in Strathclyde is to be found Dumfries — 'the Fort of the Friesians').

Urien Rheged was the most able soldier among the Men of the North, and it was to him that Taliesin sang. It is this Urien who is described in battle by the poet of Llywarch Hen —

> Ac ar y fron wen frân ddu.

> And on the white breast a black crow.

When Morgant and his legion attacked this gallant man,

> Llyc a grafai wrth glegyr;

he was like 'A mouse scratching against a rock'. He is depicted by Taliesin as a fine military leader who was no statesman. In the words of Ifor Williams: 'He is a warrior to the end, until he is white-haired, until he is old'. We see in him too the arrogant temper of the lord who does not want a competitor: he was a 'teyrn' (autocrat) in the modern sense of the word; they were afraid of him in his own court as well as outside. It is easy to credit and understand how a rift opened in his alliance against the English of Ida's time: he did not know how to lead his peers fairly. Because of him the unity which could have saved the north was dissolved. According to Nennius, Morgant and the others sulked and left him 'because of jealousy', and he died on the battlefield. If he was for some time king of Catraeth (Catterick), he was lost when Deira and Bernicia grew in strength. Incidentally, the fact that Taliesin refers to him as Gwledig Catraeth shows that Taliesin wrote before Aneirin. Towards the end of the century these two kingdoms united to form Northumbria, which remained the strongest kingdom of England until it was supplanted in the eighth century by Mercia — which was, like Northumbria, a little larger than the whole of Wales.

It was against Catterick, which was now enemy territory, that Mynyddog the king of Gododdin prepared his famous attack, which is celebrated in the poem by Aneirin. For a whole year three hundred chosen men had been lodged and trained by the king. They included soldiers from other countries, such as Owain Môn of the lineage of Maelgwn Gwynedd — 'detholwyr pob doeth-wlad' ('chosen men from each wise land').

All three hundred were killed with the exception of one or two. The poet praises the wonderful bravery of the young and handsome men who were faithful unto death, but he does not praise them collectively as an Army. Aneirin describes and praises them as individuals whom he knew personally; he praised each of them for his courage and loyalty to his overlord, giving a vivid picture of men whom he had seen with his own eyes.

This was the last attack of the Men of the North against the English: from now on they gradually lost their territory. As a result of the battle of Catraeth, Northumbria was strengthened and it cast its net further west. Nennius records that Oswy, king of Northumbria from 641 to 672, married Rhiainfellt, the great-grand-daughter of Urien Rheged, and that the kingdom of Rheged thus came into his possession: it was through this fateful marriage and not through conquest that Rheged disappeared. This brought English political authority to the edge of Strathclyde. Northumbria also extended its rule northwards up to the river Forth into the territory of Gododdin.

The spread of the English language accompanied the spread of English rule. People are inclined to accept the language of their masters, just as they often accept their religion; it was no use telling them to speak Welsh on the hearth. Whole generations have been seen to change their religion with a change of government or a change in the mind of a government. The spectacle of people accepting the language of their rulers is even more familiar. It is the government and the establishment and not the hearth that usually determines a people's language. Among the Celtic peoples this is the rule even in the centuries long before educational developments and modern techniques were able to force the language of the government on the people.

Strathclyde was now the only Welsh kingdom left in the north. It remained strong until it too was incorporated into Scotland in the eleventh century. Nor was this the result of conquest: the kingdom was inherited by the unfortunate king Duncan who is portrayed in Shakespeare's *Macbeth*.

Cornwall lost its freedom in 836, so that Wales became the only self-governing member of the Brythonic nations of the island. As a consequence, Wales alone preserved its national tradition. The Men of the Old North had fought bravely: 'Dros ryddid collasant eu gwaed' ('They lost their blood for freedom'). But they also lost their freedom. For that reason the old language did not survive among them, and when they ceased to speak Welsh they ceased to be Welsh. Welshmen looked in vain over Offa's Dyke for companions in Welsh nationhood. In Rheged and Devon, Strathclyde and Cornwall,

'Llefarai dewr arglwyddi ein cadarn heniaith ni,
Parablai arglwyddesau heirdd ei pheraidd eiriau hi.'

Our vigorous old tongue was spoken by brave lords,
with lovely ladies eloquent in its sweet words.

But for centuries the language has been silenced there. Their freedom was over. Where there was no national freedom the people perished.

Saint David — Dewi Sant by John Petts

Page from *The Book of Kells*

Christian Wales

I. FROM HELEN TO CADOG

IN SPITE of the magnificence of its culture and the high evolution of its economy, Rome's yoke on Wales had been light. Since the time at the end of the 4th century when the Welsh had to accept responsibility for themselves, their traditional life developed and flowered. Materially life in Wales was still harsh; comfort and bodily luxury were in very short supply. Compared with the standards of the twentieth century, life in the fifth century was very primitive indeed, although it was no worse in Wales than in the greater part of Europe, and no doubt better than in many other parts. In spite of this the two hundred years which followed the departure of Macsen Wledig (Magnus Maximus) was the period most like a golden age in the whole history of Wales. What makes the deepest impression is the dynamism of these two centuries: the physical and the mental and spiritual energy, the creative power. Impressive industry is to be observed at that time: politically, intellectually and culturally, and above all in religion.

Strong, well-ordered states were created; Brittany was established, the native culture developed, and some of the Roman culture and learning was assimilated; an excellent language was formed, and the creating of a language is the greatest feat of man; and as if this were not enough, spiritual life was revolutionised and throughout the land people were imbued with Christian values as the life of no other nation was imbued. This early it was demonstrated that freedom and responsibility can do more than secure that the tradition of the nation continues and develops according to the characteristic talents of the society: they can also stimulate and excite the development of all the resources of the people, morally, mentally and materially.

L F—F

Christians had been living and worshipping in the south-east of Wales in the fourth century, and it is possible that Chrisianity had reached Wales much earlier than this. About 20c A.D. Tertullian's testimony, supported by Origen, is that there were 'places in Britain, although they were too inaccessible for the Romans, which had yielded to Christ'. These areas could include parts of Wales and Scotland, which missionaries had reached by sea from the West. However, at the end of the fourth century the great revolution started under the leadership of the royal families. Christianity was an aristocratic religion in Wales in this period. Three families in particular are to be seen in the forefront: the families of Macsen Wledig, Cunedda and Brychan Brycheiniog; Magnus the Roman soldier from Spain, Cunedda the leader from Scotland, and Brychan of Irish descent.

Macsen's connection with the new movement is particularly interesting and significant, for he obtained the support and friendship of Saint Martin of Tours, the patron saint of France, when he went over to the Continent in 383. It was Martin, who had had a vision of Christ when he was a soldier, who was the main supporter of the ascetic and militant monasticism which caught the imagination of the Welsh saints. It was in Wales that this form of Christianity saw its fullest develop-ment: the saints were monks living in this manner; this was David's way of life. Their way of life was very different from the Roman mode of Christianity in England. The Roman-English pattern was priestly and urban: in Wales it was monastic and rural; but Latin was the language of both systems. Bearing in mind the connections with Gaul there is nothing unlikely in the tradition of Elen the daughter *circa* of Eudwy of Gwynedd returning to Caernarfon after 390 the killing of Macsen her husband — with her two A.D. sons, Cystennin (Constantine) and Peblig (Publicus), who were both monks who had learnt their monasticism from Martin. Many churches are dedicated to Elen including, suitably enough, one in Anglesey and another in Gwent. There is a church at Llangystennin in Caernarfon-shire, twenty miles to the east of Llanbeblig, and another in a place now called Welsh Bicknor near the border in Hereford-shire. These are the very first Welsh saints known to us. Others came afterwards from Macsen's family — in all there are nearly 40 churches dedicated to them.

It was the south-east of Wales, the region that came most heavily under the influence of Rome, that first saw the great increase in the monastic and evangelical movement. The pioneers there were the family of Brychan Brycheiniog, a contemporary of Cunedda and Vortigern. Brychan, whose kingdom included Breconshire (Brycheiniog) had quite a large family — assuming that they were all children of his own flesh and blood — and many of them became saints. Among the boys are Clydog, Cynog and Berwyn; the names of the daughters shine like a cluster of stars — Gwladys, the wife of Gwynllyw and the mother of Cadog; Tudful in Merthyr Tudful (*Merthyr* corresponding to *Llan* in those days); Tybie in Llandybie; Dwynwen in Llanddwynwen; Cain in Llangeinor; Ceingar the mother of Cynidr; and Meleri the grandmother of Dewi.

A saint who was connected with Brychan's children was Peulin (Paulinus) who has two chapels called after him in the parish of Llandingad, Llanymddyfri (Llandovery). Dingad was

circa
420
to
490

another of Brychan's sons. Peulin had been a pupil of Garmon and was therefore a link with Roman Christianity. He was a learned man, the head of a monastic school, similar to the school of Illtud, where Dewi and Teilo sat at his feet. Dewi was thus educated by a man who had been taught by Saint Garmon. In Cynwyl Caeo, Carmarthenshire, in that part of the country where his influence was strongest, a memorial column (now in the Carmarthen museum) was found bearing the name of Peulin. Although there is no certainty about this, it is quite likely that it is Saint Peulin whom it commemorates; the likelihood is strengthened by its location and the type of metrical inscription on it. It says, in Latin, 'Protector of the Faith and consistent lover of his country, Peulin lies here: he followed faithfully what was right.' It is proper that these words are found in the natural fort of Cantref Mawr on the memorial stone of a great Welshman of the fifth century, in the neighbourhood of Llywelyn ap Gruffydd Fychan of Caeo who was executed in Llanymddyfri in 1401 in the presence of Henry IV because of his support — with his sons — of Owain Glyndŵr; and not very far from Rhydcymerau, where the remains of another patriot were laid to rest almost fifteen hundred years after the time of Peulin. Peulin's epitaph would have been wholly appropriate to D. J. Williams: 'Protector of the Faith and consistent lover of his country: he followed faithfully what was right.'

One of the members of Brychan's circle was his friend and chaplain, Brynach Wyddel (Brynach the Irishman), after whom a dozen or more churches, mainly in Pembrokeshire, are named. Another Irishman among the early saints was Tathan, the teacher of Cadog, who settled in Gwent in the first half of the 5th century. His father was King Tuathal (Tathalius), who possibly reigned in the north-west of Wales. Tathan established a monastery in Caer-went on land he received from Caradog, the king of Gwent whose dynasty reigned there for nearly six hundred years. Of him J. E. Lloyd writes: "All the men of Gwent revered him as the father of their land, its guardian and the avenger of its wrongs."

circa 420 to 490

The most energetic evangelist of all the great men of the fifth century in the south-east was Dyfrig, who can be placed fairly clearly in time as it is known that he was a little older than Illtud. The area of his influence was the foundation of the diocese of Llandaf. He too was a scholar and teacher; he received pupils from all parts in his monastery at Henlan in the Vale of Wye. Like so many saints who exhausted their energies in very heavy work, Dyfrig withdrew as a hermit to the Island of Enlli (Bardsey) where, like Padarn and Deiniol before him, he lies buried. It was the practice of the saints to retire into 'the desert' like this, but they were not allowed to go before they had completed their evangelical work. Enlli attracted more of them than any other lonely island near the Welsh coast, and for that reason it was looked upon as a holy island.

circa 410 to 480

It became the haunt of pilgrims. Three pilgrimages to Enlli were considered equal to two to Saint David's and one to Rome:

> Mae yno ugain mil o saint
>   Ym mraint y mor a'i genlli,
> Ac nid oes dim a gyffry hedd
>   Y bedd yn Ynys Enlli.

> And there are twenty thousand saints,
> honoured where the seas lave,
> and nothing comes to mar the peace
> of Bardsey's quiet grave.

Thus T. Gwynn Jones. But he would not have been thinking of Dyfrig, for in May 1120 his grave was plundered by priests of Llandaf who claimed him as a bishop, and carried his remains to the cathedral in Llandaf. Thus it is not 'yn nwys dangnefedd Enlli' (in the solemn peace of Enlli), that the dust of Dyfrig lies but somewhere in the bosom of the noisy city of Cardiff.

It should be noted in passing that Christianity had rooted itself in Ireland and Scotland, as in Cornwall and Brittany too, in this period. Patrick of course is the great name in Ireland. It may be that it was from the Vale of Severn that he was taken there as a slave. His father and grandfather were Christians who spoke Latin. Since he died in 461 it may be presumed that there was Christianity in the region where he was reared in the middle of the fourth century. Ceredig Wledig brought some of Patrick's converts as slaves from Ireland. In a letter chastising him Patrick refers to the fact that Ceredig claims to be a Christian and a patron of the church and the monks. This proves that Christianity had reached the Vale of Clyde (Clud) early in the fifth century. Further north Nynio had been working among the Picts a century and more before Columba crossed from Ireland in 565.

We must now bring into the picture the biggest names among all the saints of the south-east, Cadog and Illtud, the greatest scholars of the fifth century in the Celtic countries. Cadog's father was King Gwynllyw and his mother Gwladys

was the daughter of Brychan. Educated by Tathan in Caer-
went, he was a notable example of the royal lineage of so
many of the saints. It is a tribute to his position that Liffrig,
who wrote one of the Lives of David, considered him as the
chief rival of his hero; but Cadog was long dead when David
was born. Very few travelled more than Cadog did along the
Roman roads which were so extensively used by the saints.
He made a great name for himself as a wise and well-informed
teacher in the monastery which he established in Llancarfan
in the Vale of Glamorgan, near which Iolo Morganwg was
born thirteen hundred years later. From there his influence
spread throughout Wales, and beyond its shores to Cornwall
and Brittany, Ireland and Scotland. It is worth noticing that
neither he nor any of the other Welsh saints worked to the
east of Gwent and Hereford. They were not enticed along the
Roman road in that direction. Why not, one wonders? A
difficulty of language? English, Pictish or Scottish raids?
Social disturbances? A mystery indeed.

II. ILLTUD AND EDUCATION.

ALTHOUGH the poets made a rich contribution to education,
the great teachers of the age were the saints. Between them
they fulfilled the educational function of the druids. It was in
Morgannwg and Gwent that the educational tradition was at
its strongest, perhaps because the influence of the Romans was
greatest in that area. It is not too much to see in the great
schools of the saints there the shoots of the marvellous schools
that rose later on the continent of Europe, although it was
Irish scholars and evangelists, rather than the Welsh, who
laboured most on the Continent and outside the Celtic
countries.

Among the saints there is only one who in his time was
more famous than Cadog, who was known as Catwg the Wise
because of his learning and wisdom. Illtud was the most
learned among them. He was another of the brilliant students

of Saint Garmon, whose influence, directly and indirectly, was so strong on the political and religious life of Wales. According to his biography, Illtud was the son of King Glywys and the grandson of Amlodd Wledig. He had been a soldier and captain of the guard, but on the banks of the Dawen (Thaw) in the Vale of Glamorgan he had a vision and heard a voice saying: 'It is your love for a woman which is preventing your turning to the Lord.' He became a monk and his wife a nun. In the same area, about ten miles to the west of Llancarfan, he established at Llanilltud Fawr a monastery which became the haunt of many great men of the period. Maelgwn Gwynedd, a descendant of Cunedda Wledig, would never have been sent there but for the belief of the royal house of Gwynedd in the education offered in the Vale of Glamorgan.

It is fortunate that there is a description of Illtud to be found in the biography of Saint Samson, who was one of his famous pupils, which was written in the beginning of the seventh century. It says there that he, 'amongst all the Brythons was the greatest scholar in Holy Scripture, the Old Testament and the New, as well as in every branch of knowledge, such as geometry, grammar, arithmetic and a knowledge of all the arts; and he has the ability to foresee occurrences.' To these could be added a knowledge of Latin texts, and even Greek, for there is testimony enough that the early saints knew Greek. Indeed this, as well as their way of dating Easter, is part of the argument for believing that the Christianity of Wales had its roots in the east of Europe rather than in Rome.

Latin was the chief means of communication between the saints of the different countries, and also the language of the services of the monasteries. Welsh, no doubt, was the language of communication within the cloisters, but there is no mention of a Welsh Bible, nor of using Welsh in the services. Such famous Brythons as Pelagius and Faustus, Ricocatus and Fastidius, Gildas and Padrig, wrote in Latin, although there is proof that Pelagius was fluent in Greek also. Since the communication between the monks of the Celtic countries was so close, they developed a distinctive Latin style of their own

But of course they could not evangelise the people through the medium of Latin; they had to speak to them in their own language, and Welsh was the language of the great majority of the Welsh people. Hence very few Irish saints, fervent and energetic missionaries though they were, came to work in Wales; and since not many of the Welsh saints could speak Irish, very few of them laboured in Ireland. Perhaps this helps to explain why they did not work in England, even as early as this: they could not speak English.

A story relevant to the position of Latin among the saints is told about Gildas and Cadog on a desert island near the southern shores of Brittany, where Cadog was building a monastery. One day, while he was walking along the shore with Gildas, his Virgil under his arm, Cadog wept at the thought that the author whom he admired so much was in hell. Gildas bluntly reproved him. At that the Virgil was blown away by a strong gust of wind. Cadog returned sadly to his cell. In his sleep he heard a voice (from purgatory, he thought) saying: 'Pray for me; do not tire of praying.' Next day he received a fish as a gift from a fisherman, and inside it he found the Virgil he had lost. This story reflects the tenderness and liberal nature of Cadog as well as his love of the great pagan Latin poet.

The list of disciplines of which Illtud was master shows that the colleges of the saints contributed much more than a scriptural and theological education, although this list does not exhaust the syllabus; for example manual skills and work on the land were essential parts of the educational course. It was not only academic subjects which were taught at these comprehensive schools. They taught very little pagan literature, but a prominent role was given to philosophy. This field was of necessity divided into three parts; three has been the most important number for the Welshman who always gets 'tri chynnig' (three chances) since the days of prehistory when the Celts thought in threes about the supernatural beings who ruled their world; and through the triads of the poets up to the three inevitable headings of the preachers of the 'Hen Gorff', the Calvinistic Methodists. The three fields of the philosophers in the schools of the saints were physics, ethics and logic.

A syllabus was prepared for laymen as well as monks, and women as well as men, and children as well as adults. However, parents sometimes doubted whether it was wise to send their children to these schools. They feared that the militant Christian spirit of the school would turn their children away from the path of political or military service into the Church, for it was the Church which attracted the most able people at that time. This is precisely what happened to Samson. He was sent to Illtud by his father, Amwn Ddu of Dyfed, to be prepared for a political career. Amwn hesitated before sending him there; he feared that Llanilltud Fawr would make a monk of his son. He had discussed the possibility of having him educated at home with his wife, Ann of Gwent; that too was possible at that time. But it was to Llanilltud Fawr that Samson went, and there he found himself among such pupils as Gildas and Paul Aurelian, the founder of Saint Pol de Leon in Brittany. His father's fears were proved true. Samson became one of the greatest missionary saints of his time.

There were in Wales schools other than the monastic ones: these were the schools of the poets, which descended more directly from the druids. Eoin MacNeill believed that the last Brythonic schools of the classical *rhetores* could be found in Dyfed in the sixth century. If this is correct then certainly these schools were connected with the old druidic schools, and no doubt it was the poets who were in charge of them. Saunders Lewis raises the question of whether the schools of the lawyers and *tafodogion* (barristers) were a continuation of the Latin *rhetores* in the middle ages.

Illtud was the greatest and most distinguished of the assembly of great men who developed and enlightened the educational tradition of the druids in the spirit of Saint Colomba who said 'Christ is our druid.' Through their schools they gave great confidence to the saints and a new energy to their culture. It was they who laid the intellectual foundations of the Celtic Church, which was to be the most splendid establishment of the nation.

III. DAVID (DEWI) AT THE CENTRE OF
THE SURGE.

DURING the two centuries of the spiritual revolution
which recreated the life of Wales, the nation
circa was like clay in the hands of the potter. The
515 surge of the Christian tide reached its zenith
to in the age of David (Dewi), who was born
585 about a century and a quarter after it began to
rise and who died about a century and a quarter before
it receded. In more than one sense David was in the middle
of it.

By his day the character of the Church of the Welsh had
been established, and David was a mirror of that character.
Nine statements can·be made about it: (*i*) it was a monastic
not a priestly church; (*ii*) it was a missionary church — the
saints went out into the highways and byways to convey their
vision of God in Christ; (*iii*) it was learned; (*iv*) its languages
were Welsh and Latin; (*v*) it was Celtic in its connections;
(*vi*) it was of a high spiritual level; (*vii*) it was ascetic in its
discipline; (*viii*) it was decentralised and effective in its organisation; (*ix*) it was a Church for the whole of Wales.

David was a learned monk, an ascetic man of high purity
and devotion, who stimulated the foundation of a great community of free churches in Wales, who maintained contact
with the other Celtic countries, and who became the patron
saint of his country. Of the patron saints of the four main
nations of these islands, he alone was brought up in the land
which he protects as patron saint. He was reared in Henfynyw
in Ceredigion, the kingdom of Ceredig, on the banks of
Aeron. He united in his person two of the most important
families connected with the saints, the one in the north-west
and the other in the south-east. He was descended on his
father's side from Cunedda, and from Brychan Brycheiniog
on his mother's. His father was called Sant, and his grandfather
Ceredig. Meleri the daughter of Brychan was his grandmother, and Cunedda his great-grandfather. His mother was
Non, the daughter of Cynyr of Caeo — the land of Peulin

in the Cantref Mawr; and it was from Peulin that he got his education. He was thus related to many of the most prominent saints and princes of Wales. If the Church of the Welsh was embodied in his person, the history and geography of his country were united in him too.

He founded a monastery in Glyn Rhosin, a place well sheltered from the sea and extremely convenient for the saints from Brittany, Cornwall, Ireland and Scotland. Irishmen mixed freely with the Welsh in this area, and no doubt David knew Irish as well as Welsh and Latin. Gwynfardd Brycheiniog refers to his Welsh in his well-known *awdl*. His emphasis was different from that of the saints of the south-east. Although Illtud and Cadog, Peulin and Tathan were evangelists, their emphasis lay upon education. David and Teilo were men of learning, like Padarn whose influence spread throughout mid-Wales from Llanbadarn Fawr, but their stress was on evangelisation. They were teachers, but their main work was preaching the gospel. In this too they reflected the nature of the people of Wales. Just as there was a great respect for education in the time of the druids, so the intense preaching of the saints seized upon the love of the spoken word revealed in the ancient love of rhetoric and poetry, which was always delivered by word of mouth: 'Two things they are intensely concerned about,' says Cato the Elder, of the Celts of Gaul; 'to be brave in war and to speak well.'

They learnt their lessons word by word and committed them to memory; that is what the pupils of the druidic schools and the schools of the saints did. Producing a generation of inspiring teachers and great preachers was part of an old pattern, the continuation of an ancient tradition. As the Folk Schools of Denmark depended on what their prophet Grundtvig called 'The Living Word' which awoke and enlivened, so also did the early peaceful missionaries of Wales. We read in Rhygyfarch's biography of David about the land rising under the saint's feet when he was preaching at a Synod of Bishops in Llanddewi Brefi: this is the author's colourful way of showing the power of his hero's personality, the depth of his conviction, the strength of his reasoning and especially the influence of his great ability as a preacher.

David travelled the country tirelessly as the great revivalists did in the eighteenth century. As the travels of Paul and his companions were made possible around the Mediterranean by the Roman peace, so also in Wales the roads and the internal peace were conditions of the work of the saints. It is quite likely that it was easier for David to travel in the sixth century than it was for Pantycelyn in the eighteenth. He met many of his fellow evangelists on his journeys whose names are known to us. The names of five hundred saints from these two wonderful centuries survive, and it is notable that they are Welsh not Latin. The burden of their message was the same in every generation, in every province in Wales, in every country: honour God and praise Christ and glorify the Holy Trinity. Twelve hundred years later a succession of great preachers and hymn writers (Titus Lewis) would be conveying the same message to the same country, and in the same language.

> Mawr oedd Crist yn nhragwyddoldeb,
> Mawr yn gwisgo natur dyn;
> Mawr yn marw ar Galfaria,
> Mawr yn maeddu angau'i hun;
> Hynod fawr yw yn awr,
> Brenin nef a daear lawr.

> Great was Christ once in eternity,
> great in human nature dressed,
> great in dying upon Calvary,
> great when death he there suppressed;
>   very great is he now,
> king of heaven and earth below.

A close worker with David was Teilo, also a pupil of Peulin and Dyfrig, who founded a central monastery at Llandeilo Fawr near the place where the Lord Rhys was to build his castle of Dinefwr above the Tywi river six centuries later. Between them Teilo and David founded a number of monasteries and about a hundred churches bear their names. Teilo was born in Penalun (Penally) in Pembrokeshire during the reign of Aircol (Agricola) Lawhir, who was a good patron of the Church. His name shows the Roman influence in Dyfed. The son of Aircol was Vortiporex, one of the five princes who came under the lash of Gildas, to whom there is a memorial bearing a Latin inscription in Castell Dwyran.

A great part of this territory was included in the see of St. David's. In their day there were no territorial dioceses: this conception was taken over from the Continent later on. The two were bishops but they did not possess central control. Although it was a national and civil power, the Celtic Church Although it was a national and civil power, the Celtic Church, like the political order, developed in a notably decentralist way. Centralised authority was never compatible with the Welsh temperament, neither in religion nor in politics. It was decentralisation every time.

Another difference between the saints of the two provinces and the two periods was that the monasticism of the western and later ones was stricter in its discipline. It appears that David, who was called Dewi Ddyfrwr (David the Water-drinker) was the leader of a puritanical movement in the Church. His followers abstained from wine and meat; they rationed their bread; they were not allowed to have any possessions — a man was punished if he talked about 'my book'. They held everything in common. They worked extremely hard on the land, the monks themselves pulling the plough instead of oxen. Gildas, who belonged to the more Roman school, believed that they went too far, and that their extreme discipline led to a pharisaic spirit which, in his opinion, was worse than the sins of the flesh.

The monks used to live in their own tents, and perhaps it is fair to see in the monastic system a tendency towards individualism and decentralisation coming to the fore. Every building, including the church, was constructed of wood, sticks and turfs, so that there are no tangible archaeological remains to be found. Everything was collected inside the *llan*, which means a place enclosed like *ydlan* (rickyard) or *gwinllan* (vineyard). When Saunders Lewis puts these words into the mouth of Emrys Wledig in *Buchedd Garmon:*

Gwinllan a roddwyd i'm gofal yw Cymru fy ngwlad
I'w thraddodi i'm plant
Ac i blant fy mhlant
Yn dreftadaeth dragwyddol;

A vineyard given to my care is Wales my country,
to pass on to my children
and to my children's children,
an everlasting heritage.

no doubt the two syllables in the word *gwinllan* (vineyard) have
an ambiguous quality, (*gwyn* can mean blessed). It was inside
the *llan* that the monks prayed and sang, worshipped and read,
meditated and wrote; and it was on the surrounding land
that they sweated at their labours.

In the fellowship of their Christian encampments, which
always had a living relationship with the society around, the
local church with the local settlement and the mother church
(*clas*) with the kingdom, each individual had his role to play
under the abbot; and the day was divided into periods, each
with its special duties. As a rule the abbatial office was in the
hands of a family of aristocrats, and the position was passed
on from father to son. The abbot was allowed to marry and
bring up his family inside the monastery. This was an offence
according to Continental reformers in later centuries, but in
it can perhaps be observed the characteristically Welsh
attitude towards women and sex and family that is evident
in the system and law and mythology of Wales. In the early
and middle ages the Manichean point of view did not make
much impression on the Welsh.

The Welsh word for this establishment was *clas*; it can be
compared in some ways with the kibbutsim in Israel which,
in our own times, have made the desert flower like a rose.
They exemplify at their best the same close co-operative
society which was found in the *clas*. In the kibbutz today, as
in the *clas* of the past, the members hold possessions in common.
The two establishments have the same deep sense of moral
duty towards the nation. Without a complete dedication to
their Lord and country the members could not live such a

disciplined and self-sacrificial life. The *clas* arose in a heroic age in Wales, just as the kibbutz has done in Israel.

Three notes struck by David in his sermons were joy, faith and discipline. 'Lords, brothers and sisters,' he said in his last sermon — and note the presence of the women — 'Be cheerful and keep your faith and belief. And do the little things which you have seen and heard from me.' The old saint maintained nobly to the end of his days that Christian joy should temper the discipline of the life of *clas* and society. We do not know the year of his death (possibly it was in 588), but we do know that March the first was the day. This day is kept as a national festival. On one day every year everyone, even those 588 who would not lift a little finger to uphold the traditions which cost so much to so many people, remember that they are Welshmen. That is Saint David's day.

David was recognised as our patron saint very early on, and this for national reasons when Wales was fighting for its life against the Normans. It was then that Rhygyfarch wrote his *Buchedd Dewi* (Life of David). R. T. Jenkins has this to say about him:

'He (Rhygyfarch) did not want strangers to interfere with his beloved Church. He believed that he should write to prove that Wales had as fine saints as any section of the Catholic Church, and that St. David's had spiritual jurisdiction over the whole of Wales, and an older title than Canterbury. He considered that it was essential for him to prove this by chronicling the many miracles of the saint, his ordination by the Patriarch of Jerusalem, his election as Chief Bishop in Wales after the miracle in Llanddewi Brefi . . . A century after the death of Rhygyfarch a half-Norman archdeacon will be fighting the battle of St. David's against Canterbury, employing 'facts' out of Rhygyfarch's book as ammunition. In this way the see of St. David's became a sort of symbol of the independence of Wales (Llywelyn Fawr ap Iorwerth saw the significance of the battle), and hence David was elevated as Patron saint of Wales.'

St. David's became the haunt of pilgrims and the centre of the hopes of the nation. Pope Calixtus II announced that two pilgrimages to St. David's were equal to one to Rome. Up to the days of Glyndŵr patriots stood for its rights and for the independence of the Church in Wales from Canterbury.

It is impossible to think of a more worthy patron saint for Wales than David. He is one of us, a Welsh-speaking Welsh-man who worked amongst us and who suffered for us. In the liturgy of the Church in the middle ages it is said of him, 'He is the champion of the Brythons, leader and educator of the Welsh, and he is of the company of the citizens of God.' About 930 A.D. a great prophetic song, the *Armes Prydain*, was written calling upon all the Celts to unite to expel the English from Britain. The poer foresees that they will be following David as their leader.

'A lluman glân Dewi a ddyrchafant.'

And they will raise the pure banner of Dewi.

As early as this, over a thousand years ago, David's place in the minds of the Welsh was safe.

IV.　THE SATURATION OF GWYNEDD AND POWYS.

IT is the return of Macsen's widow, Elen, with her two sons to Wales which dates the beginning of the age of the saints. But although it is in Arfon that the earliest Welsh saints came into the light of history, it is in the south of the country that the extraordinary surge, which completely changed the appearance of the nation by extending its steadfast hold to Gwynedd and Powys within two or three generations, was first experienced. This may well be an example of W. J. Gruffydd's observation that it is the south which begins things and the north which conserves them. Members of Cunedda's family were to the fore in the north, and amongst them Seiriol, Einion Frenin, Meirion, Eurgain and Edern. The reign of Maelgwn Gwynedd, when David was at his prime, was the golden age of religion in Gwynedd. This is the epoch of Cybi, Seiriol, Cadfan and Deiniol.

Cybi came from Cornwall, the son of Selyf ap Geraint who was a military leader in the court somewhere between the

Saint David's Cathedral — Prifeglwys Tyddewi

"David the Waterman Pray for Wales"—by *David Jones*

rivers Tamar and Llynher; J. E. Lloyd suggests that the Gelli-wig connected with Arthur is possibly the place. Cybi had been evangelising in Ireland after coming to Anglesey, where he made a great name for himself. His influence spread far. There are churches dedicated to him in Monmouthshire and Cornwall as well as in Arfon and Ceredigion. When necessary, he stood firm against Maelgwn Gwynedd. On one occasion his defence of a wild goat caused a quarrel between them. (It is worth noting how frequently there are references in the Lives of the Saints to their gentleness with wild creatures.) Although the two did not always see eye to eye, Maelgwn was very generous to Cybi. It was he who gave him the land of the Roman fort on which to build a church. This *clas* survived in Caergybi (Holyhead), Cybi's principal settlement, as a collegiate church throughout the middle ages, with sixteen prebendaries in the sixteenth century: an unbroken history of a thousand years following the centuries of the Roman fort.

The founder of the cathedral in Bangor, and the first of its bishops, was Deiniol, the son of Dunawd of the lineage of Urien Rheged and Coel Hen. The likelihood is that Pabo, his grandfather, had come to Wales from Scotland with Cunedda. Asaff, to whom the cathedral church of Llanelwy (St. Asaph) is dedicated, was a cousin of his. Deiniol was educated by Cadog or Illtud at the same time as Maelgwn Gwynedd. He is called Deiniol of the Bangors because he founded Bangor Iscoed as well as Bangor in Caernarfonshire. The name Bangor refers to the strong defence of poles raised around the *llan* to protect it. The monks of Bangor Iscoed would have been glad had the *bangor* around them been strong enough to protect them after the battle of Chester in 617, when twelve hundred of them were killed. This number may appear to be exaggerated, but Bede says that the number of monks in Bangor Iscoed was so great that the monastery was divided into seven with three hundred men in each part living on the fruits of their labours. It was from this monastery that monks went to meet Saint Augustine at the Synod of Chester, and to be condemned by him.

Beuno lived two generations after Deiniol. He died in about 642. He was born in Llanymynech in Powys, near the river Severn. Beuno's *Vita* says that he left Berriw on the Severn when he heard the sound of English on the other side of the river. He was descended from Macsen Wledig on his father's side and through his mother he belonged, like Deiniol, to the family of Urien Rheged and Coel Hen. Dozens of saints belonged to these great families. There are numerous churches named after him in Gwynedd and Powys.

The only prince of this period whom we hear of as breaking the peace of Wales was Cynan Garwyn. At a time when he was strong and successful he attacked a number of Welsh kingdoms. He made Powys so unpopular that it had to stand alone facing the English in the great battle of Chester in 613. It was from Cynan Garwyn that Beuno had the gift of land in Gwyddelwern. His chief patrons were the kings of Gwynedd, Cadfan and his son Cadwallon, although there are tales of bitter quarrels with them too. Gwyddeint, the cousin of Cadwallon, gave him his inheritance in Clynnog in Caernarfonshire, and there Beuno established the monastery referred to as *Clas Beuno* in the Laws of Hywel Dda. Of all the saints of Gwynedd he is the one who most resembles David.

Another great saint of Powys was Tysilio, brother of Cynan Garwyn and son of Brochfael Ysgithrog, the most famous scion of the ancient lineage of the princes of Powys, who had a seat in Pengwern, Amwythig (Shrewsbury). Tysilio *circa* was educated in Meifod by the abbot, Gwyddfarch, 560 and there he established his main church. There are to many churches dedicated to him in mid-Wales, and 630 others in Caernarfonshire, Ceredigion and Pembrokeshire. Tradition has it that he too travelled to Brittany. He must have made an impression on people's imaginations for Cynddelw addressed a poem to him in the twelfth century. In this poem he says that Tysilio was present at the great battle in 642 when Oswald, the king of Northumbria, was killed. The saint continues to fight from heaven, says Cynddelw, just as *Armes Prydain* says Saint David will be fighting when the Welsh come to their kingdom.

V. THE CELTIC COMMUNITY OF CHRISTIAN NATIONS.

A SPECIAL characteristic of the labours of many of the saints is that they were not confined to Wales. It is true that they never had anything to do with any part of England until the kingdoms of Bryneich and Deifr rose in the north; there is no mention of any Welshman penetrating into the country lying next to Wales further than the Welsh parts of western Cheshire, Shropshire, Hereford and Gloucester, and very little even in those parts. But when we turn to the west the picture is refulgent and cheerful. The relationship with the Celtic countries is close, lively and fruitful. For centuries the life of Wales was completely separated from that of England and tied to the life of Brittany and Cornwall, Ireland and Scotland. Discoveries of Mediterranean pottery from this period in Wales and the Dumnonian peninsula, but not anywhere in England, show that there were also commercial contacts with the Mediterranean. In the Lives of many of the saints — and their Lives are as frequent as the biographies of ministers in the last century — we hear of journeys across the Irish Sea, which was for so long the lake of the saints.

Take for example Samson, about whom we have
485 more certain facts than any other saint because his
to biography was written carefully after a great deal of
565 research about 610, i.e. within a generation of his
death in 565. The author is a Breton, and he was persuaded to write it by the abbot of the Monastery of Dol in Brittany, which was established by Samson. The author had been to Cornwall on his mission of research, staying in a monastery there which had been founded by Samson and which was still ruled by one of his family, and also in Wales, in Llanilltud Fawr (Llantwit Major) and Ynys Byr (Caldey Island) and other places. It is he who tells us that Samson was the son of Anna of Gwent and Amwn of Devon and that Amwn was a foster father to kings.

When he was still quite young Samson was created abbot

of Caldey, and in the biography a company of learned Irishmen are said to have called there on their way back from Rome. That in itself is enough to prove that the claim that Wales was completely out of touch with Rome cannot be taken seriously. Samson accompanied them to Ireland where he became the abbot of a monastery near Dublin. There are churches dedicated to him in Ballygriffin near Dublin and in Bally Samson in the county of Wexford. When he returned to Wales he lived the life of a hermit for a time on a sea shore in Pembrokeshire. He walked from there in the company of an Irish abbot to Gwent, where he established a church somewhere on the top of a fort. He was made bishop, and consecrated in the office by Dyfrig and others, and thereafter he became abbot of Llanilltud Fawr, which was 'founded they say by Saint Garmon' according to his biographer.

One day, when he was standing beside the altar in Llanilltud Fawr, a message came to him from heaven saying that he should be a pilgrim: 'You will be very great in a Church across the sea,' said the voice. On Easter Sunday he crossed the Severn in the company of the Irish abbot to the monastery of Dochau in Cornwall, which was founded by Dochau, a cousin of Illtud and Arthur. He left behind him in Cornwall, after a long stay, four foundations, and still another on the isles of Scilly. From there he went to Brittany. The most famous of the monasteries that he founded there is Dol, where he spent the rest of his life. It is known that all this happened before 547, for it was then that Teilo went to him, having fled from the yellow fever that killed Maelgwn Gwynedd in that year. It is believed that this great plague of the middle 40's killed off one-third of the population of Justinian's Roman Empire. While he was in Brittany Samson succeeded in freeing Idwal, a young prince of the north of Brittany, who was kept imprisoned in Paris by Chuldebert, the French king. He went again to Paris to visit the senate of the bishops of France. One Welshman at least was in touch with the Church in France.

Wade-Evans draws our attention to an interesting fact: the pioneers of the Welsh settlement in Patagonia landed on the inhospitable shores of that country on the feast of Saint Samson, July 28, 1865, one thousand and three hundred years after the death of the man who became 'very great in a Church across the sea.'

David had contact with a host of saints and people in the Celtic countries. They communicated with each other in various ways, and many of the saints of other countries had their education in Wales in the monasteries of Samson, Cadog, Illtud, Dewi and others. P. A. Wilson says:

> 'All the great names of the first century of the age of the saints in the Irish church concerning whom any useful information has come down to us were British-trained, either directly, or at one remove, or in the case of Saint Columbus at two removes.'

'British-trained' included Scotland of course. We have seen that the difficulty of language explained the scarcity of Welsh missionaries in Ireland and of Irish saints in Wales, but in spite of this many did come to Wales. Some of the saints who used to be thought Welsh were in fact Irish: e.g. Ffinian, Cennech, Myllin, Aeddan, Sannan, Caron, Colman, and of course Ffraid (Brigid). A considerable number of Welshmen went to Ireland as pupils or as teachers, and a few (such as Samson and Cybi) founded churches there. David counted amongst his friends some of the most prominent Irish saints, among them Ffinian, Ailbe, Aiden, Maedoc, Senan, Molag and Brendan. Ffinian was the greatest teacher in Ireland, and had been like Cennech a pupil of Cadog in Llancarfan. Brendan too paid a visit to Llancarfan. The Irish and Welsh monks exchanged books and other treasures constantly. Indeed the relationship between them was so close that they adopted the same type of script and orthography. In an article in the *Welsh History Review* for December 1966, already cited, P. A. Wilson includes this quotation from the work of Eoin MacNeill:

> 'Perhaps the most remarkable trait of the British-Latin Culture influence in Ireland is to be found in the orthographic system of Old Irish, in the phonetic values of the consonants . . . The spelling of the

manuscripts is not derived from the spelling of the oghams. The oghams express the sound b, d, g, by their normal symbols for b, d, g . . . At the time when the manuscript spelling was established, p, t, c, following a vowel in Latin, were read and pronounced b, d, g. This pronunciation of Latin came from Britain, and it becomes universal in the Latin schools of Ireland.'

After summarizing the testimony which supports the belief that here was an unbroken continuation between the Christianity of the Celtic Church and Christianity in Roman Britain, P. A. Wilson refers in the same article to another conclusion which bears witness:

'It also points,' he says of this testimony, 'to another conclusion hardly less important: it suggests that Wales, and more particularly southern and western Wales, was the epicentre of that "great missionary effort", as Dr. Radford has called it, which spread by the western sea routes to Iceland and to Spain, and which we think of as Celtic Christianity. That it was in Ireland that the Celtic Church achieved its greatest renown is beyond dispute, but the initial impetus came from sub-Roman Britain. Direct evidence is almost wholly wanting, but indirectly all the indications point this way . . .

That the Celtic Church adhered to peculiar customs in regard to the tonsure, the celebration of Easter, and other matters not fully understood, is well-known. The term 'Celtic particularism' has come to stand for these peculiar customs, and for the tenacity with which they were maintained. That the British Church apparently succeeded in imposing these customs upon the Irish Church, which owed its origin, at least in part, to a different and opposed tradition, is itself evidence of this tenacity. It is tempting to suggest that this feature, a special tenacity, even obstinacy, in adherence to ancient customs, is perhaps more peculiarly British than Irish. The majority of the Church in Southern Ireland began to conform to the Roman usage on the Paschal question in the 630's; not for nearly a century and a half thereafter did any of the churches of Wales conform.'

Had they not reverenced their tradition and clung stubbornly to it, the life of Europe would be the poorer. In the fifth and sixth centuries the civilisation of Europe was enriched by this small, out of the way society because it struggled confidently and heroically to live its own life.

VI. THE CONTINUITY OF THE TRADITION IS UNBROKEN.

THREE things have become obvious in this discussion: that the tradition of Wales had its own clear and strong character; that it received a great deal from outside — particularly Christianity and the culture of Rome — which was compatible with the Welsh mind and nature; and that the Welsh character set its own stamp on what was received, forming a synthesis which can be called the Welsh way of life.

Consider what happened in the period under review. Christianity was received in a monastic form, but it was an aggressive and learned monasticism which laid great stress on educational preaching. It was different from the order on the Continent in that it was decentralised, both on a local and on a national level. The Church in Wales had no centralised system but it had 'unity of organic intention' throughout the whole country. Locally in the *clas* the monks lived apart in their own dwellings. The mind behind the order was deeply rooted and the energy which created it completely confident, as can be seen when the centralised continental order in Brittany was swept aside — a system which had been there for centuries before the saints crossed over to establish the Welsh system in the region. Referring to Celtic art, Gwyn Williams has said, 'what happens in a corner is as important as what happens at the centre, because there is no centre.' So in church order: there was no centre.

The *clas* was usually ruled by a married abbot and the family succession was continued as in politics. The attitude to sex was different from that of the churches in countries which came strongly under the influence of Augustine and Manichaeism: and women were accorded more respect than in most countries. They received an education, sometimes by the greatest teachers. Children too were given an education: thus people of both sexes and of all ages were respected. Indeed wild creatures too were given consideration, and the saints often took pity on them.

The respect which was accorded the individual person can

be seen in the fact that penance and confession were personal and private. P. A. Wilson says:

> 'Among the early Christians confession and penance were alike public; the earliest evidence of private confession and private penance seems to come from the Celtic Church. It has been thought that private confession may have been a pre-Christian Celtic practice. St. Patrick's confession to his greatest friend of a sin committed in early life is of interest in this context; while the prominent place taken by penance in the devotions of the British Christians in the late sixth century seems to find an echo in the Gododdin poems.'

After referring to the oldest documents which discuss penance, he says:

> 'It would appear that this particular penitential system originated in Wales, and that it was adopted and further developed in Ireland.'

The giving of the names of their founders or their native patrons to churches in the Celtic countries is a form of respect for the individual worthy of note. This is unusual in Europe. It is uncommon to give so much honour to a prophet in his own land, but it was customary in the Celtic countries. Alice Stopford Green says of the Church in Ireland:

> 'Never was a church so truly national. The words used by the common people were steeped in its imagery . . . In their dedications the Irish took no names of foreign saints, but of their own holy men. St. Bridgit became the "Mary of the Gael". There was scarcely a boundary felt between the divine country and the earthly, so entirely was the spiritual life committed with the national.'

Together with the respect accorded to individuals, whatever their age, and to women, it can be seen that the family too had a central place in the Welsh Christian society. This fact is reflected in the inscriptions on early graves. The usual practice on the continent was to put only the name of the deceased on the stone, but in Wales his father's name was also recorded. Leslie Alcock says: 'This stress on filiation was alien to orthodox Christianity of the time, whereas it was natural for the tribal society of the Celts.'

Pelagius takes his place as naturally in this pattern as did

Abelard the Breton heretic in the twelfth century, who was expelled from the University of Paris to whose fame and popularity as an intellectual centre he contributed so much. Pelagius was a Brython, or at any rate a Celt who had received his education in Brythonic monasteries, and his teaching was greatly welcomed among the Brythons. When he went to Rome Pelagius was disturbed by the low moral standard of the life of the city. He was told when he protested that the weakness of human nature explained the situation. Attempting to show that there were great powers in the human personality, he discovered that Augustine of Hippo's teaching about the complete corruption of human nature cut the ground from under his feet. The argument became embittered because it was thought that Pelagius tended to say that man could save himself without the grace of God, while the Church claims that God takes the first step and that he alone can save man. Pelagius's most profound conviction, however, was in the dignity of human nature. He believed that people can live good lives, free from the pride which for him was the essence of sin. This is what made him so congenial to the Welsh and Celtic mind.

The Celts had been groping constantly in the same direction. What is known of the druids and the pre-Christian mind in old mythology indicates the direction of the mind of the Celts. There are two fundamental characteristics: the belief in the immortality of the soul, and a profound sensitivity to life. What disposed people to give great value to the human person more than the belief in the immortality of his soul? And is this not completely consistent with the consciousness that all life is one and that divine energy 'is like a flood pouring down on us' as Gwilym Hiraethog's great hymn has it?

According to Pennar Davies, in *Rhwng Chwedl a Chredo:*

'A consciousness of the mystery of the universe and an awareness of the unity of life — this is the experience which lies beneath all the symbols, all the correspondence, all the interchanges, which are seen in the ancient legends of the Celtic nations; and certainly it is an important part of the distinctive nature of the mythological literature of Wales. Every occurrence, every soul, every idea, every condition is incomplete in itself. We move nearer to the truth through examining the relationship of everything to what resembles it, and to what is its opposite, and honour the mystery which broods over our life; and through this exploration and this reverence we come to some recognition of the unity of the whole . . . the consciousness of the unity and inter-relationship of the universe is ever present. The debate and the dialogue between two worlds symbolize one all-embracing world . . .

'In it (the pre-Christian polytheistic religion of the Brythons) the communication between the two worlds is extraordinarily close and mysterious. Between the dark and the light, between the great and the small, between the living and the dead, between the happy and the sad, there is continual intertwining and opposition, and the gods move in some enchanted land which yet interpenetrates this earth.'

The Celts were in the twilight, not in darkness: the twilight of the morning not the evening. When the dawn broke with the good news that God had revealed himself in Christ, it was found that the way had been prepared for the Welsh to accept the rule of his law. Our whole life was united in him: 'For you are all one in Christ Jesus'.

Circumstances joined together in a mysterious way to prepare Wales for the coming of the Gospel; the internal peace, the Roman roads, the Latin language and the intellectual background. Here, in the fullness of time, Christianity arrived in its strength.

VII. THE CONSEQUENCES OF THE CHRISTIAN REVOLUTION.

WALES was given a vision of goodness, human and divine, which can never be utterly lost unless the Welsh tradition is erased from the face of the earth. The saints proclaimed the good news that this world is God's world, that it is he who rules and that his nature is to be seen in the Christ who is the way, the truth and the life. Yeats regretted that good people were lacking in passion. The saints were good people; they were also passionately enthusiastic: they were 'ministers who were a flame of fire'. In the bright light of their zeal Wales was reborn a Christian nation. In the great heat the old tradition melted into a pattern of Christian values, and from this fusion emerged a finely tempered way of life and thought. This is the beauty which past and present have felt it their duty to guard for future ages.

Ever since the age of the saints Welsh patriotism has been a buttress of the Church. Everyone brought up in the Welsh tradition was nurtured in the values it embraced. This tradition is the best possible Welsh education in any age; it is an education in values. Its splendour imposes upon every Welshman the solemn duty of maintaining it, and ensuring the conditions which make possible its transmission to the future.

Christianity bestowed a conviction of divine providence, and that there is a meaning and purpose to a man's life; that each person and each nation have a significance and a destiny. It gave to every human being an eternal value. It taught the Welsh that however important objects and institutions might be, the human personality and the quality of human life were more important. Every institution existed for man, even the state. Christ and his love, in his life and death, brought a wellspring of strength: the basis of the relationship between man and man, the foundation of art, and the standard by which to value everything. The conviction took root that human life is a life to be lived for others, and that we are servants of one another; the only Christian leadership is service: 'A fo ben bid bont' — let him who would be head be a bridge.

The Welsh have been sadly unfaithful to this Gospel, and by our own day only a minority are united with the Christian Church; but while the Welsh tradition exists no one in Wales can escape it. It is an essential part of our way of living and thinking. It is good that we are reminded daily of its demands upon us by the names of the great men who proclaimed it with such power, names which have rung like bells about us since the days of the infancy of the nation.

If Welsh patriotism has been a buttress of the Church, the Church too strengthened Welsh patriotism. Each was united to the other. The saints were the Fathers of the Church: they were also the fathers of the nation. The Church created a close-knit society; it was the institution which did most to give the nation structural unity. Christianity deepened the awareness of the separateness of Wales. It bestowed a vivid and luminous distinction when comparison was made with England. G. M. Trevelyan observes:

'The Welsh of the fifth and sixth centuries came to regard Christianity as their distinguishing mark which, together with their love of bardic music and poetry enabled them still to feel superior to the Saxon savages.'

In standing firm for the Church we also stand firm for Wales; in contending for Wales we also fight for Christianity.

Thus by the beginning of the seventh century there was in Wales a society composed of people who had close communication with each other. Though it would be anachronistic to impute to them a national consciousness, they were in fact a national community. They possessed a country and they possessed roots. They were descended for the most part from those who had lived amid the same enchanting beauty a thousand years earlier. And they possessed a history which united them. They also possessed a language, and a magnificent literary language at that. They possessed a culture, venerable and rich. They possessed a Church in a position of unusual strength in relation to the state. And they possessed a sublime religion. Over five hundred years had passed since Ostorius and the Romans launched their assault upon Wales, and after their departure Wales underwent the sustained and shattering experience of the two most remarkable centuries it was ever likely to see. From this majestic experience it arose as a Christian nation, a Welsh nation, and a cultured nation.

The miracle of all this is underlined by the contemporary situation in England, the land which was to conquer Wales six centuries hence, to engulf it in eight and a half centuries, and to come near to destroying it in fourteen. In England there was a complete break in the tradition. Roman civility disappeared and the lights of Christianity went out. The people slipped into a dark period of their history. When the mists began to clear, a barbaric, pagan English people was to be found there. In the east the sun of civilisation set; but in the west the dawn broke.

Facing the English

I. THE SAINTS OF BANGOR ISCOED AND AUGUSTINE.

DURING the age of the saints Wales seems to have had two remarkably peaceful centuries. There was some disturbance involving the Irish at the beginning of the period, and Cynan Garwyn of Powys let his weight be felt towards the end, but there is no record of the kind of war and turmoil which the Men of the Old North had to face in the days of Urien Rheged who was a younger contemporary of Saint David. The saints and the poets, the craftsmen and the singers, moved in peace around the country; and the sea too was sufficiently free of pirates to allow movement from one Celtic country to another. This period followed three centuries of Roman peace, and two more quiet centuries were to follow again, apart from the fighting against the English, mainly, on the border of Powys. In 800 it would be possible for the Welsh to look back on seven centuries of comparative peace which contrasted favourably with the following seven hundred years.

In 600 the ruling families had been in power for two hundred years or more, and they were to remain for centuries yet in Gwynedd and Powys, Ceredigion and Dyfed, Brycheiniog, Morgannwg and Gwent — the seven kingdoms of Wales. This is a very different picture from the one usually drawn of a Wales divided and ripped asunder by bloody and barbaric civil wars. If the statistics were known, it would no doubt be found that far fewer Welshmen lost their lives in battle in those centuries, and that less time had been given to war, in proportion, than during two centuries of the modern period. And from the point of view of the barbarity of war they had nothing to teach us. Moreover, it was to defend their way of life and their language and their tradition, and for institutions essential for their freedom, that the Welsh of the seventh and eighth centuries fought. The comparison with recent centuries is striking. From 1750 to 1950 scores of thousands of Welshmen lost their lives in war. And for what? Was it not for an order which was destroying their way of life, their language and their tradition? It was not for their national freedom that they lost their blood: Welshmen of recent times have not had one iota of that to defend.

At the beginning of the new century there occurred the sort of meeting which changes history. There were in fact two meetings, and it was the second which led to bitter contention: possibly it was among the reasons for the war which broke out a few years later. The disagreement was between the Church of the Welsh and the Roman Church in England; the war was between the Welsh and the English. During the ensuing four centuries there was quite a lot of fighting against the Scandinavians, but more frequently it was against the English, and it was not the Welsh who began the fighting.

A Christian mission under the leadership of Augustine of Kent came to England in 597. He received a welcome there from Ethelbert, the king of Kent, and an invitation was issued to the Celtic Church to send a delegation to meet Augustine. This invitation was accepted and a congress was held half way between Wales and Kent, probably 602-3 in Wiltshire, in 602-3. Bede tells the story and his detailed knowledge shows that he was writing from contemporary sources.

The purpose of the congress on Augustine's side was to try to secure three things: first, to get the Welsh to lay aside the distinctive usages of the Celtic Church, such as their way of dating Easter, their mode of baptism and of tonsure; secondly, to get them to obey him as the Archbishop of Canterbury; and thirdly, to get their help in evangelising the English. There was a long discussion which was spiritually and physically tiring, but no agreement was reached. Bede makes a very significant observation about the way this futile congress ended: 'The Brythons said they could not give up their customs,' he said, 'without getting their people's consent.' They returned to Wales to discuss matters with them.

The second meeting was the fateful one. According to Bede seven Brythonic bishops went to this one. Since there were not that many in Wales, some perhaps went from Scotland and Cornwall. He also says that a number of learned men went with them from the great monastery of Bangor Iscoed. He gives a detailed account of the organisation of that establishment, which had grown greatly in size and importance.

604   Although we do not know when this second conference took place, it could hardly have been before 604 because the discussion in Wales would have taken some time, and it happened before Augustine's death in 605.

This time the Welsh consulted a wise hermit and accepted his advice. 'If he is a man of God,' said the hermit about Augustine, 'follow him.' But how were they to know whether he was a man of God or not? The hermit's answer to this question was a quotation from the Gospel according to Saint Matthew — and it is Bede who is telling the tale: 'Shoulder my yoke and learn from me, for I am gentle and humble in heart.' If he were gentle and humble he should be followed; if he were proud and severe, Christian truth was not in him and his leadership should not be accepted; that is, he could not be recognised as their archbishop. How to judge? 'Arrange that he and his companions arrive first,' said the hermit. 'If he gets to his feet when you come to him, listen humbly to him, for he is the servant of God; but if he scorns you by remaining seated and not rising when you arrive, you being accompanied by a greater number than he is, then you must treat him with contempt.' Augustine did not rise to greet them, and the Welsh did not accept him as archbishop nor agree to any of his suggestions.

This throws light on the standards of the two sides. In the opinion of the Celtic Church, spiritual pride was the worst sin; it regarded spiritual sins — and this is often seen in its history — as being more dangerous than sins of the flesh. It does not appear that humility and gentleness, which reveal love and respect for others, were regarded in the same way by the imperial Church order. Augustine was extremely agitated by the attitude of the Welsh, and used severe threats against them. If they did not do what he asked, according to Bede's report, they would have to face war against them from their enemies. If they did not unite with him to evangelise the English they would suffer the vengeance of death at their hands.

And that is what happened. In ten years' time Ethelfrith, the king of Northumbria, who had already attacked the Welsh Brythons of Scotland, launched a heavy attack on the borders of Powys. It is noteworthy that this first attack of the English upon the Welsh came from the North-east of England and not from the country bordering Wales. A great battle was fought near Chester in 615 and Selyf, who followed Cynan Garwyn as king of Powys, was killed there. There is a closer connection than this between the war and Augustine's threat, and this is the Massacre of the Saints. It was not only soldiers who were killed in this battle, but also twelve hundred of the monks of Bangor Iscoed, the great monastery which sent learned men to meet Augustine. Bede tells the story with relish; obviously he preferred the pagans of England to the Christians of Wales. He calls the Welsh 'treacherous men' and their army an 'atrocious militia'.

> 'It shows Bede's national and political prejudices,' says Plummer, 'that he should apply such an epithet to men who were only defending their own country against attack.'

Bede quotes the words of Ethelfrith when urging his army to murder the saints who were kneeling in prayer:

> 'If they call upon God against us they are fighting against us as surely as those who bear arms.'

Bede is used as their final authority by English historians. His able work, written about 710-30, is their chief source for the history of England in the centuries after the departure of the Romans. It is he who gave circulation to the myth that a great English invasion had sent the Welsh fleeing to the mountains of the west. He could not hide his pleasure at the fact that the attack on Powys and the Massacre of the Saints had followed Augustine's threat. Perhaps Augustine and his followers had not interfered in politics as Garmon did; but whether the churchmen had anything to do with Ethelfrith's attack or not, that ambitious king would not have needed much encouragement. He had already overcome the Brythons of the north, and the increasing power of his kingdom gave him hopes of becoming Bretwalda — Prince of England. If his intention was to defeat and rule Powys he failed, for his army did not penetrate into the heart of the Welsh kingdom; this suggests the strength of the Welsh defence against the army of the man of whom Bede says with pride that he had routed the Brythons more cruelly than that of any other English king, annihilating or enslaving them and taking their lands. It would have been to his advantage to try and break the spirit of the Welsh by murdering the saints who gave spiritual sustenance to their cause. Killing or imprisoning scholars, or stifling them, has been the first step of the oppressors of every nation. In this there is a remarkable resemblance between the Massacre of the Saints and the Massacre of the Druids in Anglesey more than five centuries earlier.

Politically the Battle of Chester was without result. The position of Wales remained unchanged. Ethelfrith retreated to Northumbria. In the following year, in a battle in the east of England, he was killed, the first English king to attack Wales. Perhaps there was an echo of the fighting, which followed the pattern of the heroic effort of the Men of the Old North some years earlier, in the magnificent poetry of the ninth century. Although Selyf became a figure of importance in heroic poetry, we have lost all the work of Arofan, the court poet who celebrated him as Taliesin had celebrated his grandfather Brochwel Ysgithrog and his father Cynan Garwyn. Perhaps we have lost a body of work like the *Gododdin* which celebrated the same sort of heroism. Selyf deserves our remembrance: the first Welsh king to give his life defending his country against the English.

II. CADWALLON AND THE WELSH DEFENCE

IT was on the borders of Powys that the struggles of this period occurred; the men of that province bore the heat of the day. The fiercest fighting took place around the Severn; at this time, in the middle of the seventh century, Pengwern and the lowlands around Shrewsbury were lost. To the west of the Severn, Beuno and Tysilio continued to evangelise in tranquil, undisturbed country, and the life of Gwynedd is reflected by what is seen on the memorial stones of the period. Of the 190 memorial stones with Latin inscriptions that have been found in this island it is significant that ten are in the Brythonic North, forty in the Dumnonian peninsula (of which 25 are in Cornwall) and 140 in Wales. In the church of Llangadwaladr in Anglesey a memorial stone was erected to honour Cadfan, the king of the line of Cunedda who died in 613. In the most magnificent inscription that is found on any ancient stone in Wales, it proclaims in Latin that Cadfan was 'the wisest and most renowned of all the kings'. There are other memorial stones still standing in Gwynedd. The inscription is always in Latin — one refers to 'a citizen of Gwynedd', another to a justice of the peace, others to priests, and one to a physician, 'Nelius Medicus', which shows that the medical profession was held in high regard in Gwynedd. The Penmachno inscription tantalisingly records that the memorial was made 'in the time of Justinus the Consul'. Justinus was Consul in 540. Altogether these stones reflect a civilised and sophisticated society.

There is strong testimony that Cadfan was the foster-father of Edwin, who became king of Northumbria when he was young and on the run. In a generation Edwin would be attacking Wales and meeting his end in a battle against

Cadwallon and his son Cadfan. Cadwallon is the greatest of the military and political leaders of Wales since the time of Maelgwn Gwynedd; all down the centuries to the end of the middle ages political leaders had, of course, to be *circa* military men; war was the only way men knew *575 to* to change and defend the politcal order. From the 633 third century on the Church throughout Europe gave its blessing to the most shameful behaviour of man towards his fellow-men in war if he fought under the patronage of a state and in a good cause. Cadwallon, who ruled Gwynedd at the time of the Northumbrian attack on Powys, was a Christian, as was Edwin his foster-brother who took over the government of Northumbria the year after the Massacre of the Saints. These two Christian foster-brothers became rivals, each doing his best according to his lights for his own kingdom. Edwin conquered the little kingdom of Elfed in Yorkshire, and established his authority throughout most of the English kingdoms. Then he turned his attention to Wales. Having assembled a navy in the estuary of the Dee, he probably attacked Gwynedd and Anglesey and the Isle of Man. A triad refers to him as one of the 'three chief attackers of Anglesey who were reared on the Island'. This was the second heavy onslaught on Wales, and the first to penetrate deeply into the country. In spite of the long and vigorous defence of Cadwallon, he had to flee to Ireland with his retinue, and there according to another of the triads he remained an exile for seven years.

But Cadwallon was a man of many resources, and in 632 his luck changed. He made an alliance with Penda, the king of Mercia. This is the first mention of Mercia in history and it is in an alliance with the Welsh that it comes to light. Perhaps Penda himself, as his Welsh-sounding name implies, was of Brythonic descent. Cadwallon has been blamed by Welsh historians for making an alliance with him, but his first obligation was to defend his kingdom against the greatest danger, and that was the powerful onslaughts of Northumbria. By attacking Northumbria he could hope to weaken it and prevent it from attacking Wales in the future. He succeeded,

and there was not a single attack on Wales from Northumbria
after this. With the help of the Roman roads the
632   allies advanced quickly and met Edwin's army at
Heathfield. Wherever Heathfield may be — near
Doncaster according to J. E. Lloyd — it was there that the
greatest Welshman and the greatest Englishman of the century
came face to face: two Christians and two foster-brothers. The
Northumbrian army was beaten and Edwin killed. The
Welshmen and the men of Mercia moved forward, and in the
battles which ensued the leaders of Bernicia (Brynaich) and
Deira (Deifr), the two kingdoms which had united to form
Northumbria, were killed, leaving the land at the mercy of
Cadwallon and Penda. Two and a half centuries after the
departure of Macsen Wledig, the Welsh were strong enough
to penetrate to the northernmost point of England and
vanquish its strongest kingdom, the kingdom which had
possessed the land of Cadwallon's forefathers and had murdered
hundreds of Welsh monks. But the joy of the Welsh was
short-lived. They had to ravage the country to
633   prevent the kingdom from being built up again,
and Cadwallon was in the process of doing this when
he met an English army under the leadership of Oswald, the
son of Edwin. In a sudden attack near Hexham in 633 the
Welsh were overcome and Cadwallon killed.

Oswald himself met his end in 642 fighting against Penda
on the borders of Wales, probably near Oswestry. Although
that part of the country had belonged to England since the
first half of the seventh century, until today Welsh has
remained the speech of families on the English side of the
border, and on market day the cadences of the old language
are heard on the streets of Croesoswallt (Oswestry), thirteen
centuries after the killing there of Oswald, king of Northumbria, in a battle against the king of Mercia. Seven centuries
after this battle, Owain Glyndŵr was bred at Sycharth within
a few miles of the spot.

III.   THE END OF RHEGED AND GODODDIN

ALTHOUGH Northumbria did not attack Wales after this, the history of that English kingdom remained of importance to Wales, for it was Northumbria that destroyed three of the states of the Men of the Old North — Elfed, Gododdin and Rheged. Rheged was easily overcome without wasting a drop of blood, through the marriage of Oswy, the son of Oswald and Rhiainfellt, the great-grand-daughter of Urien *circa* Rheged. This political marriage had all-important 640 consequences; through it the Welsh kingdom came under the rule of Northumbria, whose authority stretched from sea to sea, from the North Sea to the Irish Sea and from the Humber to the Firth of Forth. It was almost three times the size of Wales.

The consequences to the language and culture of the Welsh kingdom were tragic. Although Welsh no doubt persisted in many parts for centuries to come, it was the English language and English culture which took over in the greater part of the country. The sun set on Rheged, the land of heroic men: there was no dawn ahead. The light of the old language disappeared for ever. The nation of the generous host of men who went to Catraeth was to die, and when a nation dies there is no resurrection.

IV.   THE AGE OF CADWALADR

CADWALLON left an heir, his small son Cadwaladr, but during his childhood it was Cadafael who ruled Gwynedd. Under his leadership the army of Gwynedd was dragged once again, for the last time, to the north of England to fight against Oswy, the king of Northumbria. It is not known why; perhaps it was connected with the attack made by Oswy on the Brythons about 645. With Rheged now part of his kingdom, perhaps Oswy was trying to extend its boundaries still further. The attack of the Welsh in 654 was in many ways very 654 similar to Cadwallon's effort eighteen years before. Again Penda was the ally; and this time he was the principal general. Once again they penetrated to the heart of the kingdom of Northumbria, advancing this time to its furthest point on the banks of Abergweryd (Firth of Forth). Once again they won a brilliant victory, seizing the royal treasure and taking it back with them. Once again the army of Northumbria attacked suddenly when they were on their way home. And again the allies were overcome — on Winwaed Field in Yorkshire — and once more their leader was killed on the battlefield. Penda met his end fighting against Oswy.

It was regarded as a matter of shame by the Welsh that Cadafael and his men did not take part in this battle. This is what won for him the name Cadafael Cadomedd, that is 'the battle-maker who evades battle'. But if, as is said, the Welsh were on their way home, having left Penda the previous day, and if Oswy's attack was very sudden and unexpected, Cadafael may have had sufficient reason for his absence.

Historians like to say that Wales was finally separated from the North by the Battle of Winwaed Field. This can hardly be true. It is difficult to believe that it made much difference to the situation, apart from strengthening Northumbria at the expense of Mercia. We have already seen that Northumbria stretched from sea to sea after the marriage of Oswy and Rhiainfellt had given it Rheged. From about 640 Northumbria thus lay across the path to Strathclyde — the only Welsh kingdom left in the North. The Welsh, however, had made little use of this route, for the reason given by Nora Chadwick in her article 'The Battle of Chester' in *Celt and Saxon*:

> 'The land route north through Lancashire,' she says, 'although not impossible, as we know from references in Welsh bardic poetry, was at all times a difficult one, unsuitable for movements of large bodies of men. The south was forest-clad; the centre boggy and water-logged; the rivers ran from east to West, and were not easily forded in their lower courses. To the east the Pennines stretched from north to south, inconveniently steep to the west. The more natural route from Strathclyde or Cumbria would have been across Morecambe Bay, though this route would, of course, be conditional on the Isle of Man being in friendly hands.'

Since communication with the North was mostly by sea, the Battle of Winwaed made little difference to Wales, nor to its relationship with Scotland. What changed that relationship was the disappearance of Gododdin and Rheged in the seventh century and the increased presence of the Northern 'Black Pagans' from the eighth century on.

After Maes Winwaed, Cadwaladr came into his inheritance in Gwynedd. His reign was short, for he died young of the yellow plague in 664. In spite of this he made a deep impression on his age, and his name remained great among the bards who kept his memory alive in the country.

664

In *Armes Prydain*, which was composed about 900, and in other prophetic poems there is a prophecy that Cadwaladr will return to lead the Welsh to victory over the English. Cadwaladr must have been a fine military leader in order to leave such an impress on the folk memory; and it can be assumed that he was also a man of learning and culture. He gained the name Cadwaladr Fendigaid (the Blessed), which suggests that he finished his days as a monk; his name is found attached to churches in Anglesey and Monmouthshire and in Denbighshire. It was he in all probability who erected the memorial stone to his grandfather Cadfan in the church of Llangadwaladr. This stone shows that his court was in contact with the culture of the Continent; the letters of the words are carved in the most recent mode of script.

Detailed knowledge of the enterprises which made Cadwaladr's name so great was lost, but *Brut y Tywysogion* (the Chronicle of the Princes) mentions three battles in 721, in connection with the name of his grandson Rhodri Molwynog. Two are in the south of Wales, in Pen-coed and Garth Maelog, the second in Radnorshire probably and one, Brwydr Heilim, in Cornwall. About these it says: 'And in those three battles the Brythons won'. We infer from the wording that they were fought to defend Wales and Cornwall against the English. Rhodri Molwynog died

754

in 754 having done the most important thing that any Welsh leader could do; he successfully defended his kingdom and passed on his inheritance to his children.

V. THE CHURCH OF THE WELSH

ALTHOUGH the enormous energy of the past centuries had ebbed, vigorous life still flowed through the Church. Only when compared with its heroic age did it appear quiescent. In Morgannwg for example the records of the Book of Llandaf, the *Liber Landavensis*, show that the great monasteries which gave the leadership to the fifth and sixth centuries remained prosperous between 600 and 750. The abbeys of Llanilltud Fawr, Llandochau and Llancarfan worked happily and consistently in co-operation with each other, but later on the destructive attacks of the Danes interfered terribly with their lives. It became necessary too to withstand an occasional attack by the English; a gift is recorded to the church by Athrwys, the king of Morgannwg and Gwent, to celebrate a victory he had won over the English in 680. They had come to the borders of the diocese in the middle of the century when Hereford had been annexed. Athrwys had followed his father, Meurig, as king; when Meurig reigned the bishop was Oudoceus, the nephew of Teilo, who maintained the continuity with the age of the Saints. The son of Athrwys was Morgan Mwynfawr who gave his name to the kingdom in its Welsh and English forms, Morgannwg and• Glamorgan — the Country of Morgan. He came to the throne at the beginning of the eighth century.

600 to 750

680

circa 700

All the largest churches were in the form of monasteries. The *clas* remained a community of monks right up to the middle ages: and according to Welsh law, the canons of the church were the *claswyr*, with the abbot — 'dwyfol lythyrwr' (divine letterer) — as head. In the four cathedrals later on the office of abbot melted into the office of bishop. In the ninth century the canons were usually married men, and this remained so through the following centuries, to the great indignation of the reformers of the twelfth century. But some communities of saints, especially on an island like Enlli (Bardsey), kept to the old ascetic discipline in all its severity; no woman was allowed to come near its shores.

There was much humanity in the Welsh Church, and its history and order give the impression that it was somewhat less inclined to foster spiritual pride, the besetting sin of the Church in all ages. Its leaders appear as humble men rather than proud prelates, although so many of them came from noble families. We noted a striking illustration of this in the readiness of the leaders who met Augustine to accept the advice of a hermit who lived in quiet solitude, far from the noise of the world's pain.

For a century and three quarters after that fateful meeting the Church of the Welsh adhered to its own usages against all pressure from those who wished it to conform. It was a non-conformist church during these centuries. The bones of contention were the differences about the dating of Easter, baptism, and the tonsure; but beneath these comparatively small matters lay issues of great importance to the two sides. The Roman Church believed that its continued existence depended upon its complete supremacy throughout Christendom, upon securing perfect unity in the one fold, and unquestioned obedience to the one shepherd. Although the Church of the Welsh was part of the Roman Church, it stood for a measure of spiritual independence and therefore its right to its ancient and venerable customs. It insisted on clinging to the old tradition that had been passed down for generations since the days of the early fathers.

No doubt politics had something to do with the situation. The fathers of the Church were also the fathers of the nation which had struggled against the attacks of the English, with whom the alien customs of Rome were associated. In the opinion of Wales it was a question of the Church of the English bringing pressure to bear on the Church of the Welsh: the resistance was to Canterbury not Rome. This probably explains why the Welsh clung more fervently than the other Celts to their different customs, although they were so close geographically to the ones who brought the pressure to bear. It was not so much Rome as the English that Wales was resisting; it was not only their Church but their way of life that the Welsh were defending.

The southern Irish part of the Celtic Church yielded first, between 625 and 638; and they were followed by their fellow countrymen in the north before the end of the century. About 705 the men of Devon and Cornwall were persuaded to conform. Iona in Scotland resisted until 718, and it is likely that Strathclyde gave up its stand about the same time. One cannot talk of the Celtic Church after this date. It was only Wales that stood firm now, and the strong unity of its stand is proof of the close communication among all parts of the country, showing again the great importance of the role played by the Church in welding Wales into one national com-

768   munity. The situation remained a lively point of discussion until in 768 it was decided to conform.

The man who persuaded the Welsh to conform was an unusual person. Elfodd was a monk from Caergybi (Holyhead), a learned and able man, whom Nennius proudly claimed had been his pupil. He must have been quite young in 768 for he did not die until 809, an old man, deeply respected as the 'chief bishop in the land of Gwynedd'. The reasoning power of this young man's sharp and scholarly mind succeeded in convincing the Church that there was nothing further to gain from adhering to the old usages which had characterised it for almost four hundred years, and which had been the subject of the disagreement with Augustine. Although they were allowed to go, other differences remained which were much more important than the ones which caused such bitter strife.

This quarrel was consciously associated in Wales with the dispute with Augustine. The Welsh knew about the contents of Bede's book *The Ecclesiastical History of the English People* where detailed accounts were given of the conferences between Augustine and the Welsh. This showed the Welsh that the archbishops of Canterbury had no more authority over Wales than they had over Ireland, where they had none at all. Wales lay completely outside their jurisdiction. Wade-Evans suggests that this knowledge helped Elfodd to win the day. He made clear the situation between Wales and Canterbury; there was no formal relationship. Since this fundamental point was established the Welsh could afford to yield on the other issues, which had become unimportant.

What underlay the dissension most of the time was the relationship between the Church of the Welsh and the Church of the English. The relationship of the Welsh Church with the Roman Church was never in doubt. This resembled the relationship with the king of England that the Welsh princes tried to develop. The little Church was happy to recognise the supremacy of Rome while its own character was respected. The Church in Wales continued to possess its distinctive Welsh character for hundreds more years, drawing spiritual nourishment from the tumultuous experiences of the age of the saints. Of the struggle of these centuries with Canterbury it can be said — as Llywelyn Williams said of the struggle to disestablish the Church of England in Wales twelve hundred years later — that it was Welsh nationalism in religious dress.

VI. THE GOLDEN AGE OF IRELAND

ALTHOUGH there was much learning and culture in Wales, Irish civilisation attained a still higher level in the seventh and eighth centuries, as is demonstrated, for example, by the Books of Kells. With the blending of Christianity and the native Celtic culture, the genius of the Irish flowered into a splendour which was an inspiration to much of Europe. Its great monasteries drew people from many lands. Its evangelists and teachers went to England and Scotland, France and the Netherlands, Germany and Austria, Switzerland and Italy; as far east as Syria, and to Iceland in the north. Wales gained much from their visits. For centuries they streamed out into the world, infusing it with their learning and godliness. These Irishmen did not attempt to conquer anyone; no bloody religious crusade was fought by them. They used only mental and spiritual persuasion: their aim was to bring the world to Christ.

But their civilization was brought to ruin by wave after

wave of invaders, Danes, Normans, and finally, the English, together with, sad to say, some Welsh, and many Scots. Since the age of Elizabeth, and throughout Cromwell's time, the history of the villainy of the English government is incredibly cruel, reaching the nadir of barbarity in the eighteenth and nineteenth centuries. It would be impossible to find a greater contrast than that between the wretched state of Ireland in the eighteenth century and the glory of its golden age in the eighth. The history of Ireland under English rule is tragic and anguished.

VII.   OFFA'S DYKE AND BEYOND

THE most important political development in eighth century Wales came as a result of English pressure on its eastern border. In the seventh century the border had been pushed further west in many places. This occurred with the increase in power of Mercia after the Battle of Chester, and Powys was the principal but not the only loser. We have seen that the location of the battle between Penda and Oswald in 642 suggests that the Oswestry area was already part of Mercia. The fact that Bede gives Bangor Iscoed an English name shows that the English border had reached the Dee by the beginning of the eighth century. The son of Penda, Wulfhere, gave his name to Wulheresford near Llanymynech about 660. The English convent which was established in Wenlock near Shrewsbury shows that that area too was in English hands in the seventh century; and in the same century a large part of Herefordshire had been occupied, although there is no proof that more than the western side had ever been part of a Welsh kingdom. Erging, the Welsh part that was lost, remained Welsh-speaking at least until the end of the middle ages; and there was a Welsh service in the church of Llanfair Waterdine, in Herefordshire, right up to the middle of the nineteenth century.

The border of Powys no doubt saw much fighting before

one inch was yielded. Although there is no mention of this, perhaps it is reflected in the magnificent poetry of Llywarch Hen in the ninth century. Neither the battles nor the victories were one-sided. The Latin biography of an English saint, Guthlac, refers to heavy attacks by the Welsh on Mercia between 705 and 709, when the country was razed by them, and the words on Eliseg's memorial suggest that the Welsh had regained territory from the English by the beginning of the eighth century. The two victories which were won, probably by Rhodri Molwynog in 721, have already been mentioned. By then the border had been established and it remained in the same place until the Welsh, under Owain Gwynedd, won back a substantial amount of land in the north-east in the twelfth century.

705
to
709

721

Offa, the king of Mercia from 757 to 796, was the most powerful ruler produced by the English up to this time. When Northumbria fell into anarchy it came under his rule; his authority stretched over a great part of the south of England too. He also came to attack Wales. *Brut y Tywysogion* says, about 776, 'and then there was great destruction of the South by King Offa', and it also refers to his ravages in Wales in the summer of 784. He is the king who defined and noted the only territorial boundary of Wales, at the same time the western boundary of England. Ever since then England has been for the Welsh 'the land beyond Offa's Dyke'. And this was indeed the purpose of the dyke. 'Offa's dyke marked a boundary, a frontier: it was not a military barrier,' says Cyril Fox in his great volume about the dyke, which was described by F. M. Stanton as the 'outstanding memorial of its type and period in north western Europe.' It is a tribute to the spirit of the Welsh that part of Mercia which lies east of Offa's Dyke is today a part of Wales.

776
784

VIII. THE TENACITY OF THE STATES

Powys of necessity faced the worst English onslaughts at this period, but although it decreased in size it remained a strong and vigorous kingdom. Its confidence and spirit are shown by the memorial raised in the Vale of Llangollen at the beginning of the ninth century by its king, Cyngen. The column commemorates the crucial victory of his great-grandfather, Elisedd, against the English. Edward Lhuyd, the famous antiquary of the seventeenth century, copied the inscription and proudly claimed that it was Elisedd who saved the heritage of Powys from the English. Elisedd was descended from the Selyf, of the lineage of Brochwel Ysgithrog, who lost his life in the battle of Chester. The reign of Cyngen, who came to the throne in 808, was characterised by hard fighting on the border; and as the spirit of the memorial to Elisedd shows, he succeeded in defending his patrimony, which reached as far as Iâl (Yale). After a long life he went to Rome about 854, the first Welsh king to go on that arduous pilgrimage, and there in Rome he went to his long peace.

808

Gwynedd too had to withstand English attacks. In one of them, in 798, King Caradog was killed. In 817, the year King Cynon died, the English penetrated into the heart of Arfon. The *Brut* says, 'and the English laid waste the mountains of Eryri'. Again in 823 the burning of the Castle of Dyganwy (where the court of Maelgwn Gwynedd had been) is noted and the ravaging of Powys by the English. By this time the misery of the situation was increased by attacks from the Norsemen. The Vikings and the English came by sea to Gwynedd, the English from the east and the Norsemen from the west, and thus it was the coast that suffered most. This was the period in which the Norsemen took possession of all the islands of Scotland and of Caithness, Argyle and Galloway on the mainland. They occupied the Isle of Man and parts of Ireland, inaugurating there a time of anarchy which brought the splendid civilisation of the seventh and eighth centuries near

817

to ruin. Although Wales had more success in preventing Norse settlement than did Ireland, Scotland and England, yet she suffered grievously and lost treasures of incalculable value from her churches and monasteries in the raids. The Welsh had to fight on two fronts. In addition to the Viking attacks they had also to cope with the adjacent English.

The shores of Ceredigion and Dyfed suffered many attacks, particularly from the Danes, but they did not succeed in making strong settlements. In the middle of the eighth century there had been quite a lot of vigour in Ceredigion. When its king, Seisyll ap Clydog, was in his prime about 730 he occupied the three cantrefs or hundreds of Ystrad Tywi, which lay between the Teifi and the Tawe, and which had once been part of Dyfed. These three cantrefs formed with Ceredigion the kingdom which was called Seisyllwg after the king. The story occurs in the tale of *Pwyll Pendefig Dyfed* in the *Mabinogion*. It was out of this kingdom that the Deheubarth of the princes of Dinefwr grew.

The king of Dyfed at this time was Rhain ap Cadwgan, and his kingdom is sometimes called Rheinwg. Amongst the ancestors of Rhain was Aircol, who reigned in the time of Teilo; and Vortiporex, who is commemorated on the column in Castell Dwyran; and Eochaid Allmuir, the Irish prince who settled in Dyfed in the third century. The family came to an end with the death in 796 of Maredudd the grandson of Rhain. About the same time as Seisyllwg was founded and Rheinwg named, Morgannwg got its name; of these three, two have disappeared and only Morgannwg remains.

Another Rhain, also of Irish descent, reigned in Brycheiniog in the fifth century. He was the son of Brychan who founded the kingdom. Like the family of Eochaid Allmuir, Brychan's family was of long continuation; it persisted for generations after the death of Maredudd, the last of the old line of Dyfed. It also remained aware of its Roman and Latin connections: Awst (Augustine) who ruled Brycheiniog in the seventh century was a member of this family.

IX. ART, LITERATURE AND EDUCATION

THE interest in the things of the mind continued throughout these centuries. People were constantly emerging who had an eye for discovering the beautiful and who could create fine compositions out of substance and sound. Words were the main media of the artists; in any event more of the work of the bards has remained than that of other artists. Although it is not of the standard of the glorious Irish work, what remains of the work of the Welsh monks in the Gospels of Chad shows that they could create remarkably fine manuscripts. Examples are found too of metal work by Welsh craftsmen dating from the fifth to the eighth centuries. These show the characteristics of Celtic work everywhere, the love of abstract patterns rather than natural forms from the world of nature, and the tendency towards geometric patterns and looped and winding curves which flow easily on metal and stone. It is not anything that can be found in nature which is reproduced, although the inspiration comes from nature; we see creations of the imagination, remarkably gentle, and never coarse. As in the world of the Celtic mind, we see here a consciousness of the unity of life; leaves or fruit in metal, for example, can develop into heads of animals. Many of the most beautiful things which have been discovered are household implements or military accoutrements.

Music played an important part early in the life of the Welsh. There must have been a very long tradition behind the famous comments of Gerallt Gymro (Giraldus Cambrensis) centuries later:

> 'On their musical instruments they attracted and enchanted the ear with such sweetness of sound, they moved with such swiftness and purity of key, and they composed such *cynghanedd* under the quick and eager touch of disunited fingers . . . and through an art that lacked nothing, on tunes of varied movements, with such sweet speed, such immoderate moderation, and such discordant harmony, they finish and complete the melodies in consistent tones. Whether they be fifths or fourths which resound from the strings, they nonetheless begin every time in B flat and return to it so that the whole thing finishes on a pleasantly sweet note. . .

They use three instruments: the harp, the pipe and the crwth.

In their song melodies, they do not sing in unison as they do in other countries but in many modes and keys. And thus in a company of singers, as is usual among this nation, you hear as many different pitches and voices as you see heads, and all of them in the end uniting in one alliteration in the sweetness of the key of B flat, and in perfect harmony.'

Perhaps Gerallt was exaggerating about the B flat, but the love which has continued down to our day for the minor key and for singing in harmony reflects the basic truth of the words of this keen observer. The musical gift which was so obvious in Wales must have produced music of value long before the twelfth century, but nothing has survived which can with any certainty be attributed to a very early period.

A small quantity of poetry survived from the seventh, eighth and ninth centuries: an occasional song of praise, such as the one to Cadwallon; the marvellously subtle compositions of Llywarch Hen and the *englynion* pertaining to death.

> Stafell Cynddylan ys tywyll heno,
>   Heb dân, heb wely,
> Wylaf wers; tawaf wedy.
>
> Stafell Cynddylan ys tywyll heno
>   Heb dân, heb gannwyll.
> Namyn Duw, pwy a'm dyry pwyll?
>
> Stafell Cynddylan a'm gwân i'w gweled,
>   Heb doad, heb dân.
> Marw fy llyw; byw fy hunan.
>
> Stafell Cynddylan ys tywyll ei nen,
> Gwedi difa o Loegrwys
> Gynddylan ac Elfan Powys.
>
> Stafell Cynddylan ys tywyll heno
>   O blant Cyndrwynyn—
> Cynon a Gwion a Gwyn.
>
>
> Cynddylan's hall is dark tonight,
>   no fire, no bed;
> I'll be still when these tears are shed.

Cynddylan's hall is dark tonight,
    no fire, no taper;
God's the only patience-giver.

Cynddylan's hall hurts me to see,
    no fire, no roof;
my chief is dead, I live aloof.

Cynddylan's hall is dark of roof-top
    since the English ruined
Cynddylan and Elfan of Powys land.

Cynddylan's hall is dark tonight;
    of Cyndrwynyn's breed,
Cynon and Gwion and Gwyn are dead.

The series conveys the sustained anguish of the poet with the
same economy as is shown in *Canu Heledd*, *Celain Urien*,
Marwnad Gwen and others Here is a verse from *Can yr Henwr:*

Y ddeilen hon neus cynired gwynt,
    Gwae hi o'i thynged!
Hi hen; eleni ganed.

The wind carries away this leaf—
    alas for its fate!
It's old, though born only this year.

Just as the filid in Ireland were historians, and the druids
before them, so also were the Welsh bards They were the
keepers of the pedigrees which were so important in the
history of the royal family around whom the kingdom
revolved. It has been proved that these genealogies were
remarkably correct as far back as the middle of the fourth
century. From this it may be deduced that it was immediately
after the departure of the Romans that they began to be
assembled, orally of course, and this consciousness of history
showed the new self-respect and self-confidence of the period.
Here is the beginning of the nurture of what may be called
national consciousness. The history which was embodied in
the genealogies was used, according to a custom that went
back a thousand years and more, when singing the praises to
the Prince. Gwyn Thomas says in *Yr Aelwyd Hon:*

'The essence of the tradition was that the bard sang to the leaders of his society. He composed verses of praise to a lord, during his lifetime celebrating his heroism, his generosity and his lineage in particular; and after his death he would compose an elegy upon him. In the early period . . . the leaders of society were warriors: to a great extent that is why so much of our early poetry is war poetry. Through his praise of his lord the bard proclaimed his heroism, praised his achievements and gave him the courage to carry on. And in the period written about we should remember that the life of the people depended literally on the ability of their lord to protect them . . . Thus the bard, dealing with life and death in his community, sang to the one who stood for the people. He also sang on behalf of his society, conveying their hopes and their fears.'

The bards praised the qualities upon which depended the continuation of the kingdom, and treasured that which gave roots and unity and strength. There was an essential social purpose to the story they narrated; it was not an academic study. No doubt the *cyfarwyddiaid* too inspired their listeners, as well as entertaining them with their stories. The *Mabinogion* has handed down some of the fruits of this skill, which had developed throughout Wales by the ninth century.

It was in Wales that history was most carefully preserved, including the history of the princes of the Old North; it is here that we have the poetry, the genealogies and the *Brutiau* or chronicles. And Nennius, upon whose *Historia Brittonum* we depend so much, was a Welshman. His book, written about 800, was an attempt to put on record the history of the Welsh and the other Brythons from the landing of Julius Caesar to the end of the seventh century.

Of all the courts in Wales the one that attributed most importance to the history which poets preserved was Gwynedd, especially under the rule of Merfyn Frych. And it is to this unusual man that we now turn.

X. MERFYN FRYCH

WITH Merfyn Frych Wales takes a great stride forward. In him Gwynedd had a king of wide culture and penetrating political insight. He reinvigorated the culture of Gwynedd;

he defended it successfully in a time of turmoil; he gave it strength to withstand the fierce attacks which tore at it from every side. The Norsemen conquered a large part of England in the ninth century; they held the Isle of Man and had established a powerful kingdom in Ireland around Dublin, only a few score miles from the shores of Wales. In the first half of the tenth century they almost completely ruined the fabric of western European civilisation. No Norse kingdom, however, was established on Welsh soil. They were successful only in giving their names to ports and islands such as Swansea and Anglesey, Fishguard and Bardsey, Milford and Flatholm. For this we have to thank the succession of outstanding leaders which Wales had in the ninth and tenth centuries — Merfyn Frych, his son Rhodri Mawr, his grandson Anarawd and his great-grandson Hywel Dda. In the eleventh century the whole of England was conquered by the Danes but Wales remained a free land, living not under 'Dane-law' but under the laws of Hywel Dda, thanks to Gruffydd ap Llywelyn and the loyalty of the people of Wales to their leaders.

Merfyn came from the Isle of Man, the only Welsh king to do so. A stone cross from this period has been discovered there which may be a memorial to his father, Gwriad. Gwriad married Esyllt the daughter of Cynan ap Rhodri Molwynog, of the family of Maelgwn Gwynedd and Cunedda. In 818 Hywel ap Rhodri, Cynan's brother, died and Merfyn became the king of Anglesey, which is more open than any other part of Wales to attacks from the sea. Perhaps his lineage would not have been sufficient in itself to give him the crown, were it not for his natural ability and the strength of his personality. At the death of Hywel ap Caradog in 825 he added the cantrefs of Arfon to Anglesey, reuniting the heritage of the descendants of Cunedda in Gwynedd. Merfyn made a great enough name for himself for the English to call Caer Segeint, in Arfon, Mirmanton — Merfyn's town. He married Nest, the sister of Cyngen, the king of Powys who raised the memorial near Llangollen. One of the sons of this marriage was Rhodri Mawr, who united the two kingdoms. Merfyn strengthened

the tendency for large parts of Wales to recognise the authority
of one prince, a tendency which developed as the pattern of
political development in the ensuing centuries. Nora Chadwick
refers to

> 'the gradual approximation to a Wales united under a single family.
> It is I think the most remarkable feature of early Welsh history that
> the union of most of these kingdoms should have come about gradually
> with no record of conquest and no bloodshed. Those historians who
> speak of the Welsh as a warlike people see Wales only through the
> eyes of the Norman conquerors, when the whole country became an
> armed fortress on the defensive. The early history is very different —
> a history of peaceful development, of gradual unification by policy,
> and by a series of royal marriages.'

Another branch of Merfyn Frych's family is also of considerable interest. On his father's side he was descended from
Llywarch Hen, a prince in the North in the sixth century and a
central character in the fine poetry which was composed in
the middle of that century in the time of Rhodri Mawr. The
poet located many of the incidents in his poems on the English
border of Powys, but other poems describe events in the Old
North. In her excellent essay *Early Culture and Learning in
North Wales*, Nora Chadwick draws attention to the striking
fact that a character of the same name as Gwriad, the father of
Merfyn Frych, is mentioned in the Red Book of Hergest as a
king in the North, and that his name also occurs more than
once in *Englynion y Beddau* side by side with that of Urien.
In one *englyn* Gwên is connected with them: Gwên was
Llywarch Hen's youngest son; he was killed defending the
border against the English.

> Y beddau a wlych cawod:
> Gwŷr na thrawyd yn lledrad—
> Gwên, a Gwrien a Gwriad.

> The graves that a shower wets:
>   men not struck down whilst thieving—
> Gwên and Gwrien and Gwriad.

The implication is that because Merfyn was descended from
Llywarch Hen and the princes of the Old North, the court of

Merfyn Frych and Rhodri Mawr set great store upon the relationship with the North and the history and poetry of its Welsh kingdoms, gathering together every tradition, manuscript and heroic ode about them which remained. This is the period of the composition of the *Annales Cambriae* and the writing of the *Historia Brittonum* by Nennius. Nennius had had a connection with Gwynedd as a pupil of Elfoddw, its chief bishop, although his home was originally in the southeast. Elfoddw was naturally concerned with the interests of Gwynedd, but he had, as a bishop, another reason for taking an interest in the traditions of the north: the first bishop of Bangor was Deiniol and he too, like his cousin Asaff, was of the lineage of Urien Rheged and the princes of the North, and this could have led the interest of Nennius into the same channels.

This great interest in history was a form of patriotism and an indication of a many-sided culture. It has already been seen that there was evidence of quite a rich culture and sophisticated life in Gwynedd, and that this was true of the whole kingdom. For that matter, it must have been true of all the kingdoms of Wales: of Morgannwg, where a vigorous life persisted in the great learned monasteries; of Dyfed, the land where the art of the *cyfarwydd* was shown in some of the tales of the Mabinogion; and of Ceredigion, where Llanbadarn Fawr was developing into one of the most important centres of learning in the whole country.

The wide diffusion of intellectual life is one of the advantages of a decentralised political system in which many centres of learning and culture, rather than one large centre, receive the support of the state. In the military sphere the vigour of local patriotism was one of the fundamental reasons why neither the Norsemen nor the English were able to establish more than a foothold in Wales. Local defence was more effective because people were able to understand what they were defending, and because there was great loyalty to the little kingdom and its leader. Moreover when one kingdom was being attacked, the whole of Wales was not disturbed at the same time. In a centralised system, when the centre fails the whole falls.

Among the examples of the cultural position in the royal court of Gwynedd given by Nora Chadwick is a manuscript in Bavaria founded on a letter sent by Merfyn to his brother-in-law Cyngen. This letter, in polished Latin, begins with a greeting from Merfyn to Cyngen, and shows that two Celtic languages were spoken in the court of Gwynedd, and that there was also a knowledge of Latin and Greek there. The letter includes a cryptogram sent by four Irish scholars to one of their teachers. They ask for help in solving it so that they will not have to blush with shame in the presence of Merfyn, 'the magnificent King of the Brythons'. By tracing the names and connections of these scholars Nora Chadwick shows that it was likely that the Court of Gwynedd was a staging-post for Irish scholars on their way to the Continent and back: that in all probability it accommodated all the needs of men of learning and culture: that through these inter-mediaries Merfyn communicated with the court of Charles the Second, Charles the Bald, the son of Charlemagne; and that there was at least one learned Welshman in France, a bishop living there as a hermit, who was in contact with the court of Charles. One of her general conclusions is that the sea still united the Celtic countries and especially Wales and Ireland, but that Wales now received more from the Irish than it gave to them. She adds:

'Round about the beginning of the ninth century there seems to have been a heightened intellectual activity and a keen sense of nationalism throughout all the Celtic countries, one important manifestation of which was a keen interest in the past resulting in widespread gathering and recording of early traditions, and antiquarian speculation and inference.'

Merfyn encouraged this cultural life, but enlightened patronage would have been of no value if it had not been able to count upon a political order which created the conditions of its success. He passed on the system and the tradition in its entirety, strengthened and enriched, to his son Rhodri.

XI. RHODRI MAWR

IT is Nora Chadwick's firm opinion that Rhodri Mawr was
the greatest of all the Welsh kings. She says that he was put
to a more rigorous test than anyone else in the early history of
Wales, with the English increasing their power in the east,
and the Scandinavians a growing threat in the west. Rhodri
succeeded in wrestling with this serious situation and, in spite
of all the difficulties, in building a still more powerful kingdom.
.He was a man of culture who promoted scholarship and art.
During his short lifetime the poetry of Llywarch Hen was
composed. He was the first to be given the epithet 'Great'. Only
one other in the history of Wales received the same honour,
Llywelyn Fawr.

When Cyngen, the King of Powys, died without a
son in 955, Rhodri inherited the kingdom as the son
855   of Nest, Cyngen's sister. The men of Powys were
doubtless glad for him to have their throne
because they had had a hard time fighting against
Mercia. In England the terrible onslaught of the Danes
853   was driving Mercia and Wessex closer together, and
there were united attacks on the Welsh by the men
of the two strongest English kingdoms. In 853 Ethelwulf, the
father of Alfred the Great, united with Burgoed, the king of
Mercia, in an attack of this kind. Ifor Williams believes that
this was the background of some of the poems which were
attributed to Llywarch Hen. However there is no proof that
the Welsh lost more territory. Indeed they even won back
some which had been taken earlier. In the same year the
'Black Pagans', as the Danes were called in the *Bruts*, were
plundering Anglesey.

In 856 Rhodri won a great victory in a battle in which the
leader of the Danes, Horm, was killed. This Dane
856   gives his name to the Great Orme (Trwyn y Gogarth)
near Llandudno. In an Irish *brut* this great event is
recorded, and the news reached the court of Charles the Bald
in Liège, for a poem was composed on this theme by Sedulius

Scottus, an Irish poet and scholar who was a member of the court. Nora Chadwick believes that Sedulius was a friend of one of the four Irish scholars referred to as being at the court of Merfyn Frych.

Rhodri married Angharad, the sister of Gwgon, the king of Seisyllwg, the kingdom which united Ceredigion and Ystrad Tywi. When Gwgon was drowned in 872, it 872 was Rhodri who succeeded to this throne too. He was, therefore, ruler now of nearly two-thirds of the country, with more power to withstand the enemies who had conquered much larger kingdoms than Wales. No doubt this degree of unity deepened the national consciousness, which continued to influence a number of the descendants of Rhodri in Deheubarth and in Gwynedd until Wales lost its independence. It is worth noting that the word 'Deheubarth' (the Southern part) implies that Wales is one land.

Until the end of his days he fought against the 'Black Pagans' and the English. In 876, the year before the Danes 876 overcame Wessex and drove Alfred into the hills of Somerset, Rhodri was fighting in a battle against them on a certain Sunday, according to the *Brut*. He had to flee to Ireland. After his return he is found in a battle again, against the English of Mercia this time; but this was his last battle. He and his son Gwriad were both killed in it, a sad blow for the Welsh. His life was of great value to his country; he defended its territories in the face of powerful enemies; he maintained its tradition. The history of Wales would be very different but for his premature death; he left an enormous gulf. The Welsh recognised the extent of their loss, and when the English were beaten by Anarawd, Rhodri's son, in a battle near Conwy three years later the Welsh looked upon this victory as 'God's revenge for the killing of Rhodri'. They were fortunate indeed in having so courageous a man to lead them in such disturbed times. Because of him they were able to face the future with more courage.

Rhodri left six sons, among them Anarawd, Cadell (father of Hywel Dda) and Merfyn, to carry on his work, and although the kingdom was divided among them in the way required by Welsh law, they co-operated vigorously according to the testimony of no less a person than Asser, the Welsh scholar from St. David's who was attracted to the court of Alfred the Great. While Rhodri was spending his last years in battle, Alfred was heroically building up Wessex in the teeth of the attacks of the Scandinavians: the most able military leader they encountered. He was also a statesman of vision and a man of wide culture. Asser's laudatory biography was written for Welsh readers in order to persuade them that Alfred was a Christian, civilised monarch deserving of their co-operation. It is strange to think that the children of England and Wales would not have heard about Alfred and the cakes but for this famous book compiled by the monk from St. David's. In Alfred, of course, he had a magnificent subject, the greatest national hero that the English ever had. Winston Churchill writes thus about him:

'This sublime power to rise above the whole force of circumstances, to remain unbiased by extremes of victory or defeat, to persevere in the teeth of disaster, to greet returning fortune with a cool eye, to have faith in men after repeated betrayals, raises Alfred far above the turmoil of barbaric wars to his pinnacle of deathless glory.'

XII. ANARAWD

IT was Anarawd who ruled Gwynedd, and probably Powys too, after the death of his father; while Ceredigion and Ystrad Tywi, the kingdom of Seisyllwg, was ruled by Cadell, the father of Hywel Dda. According to Asser, who gives a clear description of the Welsh political scene in the last quarter of the ninth century, the power of Anarawd and Cadell was much feared by the other Welsh kings in Dyfed, Brycheiniog, Gwent and Morgannwg; although Hywel ap Rhys in Morgannwg, and Penfoel ap Meurig in Gwent had much more reason to fear the Mercians. A striking characteristic of Welsh life through all the centuries of freedom is the peace which Gwent, Morgannwg and Brycheiniog enjoyed. Elisedd ap Tewdwr, of the old lineage of Brychan, ruled Brycheiniog.

Dyfed was ruled by Hyfaidd ap Bledri, who had troubled the
men of the great *clas* of St. David's. Whatever the reason, the
kings of these four small kingdoms were glad to have the
patronage of Alfred, giving Asser the opportunity, he said,
of serving St. David's better in the court of Wessex than he
could have done at home.

The duty of Anarawd was to protect his kingdom against
the greatest danger facing it. When this came from the side of
the English, the prince made a treaty with the Danes, forming
an alliance with their king in York whose kingdom stretched
across England as far as the banks of the Mersey. However,
when the threat from the Danes increased Anarawd turned to
Alfred, who was very ready to welcome the co-operation of a
king whose kingdom had withstood the Danish attacks so well.
Anarawd paid a visit to the court of the famous English king
— the first time for a king from Wales to visit an English
court — where he was received with every courtesy and
honour by Alfred, who acted as sponsor for him when he
received the sacrament of confirmation. Later on, however,
this visit was turned into an argument by the English kings
for demanding the homage of the kings of Wales.

Everywhere at this time the foundations of European
civilisation were crumbling. In Rome itself between
896 and 904 there were ten popes. In England in 892
the pressure of the Danes increased dangerously when
their army crossed over from the Continent. Between 892 and
896 they overran central and southern England from sea to sea,
and reached the Welsh border in 893 at Buttington, the con-
fluence of the Severn and the Wye. There they were resisted
by a large army of Welsh and English, the men of Gwent and
Morgannwg uniting with the men of Mercia and Wessex.
A great number were killed before the Danes were finally
driven back from the Welsh border. In 894 they
occupied Chester and then attacked north-east Wales,
but were repulsed by Anarawd. It is believed that he
had some English help, and when he attacked
Ceredigion and Ystrad Tywi in 895 there were a
number of Englishmen amongst his soldiers. At the end of that

892

894
895
896

year the Danes are seen again in the Vale of Severn, and in 896 they attack Brycheiniog, Gwent and Morgannwg. They must have been sorely disappointed for their great army collapsed that summer, and those who had settled in the north of England returned to their homes there. Once again the opposition met by the Black Host was stronger in Wales than in England, which failed on the whole, with the brilliant exception of Alfred, to produce a system or leaders who inspired confidence.

> 'The richest and most populous part of old agricultural England — East Anglia — had failed in the race for leadership,' says Trevelyan, 'because it had no prince of the calibre of Edwin of Northumbria, Penda of Mercia or Alfred of Wessex. The Danes soon found how safe it was to land on the shores of helpless East Anglia and thence to overrun decadent Northumbria and declining Mercia.'

Had the little Welsh kingdoms been as helpless as these great English ones, Wales would have ceased to exist centuries ago.

The Welsh remained on their guard, their morale high. They had to defend their country by costly efforts over and over again during the years that followed, especially after the coming of the Danes in strength from Ireland in 902.

902
915
They came from the west, the north, the east and the south. In 915 an army of the Black Host, which had founded a powerful kingdom in Normandy, sailed from Brittany to the Severn; but although they plundered the shores of Severn in Gwent and Morgannwg, they failed to colonise there, and so sailed on to Ireland. Nor did the English cease their onslaughts, as is shown by the story of their attacks in 916 on the royal fort of Brycheiniog,

916
near Llyn Safaddan (Llangors Lake). When Anarawd died in that year, after reigning for thirty-eight years, the territory of Wales was as intact, and its tradition as secure, as it had been in the time of his father. Anarawd was a worthy successor to Rhodri Fawr.

XIII. HYWEL DDA

Two years after the death of Anarawd, Idwal Foel, his son and
successor, went to pay homage to King Edward, who
918 spent most of his life, like Alfred before him, fighting
the Danes. With Idwal at this time went Hywel Dda
and Clydog his brother, who between them had inherited
Ceredigion and Ystrad Tywi from their father, Cadell. When
Clydog died in 920 Hywel, who had been reigning
920 since about 909, became king of the whole of the
kingdom of Seisyllwg. He was married to Elen, the
daughter of Llywarch, the king of Dyfed. When
928 Llywarch died without a son in 904, that ancient
kingdom too came under his control. The grandson
of Rhodri Mawr was now king of the whole of the southern
kingdom of Deheubarth. This was the position when he went
on a pilgrimage to Rome in 928.

The great achievement of Edward, who ruled Wessex for a
quarter of a century after his father, was to bring under his
control a great deal of the country conquered by the Danes.
This brought Wessex to the border of Wales. Clearly, therefore, it was of benefit to Hywel Dda and the other Welsh
kings to be on good terms with him. What any government
must avoid if it possibly can is a war on two fronts; that had
been Rhodri's predicament. Wessex would have been just as
anxious as the Welsh states to avoid this. Hence Hywel went to
pay homage to Edward, and for this reason Edward
926 too desired an understanding with Hywel. It implied
no more than that. 'Their kings and princes', says
Trevelyan about the Welsh and the kingdom of Strathclyde
which was still a Brythonic kingdom, 'sometimes acknowledged a vague supremacy in Athelstan and Edgar'. Hywel
acknowledged the 'vague supremacy' of Wessex.

The relationship between these kingdoms in the tenth
century can be compared with the relationship between the
countries of the Commonwealth today. They accept the
English crown as a connecting link, but the Commonwealth
is by definition a society of 'free and equal nations'. This

equality refers to their constitutional position. In the tenth century the Welsh states were free and equal members of a loose association. What was important for Hywel was the essential freedom of his position. Paying homage to the king of Wessex did not worry him at all since it did not take away any of this freedom, any more than recognising the crown today diminishes the freedom of the countries of the Commonwealth.

This proved distasteful to those who laid great stress on symbolic appearances. It was more difficult for Idwal Foel of Gwynedd (killed fighting against the English in 942) than for Hywel. Naturally hatred of the English flourished amongst some, especially if they believed the legends of Bede and Nennius about the great English conquest which had sent the Welsh fleeing to the mountains of the west. It was as a result of the tension which was felt in Wales that the *Armes Prydain* was composed about 930, the greatest 'prophetic' poem in our language, a poetic composition which conveys the bitter enmity towards the English which burned in the hearts of some of the Welsh. This long exciting poem is founded on the belief that the Welsh have a right to the land of England: that the whole of Britain is really *their* land. With consuming passion the poet appeals to the memory of the heroes of the magnificent past, showing how profound was the consciousness of history at that time, more than a millennium ago. The princes advance from the past, Arthur at their head, to lead the nation on a crusade. The Celts are called upon to unite — the Welsh with the Men of the Old North as well as the Irish, the Bretons with the men of Cornwall — to hurl the English into the sea. Unity is even called for between the Celts and the Picts and the Black Pagans. The purpose of this unity is to rid the island of the English.

942

> A chymod Cymry a gwŷr Dulyn,
> Gwyddyl Iwerddon, Môn a Phrydyn,
> Cernyw a Chlydwys, eu cynnwys gennym.

> And a pact between the Welsh and the men of Dublin,
> and Irish of Ireland, Anglesey, the Picts,
> Cornwall and Strathclyde, they'll all be in.

There is no clear proof that this had ever been the policy of any Welsh king, nor that any responsible leader in Wales had ever dreamt of regaining England. But the supposed right of Wales to England was a constant theme of the poets throughout the middle ages and the historical annals constantly refer to the people as Brythons rather than Welsh. Great importance is given to the legend of Hengist and Horsa and Gwrtheyrn and the great English conquest. All this had a bad psychological effect on the Welsh: first of all, it made them dream paranoic and completely unrealistic dreams about their future. Secondly, it made them a ready prey to the ravages of Britishness which went from strength to strength after the Battle of Bosworth and the triumph of the Tudors — connected with the same dream — and which reached its climax in the age of Victoria. Thirdly, the spirit of the Welsh was sorely injured by the belief that they had lost their fine big country and were having to live like 'gwehilion o boblach' (human refuse) on a peninsula which was —

Yn ddim byd ond cilcyn o ddaear mewn cilfach gefn
Ac yn dipyn o boendod i'r rhai sy'n credu mewn trefn.

Nothing more than a fragment of earth in a back cove
Causing quite a bit of trouble to those who believe in order.

The policy espoused by the author of *Armes Prydain* — probably a monk of Deheubarth — did in fact bring the kings of Scotland and the Welsh kingdom of Strathclyde together in unity with Olaf of Dublin in opposition to Athelstan. But the English king decisively defeated the allied armies in 937 in the Battle of Brunanburh. However, Hywel Dda was too wise to be bewitched by this silly dream. He pursued his policy with a sure touch and remarkable success, and this without killing, as far as we know, a single Englishman or Welshman. Only a statesman of consummate ability could have united Gwynedd and Powys, as well as Deheubarth, on the death of Idwal Foel in 942, without shedding blood. For Idwal had sons, and by supplanting them Hywel broke roughly with the custom of centuries. Nevertheless his unbending resolution at this time shows how mistaken it is

942

to think of him as a soft man. His action was accepted peacefully; he was welcomed as king of the whole of Wales except
the south-east, because the Welsh needed one man to lead
their defence. He ruled from Caergybi (Holyhead) to Cydweli,
and from Llanelwy (St. Asaph) to Tyddewi (St. David's).
He minted money with his name on it as one who ruled all
Wales.

More important than anything else, this great man summoned an assembly to ensure one body of law common to
every commote and hundred of the land. The manuscripts of
these laws — the earliest of which belong to the twelfth
century — record that Hywel called to Hendy-gwyn-ar-Daf
(Whitland) six men from every commote in his kingdom.
Although the Church was accustomed to summoning synods,
this one would have been on a larger scale than anything ever
seen before. It included political and ecclesiastical leaders,
nobles and bishops, priests and magistrates, lawyers and abbots.
Its main purpose was to consider the laws of the land; and
calling these men together was the greatest national event that
Wales had ever witnessed. If representatives were called from
every region then it was in reality a parliament. J. E. Lloyd
thought that it was a man from Gwent, Blegywryd, who
was the leader — 'the most eloquent scholar in the whole of
Wales' — but recent scholars are more than sceptical on this
point.

Thirty-five manuscripts of Hywel's laws in Latin and Welsh
survive from the Middle Ages, which compares remarkably
well with the number of copies of English laws from the same
period which remain in England — twenty-seven of Glanvil's
volume and forty-six of Bracton's. Because law changes from
generation to generation most of the contents of these manuscripts belong to a later age than Hywel's, and it is difficult to
decide what part goes back to the tenth century, when it was,
in all probability, written in Welsh. In his book *Cyfraith
Hywel*, Dafydd Jenkins comes to this conclusion:

> 'There must have been a close connection between Hywel Dda, the
> king who died in 950, and the Laws of Hywel . . . the treatises and the
> Welsh books giving a clear indication that they were derived from one

source; all this suggests that the law of Wales underwent some great reform at a period which (compared with the period of the reform of Irish law) was comparatively recent, and it is reasonable to suppose that this occurred under the leadership of some king. This is indicated by the way the Welsh books take it for granted that there was only one law in Wales although it embraced many countries (or many states as we would say today), and the same material is found in books copied out in different parts of Wales . . . he must have been a king whose authority extended over most or all of Wales; and Hywel Dda is the only king who had such authority in a sufficiently peaceful period and for a long enough space of time to have the opportunity to give such a leadership. Some of the characteristics of Welsh law also bear this out . . .'

The characteristic of the law which had the greatest effect on the history of Wales was that the land of the father must be divided when he died between all his sons, and not pass in its entirety to the eldest son of the legal wife, as in England. It is noteworthy that the land was divided among *all* the sons; this included the son of an unmarried woman if the father had accepted him as his son. It was not only the inheritance of the individual person which passed on according to the law of portion (gavelkind), but the kingdom too: this was the feature which prevented the uniting of the kingdoms. Hywel's law excelled from the point of view of justice, but the law of England was possibly sounder from the point of view of political strength. Welsh law was more civilised but it weakened the State. It was when faced with united and imperialistic England on the attack that the Welsh suffered most from the weakness caused by its civilised character.

In the position of women under the law in Wales we see justice which was rare in the Middle Ages. Marriage was a real partnership, a union — the laws do not actually mention marriage which was a contract rather than a sacrament. When a girl married she received property which then remained completely and absolutely hers thereafter. She had the same rights as her husband about divorce, and if a husband and wife separated after seven years of marriage she had the right to half his property. The widow had the same right on her husband's death. A wife could transfer this property in a will.

In England a wife did not have the legal right to hold property apart from her husband until the Married Women's Property Act, 1882.

The body of the laws left its mark on Wales; not only did it reflect the national character but also contributed to its creation. It strengthened the unity of the country, deepened its national consciousness, and contributed to its confidence. When Wales was free to create its own laws, it did at least as well as its conqueror. Giraldus Cambrensis refers to the talent of lawyers in courts:

> 'In cases and actions of the law in the courts of justice,' he said, 'they do not neglect any part of rhetoric, which is completely natural when ensnaring, insinuating, devising, conveying, refuting and confirming.'

In parenthesis one may note that in an essay competition arranged on the subject 'Hywel Dda and his Laws' by the National Eisteddfod in Caernarfon in 1886, the two adjudicators were Thomas Powell, professor of Celtic in University College, Cardiff, and Gweirydd ap Rhys, the scholarly Welsh weaver who only had four days of formal education. The two winners were Edward Owen, an erudite civil servant from London, and Charles Ashton, a learned policeman from Dinas Mawddwy.

The Laws of Hywel Dda have drawn the attention of noted scholars of England and of the Continent. F. W. Maitland made a valuable study of them, noting the striking fact that the laws gave great prominence to the idea of nationhood. Joseph Loth comes to this conclusion:

> 'From an intellectual point of view it is the laws which give the Welsh the greatest claim to fame.'

And in a masterpiece in the middle of the last century, *Das Alte Wales*, Ferdinand von Walter of Bonn says:

> 'From this point of view, the Welsh outdistance all other people in the Middle Ages . . . In Wales justice and right blossomed, founded on the laws of Hywel Dda, into a perfection of beauty unlike anything found among other people in the Middle Ages.'

The laws as a Welsh language classic were also in the mind of the Frenchman Jacques Chevalier, who made a study of religious life in Wales in particular, when he came to this conclusion:

'Wales was the only nation in Europe in the tenth and eleventh centuries which had a national literature, apart from an imperial one in Latin. The people of Wales were the most civilised and intelligent of the age.'

What is certain is that to be in possession of a national code of law had deepened the national consciousness immeasurably. In the middle of the tenth century, when nine hundred years had elapsed since the onslaught of Ostorius and the Romans, the Welsh still had their own country and language, their own church and institutions, their own history and traditions. And on top of this they had their own legal system. What wonder that when he went to his grave in 950, after reigning for about forty years and leading his country with remarkable success, *Brut y Tywysogion* proclaimed Hywel Dda 'Pen a Moliant yr holl Frythoniaid' (Head and Glory of all the Brythons).

XIV. THE AGE OF MAREDUDD AB OWAIN

WELSH culture was now like a healthy young tree, fruitful and deep-rooted, many-branched and bearing its fruit in due season. The main work of future leaders would be to defend this vigorous growth and create the conditions in which it could attain its full maturity. During the four generations that followed Hywel Dda, before the coming of the Normans, the task would be a heavy and complicated one. That period saw more chaos than Wales had ever seen before; again and again the maritime regions were ravaged by the Danes and the English and numerous mother-churches near the seaboard were despoiled. In one period of only half a generation, between 982 and 999, St. David's was ravaged four times, and its bishop killed on one occasion; in one year, 988, Llanbadarn Fawr, Llandudoch, Llancarfan and Llanilltud Fawr were all destroyed; in one attack in 987 two thousand people from Anglesey were taken slaves; and on top of all this, and perhaps as a result of it, there were many internal skirmishes. But in spite of it all, and although the Scandinavians succeeded in getting footholds in the south of Pembrokeshire and in the Vale of Glamorgan, and establishing themselves as merchants in Cardiff and Swansea and a few other places, the resolute resistance put up by the small kingdoms prevented them occupying any big tracts of land.

In England chaos had been the order of the day for centuries. 'War, invasion and bloodshed', said Trevelyan, 'were normal conditions of life in Saxon England'. There, Vikings and Danes were in possession of a great deal of the country, which was ruled by them from cities between Chester, York and London, towns such as Lincoln, Leicester, Nottingham, Derby and Stamford. It was *they* who were the soldiers and the merchants, it was *their* language which was heard spoken; and *their* law administered. Eventually this was to enrich the life of England greatly; the Scandinavians were sufficiently like the English for them to fuse into one nation without too much despoiling of tradition. But bringing this wide territory under Saxon control by Wessex cost the people dearly, and no sooner had they succeeded than there came another wave of Danes to plunge the country into war again for a quarter of a century, until the accession of Cnut (Canute) of the Danes to the English throne in 1016.

As usually happened, the princes of Gwynedd would not accept the continuation of the unified order created by Hywel Dda. As a result there was ceaseless friction between them and Owain Maredudd and Hywel's other sons for four years when these attempted to force that order on Gwynedd. In the ensuing struggle the men of the south were defeated 951 in the battle of Nant Carno by Iago and the sons of Idwal Foel. An attack by the men of Gwynedd on Deheubarth is recorded for 952, and another by

Owain on the north in 954, but these led to no change.
Although the sons of Idwal Foel were an undisting-
954   guished quarrelsome lot, Iago did manage to maintain
strong government in Gwynedd — and probably
979   Powys as well. He kept the two kingdoms intact
until 979 when they were seized by his nephew
986   Hywel, who ruled until he was killed in 986. This
was a substantial achievement in the dark days of
constant Danish and English attacks, and one not to be under-
estimated.

Deheubarth, the southern kingdom, remained intact
throughout the long reign of Owain (the son of Hywel Dda),
who ruled from 950 to 988. Between them, father and son
had reigned for over three quarters of a century. Owain's son
Maredudd took over and ruled until 999. From 988 to 999
Maredudd was also the king of Gwynedd, and probably
Powys as well. When these periods are added to the reign of
Hywel Dda and Idwal Foel and their predecessors it can be
seen that during most of a century of great disorder in
England, Wales enjoyed strong and stable government.

After the attacks of Owain on Gwynedd early in the fifties
there is no further mention of his attacking any of his fellow
Welshmen until his invasion of Morgannwg in 960 and on
English Gower in 970 and 977. By this time he was
988   ageing; when he died in 988 he had ruled Deheubarth
for thirty-eight years. His long and successful reign
places Owain ap Hywel Dda high amongst the benefactors
of Wales.

But more notable than even Owain is his son Maredudd ab
Owain, grandson of Hywel Dda, and great-grandson of
Rhodri Mawr, although he only ruled for eleven years.
Maredudd had shown his military capacity in the attacks on
Morgannwg. The later course of his life perhaps makes
clearer the purpose of these attacks. Two years before the
death of his father, he had led his army to Gwynedd to depose
Cadwallon ap Ieuaf, who was also a great-great-grandson of
Rhodri Mawr. In this way he succeeded in uniting Gwynedd,
Powys and Deheubarth again as his grandfather Hywel Dda

and Rhodri Mawr had done before him. In all probability
Brycheiniog too recognised his supremacy, thus giving him a
wider authority than Hywel had had. Throughout his reign
almost the whole of Wales was united. The exceptions were
Gwent, where the family of Noe ap Gwried had been reigning
for sixty years, and Morgannwg where the grandsons of
Morgan Hen, who had been king there for a quarter of a
century from 949 to 974, continued to rule.

Maredudd resisted both the English and Danes with great
success, and even made a counter-attack on Mercia. When
some of his men were taken as slaves by the Norsemen he
had enough moral and material resources to buy them back.
In troubled times he pursued a powerful national policy; he
stood firm when it was necessary to make a stand; he acted
vigorously when action was necessary; he sustained the spirit
of the nation and safeguarded its tradition for the future.
When he died in 999 he had earned the title the chronicles
bestowed upon him: 'Clodforusaf frenin y Brytaniaid', Most
glorious king of the Brythons.

The century saw noteworthy literary achievement, some
of it of a very different kind from the heroic poems and
chronicles of the past centuries. There are nature poems, for
example, such as 'Yr Addwynau', (The Gentle Things), a poem
about the things that the poet found tender and desirable:

> Addwyn Aeron yn amser cynhaeaf,
> Arall addwyn, gwenith ar galaf . .
> Addwyn eryr a lan llif pan llanwy,
> Arall addwyn, gwylan yn gwarwy . . .
> Addwyn Mai i gogau ac eaws,
> Arall addwyn, pan fydd hi'n haws . . .
> Addwyn grug pan fo ehoeg,
> Arall addwyn, morfa i wartheg.
>
> Fair are fruits at harvest time
> and fair the wheat upon its stalk,
> fair on high tide's edge the eagle,
> fair, too, in its play the seagull . . .
> May is fair for cuckoo and nightingale
> and it's fair when things get easier . . .
> Heather's fair when it grows purple,
> coastal grass is fair for cattle.

There are descriptions of nature in the different seasons, such as the series of *englynion* which starts thus:

> Llym awel, llwm bryn, anawdd caffael clyd,
> Llygrid rhyd, rhewid llyn;
> Rhy saif gŵr ar un conyn.

> Sharp wind, bare hill, shelter is hard to find,
>   the ford is foul, frozen the lake,
>   a man may stand on a single stalk.

A fine little poem, very different from the type of poem usually preserved is the lullaby sung by the mother of Dinogad. The song is about his father's feats as a hunter and draws a delightful picture of a happy home.

> Pais Dinogad, i fraith fraith,
> O grwyn balaod ban wraith:
> Chwid, chwid, chwidogaith
> Gochanwn, gochenyn' wythgaith.
> Pan elai dy dad di i helia,
> Llath ar ei ysgwydd, llory yn ei law,
> Ef gelwi gŵn gogyhwg—
> 'Giff, gaff; daly, daly, dwg, dwg,'
> Ef lleddi bysg yng nghorwg
> Mal ban lladd llew llywiwg.
> Pan elai dy dad di i fynydd,
> Dyddygai ef pen iwrch, pen gwythwch, pen hydd,
> Pen grugiar fraith o fynydd,
> Pen pysg o Raeadr Derwennydd.

> Dinogad's speckled petticoat
> is made of skins of speckled stoat:
> whip, whip, whipalong,
> eight times we'll sing the song.
> When your father hunted the land,
> spear on shoulder, club in hand,
> thus his speedy dogs he'd teach,
> Giff! Gaff! catch her, catch her, fetch, fetch!
> In his coracle he'd slay
> fish as a lion does its prey.
> When your father went to the moor,
> he'd bring back heads of stag, fawn, boar,
> the speckled grouse's head from the mountain,
> fishes' heads from the falls of Oak fountain.

There is no better poem to start the tenth century that that written in praise of Dinbych-y-Pysgod (Tenby) — 'Addwyn gaer y sydd ar glawr gweilgi' (There is a gentle fort on the ocean dyke) and describing the cheerful life of the fort. And this is written in the beautiful Welsh spoken at that time in the south of Pembrokeshire.

The country continued to produce scholars. Sulien, born at the beginning of the next century shortly after the death of Maredudd, is a fine example of their quality. Sulien came of a family of priests from Llanbadarn Fawr, where there was a tradition of scholarship which was overshadowed by the fame of St. David's, fifty miles to the south. Sulien was a non-resident bishop of St. David's; his scholarly background was Llanbadarn Fawr, and it was there that he spent most of his life. However, he passed some time in centres of learning in Ireland and Scotland — five years in Scotland and eleven in Ireland — a good example of the habits of the fifth, sixth and seventh centuries continuing into the eleventh. His four sons inherited the scholarly tradition, each showing great ability; likewise his grandson, Sulien the Second, who was a teacher, a judge and a distinguished diplomat. Ieuan ap Sulien wrote a long Latin poem in praise of his father on the back of a copy of Augustine's *De Trinitate*, which is now in the library of Trinity College, Dublin. This poem gives much of the background of the family and the history of the area. Another son was Rhygyfarch, the patriot who wrote the earliest biography of St. David. It was Ieuan who painted the first letters in the book. The *clas* of Llanbadarn, which remained vigorous until the fifteenth century, thus survived Danish despoilation although the Danes must have destroyed many priceless manuscripts.

XV. GRUFFUDD AP LLYWELYN

THE pattern in which disorder followed the death of a king who had united the country is found again after the death of Maredudd ab Owain ap Hywel Dda, but it did not last long.

The land was once more united by Llywelyn ap Seisyll whose marriage to Angharad, daughter of Maredudd, gave him a legitimate claim to the throne of Gwynedd. For fifteen years Gwynedd had been ruled by Aeddan ap Blegywryd.

1018   It was by defeating him in battle in 1018 that Llywelyn extended his rule over the ancient kingdom of Cunedda. The three kingdoms of the south-east continued to live quietly and undisturbed under their old ruling, families, but Llywelyn completed the conquest of Deheubarth by overcoming Rhain, an Irish pretender who claimed

1022   to be a son of Maredudd. The decisive battle was fought in 1022 at Abergwili in the Tywi valley. By the time of his early death in 1023 this powerful and ambitious man had united Gwynedd, Powys and Deheubarth as Rhodri Mawr, Hywel Dda, and Maredudd had done before him.

The achievement of Llywelyn ap Seisyll made a deep impression. The account of him in *Brut y Tywysogion* is by far the fullest until then. It includes a description of the battle of Abergwili and of Rhain the Irishman. The most notable thing is the account of the condition of the country during this reign:

> 'In his time, as the elders of the kingdom used to relate, the whole country from sea to sea was full of an abundance of animals and men, so it is not supposed that there were poor people nor anyone in need in all his lands, nor one town empty nor waste.'

Once again, alas, Wales lost an able leader too soon. But a still greater man was to take up his work. It was Llywelyn's example no doubt that inspired his son Gruffudd ap Llywelyn to live a life of heroic effort which left a deep impress on the whole of Wales. When Gruffudd was a youth the last thing that anyone would have expected of him was a life of strenuous dedication. Gruffudd was rather a cowardly boy, lazy and unadventurous, according to Gwallter Map, the writer from Herefordshire, who tells an interesting story about the night the late king's son decided to mend his ways. One New Year's Eve, when he had been teased by his sister about his laziness, he went out into the open air; while he was leaning against the wall of a house where the cook was cooking in a cauldron great pieces of beef for the family, he heard the cook saying, 'That's odd: one piece of meat insists on rising to the surface, no matter how often I push it down.' These words went straight to Gruffudd's heart: they were prophetical words for him. From that moment he was a changed man; so changed indeed that *Brut y Tywysogion* could state, when recording his accession to the throne of Gwynedd in 1039, 'and from first to last he harried the English and the other nations.'

'The other nations' were usually the Danes; there is no mention of Gruffudd losing against them. Yet it was the English whom he met most frequently. He was probably King of Powys before he became King of Gwynedd after the death of Iago ab Idwal, and he had the responsibility of defending the English border. It was by doing this that he came into prominence in 1039 in a battle against Leofrig of Mercia near Rhyd-y-Groes on the Severn, where he defeated the English with great bloodshed. An English chronicle recounts that the Welsh were attacking in the region of Offa's Dyke at that time, and adds 'They are too strong while Gruffudd is king over them.'

Having defended the border in this way, he turned in another direction. His great ambition was to unite Wales as his father, Llywelyn ap Seisyll, had done. No one was allowed to stand in his way for long. He was not a merciful man. Anyone whom he judged to be a threat was removed either by imprisonment or death. This streak of cruelty in him perhaps had something to do with his own end. 'Do not talk about killing,' he said when justifying himself; 'I am only blunting the horns of the progeny of Wales to prevent them from injuring the ewe.' He was not unique in history in believing that the end justified the means. He was more of a soldier that a statesman. Perhaps a good measure of the political talent of Hywel Dda would have enabled him to avoid much of the bloodshed. But Hywel Dda had the great advantage of being the grandson of the illustrious Rhodri Mawr. The people of Gwynedd and Powys had been readier to accept his overlordship on account of his grandfather. Gruffudd lacked the ancestry which compelled nationwide loyalty; he had seized the reins of power through violence

as his father had done. He was a soldier, violent in manner and
cruel of temper. He used the only means he knew to change
the political order, and that was war. He had great virtues:
he was single-minded, brave, devoted, a man of imagination
and vision; and he pursued this vision with an ability far
beyond the ordinary.

The two who stood most firmly in the way of the realisation
of his dream of a united Wales were the able and determined
kings of Deheubarth: first, Hywel ab Edwin, until 1044, and
then Gruffydd ap Rhydderch until 1055. The first, a great-
grandson of Hywel Dda, spent much time defending Deheubarth against the Vikings and Gruffudd ap Llywelyn. After
his victory against the English in Rhyd-y-Groes on the

1039   Severn, Gruffudd had turned on Ceredigion and
plundered the lands of the *clas* of Llanbadarn Fawr
where Sulien may have been working on his books.
He failed to destroy Hywel's strength by this attack, for within
two years the two were facing each other in battle again, this
time at Pencader. Hywel was beaten and Gruffudd carried
his wife back to Gwynedd. Despite this second disappointment,
Hywel continued strong and vigorous, as is shown by his

1042   victory the following year over an army of Danes
near Carmarthen. Later he was defeated again and
had to flee to Ireland. He returned in 1044 with a
Danish navy. Gruffudd was down by the mouth of the Tywi
to meet him. In the battle which ensued Hywel was

1044   killed. At last Gruffudd had reason to think that
he had won the crown of Deheubarth.

Yet although he had got rid of his main obstacle,
his road was not yet clear. Gruffydd ap Rhydderch of
Deheubarth still stood in his way, with the same determination
and even more military ability than Hywel; and it was
obvious that the people of Ystrad Tywi and Ceredigion were
behind him, although his family came from Gwent and the
foundation of his power from Morgannwg. Gruffudd ap
Llywelyn went so far as to gather Englishmen from Mercia
to help him suppress Gruffydd ap Rhydderch; but all that he
attained was one year of peace. The following year a hundred

and forty members of the prince of Gwynedd's retinue were killed in Ystrad Tywi, and although he plundered Deheubarth to avenge this defeat, he had lost his authority there, and for eight years Gruffydd ap Rhydderch ruled without opposition. In 1049 Gruffydd is seen repulsing a heavy attack by the Scandinavians on the kingdoms of the south, and then making an agreement with them for a joint attack on the country in the upper reaches of the Severn Sea, on the Welsh as well as the Gloucestershire side. Perhaps he wanted to secure his hold on the country of his grandfather.

1049

Gruffudd ap Llywelyn turned his attention towards the east. This was probably the time when early English settlements at Wrexham, Bersham, Gresford and Allington were engulfed in the Welsh tide. In 1052 he defeated a mixed army of English and Normans near Llanllieni (Leominster) in the first battle in which the Welsh met a Norman army. They had been brought to Herefordshire by the policy of Edward the Confessor. Gruffudd is seen forming an alliance with Aelfgar of Mercia in 1055 to attack the Normans and the English of Herefordshire and Gloucestershire again. After he had totally vanquished them he set fire to the town. This alliance with the Earl of Mercia appeared at the time to be a stroke of genius, but by frightening Earl Harold, it cost Gruffudd his life. Harold gathered a great army together from almost every part of England and assembled it at Gloucester. His movements at this time were only defensive, intended to counter the growing Welsh power which was now feared in Mercian territory.

1052

In 1056 the Normans and the English took the initiative in aggression. Harold had put the defence of Hereford in the hands of the bishop — an old English policy — and he appointed as bishop a man by the name of Leofgar, who was more of a soldier than a priest. Leofgar sought to show his military prowess by personally leading an army over Offa's Dyke into Wales. He was met by Gruffudd, defeated and killed. Clearly the bishop had never preached on the text, 'All those who take up the sword shall perish by the sword.'

1056

In the meantime, in 1055, Gruffydd ap Rhydderch too had been killed, though it is not stated how or where. Gruffudd ap Llywelyn seized control of Deheubarth again, and with it authority over Morgannwg and Gwent. The area of his government was now greater than that of his father, of Maredudd ab Owain, of Hywel Dda, or of Rhodri Mawr. From Anglesey to Gwent (Gruffydd had established his power firmly in the south of Gwent) the whole of Wales was united politically. For many centuries Wales had been a nation. From 1055 until the death of Gruffudd in 1063, it was in a sense one state: a loose union of kingdoms — these had not disappeared — a confederation which came into being through the might of Gruffudd, with every kingdom recognising the supremacy of one Welsh crown.

Had Wales been allowed to develop in its own way perhaps a type of federalism, like that of Switzerland, would have emerged; this is what would have been natural in view of the remarkable resilience of its little states which had such strong social cohesion. The fate of Wales, however, was to be the neighbour of a nation a dozen times its own size, which developed into a unitary, imperialist state intolerant of the life of the small nations adjoining it. England explored every way of sowing disunity within them by dividing and ruling, and then incorporating them. Contemplating all the reasons for disunity in Wales — its legal system, its mountains, the strength of its tribal life and even the character of its people, it is apparent that the most fundamental explanation lies in the frightening presence of its powerful neighbour.

In the penetrating chapter of his *Description of Wales* entitled 'How this nation is to be conquered', Giraldus Cambrensis gives wise advice to the Norman government: 'Let their strengths be divided, and by bribes and promises endeavour to stir up one against the other, knowing the spirit of hatred and envy which generally prevails amongst them.' All down the centuries the Welsh were confounded by England's dividing them and enticing them 'by bribes and promises'.

It was usually towards the end of their lives that past leaders

had succeeded in uniting Wales, and this was repeated in the
story of Gruffudd ap Llywelyn: the end was near, he lived only
eight years after achieving his aim. His alliance with Earl
Aelfgar, whose daughter Gruffudd married, had frightened
Harold. He determined to destroy the Welsh power. In the
middle of winter, early in 1063 he made a sudden
1063   attack from Gloucester on the Welsh fort at Rhuddlan.
He failed to find Gruffudd, who escaped by sea to the
mountains of Eryri. By May Harold and his brother Tostig
had made extensive preparations to attack the heart of
Gwynedd. Harold and his fleet sailed from Bristol. Even then
he might not have succeeded had he not taken other, more
stealthy steps. He succeeded in bribing Welshmen close to
Gruffudd to murder their prince. They did so and sent his
head to Harold. It was weakness from within rather than
strength from without which brought about his tragic end.
Brut y Tywysogion records:

> 'Gruffudd the son of Llywelyn, the head and shield and defender of
> the Brythons, fell through the treachery of his own men. The man who
> had been invincible before was now left in the wilderness, after vast
> plundering, and uncountable victories and innumerable riches of gold,
> silver, gems and purple garments.'

Disorder once again followed the fall of the strong leader,
and in the middle of the confusion the Normans appeared.
Wales however had one more name to add to her gallery of
heroes. With all his weaknesses, Gruffudd had brought power
and confidence and vision to the life of an ancient nation.

> 'He founded no dynasty,' says J. E. Lloyd, 'but he bequeathed to the
> Welsh people the priceless legacy of a revived national spirit; in his
> vigour and daring the nation felt its youth renewed and no longer
> harboured the hidden fear that it had grown old and effete among the
> peoples of the earth.'

England, too, was thrown into disarray with the death of
Edward the Confessor; and three years after organising the
death of Gruffudd, Harold himself was killed. The Danish
conquest was followed by the Norman conquest. Having been

part of the Danish empire, England became within months of the landing of William the Conqueror part of a Norman empire. Having seen the Danish language in the ascendant in its literary life, it now saw French becoming the official language. But Wales, with Ostorius the Roman in his grave for more than a thousand years, remained whole, free and Welsh-speaking.

Facing the Normans

I. THE POWERFUL NORMAN SURGE

THE next two centuries are dominated by the fateful struggle between the powerful Normans, who had so completely demoralised the might of England, and the two hundred thousand people of the little Welsh nation. The story is told in the second volume of J. E. Lloyd's great book. Of all the countries of that period in Europe it was Normandy that created the strongest political order and was the best prepared for war — and it was strengthened by the close alliance of the Church, as Wales saw to its cost. The Normans, descended from those Northmen who had settled in northern France and had adopted the French tongue, had little culture at this time: the noblemen could neither read nor write; there were no lawyers among them and hardly any professional men apart from the priests. They hunted 1066 and organised, they feasted and fought; these were the pursuits dear to the hearts of the men who landed near Hastings on October the 4th, 1066. Although they put up a brave fight against them that day, the English lost, and their national resistance ceased there and then:

'The shock of the battle of Hastings would have rallied the forces of a well-organised feudal kingdom, and stirred the patriotic resistance of a nation,' says Trevelyan. 'It had no such effect on the Anglo-Danish realm. Earls, thegns, bishops, sheriffs, boroughs thought only of making their private peace with the conqueror . . .

There had been no general movement of patriotism, no Wallace or Joan of Arc. England was still a geographical expression, an aggregation of races, regions and private jurisdiction. She still needed to be hammered into a nation, and she now found masters who would do it.'

The south of England yielded at once, led by Winchester. Within a few weeks William the Conqueror was invited by

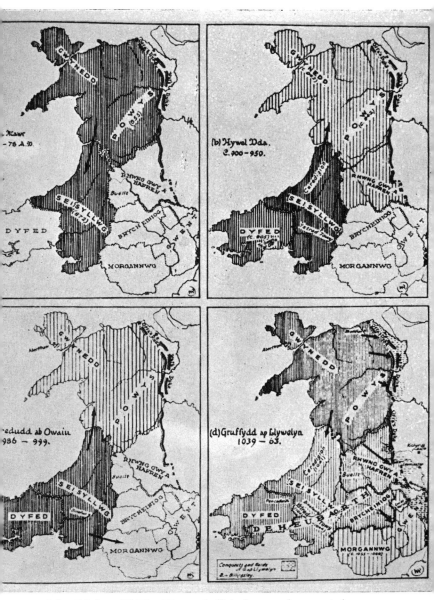

The Wales of "The Heptarchy" (9th to 11th centuries)
from "A Historical Atlas of Wales" with permission of Professor William Rees and Faber & Faber

The Lord Rhys

the city of London to be crowned in Westminster. Everywhere he nailed his military authority on the country. Huge mounds and timber castles were built by English peasants some of whom would shortly be following their Norman masters to Wales. But Wales was not so easily conquered.

What William did was to place three of the most powerful earls, with their armies, in three strategic positions along the Welsh border. First of all he created FitzOsbern, his second cousin, Earl of Hereford, in the border area where Gruffudd ap Llywelyn had shown his strength four years earlier. In 1070 Hugh of Avranches was created Earl of Chester; and in 1071, Roger de Montgomery was created Earl of Shrewsbury. Mercia, Northumbria and Wessex disappeared; the whole of England was divided into shires, each one under the control of the King's officers. There were only three exceptions to this type of control: one in Durham, on account of its proximity to the Scottish border, and the other two in Chester and Shrewsbury, near the Welsh border. He created a Palatine county in Durham, and two Palatine earldoms in Chester and Shrewsbury, to exercise military oversight over the Scots and the Welsh like the system created by the Romans a thousand years earlier with one legion in the north of England and two on the Welsh border.

The little states founded on the borders of Wales were more or less independent, each with its own government and independent court of justice, its chancery and its treasury; and of course each also had its own powerful army which sometimes surpassed the armies of the Welsh princes in strength and number because they were better trained and armed at the outset, and had a strong cavalry unit. If they conquered a Welsh king or prince, as they quickly did in Gwent, Morgannwg and Brycheiniog, they would take away all his rights and powers. The Norman king had small power to interfere in the matters of these states which had been created to solve the Welsh problem. The political order he developed had federal characteristics, with the Norman Lords of the Marches like little kings responsible for almost the whole internal disposition of their small states, and the London government responsible for the foreign policy and the defence of the large state.

Their way of solving the Welsh problem was to mount fierce attacks on the kingdoms of Wales in order to conquer the country by degrees. It was natural for William to think that all serious opposition would disappear in Wales, as it had done in England, if substantial pieces of territory were conquered. He did not know what it was to fight against a nation; he did not dream that people would be ready to sacrifice everything for their country. Because of Wales's indisputable nationhood Llywelyn the Second, in 1267, exactly two hundred years after the settling of FitzOsbern in Hereford, would be making an alliance with the King of England who had recognised him as Prince of Wales.

The Normans started in earnest on the work of solving their little local problem; the Welsh showed tenacity in their opposition, uniting for three years in succession with the chiefs of Mercia when the latter rebelled. When Mercia submitted to William, the Welsh stood completely alone in their opposition.

In the beginning the Normans won many resounding and important victories. Gwent was the first to fall. From his centre in Hereford, FitzOsbern built the castles of Wigmore, Clifford, and Ewyas Harold, first of wood and later of stone, like all the Norman castles. After this he established himself strongly in Monmouth and Newport. This gave him five castles on the border. From these he pressed forward towards the river Usk along the old Roman way and settled in Caerleon. In a few years six centuries of political order came to an end with the disappearance of the old Welsh kingdom.

But Gwent remained Welsh. In the nineteenth century the coal-fields of Gwent were to give Wales her greatest poet in the person of Islwyn. The destructiveness of the capitalism and philistinism of that century did not blunt his vision of the interwoven fabric of the history of Wales, its society and its land:

> "All, all is sacred, and the heavenly muse
> Of poetry has crowned these lofty hills,
> And if my partial strains of patriot love
> May aught avail, I bid them now reveal

Our kindred old, and fathers we revere,
Whose names no more we know, whose fame is silent
Mist curling around the age-old mountain peaks —
How on these heights on many a flaming noon
They sang or sorrowed as they found life's way.
Bitter or sweet."*

If FitzOsbern, the Earl of Hereford, had his successes in Gwent, the movements of Hugh, Earl of Chester, came even earlier and were still more of a threat. 'Huw Dew'— Fat Hugh — as he was called, was to be the most potent figure in the northern border country for thirty years, with his cousin, Robert of Rhuddlan, as his chief lieutenant. Robert was able to take over Rhuddlan and the cantref of Tegeingl, in effect, the greater part of Flint, three years after Hugh had settled in Chester, and add it to the state of Earl Hugh in Cheshire. Thus Flint and Gwent fell into the possession of the Normans very early on. But just as life in Gwent remained Welsh until the second half of the last century, so it was in Flint. Gwent produced the greatest poet of the century, Flintshire the greatest novelist, Daniel Owen, who was born and bred and lived in Mold, within three miles of the English border, where, in the land occupied by the Normans over eight hundred years earlier, he died in 1895. This is an impressive tribute to the resilience of the Welsh civilisation: that the border country had kept the language until such a recent period and that their society still had in it the energy to produce the two greatest literary men of the last century.

The Earl of Chester occupied the Vale of Clwyd, and a great part of the cantref of Rhos and Rhufoniog came into the possession of Robert of Rhuddlan, who built a castle in Dyganwy as a step towards realising his ambition of becoming lord of Gwynedd; thus a large part of Denbighshire 1081 was annexed. In 1081 when Trahaearn, the king of Gwynedd, was killed and when Gruffudd ap Cynan was taken prisoner to Chester by Earl Hugh, the Norman government recognised Robert of Rhuddlan as overlord of all Gwynedd.

* Translated by D. M. Lloyd.

The third earl, Roger of Montgomery, Earl of Shrewsbury, was also successful in his attacks. His two main centres when attacking Wales were the castles of Oswestry and Montgomery Before long the cantrefs of Cydewain and Arwystli, that is, a third of Maldwyn, came into his hands. From Oswestry he captured the cantref of Cynllaith in the north of Maldwyn, Nanheudwy around Wrexham and Llangollen, and Edeirnion in the east of Meirionnydd. This was the position of the Normans when William the Conqueror died in 1087 1087. Although they had taken almost twenty years to attain it, the might of Gwynedd and Powys was rocked by them. To all appearances, it was a matter of a comparatively short time before Wales would be taken over as completely as England.

II. RHYS AP TEWDWR

DURING these twenty years other important political developments were taking place in Wales. Maredudd ab Owain, a descendant of Hywel Dda and Rhodri Mawr, had become king of Deheubarth after the death of Gruffudd ap Llywelyn; he was a man of great energy, as were the two who became kings of Morgannwg and Gwent, Cadwgan ap Meurig and Caradog ap Gruffydd — although they were not strong enough to withstand successfully the Earl of Hereford when he overran a great deal of Gwent. Caradog used Norman soldiers to attack Maredudd, who was killed in a battle on the banks of the Rhymni in 1072. About the same 1072 time Caradog became king of Morgannwg.

Rhys ab Owain, Maredudd's brother, became king of Deheubarth on the death of his brother in the battle of Rhymni, but his rule was very short-lived. When he died in 1075, Rhys ap Tewdwr, another descendant of Hywel Dda, ascended the throne. In 1081 Caradog of Morgannwg made a powerful attempt to unite Deheubarth and Morgannwg; and Rhys ap Tewdwr had to find sanctuary in St. David's. However he enlisted the help of Gruffudd ap Cynan who had been an exile in Ireland after suffering defeat at the hands of Trahaearn, king of Gwynedd. If Caradog had Norman support, Gruffudd ap Cynan brought with him soldiers from Ireland. This force of Welshmen, Irishmen and Danes marched from St. David's with the blessing of the bishop, Sulien. In a battle on Mynydd Carn, near the Preselau on the border of Dyfed, the four most prominent Welsh leaders met — Rhys ap Tewdwr and Gruffudd ap Cynan on the one side; and Trahaearn and Caradog ap Gruffudd on the other. Rhys ap Tewdwr won the day and Trahaearn was killed.

In the year of the battle of Mynydd Carn, which established Rhys on the throne of Deheubarth, and Gruffudd ap
1081 Cynan in Gwynedd, William the Conqueror paid a visit to St. David's and was welcomed there by Sulien. The monks claimed that William had come there to honour the memory of David, but the English chronicle maintains that he came there as a general at the head of an army to free the Normans who had been taken prisoner. Even so, William made an agreement which recognised Rhys ap Tewdwr as king of Deheubarth, but on terms that meant he was a vassal to the throne of England — a precedent which was to have a permanent effect on the relationship between the English and the Welsh.

Rhys was driven out of his country again in 1088 by the young rulers of Powys. Once again he had to flee to
1088 Ireland, and once again a Welsh king brought back with him an army to regain his kingdom. Of all the Celtic countries, it was with Ireland alone that communication remained; but now the Welsh were also on good terms with their old enemies the Danes as well as with the Irish.

By now the Normans in the south-east had succeeded in pressing forward again. They occupied Brycheiniog, the old kingdom which had survived since the fifth century, and which was to produce Howell Harris, one of the greatest Welshmen of the eighteenth century. Since that part of Wales lay in the direction of Rhys ap Tewdwr's territories it was especially important for him to try and stop the advance of the Normans. There in 1093, defending his land against the Normans, he lost his life. J. E. Lloyd says:

'Whether he fell in a fair fight or by treachery is uncertain; all that is

> clear is that his death opened the flood-gates of Norman rapacity in
> South Wales, and that its trickling rills now united in one great deluge
> that swept the country from end to end.'

So died this valiant man who had guarded his kingdom
successfully in dark days: the last to be called King of
Deheubarth.

III. GRUFFUDD AP CYNAN

THE most successful king of Gwynedd during the twenty
years which followed Gruffudd ap Llywelyn was Bleddyn ap
Cynfyn, who was related to the royal family through his
mother, Angharad, the widow of Llywelyn ap Seisyll and the
mother of Gruffudd; Bleddyn was a half-brother to
1067   Gruffudd. He and his brother Rhiwallon attacked
Hereford in 1067, and in the following year succeeded
in meeting the challenge of two of the sons of Gruffudd.
He suffered at the hands of Robert of Rhuddlan
1073   and the Normans in 1073, and met his end
1075   in a battle against Rhys ap Owain and the
nobles of Ystrad Tywi in 1075.
Bleddyn was one of the few kings who reformed the Law of
Hywel, and according to the *Brut* kept in Llanbadarn Fawr,
he proved during his twelve year reign, to be the

> 'most civilised and merciful of the kings, gentle towards his enemy,
> kind and genial, generous to the poor and defenceless, and having
> respect for the rights of the Church.'

He was succeeded on the throne by Trahaearn ap Caradog,
the king of Arwystli, who ruled for six years. With the death
of Bleddyn, Gruffudd ap Cynan, of the ancient lineage of
Gwynedd, returned from Ireland to claim the throne.
1054   Quite a lot is known about this man from the
biography which was written shortly after his death.
He was born in Dublin about 1054, the son of Cynan ap Iago,
who was an exile in Ireland, and Rhagnall, of the royal family
of Dublin Scandinavians. He landed in Abermenai, received
help from Robert of Rhuddlan, attacked Cynwrig of Llŷn
and defeated him. Moving down to Meirionnydd, he met

Talhaearn on the field of Gwaeterw in the Glyngin valley, and defeated him also. He did not feel under any obligation to Robert of Rhuddlan who was endangering the independence of Gwynedd; he attacked him successfully in 1075 but failed to take him prisoner. Unfortunately the Irish members of ap Cynan's retinue were making him unpopular in Llŷn; a number of them were killed by the natives. Trahaearn saw his opportunity, and with help from Powys he overcame ap Cynan, who again fled to Ireland, thereby losing and winning a kingdom in the same year.

He returned in 1081 when he fought beside Rhys ap Tewdwr on Mynydd Carn, where Trahaearn was killed. Shortly after reoccupying his heritage, there came another quick turn in his career: through treachery he was taken prisoner by the Normans near Corwen, and kept in prison in Chester for some years. In 1088 he attacked Robert of Rhuddlan near Llandudno, and killed him. About the same time, with a troop of Scandinavians from the Orkneys, he sailed up the Severn, pitched camp on Barri Island and attacked Gwynllwg (Wentloog). A little later he again enlisted the help of the Danes to defeat the Normans in Anglesey.

Before coming to the next milestone in his career attention must be drawn to the great and sudden success of the Normans in other parts of Wales. When Rhys ap Tewdwr was killed in 1093 the bulwark which stood in the way of their advance was holed. No sooner was he dead than they occupied Brycheiniog and Buallt. Fitzhamon razed the plain of Morgannwg between Taf and Tawe, and rebuilt the Roman castle in Cardiff which is today the college of music and drama.

Roger, the Earl of Shrewsbury, occupied Ceredigion. He built a castle in Aberteifi (Cardigan) before building in Pembroke the only western castle which proved capable of withstanding every Welsh attack. Dyfed was overcome, the fourth of the old Welsh kingdoms to disappear finally into the Norman maw. The royal family of Dyfed had been founded by Eochaid Allmuir, an Irishman of the third century, when the Romans were strong in the land of the blue stones of

Côr y Cewri. The old kingdom had vanished in the age of the Mabinogion and with it a host of memories. In the middle of the twentieth century they are recalled by Waldo Williams, the greatest poet to be reared in Dyfed in the course of her long history:

Un funud fach cyn elo'r haul o'r wybren,
  Un funud fwyn cyn delo'r hwyr i'w hynt,
I gofio am y pethau anghofiedig
  Ar goll yn awr yn llwch yr amser gynt.

Fel ewyn ton a dyr ar draethell unig,
  Fel cân y gwynt lle nid oes glust a glyw,
Mi wn eu bod yn galw'n ofer arnom—
  Hen bethau anghofiedig dynol ryw.

Camp a chelfyddyd y cenhedloedd cynnar,
  Anheddau bychain a neuaddau mawr,
Y chwedlau cain a chwalwyd ers canrifoedd
  Y duwiau na ŵyr neb amdanynt 'nawr.

A geiriau bach hen ieithoedd diflanedig,
  Hoyw yng ngenau dynion oeddynt hwy,
A thlws i'r clust ym mharabl plant bychain,
  Ond tafod neb ni eilw arnynt mwy.

O, genedlaethau dirifedi daear,
  A'u breuddwyd dwyfol a'u dwyfoldeb brau,
A erys ond tawelwch i'r calonnau
  Fu gynt yn llawenychu a thristáu?

One little moment ere the sun leaves the sky,
one moment's sweetness before evening dies,
to bring to mind all the forgotten things,
lost now amid the dust of ancient days.

As the wave's foam breaks on a lonely beach,
as the wind sings there where no ear can be,
I know well that they call upon us in vain—
the old forgotten things of humanity.

Art and achievement of the early nations,
the modest dwelling-places and great halls,
fine legends scattered centuries ago.
and gods that no one any more recalls.

The little words of vanished languages,
which once were lively in the mouths of men,
sweet hearing in the talk of little children,
no tongue will ever call for them again.

O numberless generations of the earth,
their godly dreams, their brittle godliness,
is there now only silence for those hearts
which once were full of grief and happiness?

The work of Waldo, which is a proof of the continuing
strength of our national tradition in Dyfed almost eight
centuries after the Normans arrived there, is ample justification
in itself for the costly effort to maintain it there.

The Norman invasion of Wales had reached its crisis point.
In a little over a quarter of a century their power was established in every part of the country, from Dyganwy to Aberteifi (Cardigan), from Rhuddlan to Penfro (Pembroke), from
Trefaldwyn (Montgomery) to Caerfyrddin (Carmarthen),
from Cas-gwent (Chepstow) to Abertawe (Swansea), from
Conwy to Castell Nedd (Neath). Throughout the land they
built their castles as the Romans had raised their forts; and
just as small towns had grown around the Roman forts, so the
boroughs rose up around the Norman castles. The burgesses
were mostly English with a sprinkling of French and Breton.
Nationally the struggle was against the French lords; locally
it was a struggle against the English petty bourgeoisie. The
Normans and English established their mills and their fisheries,
their workshops and their shops, their mints, and of course
their Church. The Church was a strong weapon in the hands
of the Normans, and very soon it became the procedure to
appoint as bishops Frenchmen or Englishmen, or possibly
Bretons, — there were many Bretons among the invaders who
knew nothing of the old relationship between their country
and Wales.

The Hervè who was consecrated as bishop of Bangor as
early as 1092 was a Breton. Added to this the Normans
1092   often made a gift of a church or a tithe or a manor
to a church or a great monastery in England. In a few
centuries time when the castles had lost their power the towns

and the Church would continue to keep their influence as
bastions of Englishness or Britishness. A seventeenth century
Englishman, writing a travelogue of Wales, glances at the
same dilemma:

> 'Their native gibberish is usually prattled throughout the whole of
> Taphydom except in their market towns, whose inhabitants being a
> little raised do begin to despise it.'

It was not in that century however that some of the towns-
people first began to despise the Welsh language; and certainly
they did not cease, after that century, to consider themselves
'a little raised'.

To all intents and purposes it seemed to be the end of the
Welsh language, which appeared to be destined to be completely stifled by the Normans and English. Had that indeed
happened the Welsh nation would have disappeared in the
middle ages as completely as did Strathclyde. It is impossible
to appeal to economic factors to explain its continuance.
The fact is that the Welsh drew on great moral resources to
make an amazing recovery. Resistance to the invaders continued in all parts of the land for another two centuries, but
the brunt of the struggle fell on the three realms of Gwynedd,
Powys and Deheubarth.

In 1094, in the hour of their lowest degradation, they
refused to yield. They rose in Gwynedd under Gruffudd ap
Cynan and Cadwgan ap Bleddyn. They seized every
1094   Norman castle to the west of Conwy. In Coed Yspwys
they overcame an army sent to fight against them.
Gruffudd occupied the castle of Aber Lleiniog, killing a
hundred and twenty knights. In a short time the Normans
lost the whole of Gwynedd. The men of Powys rose too and
destroyed many villages and districts in Shropshire and
Cheshire, and even took the key castle of Montgomery. Down
south in Ceredigion and Dyfed the Welsh destroyed every
castle except Pembroke and Rhyd-y-gors near Carmarthen.

King Rufus himself had to prepare for a great attack to save
his feudal deputies. He did this in 1095 using the same method

as many English kings have used after him and with as little success. His hosts were forced to retreat after reaching Ardudwy. The Welsh offensive continued throughout 1096, the men of Brycheiniog and Gwent uniting to throw the yoke off their necks. They failed to take castles — that was their weakness — but they defeated an army of Normans near Ystradgynlais. Even Pembroke was in great danger that year, but Gerald of Windsor succeeded in holding on to it. This was the turning point. Pembroke castle constituted a strong basis on which to rebuild Norman strength. In 1097 a powerful and successful counter-attack was launched from there with the help of King Rufus who led another army into Wales in that year; by the end of the year, Ceredigion and Ystrad Tywi alone remained under Welsh rule in the south.

Hugh, the Earl of Chester, continued his attempts to regain his position. In 1098 the army of the Earl of Shrewsbury united with him in an attack on Gwynedd. Gruffudd ap Cynan and Cadwgan withdrew their soldiers to Anglesey and again they got the help of the Danish navy when defending the island. But the Earl of Chester succeeded in bribing the Danish navy; the Danes turned against Gruffudd and he had to flee again to Ireland. Thereupon, one of the most dramatic and timely events in our history occurred. The great navy of Magnus, the king of Norway, appeared off the shores of Anglesey; he had just restored Norwegian sovereignty in the Scottish islands and the Isle of Man. Magnus attacked and scattered the Normans, and they never again tried to colonise Anglesey.

1098

Gruffudd ap Cynan and Cadwgan returned, the one to rule Gwynedd-uwch-Conwy and the other Ceredigion and a part of Powys, where the position of the Welsh was now much easier after the total collapse of the Earl of Shrewsbury's rebellion against the king. After that the earl was exiled for life and no one took his place; the king ruled the state of Shrewsbury direct, and he also assumed control of other parts of Wales, such as Dyfed, which had been in the possession of the earl's family. Unfortunately, Cadwgan's family was torn apart by quarrels which weakened Powys, so that he was

unable to take advantage of his favourable position after the
Earl of Shrewsbury had been sent into exile.

Cadwgan was drawn into a great deal of trouble by the
action of his son Owain who fell in love with Nest, the
beautiful wife of Gerald of Windsor, the castellan of Pembroke
and the chief Norman leader in Dyfed. Nest, the daughter
of Rhys ap Tewdwr, was given in marriage to Gerald after
the death of her father. She had five children by Gerald and a
number by three other Normans including Henry I. Her
daughter Angharad, who married the Lord of Manorbier
(Maenor Bŷr), was the mother of Giraldus Cambrensis. One
son became Bishop of St. David's for twenty-eight years.
Her son by Henry was killed in an Anglesey battle against the
Welsh. Three others, Fitz Stephens and two Fitz Geralds were
the leaders of the first conquest of Ireland from this side of the
Irish Sea. The Fitz Geralds played a prominent part in
Ireland's life, and their descendants became more Irish than
the Irish. But it was with a Welshman that Nest chose to
elope, and that man was Owain ap Cadwgan. This act, which
was a challenge to the king as well as to Gerald, led to a great
Norman attack on Ceredigion, and Owain had to flee to
Ireland. He paid with his life for his rashness within a few
years, but not before his attacks on Dyfed had forced
1110   the king to occupy Ceredigion himself in 1110. As a
result this old kingdom, which is today one of the
most Welsh parts of Wales, was shared out among the Norman
lords as completely as any part of the land.

*   *   *

By now the power of the Normans had extended over the
whole of the south: Ceredigion, Dyfed, Ystrad Tywi, Morgannwg, Brycheiniog and Gwent. Their rule was confined
however to the most fertile territory, where English and
French worked on the land around the castles as well as in the
towns. There the 'Englishry' settled. The 'Welshry' were up
in the hills, where they maintained their traditional Welsh
way of life. There were differences of language and law, values
and political order, between these two factions. The distinctions
remain, to some extent, to our own day, even in political life.

It is at this time that King Henry moved a colony of Flemings to Dyfed to settle around Haverfordwest. Centuries before this, a tribe of Irishmen had settled there, and thousands more Irishmen came after them; through the centuries they mixed with the native Welsh who had continued in the majority, although an unusually large number of them belonged to the serf class. It is these people, men from the Netherlands and from Ireland who have mixed with the Welsh and Norman-French, as well as the few English burghers of Pembroke, who are the ancestors of the 'English' of Pembrokeshire's 'little England beyond Wales'. When the language of the establishment became English, the language of the whole society in the south of Pembrokeshire became English, so that for centuries the region played little part in the national life. This too is the time when a number of Swansea citizens moved out to settle in Gower. At the same time the town of Carmarthen became the administrative centre for the crown, and its castle a royal castle: for centuries it was to be an island of Englishness in the middle of a Welsh sea.

The only one who succeeded in challenging the Norman hold on Deheubarth in any degree was Gruffydd ap Rhys ap Tewdwr. He ventured to return from Ireland in 1118, where he had been taken as a child after his father was killed, to win back his heritage. He tried to get the help of Gruffudd ap Cynan, his father-in-law, but failed: on the contrary Gruffudd ap Cynan almost succeeded in delivering him into the hands of the king. In 1116 Gruffydd ap Rhys had destroyed the castle of Narberth and partly damaged the castles of Swansea and Llandovery. Even then the town of Carmarthen could be easily frightened by near-by Welsh success, and Gruffydd gave its burgesses more reason to be frightened by attacking it. J. E. Lloyd says:

> 'He had done enough to arouse the enthusiasm of his countrymen; crowds of young Welshmen gathered around him, and the authorities began to fear for the safety of Carmarthen. The plan was adopted of entrusting its defence to the neighbouring chiefs.'

He burned the town and then attacked Ceredigion. He was successful in Blaen Porth and Castell Peithyll, but failed to take Aberystwyth castle. The king tried in vain to defeat Gruffydd by ranging other Welsh princes against him, but he did succeed in forcing him to flee to the convenient refuge of Ireland. He made an agreement with the king whereby he secured a piece of the province of Caeo in Cantref Mawr. And there, in Cynwyl Caeo, he and his wife Gwenllian went to live, nearly six hundred and fifty years after the death of Paulinus, 'Protector of the Faith and consistent lover of this country'. It was there that a son, Rhys, was born to Gwenllian and Gruffydd, and known later as the Lord Rhys. At this time the continued rule of the Normans over the whole of the rest of the kingdom of their fathers seemed inevitable. But the last had not been heard of either Gruffydd or Gwenllian, and certainly not of their baby Rhys.

*   *   *

The fate of Gwynedd, with Eryri as a natural fortress, was happier than that of Deheubarth. Its power stretched south to include Meirionnydd, and east to the banks of the Clwyd, until all the land to the north of the Dyfi estuary was under Welsh rule, except for Tegeingl, that is, the greater part of Flintshire. Owain and Cadwaladr, the sons of Gruffydd ap Cynan, helped their father in this recovery. The power of Gwynedd grew to such proportions that King Henry had to lead in 1114 one of the most powerful invasions ever made into Wales. Three armies attacked from three different directions. From the south came the Normans of Deheubarth with some men from Devon and Cornwall; the king himself crossed the Berwyns with his army to meet the southern army near Trawsfynydd; the third army came from Chester, led by Alexander I of Scotland. But little fighting ensued: Gruffudd ap Cynan succeeded in making an agreement which deprived him of almost none of his power. No doubt it was this which influenced his attitude towards Gruffydd ap Rhys when the latter asked for

1114

1121

his support. The next time we hear of Henry invading Wales
is in 1121 when he set upon Maredudd ap Bleddyn
1132   of Powys, who had been attacking Chester. Maredudd
died in 1132, lord of all Powys.

When Gruffudd ap Cynan died in feeble old age in
1137 he passed down to his son Owain, after-
1137   wards called Owain Gwynedd, a large, strong
and prosperous kingdom. By dint of his heroic
character and his vigorous daring he had succeeded, under
overwhelming difficulties, in upholding, strengthening and
transmitting to the next generation the great heritage which
he loved. Our language and our poetry, as an essential part
of that heritage, were greatly respected by the king. Gruffudd
ap Cynan supported the poets generously; Meilyr's elegy to
him is the earliest example of court poetry in the middle ages.
The poet reminds us of the prince's generosity:

> Cyn myned mab Cynan i dau dywawd
> Ceffid yn ei gyntedd medd a tragawd.
>
> Before Cynan's son went beneath the gravel
> you got mead and ale at his hall table.

It is significant that the Welsh poets attributed to him the
attempt to systematize and classify *cerdd dafod*. It is good to
think that this fine man, who refused to abandon the fight
for his country when the situation looked hopeless, took such
delight in the literature and music of his nation.

IV. THE RE-EMERGENCE OF NATIONAL POWER

THE next twenty years saw a dramatic change in the Welsh
position. In every corner of the land the Normans were
driven back by the Welsh with determination and confidence
and wonderful vigour. A new energy flowed through every
part of the country; life was again surging through the whole
nation. What released this energy was the death of Henry I
in 1135. Just as the death of Rhys ap Tewdwr had left a gap

in the Welsh rampart letting the Normans through into
Deheubarth, so the death of Henry I opened the way for the
Welsh to recover much of the land they had lost. Wales
had often experienced the sort of weakness which now
overcame the English on the death of their powerful French
king, when the country was divided between Stephen and
Mathilda. In the hour of England's weakness the princes of
Wales rose powerfully.

> 'The great revolution in Welsh affairs which now took place,' says
> J. E. Lloyd, 'was long remembered by the foreign settlers as a turning-
> point in the history of their adopted country. The day of Henry's death
> was for them as fateful as was for another aristocracy in a later age the
> day of the capture of the Bastille.'

Henry died on the first day of December, 1135. Within
a month, on New Year's Day, 1136 Hywel ap Meredudd of
Brycheiniog marched to Gower where Englishmen
1136   as well as Normans had settled. In the battle that
was fought somewhere between Llwchwr and Swansea
over five hundred of the enemy were killed. This lead from
Brycheiniog was followed by the Welsh in every corner of
the country. In Caeo, Gruffydd ap Rhys saw his opportunity;
he hurried to Gwynedd to seek the support of Gruffudd ap
Cynan's sons in throwing the Norman out of Deheubarth.
While he was in Gwynedd his wife, Gwenllian, led an army
against Cydweli (Kidwelly) and its castle. Her heroism
achieved a bitter reward. Her army was defeated by Maurice
de Londres; her son Morgan was killed and another son,
Maelgwn, taken prisoner; and Gwenllian herself was killed.
On the field outside Cydweli still known as Maes Gwenllian
there died a heroine who was the daughter of Gruffudd ap
Cynan, mother of the Lord Rhys, and sister of Owain
Gwynedd.
This proved to be the only real success the Normans had
for eight years, and it was only a defensive, temporary success.
In April of that year Richard Fitz Gilbert, lord of Ceredigion,
was attacked and killed by the men of Gwent under the
leadership of Iorwerth ab Owen, the grandson of Caradog ap

Page from The Chronicle of the Princes — Brut y Tywysogion
(Peniarth Ms. 20)

Carreg Cennen Castle

Coin minted by
Hywel Dda

Owain Glyndŵr's
Great Seal

Gruffydd, when he was marching through the vale of Usk in Coed Grwyne above Crucywel (Crickhowell). As soon as this news reached Gwynedd, Owain and Cadwaladr got ready for an attack on Ceredigion from Meirionnydd where they had already settled on the banks of the Dyfi estuary. In their army there was a big company of cavalry, which shows that they were beginning to adopt Norman methods. They captured and burnt down castles in Llanfihangel and Aberystwyth near the *clas* of Llanbadarn where their praises were highly sung by the keeper of the *Brut*. Marching southwards they burnt three other castles, including Caerwedros.

Early in the spring Owain and Cadwaladr marched again on Ceredigion, this time in the company of Gruffudd ap Rhys and the chieftains of mid-Wales. Outside Aberteifi (Cardigan) they met a Norman army which had been gathered from every part of the south. The battle ended with a notable win for the Welsh, who pushed the Normans headlong into the town of Aberteifi and over the bridge in the direction of Llandudoch. The bridge collapsed under the weight of the fugitives and hundreds of them were drowned in the Teifi. The only building left whole in the town was the castle, where Fitzherbert's widow, the sister of the Earl of Chester, was living. The castle remained standing as Pembroke castle had done forty years earlier, an obstacle to overwhelming Welsh success. King Stephen arranged an attack on Aberteifi to save the situation there, but failed to advance beyond Aberhonddu (Brecon).

The following year Gruffudd ap Rhys successfully attacked Dyfed, but soon afterwards he died in the prime of his life, while his sons were still very young. This brave son 1137 of Rhys ap Tewdwr, who was also stricken down at the peak of his strength, is remembered as one who did not despair in dark times, who refused to yield when the tide was flowing most strongly against him and who kept alive the flame of freedom.

For the third time that year Owain and Cadwaladr, the sons of Gruffudd ap Cynan, marched on Ceredigion, destroying the castles of Ystrad Meurig, Llanbedr-pont-Steffan

(Lampeter) and Castell Hywel. Then after crossing the Teifi they destroyed Llansteffan castle on the estuary of the Tywi, and also Gwŷs in Pembrokeshire. And by taking Carmarthen castle they secured the key to the Tywi valley. Carmarthen had been for a generation the chief town and fort of the Normans in the south west of Wales, and its seizure was the climax of the success of the Welsh national attack. If the London dailies had been in existence at that time no doubt they would have headlined the news on the front page in bold letters, 'Welsh capture Carmarthen' as they did on July 15, 1966.

Except for a short period in the middle of the century, the Welsh kept their hold on Ceredigion for almost a century and a half. After its reconquest it was divided between two princes of Gwynedd: Cadwaladr, who was to prove a great disappointment to the Welsh cause later on, getting the area between Aeron and Dyfi, and Hywel receiving the lower part. Hywel was a man of remarkable talents, a soldier and engineer, a poet and writer, and wholly loyal to the cause.

Cantref Bychan also came into the hands of the Welsh; the Clifford family lost their authority in the Llandovery area; Maeliennydd too was taken. In a battle in Powys 1137 in 1137 the sheriff of the counties of Salop and Hereford was killed. Two days after the Feast of St. David, 1140, Bromfield castle was burnt down by the men of Powys, and Cawres castle, further south, also fell at their hands. Further down, in the lower regions of the Vale of Usk, Morgan ab Owain occupied Bryn Buga (Usk) castle, and established himself there as Lord of Caerleon. And so, the Welsh spirit proved strong enough to carry the day in a great part of Wales; and although the Normans' hold on Gwent was very firm, it failed either to destroy its Welshness or tame its patriotic spirit.

The nation was saved morally and the political situation transformed by the invigorating national resurgence of these years, and although the Normans won Carmarthen back in 1145, not all the power of England could kill its spirit any longer.

V. OWAIN GWYNEDD

It may be argued that Owain is the greatest of the four great
men who stand supreme in the history of our nation for the
next hundred and forty years. If there is reason for arguing
otherwise — and there is — and giving pride of place to the
Lord Rhys or Llywelyn Fawr or Llywelyn II, this only shows
how surprisingly fortunate Wales was in its leaders during
the twelfth and thirteenth centuries. When Owain succeeded
his father, Gruffudd ap Cynan, as king of Gwynedd
1137   in 1137, he had already demonstrated over the years
his efficiency, energy, courage and wisdom. He
continued to reveal the same virtues for thirty-three more
years. If this was a period of balanced development in all
areas of Welsh life, the thanks must go to him. J. E. Lloyd
says:

> 'it was in fact, under him that the Welsh nation attained the full
> measure of national consciousness which enabled it for a century and a
> half successfully to resist absorption in the English realm.'

Notice that it is about Wales's awareness of its nationhood
rather than the fact of nationality that J. E. Lloyd writes;
Wales was a national community seven centuries before this.

As a son of Gruffudd ap Cynan he would have been called
Owain ap Gruffudd were it not for the existence of another
prince of that name in Powys, Owain Cyfeiliog, who
married Gwenllian, one of the daughters of Owain Gwynedd.
Owain Cyfeiliog too was a brilliantly talented soldier,
statesman and poet. It was he who founded the Cistercian
monastery of Ystrad Marchell, to which he retired at the end
of his life and where he died in 1197. Giraldus Cambrensis
pays high tribute to his sense of justice, wisdom and moderation; he also mentions his eloquence and his good sense. His
poem, *Hirlas Owain*, composed in the mode of the *Gododdin*
is, according to Myrddin Lloyd

> 'the best picture we have of the life of a Welsh prince, the close
> relationship between him and his retinue, and all the zest of their
> adventurous life.'

His retinue, or 'family', was the chief tool of every prince's authority. The retinue was a small personal army of a hundred or more horsemen, pledged to defend their prince, always at his side and dependent on his generosity. The Welsh word for prince is *tywysog*; the literal meaning of the word is one who leads.

The brilliance of Owain Gwynedd's character is best seen when he is compared with his brother Cadwaladr, who inherited a large part of Ceredigion as a kingdom; the one constant, the other fickle; the one consistently building a strong and independent Welsh cause, and the other going over to the Norman enemy and scheming with them against his brother.

After the attack on Aberteifi in 1138, Cadwaladr is next heard of in Lincoln supporting one of the English parties in the Civil War in England. This was in 1141; about two years later he is back in Wales again, attacking and killing Anarawd, the eldest son of Gruffydd ap Rhys of Deheubarth. Anarawd was a young man who had an alliance with him and who was related to him by marriage. For this crime Cadwaladr was ejected from Ceredigion by Owain Gwynedd. He quarrelled with his brother again in 1152, fled to England, and when Henry II made his great attack on Wales in 1157 Cadwaladr was in the king's army. In 1159 he is found siding with the Norman earls in their big attack against the Lord Rhys. An example of Owain's magnanimity is that he accepted Cadwaladr back later and co-operated with him during their later years in the interests of the national cause.

After his successes in Ceredigion, Owain turned his attention to the north-east. There in 1146 Maelor Seisnig (English Maelor) was plundered by the men of Powys under the effective leadership of Madog ap Maredudd. Further north in Tegeingl the men of Gwynedd occupied Mold castle. In 1149 they took over Iâl (Yale) and Owain built a castle in Buddugre to guard the gap from the vale of Clwyd. This brought Owain perilously close to Madog ap Maredudd who had been reigning over Powys since 1132 and did not want to see Gwynedd reducing his power. While Owain was in the process of mastering Iâl, Madog took Oswestry and used the castle there as a fort. For years the Welsh for the first time since the early seventh century were to rule this neighbourhood again; the situation is reflected in *Breuddwyd Rhonabwy*. Madog was the patron of Cynddelw Brydydd Mawr, the greatest of the court poets of the country. Up until then William FitzAlan had been the Norman lord of Oswestry. He was the son of a Breton favoured by Henry I and brother of Walter FitzAlan, the founder of the royal family of the Stewarts in Scotland who succeeded the Tudors to the English throne — a family of Breton and Scottish origins following a family of Welsh lineage.

A new situation was created in England in 1154 when Henry II ascended the throne. An arrogant man, but powerful and able, this Norman imperialist checked the glorious surge of the Welsh. He was the worst enemy that the Celtic nations had encountered up to that time, not only in Wales but in Scotland, Ireland and Britanny too. As previous Norman kings had done he gathered together in 1157 a great army in order to attack Gwynedd, with the help of a navy which sailed from Dyfed. Owain placed his own men near Dinas Basing, across the only road to Rhuddlan that evaded the wide estuary, and he put his sons and their soldiers in the forest which stretched for fifteen miles along the ridge of Tegeingl from Eulo to Prestatyn. Henry's main army travelled along the sea road, but he himself went with his retinue through the forest intending to spring a sudden attack on Owain. He only just succeeded in escaping with his life from the Welsh onslaught. Many prominent leaders were killed and the others were scattered in confusion, although the king himself succeeded in rejoining his main army by the sea. This army pushed the Welsh back to St. Asaph. In the meantime the navy had sailed as far as Anglesey, where it came under heavy attack from the Welsh, who killed, amongst others, the son of Henry I by Nest of Pembroke.

From the military point of view Owain had the edge in this encounter but realising how powerful the Normans were under the new order, he had to make an agreement with

Henry that cost him dear. He had to yield Tegeingl; give hostages to the king; re-instate his brother Cadwaladr in his old position; and give up the title of king. This title, since the eleventh century had been confined to three courts: Aberffraw in Gwynedd, Mathrafal in Powys and Dinefwr in Deheubarth. It is not found at all after the mid-twelfth century in the Welsh Laws. Only in London will we find kings after this. In Deheubarth, Rhys was known as 'Lord', but despite this lesser title he had all the powers of past kings. From now on all the old royalty were Lords except for the Gwynedd family who used the title of Prince from the days of Owain Gwynedd on. This gave precedence to Gwynedd, which was recognised more or less as the chief royal family in the whole of Wales.

It was a matter of political policy rather than family pride. The princes of Gwynedd would pay homage to the king of England, while Gwynedd itself inclined more and more to receive the homage of all the lords of Wales. This led to the sort of situation which was starting to develop in the days of Hywel Dda before the conquest of England by the Danes. This is what Jones-Pierce says:

'Without doubt the main intention of the policy of Gwynedd from the days of Owain until the dashing of Llywelyn II's hopes was to secure for Wales, except for the Norman lordships of the south and the borders, a position as an equal member in a federation of feudal states recognising the overlordship of the English crown. Llywelyn Fawr claimed that his freedom and privilege in relation to the king of England was equal to those of the king of Scotland. Later Llywelyn II said in a letter to Edward, King of England, something like this:

"Each province represented in the empire of the king has its own rules and laws according to its usages and local traditions, such as the Gascons have in Gascony, the Scots in Scotland, the Irish in Ireland, and the English in England. I therefore hold that I too, and I a prince, have right to my Welsh law, and a right to act according to that law. According to every just principle we should enjoy our law and customs as other nations of the King's empire, and in our own language".'

The political autonomy envisaged by the princes is remarkably like that of the Welsh nationalists today. They do not demand complete independence, but ask for Commonwealth status;

they recognise the crown; and they do not want a military border, nor tolls between Wales and England. The consequence of operating this policy would be to create a close partnership of free and equal nations.

*   *   *

While Owain was holding out against the power of Henry II in Gwynedd, the sons of Gruffydd ap Rhys were busy in Deheubarth. When the Earl Gilbert came in 1145 to take possession of Carmarthen castle and rebuild it, and to build a castle near Pencader in order to restore the situation in Ceredigion, the sons of Gruffydd ap Rhys attacked Pencader and destroyed the castle. With the help of Hywel ap Owain of Ceredigion they captured Carmarthen and then Llansteffan which the Normans and the Flemings of Pembroke tried in vain to recover. The whole of the east of Dyfed was in the hands of the Welsh with Carmarthen as a centre. In 1151 however, Cadell, the eldest of Gruffydd's three sons, was incapacitated by a severe injury which he received while on a pilgrimage to Rome. Only Maredudd and Rhys remained now, but they did not falter. They captured Cydweli, and conquered the Gower; Tenby fell into their hands; they attacked Aberafan, seventy miles to the east, destroying its castle. They turned their attention too to their old heritage in Ceredigion. Hywel was driven out of the lower part in 1150 and 1151, and in a short time the whole of Ceredigion was occupied by them. Owain Gwynedd wondered whether to attack there in 1156, but the castle that Rhys built by Glandyfi helped to dissuade him. Maredudd died in 1155, a young man of only twenty-five, leaving Rhys, the youngest brother, Lord of all Deheubarth.

1145

1153

Rhys kept his lordship unimpaired for only three years. In 1158 he bent under the heavy pressure of Henry II and had to yield the whole lot to him, apart from Cantref Mawr and some other scattered lands. Ceredigion and Dyfed, Cantref Bach and Carmarthen, Cydweli and Gower were recovered by the king. Undaunted, Rhys again challenged the royal order in arms, but when Henry

1158

and his army came to the west he was forced to yield a second time. Like Owain Gwynedd he had to acknowledge that the strength of England was now far greater than his own, and that he would have to choose either to be satisfied with a little, or to be destroyed completely.

The Welsh lords accepted the situation unwillingly, of course, and a flash of their spirit is seen to gleam out every now and again. For example, in 1158, the year of Henry's march to the west of Wales, the powerful castle of Cardiff was attacked by Ifor Bach, lord of Senghennydd in the Caerffili area. His wife Nest was a grand-daughter of Rhys ap Tewdwr and a sister of the Lord Rhys. In this daring attack Earl William and his wife and eldest son were taken prisoner, giving the Norman party a scare which they were not to forget. In spite of the strength of the Normans in the Vale of Glamorgan they had not succeeded in subduing the spirit of the Welsh.

Rhys ap Gruffydd too could not be subdued for long. In the following year he is found attacking Carmarthen 1159 and the castles of Dyfed, and when an army came against him from England, under Earl Reginald of Cornwall, he retreated to the inaccessible valleys of Cantref Mawr. The attempts to supplant him were a complete failure although five great earls joined by Cadwaladr marched 1162 against him. Rhys kept his position. In 1162 he attacked Llandovery castle and it fell to him. Once again Henry was forced to lead an army through the south. Because his strength was so great he was allowed to march unopposed to the borders of Ceredigion, where Rhys placed himself in his hands. He later paid allegiance to him in Woodstock in the company of Owain Gwynedd and Malcolm of Scotland and then returned to Dinefwr (Dynevor). 1162 No sooner was he home than he attacked Ceredigion again, and with so much success that only Cardigan 1163 castle remained in the hands of the Normans. All Ceredigion was now his; and 'after that,' says the *Brut*, 'all the Welsh united to resist the French'.

* * *

Owain Gwynedd now decided to join Rhys. He timed his intervention cleverly. It was Henry's quarrel with Thomas à Becket that persuaded him that it was time to challenge the king. His son attacked Tegeingl. An alliance of the princes of free Wales was formed: Gwynedd, Powys and Deheubarth. The king accepted the challenge. He gathered an army such as had never before been seen on the borders of Wales: they came from Normandy and Scotland, from Aquitaine and Anjou, from Flanders and Poitou. They came from every region of England; the city of London gave a substantial contribution towards the cost; the Danish navy was hired from Ireland. The Norman Empire, which stretched 1165 from the borders of Scotland down to Spain, now decided to get rid of the Welsh problem once and for all. And by the end of July 1165 it was ready to strike.

Men from all parts of free Wales gathered together to face these armies. They came from Gwynedd and Deheubarth, from Powys and from the land between the Wye and the Severn, and the fickle Cadwaladr joined them too. They joined forces in Ceredigion. Rhys ap Gruffydd had come there from his battles in the province; Owain Cyfeiliog was there beside his fellow poet and prince, Hywel ap Owain Gwynedd; the sons of Madog ap Maredudd of Powys were there, and Cadwallon and Einion Clud from the Wye and the Severn. And there to lead them was Owain Gwynedd. In her hour of crisis Wales was united.

The armies of England travelled from Oswestry through the Ceiriog valley where they were resisted by chosen Welshmen — 'and many of the strongest fell on both sides' — up over the slopes of the Berwyns, and along the road which is still called 'Ffordd y Saeson' (the Englishmen's Road). And there the rain fell; it poured down incessantly; and the wind coursed like a wild thing. The floor of every camp was turned into a lake and every path flowed like a river. The soldiers were soaked to the skin by the rain, and their tents ripped by the wind. The water increased and the food decreased. Wales has often suffered from the rain; this time it profited from it. As moving forward became more and more difficult, the

Welsh awaited their opportunity to pounce. In the end the imperial forces concluded that retreat was best, and that is what they did. Full of anger Henry II avenged himself on his hostages, blinding and injuring twenty-two of them, including two of Owain Gwynedd's own sons, and Cynfrig and Maredudd, the sons of Rhys ap Gruffydd. In their fury, the king's soldiers even burnt churches.

Once again, after this tremendous victory, we see the quality of Owain Gwynedd, and particularly his capacity for restraint. Giraldus Cambrensis tells the story in his *Journey Through Wales:*

> 'The previous day the heads of the English army had burnt a number of Welsh churches, as well as villages and churchyards. So, with a host of young, lightly-armed soldiers, the sons of Owain Fawr spoke severely with their father and the other princes about this act, saying that they could never again show the same respect for English churches. And when nearly everyone was in agreement with this Owain alone, as was suitable for a man of great retraint and wisdom, amongst his people, having quietened the crowd, broke across them in the end with these words:
>
> 'I do not agree with this opinion: rather we should be grateful and joyful because of this. For we are very unequal against the English, unless we are upheld by divine aid; but they, through what they have done, have made an enemy of God himself, who can avenge this injury to himself and to us at the same time. And so let us all piously make a vow to the Lord and show from now on more respect and honour than before for churches and holy places.'

After this, Rhys ap Gruffydd succeeded in taking the key castles of Cilgerran and Cardigan. He got rid completely of the great families of Clare and Clifford who had been occupying Ceredigion and half of the Tywi valley; he restored the state of affairs that had prevailed before Henry attacked in 1162; once again he was lord of Ceredigion, Ystrad Tywi and a great deal of Dyfed.

In Tegeingl, also, Owain Fawr moved forward, destroying Dinas Basing, and, with Rhys's help, he captured Rhuddlan too after laying siege to it for three months. Gwynedd now extended from Dyfi (Dovey) to Dyfrdwy (Dee). There was political activity too. Owain carried on the fight for independence through the Church, and in defiance of the power of Thomas à Becket, insisted on the right to elect bishops. In 1162 he appointed Arthur of Enlli Bishop of Bangor. (Arthur was consecrated in Ireland — an interesting example of a continuing relationship). In this way he made it clear that he did not consider himself a vassal of the king of England. One of his last acts of importance was to send an ambassador to the court of Louis VII in 1168 offering

1168   him aid in his fight against Henry II. When he died in 1170, after sixty years of public service on an

1170   heroic scale, his country could thank him before everyone else for the degree of political and social success which it enjoyed.

Owain had a great capacity for love. He deeply loved his wife Cristin; he suffered excommunication rather than put her aside at the request of the Church. He loved his children; he almost broke his heart when his son Rhun died. He loved his country, and some of this love is also evident in the work of his son Hywel who wrote in a fine panegyric:

> Caraf ei morfa a'i mynyddoedd,
> A'i chaer ger ei choed a'i chain diredd
> A'i dolydd a'i dwfr a'i dyffrynnedd
> A'i gwylain gwynion a'i gwymp wragedd,
> Caraf ei milwyr a'i meirch hywedd
> A'i choed a'i chedyrn a'i chyfannedd.

> I love its coastland and its mountains,
> its castle near the woods and its fine lands,
> its water meadows and its valleys,
> its white gulls and its lovely women;
> I love its warriors, its trained stallions,
> its woods, its brave men and its homes.

VI. THE LORD RHYS

THE life of the Lord Rhys exemplifies what the bards knew so well, that the quality and continuation of our society depend on the one at the head, on the leader. He is a striking example of the essential importance of the personal element in the history of our nation. Rhys was born when the Normans were at the height of their success, in Caeo in the Cantref Mawr where his father, the son of Rhys ap Tewdwr, and his mother, the daughter of Gruffydd ap Cynan, were living on a small piece of the commote's land: all that then remained of the old great heritage of Deheubarth. The Normans were in control everywhere. And this, to all appearances, was how it would remain. But Rhys's father refused to accept that this was the end, and so did his mother, who was killed in battle on Maes Gwenllian when Rhys was only a boy of five. As a youth, Rhys too refused to accept the situation. In Rhys, his father, and his grandfather we have three leaders of heroic stature. If one of them had accepted the status quo as inevitable, if any one of them had argued that it was impossible even to hope to withstand the huge Norman powers and overcome them, then probably Wales would not exist today. Their heroic efforts showed the inexhaustible power of man's spirit, and that few things are impossible to achieve in a country if moral power of patriotism is sufficiently strong. Lacking the geographical advantages of Gwynedd, with little but the heroic spirit of their people behind them, these men succeeded in creating a Welsh order that supported and enriched the national tradition.

In 1170, the year of Owain Gwynedd's death, Rhys was a middle-aged man, an experienced and tried leader, who had succeeded through his ability, his courage, and his perseverance in reoccupying the land of his fathers between Dyfi and Tawe. He had been fighting on the battlefield since the age of thirteen. Four times the king of England had personally led an army into Wales against him. Eventually, after decades of harsh struggle, he succeeded in establishing political accord between Welshman and Norman throughout the southern lands. This situation in Deheubarth contrasted with the unhappy discord in Gwynedd which followed the death of Owain. Rhys continued to rule for another twenty-seven years. Throughout this time he stood head and shoulders above everyone else in Wales. 'Bri Brython, bugail Cymru' ('the glory of the Brython, the shepherd of Wales') was Cynddelw's tribute to him; and according to A. L. Poole he was 'the man who by his unceasing efforts and fine sense of patriotism kept alive the tradition of Welsh independence and nationality.' In assessing his accomplishment it must be remembered that the efficiency of England's centralised government was for generations unparalleled in Europe, at least outside the Norman Sicily of Frederick II, who has been called 'the greatest single human force in the middle ages'.

He took full advantage of every opportunity which arose from a shift in circumstances. The murder of Becket was one cause of change; another was the conquest of Ireland, which was started by a few of the men of Pembroke. The fact that such a small company of men as these went so far towards conquering Ireland shows the extent of the power the Welsh had been facing. Ironically, it was the victories of Rhys which freed the first small armies to go across. An Irish family had been ruling Dyfed in the fourth century; now the grandsons of Rhys ap Tewdwr of Dyfed went to rule in Ireland. The chief leaders, before the Earl of Pembroke went there, were three of Nest's sons. Rhys had taken Robert FitzStephen prisoner three years earlier. Nest was his mother and his father was the constable of the castle of Cardigan which Robert had defended against Hywel ab Owain Gwynedd in 1145. Rhys showed his political acumen by freeing him, after three years of imprisonment, for the Irish adventure. We thus see one grandson of Rhys ap Tewdwr, a man who had saved Wales, freeing another grandson to venture on the conquest of Ireland.

Robert crossed to Ireland in May 1160 with his nephews and some Welsh soldiers, and he soon captured
1169   Wexford. It is worth recording in passing that the monastery of Strata Florida was founded on land given by this same Robert FitzStephen to the monks. The remains of Dafydd ap Gwilym lie in the land given to the Church by the first of the Norman conquerors of Ireland, and he a grandson of Rhys ap Tewdwr and an ex-prisoner of his second cousin, the Lord Rhys. Another of Nest's sons,

Maurice FitzGerald, was the next to cross to Ireland, and before long they were joined there by Raymond FitzGerald, yet another of Nest's sons. Maurice had been lord of Llansteffan and Raymond lord of Emlyn until they were defeated by Rhys. In 1146 the two had played a prominent part in the unsuccessful attempt to recapture Llansteffan castle from the Welsh. In Ireland Maurice was established in Kildare.

In August 1170, Richard de Clare, the Earl of Pembroke (Strongbow), himself went over; then in 1172 Henry went too. It is ironic in view of subsequent history to learn that he had received the grant of Ireland from Pope Adrian IV. They very quickly captured the main towns where the Danes had settled, and before long most of Ireland was under their rule; later on many of them identified themselves with Ireland and its national aspirations. Trevelyan explains how such a complete and rapid success was realized:

> 'His (Strongbow's) partners in this last of the Norman conquests were not pure Normans, nor pure Anglo-Normans. Many of them. like the famous FitzGeralds, were sons of Welsh mothers. They were a special border breed, these 'Marcher lords'; and their soldiers were many of them Welsh or Flemings. Perhaps the Celtic element in the blood and experience of these first 'English' conquerors of Ireland helped their descendants to mingle only too easily with the native Irish and adapt their own feudal institutions to the tribalism of the Celtic world beyond the Dublin 'pale' . . .'
>
> 'But no Norman intruders in England, Sicily or Scotland ever showed themselves superior in warlike efficiency to the followers of Strongbow. His chain-clad knights were supported by archers, whose skill was then the speciality not of England but of Wales. The unarmoured infantry of the Irish tribes . . . were helpless against the best archers and some of the best cavalry in Europe . . .
>
> 'The Danes were massacred or returned to Scandinavia, making way for the conquerors . . .'

Having got rid of these uncomfortable relatives and neighbours from Dyfed, Rhys ap Gruffydd's position was a little easier. Henry II too was readier to recognise his suzerainty after such powerful lords had settled across the sea in Ireland. A favourable agreement was reached when Rhys and the king met in Pembroke in the autumn of 1171. In the following year the two met again, this time in Talacharn (Laugharne). In this meeting the very important covenant was made which recognised Rhys's general responsibility for the whole of the lordships of south-east Wales, including Gwent and Elfael. This brought the old kingdoms of Brycheiniog, Gwent, and Morgannwg together with Deheubarth, under a common but flexible Welsh administration. The Lord Rhys was now entitled Justice of Wales. If the Normans ruled all Deheubarth when he was born, Rhys was the ruler now.

Rhys gave his support to Henry when the sons of the king rebelled in 1173, and he sent a thousand of his soldiers to help in France. In return Henry was ready to listen and act when Rhys pleaded on behalf of Welsh people who lived as far away from Deheubarth as Gwynllwg (Wentloog) whose principal castle was Cas Newydd ar Wysg (the new castle on the Usk), now known in English as Newport. The bitterness of the Welsh-Norman struggle in these marchlands led to deeds of appalling infamy. One which occurred during the lifetime of Giraldus Cambrensis was so terrible that he says that he cannot bring himself to relate the details. It involved William de Braose, a powerful marcher lord in Gwent whose piety was exceeded only by his infamy. In 1176, the year of the Cardigan Eisteddfod, he invited to his castle at Abergavenny the Lord Rhys's brother-in-law, Seisyll ap Dyfnwal, chief of Upper Gwent, together with his son Geoffrey and a number of the Welsh leaders of Gwent. As they sat at de Braose's table some seventy of the best men of Gwent were murdered without warning. In the treacherous attack on their homes which followed, Gwladys, sister of Rhys, was seized and her small son Cadwaladr was murdered like his brother Geoffrey.

Such an act as this, which challenged the martial qualities of the men of Gwent, made peace impossible. Giraldus says that the Gwent men were the most experienced and valiant of the Welsh people in war, and 'the most skilful of all the districts of Wales in the art of firing a bow'. Oversight of this province therefore fully exercised Rhys's qualities as a statesman

He was wise enough to pay homage to the strongest and richest king in Europe, as he did in Gloucester in 1175, as leader of the Welsh princes. Effective power alone was important to him, and that he had. Most of the greater and lesser princes were related to him. For generations members of the princely families had been intermarrying, thus drawing the kingdoms into a close social and political relationship. With the coming of the Normans many of their lords and women also became, through marriage, a part of this social structure.

Rhys moved his chief court from Dinefwr to Aberteifi (Cardigan) in 1171, and it was in that castle, for two generations the main fort of the Normans, that the first Eisteddfod of which there is a full record was held at Christmas in the year 1176 under the patronage of the Justice of Wales. It was proclaimed twelve months beforehand, in Ireland and Scotland as well as Wales, showing that there was still some awareness of the old Celtic rapport. The winners in poetry and music were given chairs, and as it happened a poet from Gwynedd won the literary chair, and a harpist from Deheubarth won the chair for music. Welsh, of course, was the language of the festival. Welsh was the language of the court and the bard, the language of government and scholarship, the language of law and of the priests. In England at this time French was the official language; in Wales, Welsh. This old language which had been the only language of Wales for seven centuries and more was to be the only language of the majority of its people for another seven centuries.

Even the quislings of the day, those who did not stand for freedom, believed in the value of the language. Giraldus Cambrensis quotes a famous statement made by 'some old man of these people, who clung according to the weakness of his nation to him (Henry II) against the others.' He gives his own opinion at the end of the war to Henry when, in 1163, Henry was marching westwards through Pencader.

'This nation, O king,' said the old man, 'may now, as in future times, be oppressed, and greatly weakened and destroyed by your and

guydi. taliessin. brchaud.
kyffredin. vy darogan.

B reu duid auelun nerthw
ir. y scelur. ae dehoglho.
Hy rruerhir y reitir. nit
guibir ar nuygelho. Guerhed
llara llyriau niuer nidhoffer
meurer bw. Heur uum y don
un dined abun der liu guaner
gw. Hid air llauur urich din
da. ae coffa arnuy dalho. Gua
ech.

Page from Black Book of Carmarthen

Pen Gerallt Gymro.

Giraldus Cambrensis

other powers; but it can never be wholly subdued by the wrath of man, unless the wrath of God shall concur. Nor do I think that any other nation than this of Wales, or any other tongue, whatever may come to pass hereafter, shall in the day of severe searching before the Supreme Judge, answer for this corner of the earth.'

On this defiant note Giraldus closes his *Description of Wales*. How right was the prophecy of the first two sentences: Wales was 'greatly weakened and destroyed' by English government. But thank God, it was not completely annihilated. The ancient tongue is still heard in its hills.

* * *

What happened in Gwynedd and Powys was what so often happened when a very strong king died: the kingdom was divided according to the law between the sons, and the one fought against the other trying to re-establish a strong and united kingdom. In Powys, after the death of Madog ap Maredudd in 1160 the kingdom was divided among his own sons and Owain Cyfeiliog who ruled the southern part until his death in 1197. Gruffydd ap Madog, the grandson of the old hero Gruffydd ap Cynan, was the strongest of Madog's sons, who have been described as 'the chameleons of Powys.' He reunited the north of Powys before his death in 1191, and this province was thereafter called Powys Fadog. Following the marital policy of the princes he took as his wife Angharad, the daughter of Owain Gwynedd.

Gwynedd was torn by more feuds than Powys when Owain Gwynedd died in 1170, leaving seven sons fighting for the chief position. Afer Hywel, the prince-poet, was killed in a battle in Pentraeth, Anglesey, near the end of 1170, there came three years of peace. Dafydd was the strongest of the sons at that time; a marriage which he contracted in 1174 with Emma, the half sister of Henry II is proof of this. He failed to reunite Gwynedd for more than a short period. He ruled the country between Conwy and Dyfrdwy (Dee) from Rhuddlan castle until 1194, when he was deposed by Llywelyn. He then lived the rest of his life in a manor house in England, having won the admiration of the two nations, according to Giraldus, because he tried to keep the scales balanced between the English and the Welsh.

One of Owain's sons, Madog was reputed to have sailed to the West with thirteen ships until he reached America. Though the story has no historical foundations, English writers in the sixteenth century, such as Hakluyt in his *Voyages* and Sir Walter Raleigh in his *History of the World* believed, not surprisingly considering the rivalry with Spain, that Madog had discovered America.

Throughout the centuries of the Princes, the very justice of Hywel's laws was seen to promote the political weakness which followed from the principle of division: and this although there was in every princely family an heir apparent. Giraldus mentions this many times:

> 'If they decide to unite,' he said, 'they would be completely invincible. This nation would be fortunate . . . if they could accept one prince, and he a good one.'

There are two different aspects of some of the main areas of the legal, social and geographical character of Wales. Wales was united by Hywel's law; but the law which united it also divided it. The country was split politically; but it can be argued that in its division lay its strength. When one part was weak, another was strong; when one or more parts fell, others stood firm. And then there are the mountains: they divided and protected Wales, weakened and strengthened it.

* * *

However, while Rhys lived, Wales could rejoice in having one good prince who sustained the nation's confidence, although he did not rule the whole of the country.
1177   In 1177 he led all the princes of Wales to meet Henry in Oxford during a period of peace which continued into the nineties. In 1188 Archbishop Baldwin came
1188   to Wales to try and recruit soldiers for the crusades.
He did not receive much of a welcome in Gwynedd nor from Owain Cyfeiliog in Powys; he fared better in some other regions, and Giraldus Cambrensis says that three

thousand men responded, including Maelgwn, one of the sons of Rhys ap Gruffydd. The great value of Baldwin's journey for us today centres on the fact that Giraldus was his main companion, and Giraldus gives the story in a book, *Journey through Wales*, which provides, with his *Description of Wales*, a lively picture of the Wales of the twelfth century, and is also one of the most valuable source-books of European history in the middle ages. It is clear from Giraldus's description that the greater part of the country was in the hands of the Welsh.

By now five of Rhys's sons had come of age. Three of them heard Baldwin preaching in Ceredigion. In his description of Cynwrig, one of the five, Giraldus draws a picture of a Welsh nobleman:

> 'He was fair complexioned, with curly hair, handsome and tall, and according to the custom of his country and nation wore only a thin mantle and shirt, his legs and feet bare, but not bothered by the thickets nor the thorns; a man protected not by art but by nature; showing much of the dignity of a person of his rank, and very little of anything superfluous . . .'

Giraldus noticed the dignity which did not depend on abundance, the dignity of the simplicity of an heroic age, when everyone was ready to give his life to protect his country.

> 'Because of this,' said Giraldus, 'it is not only the noblemen, but all men, who are ready to take up arms; the war horn sounds, the countryman rushes to arms from his plough with the same readiness as the courtier from his court.'

In such a nation as this brave people were reared. Courage is the most handsome of all the virtues, and it comes with practice: the Welsh people of these centuries were trained in courage from their childhood.

Unfortunately great weaknesses accompanied this virtue in the people. And Giraldus saw the weaknesses too:

> 'They love their brothers more after they have died than during their life.'

But he had the sense to realise that some of the mischief was the result of:

> 'the unfortunate habit of the princes in giving out their many sons to be fostered by various noblemen from their own country; and then every one of these, after the death of the father, strives and conspires with all his might to raise his own foster son, and to raise him higher than the rest.'

Rhys ap Gruffydd suffered terribly from the consequences of this custom in his later years. His sons urged him to expel all foreigners from the country. This meant war. Rhys was a cautious man; he knew that the aftermath of war could be very different from the results hoped for by the ones who declared it. But the Welsh of the borders were also struggling against the yoke of oppression. They wanted to be as free of the Norman yoke as the men of Deheubarth were. Rhys listened to their appeal when Henry died in 1189, and he swept through Rhos, Pembroke, Gower and Carnwyllion. King Richard sent his brother John at the head of an army into Wales, but to little effect. In 1192, however, Rhys failed to take Swansea. The main reason for this was the bitter discord between his sons. Had his sons stood as firmly united as his brothers had done the history of Wales would have been different, and no doubt happier. In the course of their quarrels with each other two of them imprisoned their father, to the great delight of their enemies. The following year Rhys had to face another conspiracy of the same kind when two of his other sons seized Cantref Mawr and Cantref Bach and the castles of Dinefwr and Llandovery. His sun was setting and his lustre fading behind these heavy clouds, but the old glory flashed again, reddening the sky with a bright glow. He seized the conspirators and imprisoned them. Then he turned his energies on his enemies, as his sons should have done. He threw himself against the Normans at Carmarthen, the headquarters of royal power in the south, and burnt the town to the ground. Then he turned his attention to the borders and captured and burnt Colwyn castle, the main

1189

1192

1194

fort of Elfael Uchaf. He crossed the highlands of Clud, namely the forest of Maesyfed (Radnor), and although the Normans brought help from outside to defend it, Rhys was completely victorious. He turned then to Elfael Isaf and took Paen Castle built by the late William de Braose, the mightiest lord of the province.

This was Rhys's last effort, and he could now say, in the words of W. J. Gruffydd:

> Mi godais yn fy henaint fel hen lew
> I ysgwyd ymaith y Normaniaid mân . . .
> Ac wele 'ngoror bellach oll yn rhydd.

> I arose in my old age like an old lion
> to sweep away the petty Normans . . .
> and see — my frontiers are all free.

He did not live to such a great age as Owain Gwynedd and Gruffydd ap Cynan. He died at the age of sixty-five in 1197, the year in which Owain Cyfeiliog of Powys died. But he had been fighting on the battlefield for much of the previous half century; he had faced many great crises; he had lived a full and purposive life, every step of the way. He was a patron of the Church; he helped the Order of Saint Benedict; he supported the new Order of Premonstratensians in Talyllychau (Talley) where he built them a new abbey; he supported the convent of Llanllŷr, and the Order of the Knights Hospitallers in Slebech; and in particular he supported another great Order, the Cistercians, in Hendy-Gwyn ar Daf (Whitland), and in Strata Florida, which won a national status. And let us remember today, at a time of serious crisis for the nation and for the Welsh language, that he generously supported the language, the literature and the culture of Wales. Above all else, it was his long and heroic effort which confined the cultural influence of the Normans to the valleys and lowlands, and which led, in its turn, to a revival of the Welsh spirit in Glamorgan, Gwent, Brycheiniog and Maesyfed (Radnor). But for him the rich intellectual culture described in Griffith John Williams's *Traddodiad Llenyddol Morgannwg*

(The Literary Tradition of Glamorgan) would not have developed. The poets were right to lay such stress on the personal qualities of the leaders; society depended so much on them. It is no exaggeration to say that no Welsh would be heard in the south of Wales today had not Rhys ap Gruffydd defended the life of his country in such a masterly way in circumstances so dangerously intricate in order that his heritage could be handed down to the future.

VII. THE BARDS OF THE PRINCES AND THE STORY-TELLERS OF THE MABINOGION

THE bards made a great contribution towards the success of the princes. The high rank of the bard corresponded to his important position in society. The chief poet sat next to the king's or the prince's heir, and the family poet had his seat beside the head of the family or the captain of the guard. This exalted position reflected their social importance as the upholders of standards in ideals and education. The Order of Bards and the monastery schools were responsible for education in Wales. Like the Church, the Order of Bards had a strict discipline and order. They laid great stress on the teaching of the Welsh language, for Welsh culture depended on a detailed knowledge of it. But they were not unfamiliar with the works of the poets and thinkers of the old classical world. Boethius was the chief link that connected them and the countries of Faith.

'In his analysis of beauty,' says D. Myrddin Lloyd, 'Boethius divides it up into harmony, clarity and order. These three are prominent in Welsh poetry, and the Gogynfeirdd too (in spite of their obscurity at times, at any rate to *us*) admired clarity and lightness much more often than colours. "Ac oedd lawn o heul hirfyn a phant." ' — "The long hill and the hollow were full of the sun".'

'The Cistercian mind, particularly, was steeped in this tradition. Edgar de Bruyne says of them that they "insisted more than anyone on balance, composition and tidiness as the main attributes of beauty, and they also stress the "gracious" element which should be in all harmony. If we think of the development of *cynghanedd* in Wales, we can understand the inducement to develop it against the mental background and intellectual climate which spread throughout the countries of Faith by the teaching of the Church.'

At the beginning of the 19th century the tendency in the Welsh mind towards harmony and *cynghanedd* made an influential break-through in the social ideas of Robert Owen.

The poets were the social conscience of the country: it was they who kept in front of their leaders the ideals which gave meaning and unity to their society. They recorded the nation's past history; they inspired the leaders to ensure that there would be a future for the country. With their awareness of the past and their long hopes for the future they saw the present in perspective. These seers were of necessity determined upholders of the national tradition and social order. But they were not uncritical — they were strong for justice and showed this in their frequent rebukes to the princes for any tyrannical action.

Sometimes the poets were themselves princes, and sometimes soldiers, like Dafydd Benfras who was killed in a battle in Llangadog. There are one or two women poets among them, and an occasional monk, like Brother Madog, who wrote thus of the infant Jesus in the manger:

> Cawr mawr bychan,
> Cryf cadarn gwan, gwynion ruddiau.
> Cyfoethog tlawd,
> A'n Tad a'n Brawd, awdur brodiau . . .
> Isel uchel,
> Emmanuel, mêl feddyliau . . .
> Pali ni myn,
> Nid urael gwyn ei gynhiniau;
> Yn lle syndal
> Ynghylch ei wâl gwelid carpiau . . .
> Ei leferydd
> Wrth fugelydd, gwylwyr ffaldau,
> Engyl yd fydd,
> A nos fal dydd dyfu'n olau . . .
> Nos lawenydd
> I lu bedydd; byddwn ninnau.

> Great little giant,
> strong, mighty weakling, pale of cheek,
> poor wealthy one,
> our Father and Brother, author of brothers . . .,
> low and high, Emanuel of honeyed thoughts . . .
> He won't have silk,
> of no white weaving are his rags;
> no fine linen
> where he lies, only tatters,
> and his words
> are for shepherds, the fold-watchers;
> there'll be angels,
> like day, night will become bright . . .
> A night of joy
> for all Christendom; so let us be.

Whoever the bards were, their work shows that the awareness of artistry which was so evident in the poetry of the sixth century was also present in the twelfth.

The artistic conscience was not confined to poetry alone. It was just as evident in prose. Great literature in prose was a very rare thing in Europe in the middle ages; and in a native language it was confined to Ireland and Wales where most of the ancient kingdoms made notable contributions. Three of the romances took their literary form in Morgannwg and Gwent, where the Welsh traditions fused most closely with the Norman. Dyfed contributed some of the greatest of the Mabinogion stories. *Breuddwyd Rhonabwy*, the most mature achievement in this genre, was written by a man of Powys. *Brut y Tywysogion* (The Chronicle of the Princes) was one of the most invaluable treasures of Ystrad Fflur (Strata Florida) in Ceredigion. It is in Gwynedd that we find the best of the splendid Welsh versions of the Law of Hywel, which were prose classics. In the eleven tales of the Mabinogion, and particularly in the *Pedair Cainc* (the Four Branches) there is literary greatness. In these the craft of the *cyfarwydd* reached its apex in the age of Rhys ap Tewdwr. The *cyfarwyddiaid* were the men who kept the legends in their memories, polishing them as they delivered them. They corresponded to the Breton *conteurs* who spread the stories of Arthur in Europe. There is a picture of a poet who was also a *cyfarwydd* in the story of Math Fab Mathonwy, where Gwydion and his eleven companions went to the court of Pryderi in Rhuddlan Teifi:

> 'There was a court of Pryderi's there, and in the guise of bards they came inside. They made them welcome. Gwydion was placed at Pryderi's right hand that night.
>
> "Why," said Pryderi, "gladly would we have a tale from some of the young men yonder." "Lord," said Gwydion, "it is a custom with us that the first night after one comes to a great man, the chief bard shall have the say. I will tell a tale gladly." Gwydion was the best teller of tales in the world. And that night he entertained the court with pleasant tales and story-telling till he was praised by every one in the court, and it was pleasure for Pryderi to converse with him.'[1]

There is an excellence in the composition and writing of these brilliant tales. Thomas Parry says:

> 'It is almost impossible to over-emphasize the literary power of the man who gave their final shape to the Pedair Cainc (Four Branches). It is in the power of expression that his greatness lies. He has the first essential of a writer — in that he is a master of his medium, that is to say, the language. He knows all its idioms, and he writes it in harmony with its purest qualities . . . He forms his sentences and puts them together in such a way as to create a lively and rapid style which could not be bettered for the telling of a story. The *cyfarwydd* understands perfectly the value of dialogue for his purpose . . . When his story reaches its climax, the author knows how to set it out with short, incisive words.'

Here, for example, is the description of Branwen's death:

> 'And they came to land at Aber Alaw in Talebolion. And then they sat down and rested them. Then she looked on Ireland and the Island of the Mighty, what she might see of them. "Alas, Son of God," said she, "woe is me that ever I was born: two good islands have been laid waste because of me!" And she heaved a great sigh, and with that broke her heart. And a four sided grave was made for her, and she was buried there on the bank of the Alaw.'[2]

The legends of Wales had a great influence on the literature and life of Europe and that when Wales was continually at

1 and 2 From ' The Mabinogion.' Translated by Gwyn Jones and Thomas Jones.

war, fighting for her very existence against the violent attacks
of the Normans and the English. Arthur was the main subject
of the legends, and it was Geoffrey of Monmouth who gave
them to the world in what Koht has called, 'the most famous
work of nationalistic historiography in the Middle Ages.'
Geoffrey's *History of the Kings of Britain*, written in Latin
and published in 1136, was destined to have a tremendous
influence on Welsh thought down to the nineteenth century.
Believed by poets and scholars to be the historical truth, it
helped to sustain the Welsh people's pride of ancestry and it
reinforced their sense of a separate identity. Six centuries later
much of the story would still be told as history in the eighteenth
century classic *Drych y Prif Oesoedd* (The Mirror of the Great
Ages). Geoffrey was a member of a Breton family that came
to Gwent after the Norman conquest; perhaps the family was
returning to the land their fathers had left five or six centuries
before. He claimed that his work was a translation of an old
book in the Breton language, but A. O. H. Jarman says that
here he is doing himself an injustice:

> 'Geoffrey,' he says, 'was a great imaginative writer . . . he did of
> course use many sources . . . but nevertheless the broad conception of
> the work, its majestic sweep are Geoffrey's and Geoffrey's alone and
> constitute his title to literary fame.'

By making the Normans acquainted with the past glory of the
Welsh, Geoffrey was praising their achievement in humiliating
a nation of such excellent lineage. Ernest Reuan, the great
Breton scholar, wrote in the last century:

> 'It was through the Mabinogion that the Welsh imagination
> influenced the Continent; it transformed, in the twelfth century, the
> poetic art of Europe and realised this miracle, that the creation of a
> small nation which had been forgotten had become a feast of
> imagination for mankind over all the earth . . .
> Above all else, by creating woman's character the Welsh romances
> caused one of the greatest revolutions known to literary historians. It
> was like an electric spark; in a few years the taste of Europe was
> transformed.'

Renan goes on to argue that this was the first flowering of

chivalry which did such a lot to raise the status of women in Europe. This much is obvious: if a nation has anything to say, the world will come to know of it, however few understand its language. The trouble is that when a nation loses its language it stops having anything to say.

*   *   *

What was happening in England at this time? Bradley says:

'The crowding of the monasteries by foreigners, after the Norman conquest, arrested the development of the vernacular literature. It was not long before the boys in the monastic schools ceased to learn to read and write their native tongue, and learned instead to read and write French . . . Vernacular literature in the 12th century is scanty and of little originality . . . Romantic poetry did not assume a vernacular form till about 1250.'

*   *   *

When discussing medieval Welsh literature it should be realised that it is not in poetry or prose that much of it exists, but in the law, which was written in Welsh as well as in Latin, and not, as was general in other countries, in Latin only. Since the earliest Welsh copy belongs to the beginning of the thirteenth century, this is the place to record that the laws are literary masterpieces: according to Saunders Lewis, the Laws fashioned:

'lively forms and the mind of every poet and writer in Wales until the sixteenth century, and also directly influenced the shape and style of Welsh prose. For what is almost unbelievable about the Laws is that they are in Welsh. This implies that the language had already reached a philosphical maturity unrivalled in its period. It meant that it had a flexibility and positiveness which are the signs of centuries of culture. This means that there is a long period of development behind the prose of the *Cyfreithiau* (Laws).'

In the excellent report *Y Gymraeg mewn Addysg a Bywyd* (Welsh in Education and Life) published by His Majesty's Stationery Office in 1927, we read this:

'Later generations of Welshmen, accustomed since Tudor times to see all initiative in social, political (and, up to the eighteenth century, religious) matters originating in England, are unprepared to find in the

Welsh language of independent Wales an instrument exquisitely
perfected by circumstance and use to the expressions of whatever form
energy distinguished the life of Wales at any period in its history.

'In the early ages, the Laws of Wales were not written in Latin and
translated into Welsh, but were necessarily and inevitably first written
down in Welsh by the scholars whom Hywel Dda or some other law-
giver summoned to make the code. Reading the different versions of
the Welsh Laws, we are struck by the significant fact that here is no
striving and straining to twist word and idiom to meet the punctilious
demands of legal expression, but that, on the contrary, the language n
which the laws are written has ample reserves, and is more than
adequate to its purpose. We find, in fact, that even the Laws show the
exuberance and exultation of the artist just as truly as the *Mabinogion*
do, and that the magnificence and majesty of the Welsh Codes are the
fruit of a rich, ample, and well-ordered culture, among a people
speaking and hearing a language which, when other modern tongues
were regarded as despicable vernaculars, was exalted in its own home
to a degree elsewhere unequalled. Those who drew up the Laws were,
in the first instance, articificers of cunning Welsh, as jealous in guarding
the ancient customs and precepts of the language as in conserving the
usages and maxims of the common law; in short, it is clear that the
jewel of Welsh life and culture, during the period of independence,
was the Welsh language.'

VIII.   GIRALDUS CAMBRENSIS AND HIS BATTLE
FOR THE CHURCH OF THE WELSH

ALTHOUGH Giraldus was mainly of Norman descent he was
mentally and spiritually more of a Welshman than many a
man of undiluted Welsh blood. His father, William de Barri,
was a Norman nobleman, and his mother, Angharad,
a daughter of the famous Nest and Gerald de Windsor, and
therefore a grand-daughter of Rhys ap Tewdwr. The Lord
Rhys and many Welsh princes were related to him through his
mother, as well as the FitzGeralds and FitzStephens of Ireland.
He called himself Giraldus Cambrensis; that is how he was
known in the University of Paris where he was a student and
                  then a lecturer. When he returned from Paris he was
1184   appointed chaplain to Henry II and given the task
                  of accompanying Prince John to Ireland. There he
collected material for his first two books, *Topographia Hibernica*

(The Local History of Ireland) and *Expugnatio Hibernica* (The Conquest of Ireland), two books which are prime sources of Irish history in the middle ages.

He went on a journey through Wales in 1188 with Archbishop Baldwin to try and recruit soldiers for 1188 the third Crusade. It was then that he collected the material for his most famous books, *Itinerarium Kambriae* (The Journey thrugh Wales) and *Descriptio Kambriae* (Description of Wales). Behind the attempt to promte the Crusade on this journey the Archbishop of Canterbury had another purpose: to enforce the authority of Canterbury on to the four Welsh sees. This is tied up with the main theme of Giraldus's life. His ambition was to see St. David's an archbishopric, independent of Canterbury, and he himself an archbishop; he fought for this end for over a quarter of a century. He went to Rome three times to argue the case before Pope Innocent III; he gives the account in his autobiography. On his third visit in 1202 he gave the Pope a letter signed by Llywelyn Fawr and his nobles supporting Giraldus's case for the recognition of St. David's.

This struggle was begun, strangely enough, by Bishop Bernard, a Norman supported by Owain Gwynedd, who saw the value of an independent Welsh archbishopric. His successor was wholly subservient to Canterbury; his name was David FitzGerald, another of Nest's sons and Giraldus' uncle. Giraldus hoped to follow his uncle; he refused Llandaf and Bangor and two bishoprics in Ireland which were offered to him. In supporting him Llywelyn Fawr prophesied that the name of Giraldus Cambrensis would live as long as Wales continued to exist. Llywelyn I, like Llywelyn II after him, was strongly in favour of appointing Welsh bishops to Bangor.

Giraldus failed in his efforts, but Glanmor Williams points out in his excellent book, *The Welsh Church from Conquest to Reformation*:

> 'Gerald's unrealised aspirations for the see . . . were not without their long term effects. Two centuries later Owain Glyndŵr and his advisers seriously revived the project of an independent province with an archbishop of St. David's at its head.'

This campaign did not end until the bitter conflict over the disestablishment of the Church in Wales which ended in 1920. During that fierce struggle, seven centuries after the time of Giraldus, a dangerous degeneration into spiritual and material poverty was predicted for the Church if its connection with the British state was severed: the opposite happened. In an article which he wrote to celebrate the disestablishment the present Archbishop said:

'In an uncharacteristic weak moment, Bishop John Owen once expressed his dismay at the prospect of a disestablished Church in Wales having to cope with questions which perplexed the combined wisdom of the Church of England. The truth is that, provided it does not try to be self sufficient, a Church just like a country develops its capacity for government by accepting responsibility for its own life.'

But in the middle ages the political and national importance of the Church was too great for the Normans and the English to allow it to be independent in Wales.

The greatest service which Giraldus did for Wales was to write down a lively and perceptive description of the country and its people as he saw them. One notes that he raises no doubt about the nationhood of Wales. He describes people of one nation, not a number of provinces, and their common characteristics everywhere. Some of his comments have been quoted already. Here are some more, and first the dishonourable features:

'This nation conceives it right to commit acts of plunder, theft, and robbery, not only against foreigners and hostile nations, but even against their own countrymen.

'When an opportunity of attacking the enemy with advantage occurs, they respect not the leagues of peace and friendship, preferring base lucre to the solemn obligations of oaths and good faith . . .'

'In war this nation is very severe in the first attack, terrible by their clamour and looks, filling the air with horrid shouts and deep-toned clangour of very long trumpets; swift and rapid in their advances and frequent throwing of darts. Bold in the first onset, they cannot bear a repulse, being easily thrown into confusion . . .'

'Where they find plenty, and can exercise their power, they levy the most unjust exactions.'

'. . . and from their love of high descent . . . they unite themselves to their own people, refusing to intermarry with strangers, and arrogantly presuming on their own superiority of blood and family. They do not engage in marriage until they have tried, by previous cohabitation the disposition, and particularly the fecundity, of the person to whom they are engaged.'

'Their sons, after the decease of their fathers, succeed to the ecclesiastical benefices, not by election, but by hereditary right . . .'

In another part of his book Giraldus discusses other, more praiseworthy aspects. Here he draws a picture of people in love with life, and yet ready to sacrifice much — 'to scorn delights and live laborious days' — and, indeed, to give their very lives when necessary, for the good of their community.

'Their mind is wholly on the defence of their country and its freedom.'

'Not addicted to gluttony or drunkeness, this people show no ostentation in food or dress, and whose minds are always alert to defend their country and their property.

'No one of this nation ever begs, for the houses of all are common to all; and they place liberality and hospitality above all other virtues . . . The young men move about in troops and families under the direction of a chosen leader . . . and ever ready to stand forth in defence of their country, they have free admittance into every house as if it were their own.
Those who arrive in the morning are entertained till evening with the conversation of young women, and the music of the harp; for each house has its own young women and harps allotted to this purpose . . . In the evening, when no more guests are expected, the meal is prepared according to the number and dignity of the persons assembled, and according to the wealth of the family who entertains.'

'They are not given to drunkeness or to *cyfeddach* (carousal); they display no ostentation at all, neither in their food nor in their clothes.'

'The men and women cut their hair close round to the ears and eyes. The women, after the manner of the Parthians, cover their heads with a large white veil, folded together in the form of a crown. Both sexes exceed any other nation in attention to their teeth . . .The men shave all their beard except the moustaches.'

'These people being of a sharp and acute intellect, and gifted with a rich and powerful understanding, excel in whatever studies they pursue. And this nation is altogether more intelligent and penetrating in mind than other nations which dwell in a western clime.'

'Courtiers and men of the guard are much given to wit in their conversation.'

'Nature hath given not only to the highest, but also to the inferior classes of the people of this nation, a boldness and confidence in speaking and answering, even in the presence of their princes and chieftains . . . neither the English, nor the Saxons and Germans, from whom they are descended, had it.'

'The Welsh esteem noble birth and generous descent above all things, and are, therefore, more desirous of marrying into noble than rich families. Even the common people retain their genealogy, and can not only readily recount the names of their grandfathers and great- grand-fathers but even refer back to the sixth or seventh generation, or beyond them . . .'

LLYWELYN FAWR (LLYWELYN I)

GWENWYNWYN, the Prince of Powys, wrote of Giraldus:

'Many and great are the wars which we the Welsh have fought against England, but none was as great and fierce as that which he waged against the King and the Archbishop, when he resisted the whole power of England for the honour of Wales.'

The Welsh continued to resist all the power of England after the death of the Lord Rhys. The man who became the national leader was Llywelyn ap Iorwerth, later called Llywelyn Fawr. He moved the leadership from Deheubarth to Gwynedd where it would remain for the next three generations.
1197   Although he was only twenty-four in 1197 he was already one of the two most powerful princes of the country; the other was Gwenwynwyn of Powys, the son of

Strata Florida — Ystrad Fflur

Dynevor Castle — Castell Dinefwr

Llywelyn II
Copyright Alcwyn Deiniol with permission of City Hall, Cardiff

Owain Cyfeiliog and Gwenllian, the daughter of Owain Gwynedd. Throughout the first forty years of the thirteenth century, the name of Llywelyn was the most famous and most distinguished in Wales.

It seems that Llywelyn ap Iorwerth was born in Dolwyddelan, and bred in Powys. In 1194 he defeated Dafydd ab Owain Gwynedd in the Battle of Aberconwy; and in 1197 he took away from him the whole of Perfeddwlad, that is, Rhos, Rhufoniog, Tegeingl and the Vale of Clwyd. In the first year of the new century he added Arfon, Anglesey and Arllechwedd; in 1201, Llŷn; and in 1202 he placed his nephew Hywel in Meirionnydd. His authority stretched now from Dyfi to Dyfrdwy (Dee) bringing him face to face with Powys where Gwenwynwyn ruled the land between Tanat and Severn, the country called Powys Gwenwynwyn, to distinguish it from Powys Fadog.

1194
1197
1200
1202

Gwenwynwyn made a brave attempt to take over the leadership of Wales. He possessed the necessary personal qualifications, and had some success at first. Its geographical position along with other pressures had always prevented Powys from snatching the supremacy for more than a short period and these were the factors that defeated him now.

The struggle between the two was exploited by John, king of England, who was taking a far more direct part in Welsh affairs — and English ones too — than Richard, his predecessor, had done. John followed the classic imperial policy of pitting the strong against the weak, the principle of divide and rule. At the outset he sided with Llywelyn; then he turned to support Gwenwynwyn. But the strength and wisdom of Llywelyn proved sufficient to frustrate him. John invited him to discuss peace terms, and when the plan failed he sent the Archbishop of Canterbury and his Chief Justice to meet Llywelyn on the Welsh border in July 1201. The result was a formal agreement. In it Llywelyn undertook to pay homage to the king. In 1205 he followed this up by marrying Joan, John's daughter.

*   *   *

John had more success in Deheubarth with his policy of dividing than he had in Gwynedd, and this because of the patent weaknesses in the characters of the sons of the Lord Rhys. It was as if there were a curse on the lords of Ceredigion compelling them to turn their backs on the efforts of their own people and give their support to the Normans. That is what Cadwaladr had done in Owain Gwynedd's time, and this is what Maelgwn did now.

He turned to king John for help against his brother, Gruffydd ap Rhys, who had defeated him. On December 3, 1199 the king — that is, the government of England — affirmed

1199   Maelgwn's occupation of Ceredigion and Emlyn on condition that he yielded the castle of Aberteifi and the neighbouring district of Is Hirwern to the crown, ensuring in this that the enemy had in their hands 'Allwedd holl Kymru' (the Key to the whole of Wales) as the *Brut* calls it: 'That year Maelgwn the son of Rhys sold Aberteifi and the key to the whole of Wales for a pittance to the English.' When John proved to be a disappointment to him in 1207 he returned to the Welsh side as Cadwaladr had done before him. In the meantime, with Gwenwynwyn's help he had taken over — but only for a short time — Ystrad Tywi and the castles of Dinefwr, Llangadog and Llandovery.

In 1207 when William de Braose, one of the strongest of the border lords, fell in battle, Gwenwynwyn began to

1207   to plunder his lands. At once John responded by supporting the new lord of those lands. This daunted Gwenwynwyn, who went to Shrewsbury to seek peace. He was imprisoned there and the king took over his lands until twenty hostages were delivered to him. John was now again weighting the scales against Powys, in favour of Gwynedd.

*   *   *

Llywelyn saw his opportunity at once. He acted daringly. He occupied Gwenwynwyn's Powys and then marched to Ceredigion. He took over Maelgwn's province as far as the river Ystwyth and rebuilt the castle in Aberystwyth. The land between the Ystwyth and the Aeron he gave to the sons of Gruffydd ap Rhys, Owain and Rhys. Through all this he succeeded in keeping the friendship of John, and he showed his loyalty to his father-in-law by joining the army which defeated William of Scotland at Norham in 1209.

In 1210 Llywelyn made a bad move. While John was marching victoriously and unopposed through Ireland, he agreed to help William de Braose in his attempt to reoccupy his lordship. This proved a sad failure and de Braose fled to France. Llywelyn had to pay heavily for his error. Gwynedd was invaded by English forces under the Earl of Chester and the Chief Justice. On his march through the south of Wales when returning from Ireland, John himself assiduously encouraged the enemies of Llywelyn to strive against him. He restored Gwenwynwyn in Powys and he supported Maelgwn in a vain attempt to reconquer the north of Ceredigion; Maelgwn was defeated by the sons of Gruffydd. In addition to this, John invited all the Welsh leaders to Chester to join his army in defeating Llywelyn once and for all. That is, as the enemies of Wales have done through the centuries, he called for unity against the patriots whom he accused of a terrible crime: the patriotic extremists, he said, were splitting Wales. This ploy had great success. In this day of severe test, it was only the young sons of Gruffydd who stood with Llywelyn; these two alone were guilty of splitting the country.

Once again the great army of England marched to the heart of Wales. Once again the patriots withdrew to the mountains. And once again the king was forced to retreat with his host of hungry men and little in way of gain. This happened in May. In July John was ready to make another attempt, from Oswestry this time. He marched quickly to Conwy and on to Aber. This placed Llywelyn in an extremely difficult position. Having lost Perfeddwlad he was surrounded. It was then that Joan went to her father to intercede for him. John agreed to leave Gwynedd in Llywelyn's hands and returned to England believing that his success in Wales had been as sweeping as it had been in Ireland.

Having succeeded so well John decided on a policy of

conquest and colonisation in many parts of Wales. But this
was too much for the Welsh princes to stomach. They suddenly
realised, as so many have realised after them, that English
government never acted in the interests of Wales, that it was
less a kind grandmother than a rapacious wolf. They turned
their coats the right way round once again and gave their
support to the national cause. Maelgwn and Rhys Gryg
attacked the new castle which the king had built in
Aberystwyth and destroyed it. At the same time another
prince who had been fighting on John's side, Cadwallon ab
Ifor Bach of Senghenydd, arose and plundered Morgannwg.
Very quickly John's success was made to look like an
illusion.

Indeed, in 1212 Llywelyn spent Easter with the king in
Cambridge. That same summer he joined up with
1212   Maelgwn, Rhys Gryg and Gwenwynwyn to destroy
the new castles in Wales. In one corner of the country
Rhys Gryg burnt down the town of Swansea; and in the
other end Llywelyn recaptured Perfeddwlad except for the
castles of Rhuddlan and Deganwy. Once again John collected
the English host together in Chester finally to crush Llywelyn.
As a preliminary gesture he killed some of the hostages given
to him. But once again his daughter helped to obstruct his
purpose. After receiving a warning from Joan that there was
a conspiracy against him among the barons, all he did was to
send the navy to ravage the shores of Wales. The Pope, who
had heard a lot about Wales from Giraldus, now intervened
to secure a truce between John and the Welsh.

By now the English barons were rising against John.
Llywelyn threw in his lot with the rebels and in May
1215   1215 he captured the town and castle of Shrewsbury
for them. In Dyfed the sons of Rhys attacked the king's
castles in the west, and in Morgannwg, Rhys Gryg gave the
government more cause to fear; in Powys, Gwenwynwyn
remained faithful to the national cause. The events leading up
to the Magna Carta — which secured special rights for Wales
— gave Llywelyn his opportunity. In December the prince
appeared in the south at the head of an army taken from

every part of the free Wales: from Powys and Maeliennydd, Ystrad Tywi and Ceredigion, as well as Gwynedd. He captured the royal headquarters of Carmarthen, and then Cydweli, Llansteffan, St. Clears, Lacharn, Arberth, Trefdraeth, Cilgerran and Cardigan. 'And then Llywelyn ap Iorwerth and all the princes of Wales with him,' says the *Brut*, 'returned to their own states delighting in the victory.' They left the crown of England without a foot-hold in Wales except in the areas around Haverfordwest and Pembroke.

It was necessary to share the lands between the princes. This was done in a conference of nobles convened by Llywelyn in Aberdyfi early in 1216, 'which may be regarded', says J. E. Lloyd, 'as virtually a Welsh parliament, the first of its kind.' The decision arrived at remained in force through the time of Llywelyn and brought to an end the troubles of the sons of the Lord Rhys. The same year Llywelyn showed his strength by putting Gwenwynwyn to flight when he rebelled. This marked the end of the career of Owain Cyfeiliog's heir.

1216

> 'Gwenwynwyn had in him the makings of a patriot,' says J. E. Lloyd, 'but fate decreed that he should rule over Powys, the weakest of the three realms of Wales, and that he should be pitted against Llywelyn, whom he could not overcome and whose ascendancy he would not endure.'

In the same year came the death of king John: the supporter, the chief enemy, and the father-in-law of Llywelyn. In March 1218, the prince made an agreement in Worcester with Henry III, which ensured his hold on all he had conquered, and made him protector of Gwenwynwyn's lands and the formidable castles of Carmarthen and Aberteifi until the young king should come of age.

By this time Llywelyn had created a stronger position for himself than any one other Welsh prince had achieved since the Normans first marched into Wales. For another twenty-two years he ruled his principality with strength and wisdom bringing stability to the life of Wales. William Marshall, Earl of Pembroke, alone succeeded in impairing his hold on

the south west. This most powerful of border lords in
1223 brought an army over from Ireland which
1223   recaptured Cardigan, Carmarthen and Emlyn.
       Nevertheless Llywelyn succeeded in establishing a
new defence post of military and political importance by
winning Llanfair-ym-Muallt (Builth) in 1229, and he
       recaptured Cardigan in 1231. At this time Llywelyn
1231   felt that the officers of the king were imperilling his
       position on the borders, and he mounted a great
attack from Montgomery to Maesyfed (Radnor), through
Brecon and Caerleon, concluding with the victory in Cardigan.
This period of serious discord came to an end with the Middle
Agreement in 1234 and the rest of his reign was completely
peaceful.

*   *   *

The half century that had gone by was a period of
remarkable development in law and political constitution,
which continued through the reign of Llywelyn II. It is as
well to note what point it had reached in the time of Llywelyn
I. The meeting of the thesis of native life with the antithesis of
Norman life resulted in a Welsh synthesis which was different,
and in some ways richer, than what had gone before. As in
the Roman period, here was a progression rather than a break
in the continuity of Welsh development. After 1282 development in our institutions and law was dangerously restricted;
after 1536 they came to an end, wounding the old culture
almost unto death. Without the protection of political
institutions the national culture inevitably languished.

The lawyers of the period of the princes were firm
nationalists. They were the most powerful of the laymen who
lay behind the effort of the prince to restructure the free
Wales. It was they who were responsible for the character of
the structure. This incorporated important basic social changes.
Jones-Pierce refers to,

   'those modifications of tribal customs which made the ordinary
   tribesman more and more individually responsible for illegal acts to
   the Prince and his subordinate lords. This revision of custom, moreover,

resulted in revised codes of law which, though incorporating ideas
borrowed from the common law of England, retained the traditional
tone and form of earlier custom. There was thus produced one of the
most notable monuments of early European jurisprudence — a corpus
of customary law which continued to be associated with the name of
Hywel Dda notwithstanding the fact that so many old practices were
being entirely remodelled.'

Perhaps we should omit the word 'tribal' because it gives a
wrong impression. Ogwen Williams says:

'No tribal system ever existed in Wales, at least not since the
emergence of Wales between the fifth and the seventh centuries. It
cannot be too strongly emphasised that in its economic and social
organisation Wales was basically no different from England or France.
Its organisation was not tribal but hierarchical in character . . .'

With the developments in the law, the political
constitution was remoulded. We saw the significance of
dropping the title of 'king'. The sovereignty of the king of
England was recognised; but theoretically at least the powers
of the prince remained sovereign. The king of England had no
right to interfere. But for the imperialism of England this
would have resulted in the emergence of a confederation of
free and equal nations in these islands. This was a more
civilised answer than the primitive centralist imperialism which
won the day.

Inside Wales the princes tended more and more to accept
the overlordship of Gwynedd; a rich federal system could have
developed from this to safeguard the splendid variety we see
in the different provinces of Wales. Of course the development was a painful process, and naturally enough the other
princes fought for their rights; it was on the battlefield in the
main that such issues were settled in those days, as in our
international life today. The tendency was clearly evident
when the noblemen of Wales recognised Dafydd as Llywelyn's
heir in a second 'senedd' which Llywelyn assembled in Strata
Florida in 1238. Dafydd had already been recognised as heir
by the Pope and the King of England. This defiance of one
of the most important traditions in the Laws of Hywel —
the sharing of the inheritance between all the sons — would

have been impossible but for the general recognition that Llywelyn Fawr was 'our common leader' and 'great head of Blessed Wales,' as Dafydd Benfras has it.

Amongst the offices of state which developed, that of Chancellor was the highest. There had been a chancellor in every region, but now this office was filled by the *rhaglaw* (lieutenant), that is, the personal representative of the prince. Primarily, the Chancellor was the Prince's deputy. The Chancellorship had developed into a very busy and responsible office requiring a large staff of civil servants. Members of the staff travelled as far as Paris and Rome. Added to this, in his dealings with England, Llywelyn had a remarkably able representative in his wife Joan.

The necessity of finance to support the state and its armed forces, led to a great development in the office of Treasurer. The circumstances of the time also gave the military Chief of Staff, or Seneschal, as he was called in Llywelyn's day, great authority. This key position was filled by some of the chief counsellors of the Prince. He was fortunate enough here to have the service of men of great ability such as Ednyfed Fychan and the two sons who followed him, Goronwy and Tudur, ancestors of the Tudors who won the English crown two and a half centuries later.

We have seen that the Lord Rhys had been named Justice of Wales. This developed, in Llywelyn's day, into a great legal office, distinct from the person of the Prince. The Prince continued as president of the High Court which heard appeals against the decisions of the regional courts, but the Justice of Wales became, according to Jones-Pierce:

> 'a sort of chief magistrate of the court, having the same function as the Chief Justiciar in England. Like the court magistrates in relation to the local lord, the Justice worked, I suppose, as the chief counsellor to the Prince in legal matters, as spokesman for the high court, and as patron of the local official magistrates, and through them, he also acted as chief controller of the ordinary magistrates.'

If I may quote again what Jones-Pierce says of the high court:

> 'Here all inter-related offices met. And it was not only a Magistrates' Court in the modern sense. As the highest governing body of the

feudal state it fulfilled an administrative and political office. The letters of the princes show quite clearly that there was no essential difference between the court (curia) and the council (concilium). The letters also show, just as clearly, that it was not the custom of the princes to take an important step without seeking the advice of the chief officers of the court, members of the princely family, and leaders of the priesthood in the sees of Bangor and St. Asaph. And when it was necessary to get advice on a matter of exceptional policy, many of the lower lords (the *magnates* of the Latin chronicles) were added to the membership of the council. As far as superficial testimony counts, it is difficult to draw a difference between the ordinary council and the high court of the Princes of Wales in the thirteenth century and the contemporary parlimentum of the kings of England.'

The prince who was the chief architect of this state was Llywelyn Fawr, Prince of Aberffraw and Lord of Eryri, the able statesman and soldier who was also a patron of education and literature and religion. He ensured that Welshmen were appointed as bishops of Bangor and St. David's. When Joan died in 1237 and was buried in Llanfaes in Anglesey, he gave land to the Franciscans to build a monastery there; it was to be burnt to the ground in the fifteenth century because of the monks' support for Owain Glyndwr. He supported other Orders, but in particular he gave his patronage, like the Lord Rhys before him, to the Cistercians, the Order of Whitefriars, who fitted in so well with Wales. Did the English establishment condemn their monasteries at Aberconwy, Cwm Hir, Cymer and Strata Florida as breeding grounds of nationalists? They may well have done so, for as T. F. O'Sullivan has said, 'The Welsh Cistercian monks were not only nationality conscious, but nationalistic as well.' In his later days Llywelyn took the monk's habit in Aberconwy, and there, on April 11, 1240 he died. Let our chief historian pay him tribute:

'No man ever made better or more judicious use of the native force of the Welsh people for adequate national ends; his patriotic statesmanship will always entitle him to wear the proud title of Llywelyn the Great.'

X. LLYWELYN AP GRUFFUDD (Llywelyn II)

Llywelyn fawr passed on a strong and prosperous state into the hands of his heir, Dafydd, the son of Joan and grandson of King John. He was Dafydd II; Dafydd I was the son of Owain Gwynedd. He received the recognition of the Pope and Henry II to the succession, and in the *senedd* of Strata Florida he was accepted by the other princes of Wales. The sympathy of the Pope was sincere, but he was far away. The King of England was devious and unreliable, and he was close at hand. Soon after the death of Llywelyn, Henry began to play the old trick of the strong imperialist: he divided the country, and was rapacious for plunder. His job was easy and his success swift. The Norman lords were incited to claim Cardigan, Builth and Mold; and in Powys, Gruffudd ap Gwenwynwyn was glad of the opportunity of making a claim for his father's land. Dafydd agreed to let these matters go to arbitration, but there was delay and the king pretended that he was losing his patience. He used his strongest argument, his army. Having made sure that the Welsh princes were separated from Dafydd, he gathered his forces together in Chester, occupied Tegeingl and Rhuddlan and moved on towards Dyganwy. Without allies, Dafydd had no choice but to come to terms. And they were hard ones. They put the Norman lords back in power in the lands won by Llywelyn; Gruffudd ap Gwenwynwyn got his realm back; the king himself was to rule Tegeingl and then Carmarthen, Cardigan and Cydweli too; and Dafydd had to yield his brother Gruffudd as prisoner to be placed in the Tower of London.

There was peace for three years; but on St. David's Day 1244, Gruffudd was killed trying to escape from the Tower, and this led to a disturbance throughout Wales, perhaps because the death of Gruffudd freed Dafydd from a competitor who could be used against him by the king by appealing to Welsh law, the law that Llywelyn had contravened when he made Dafydd his only heir. But Gwynedd had not been idle. It is clear that Dafydd's representatives had been busy at work among the princes, for, showing his father's spirit and ability, he formed an alliance with all of them except the two in Powys and Gwynllwg. During the summer he was busy in every part of the country. He won back the border stronghold at Mold, and there were almost nightly attacks on Norman lands. He added diplomacy to military activity by appealing successfully to Pope Innocent IV for help. In his dealings with the Pope Dafydd showed his considerable ability as a statesman and his ambition to be a Prince who was wholly independent of the English crown. For a short time he did style himself Prince of Wales, the first to use that title.

Once again the king of England assembled his forces in Chester and marched once more to the banks of the Conwy. The fighting this time was bitter and cruel. The Normans killed their Welsh prisoners, among them one of Ednyfed Fychan's sons. An army was brought back from Ireland to plunder Anglesey. But Dafydd refused to surrender. After three months of fighting the king's armies had to withdraw without gaining very much.

1246

Then a great tragedy befell Wales. At the end of February the man who had shown in a short reign of only six years that he was a worthy successor to his father, died. Wales was left in wartime without a national leader while the English crown was in possession of so much of its land. Seizing the opportunity, a Norman army came from the south through Ceredigion, Meirionnydd and Dyganwy. The Welsh were forced to make an agreement in Woodstock which destroyed the unity which had been built up under Llywelyn and Dafydd and which had brought Gwynedd into a feudal relationship with the king of England.

1245

1247

In this black hour another hero arose, a man who quickly strode into the front rank of the great men of the nation: from the middle of the bastion of Eryri (Snowdonia) came Llywelyn ap Gruffudd, one of the grandsons of Llywelyn Fawr. In the Woodstock peace agreement he had been allowed to share Gwynedd Uwch Conwy with his brother Owain. Beginning with this small province he succeeded in rebuilding his grandfather's state and even in adding to it. This, in the circumstances, was a remarkable feat showing the wonderful resilience of this small nation whose western seaboard is only forty-five miles from the English border at the centre of its land.

In the situation that existed in 1247 there was nothing to suggest that Wales would ever taste success again. In the south a number of Welsh lords shared the hill country of Morgannwg and Gwent between them, but the finest land was held by the Normans in their strong castles; at one time there were 143 of these Marcher lords. The grandsons of the Lord Rhys had come to terms with the king, and when Maelgwn Fychan of Ceredigion refused to negotiate with him they were used to help the Normans bring him to heel. One result was to confine Maelgwn, who had been a vigorous leader, to two regions in the north of his province. The situation was further depressed when the hopes which his men had placed in his son Rhys were smashed by his early death.

> 'His men consoled themselves,' says J. E. Lloyd, 'with the thought that, though Maelgwn's day was over, his son Rhys was daily growing into the likeness of the ideal deliverer whom they hoped to see hurl back ere long the tide of English conquest. But these hopes were blasted by Rhys' early death in 1255.'

Yet the situation in Wales was not hopeless. The will to live was much too strong. That same year saw Llywelyn ap Gruffudd, the main hope of Wales, rising to the challenge in the north. The splitting of Gwynedd caused an estrangement between him and his brother Owain which brought them into conflict. On Derwin hill, in a gap between Arfon and Eifionnydd, Llywelyn won a victory which delivered
1255 Owain into his hands, and put the whole of Gwynedd under his rule. For twelve years from this until 1267 his story is an almost unbroken record of victories, and for twenty-six years his name is identified with the national struggle.

Just as his father had profited by feuds in England between King John and his lords, so now Llywelyn ap Gruffudd took advantage of the difficulties facing the English crown. By now

too the Welsh of Perfeddwlad in the north-east had had enough
of Norman tyranny. They rebelled and called upon Llywelyn
to help them. He replied with alacrity. Crossing the Conwy
he went full speed towards Chester. Within a week
1256   he had restored the borders of Gwynedd Fawr. But
he did not stop there. In the beginning of December
he overcame Meirionnydd; then moved to Ceredigion, which
had been given to Maredudd ab Owain; and then to Ystrad
Tywi, where he succeeded in supplanting Rhys Fychan in
Dinefwr and Carreg Cennen, which he gave, with the whole
of Cantref Mawr and Cantref Bychan to Maredudd ap Rhys.

He had hardly any time at home over Christmas before
setting off again for Powys to punish Gruffydd ap
Gwenwynwyn for giving his support to the crown of England.
He penetrated the valley of the Severn, occupying the land
as far as Welshpool. Without staying there any time, he
proceeded to Morgannwg where he won the support of the
Welsh of Gower. Then he secured the support of Cydweli
and Carnwyllion before returning to Gwynedd by
1257   Easter. In May he was in Powys again, where he won
a victory near Llanfyllin.

On May 31 in that same exciting year a strong Norman army
emerged from Carmarthen with the intention of re-occupying
Dinefwr. Having reached the environs of the castle they were
mercilessly harrassed for two days by sharp attacks from the
men of the two Maredudds, Maredudd ap Rhys and Maredudd
ab Owain. On June 2 they had to retreat, but they failed to
reach the safety of Carmarthen: on the way there they were
thrown into utter chaos. Just as the Welsh forwards can thrust
for the line when they have the ball at their feet in the Arms
Park in a match against England, so Rhys and Owain and their
men swept the Normans and the English of Carmarthen and
Dyfed before them that day. The Welsh attacked them every
inch of the way. In Cymerau, near Pont-ar-Gothi probably,
the final battle was fought.

'More than three thousand Englishmen fell that day,' wrote a
reverend chronicler of Talyllychau (Talley Abbey), 'very few if any
of the armed knights survived that battle.'

This was the worst disaster that the English Government
had suffered in Wales for a generation. It could not ignore it
any more than it could ignore the political victory of the
Welsh in the same neighbourhood seven hundred years later.
Nor did the victorious Welsh stay where they were; they
went on to take Lacharn, Llansteffan and Arberth. Then
Llywelyn came down from Gwynedd to join forces with
them. Trefdraeth (Newport) was taken, he attacked Haverfordwest and Rhos before marching on to Morgannwg to
conquer Llangynwyd, and back north again to defend
Gwynedd. By now all the terms forced on the Welsh at
Woodstock ten years earlier had been scattered to the four
winds.

Llywelyn's return to the north was necessary because by
now King Henry himself had been forced into action. His
forces assembled in Chester on the first of August and on
August 19 they marched out on the Welsh road. With the
aid of a navy from the Cinque ports in the south-east of
England they saved Diserth and Dyganwy, and there they
waited in vain for further help to come from Ireland.
Llywelyn's men attacked them ceaselessly and with such
resolution that they had to retreat ignominiously to Chester,
having gained almost nothing.

Why did no help come from Ireland? Was it prevented by
Llywelyn's preparations? Maurice Powicke says this about
his methods, — which included the use of small naval forces:

> 'His energy was informed by intelligence. In this war he had bodies
> of heavily armed horse-soldiers to supplement his footmen, used siege-
> engines, and protected the Welsh coasts against possible inroads from
> Ireland or elsewhere by the collection of a small fleet.'

Llywelyn was now at the apex of his strength, and after
conquering the south of Powys, he made a truce with the
king which was to last for two years. With all the princes on
his side, except Gruffudd ap Gwenwynwyn, he arranged for
them to pay homage to him as 'Prince of Wales'. Twelve
centuries had passed since Ostorius and his legion had
1258   invaded Wales but this was the first time for anyone
to hold that title. According to Maurice Powicke:

'His assumption in 1258 of the title 'Prince of Wales' was more than a gesture; it was both the answer to a challenge and a declaration of purpose.'

It gave him an authority that he did not hesitate to use; for example, when the king succeeded in weaning Maredudd ap Rhys away from him, the Welsh lord was heavily punished by Llywelyn and his allies, and more than once:

'He was to find too late,' says J. E. Lloyd, 'that the vengeance of Llywelyn had not exhausted the means of punishing the betrayer of the common cause.'

The Prince of Wales now searched for allies outside Wales:

'allying himself,' says Lloyd, 'with the national party in Scotland.'

On March 18 Earl Monteith placed a document in the hands of Gwion of Bangor, Llywelyn's messenger:

'in which they bound themselves to make no separate peace with the king of England, to give him no aid against the Welsh and to encourage trade intercourse between Scotland and Wales.'

In September of the same year a number of Welsh princes, who had convened in Emlyn, agreed to meet to hold discussion with the Norman lord of Cydweli who was in Aberteifi with a strong army. This man turned his army suddenly and traiterously against them. In the ensuing battle he was defeated and killed.

On May 28, 1259, Llywelyn showed his strength by placing Maredudd ap Rhys on trial in Arwystli before his fellow princes, who condemned him to prison for treachery. Around Christmas Llywelyn released him on Maredudd's swearing an oath of obedience to him. We see in these events Wales's progress towards a form of federalism, with a strong central power for the whole country, and considerable state autonomy:

1259

'In their own small way,' says Jones-Pierce, 'the Llywelyns deserve to rank among the European state builders of the thirteenth century, and they demonstrated in their achievements that all the pre-conditions of normal political growth existed in medieval Wales.'

In 1260 Llywelyn or his allies had successes in places as far
apart as Dinbych-y-Pysgod (Tenby), Trefyclo (Knighton)
Llanfair ym Muallt (Builth). It was this last victory
1260   which prompted the king to write from Paris to his
barons pressing them to concentrate on the Welsh
question. It was clear that Wales was as strong as it had been
in the days of Llywelyn Fawr, so that yet again it became the
target for English military power. The armed forces of
England were again assembled in two armies, one in Chester
and the other in Shrewsbury. But there was too little
zeal among the barons for war. Consequently an agreement
was made at Montgomery between Llywelyn's commissioners
and those of the king to extend the truce of 1258 for another
two years.

Llewelyn used this time to attack those Marcher lords who
supported the king. He took Elfael and Buallt (Builth) in
1260, and then in 1262 Brecon and Maeliennydd. This was
a great year for the Prince of Wales. The Welsh of
the marches had risen on his side. His authority
reached almost to Abergavenny now, although he
1263   he failed to take that lordship in 1263, and therefore
failed to conquer Gwent. Even so the king had to
gather his forces in Ludlow and Hereford to counter the
attacks of the Welsh; and an army was led by Edward, Henry
III's son, on a rather futile march to north-east Wales, a
humiliating experience he would remember as Edward I.
In that same year, when Gruffudd ap Gwenwynwyn also
capitulated, Llywelyn co-operated openly with Simon de
Montfort, the French-born noble who is a popular hero of
the struggle for English liberty. Simon took over the government of England in the following year after his victory in the
Battle of Lewes which delivered the king and Prince Edward
into his hands, and he summoned in January 1265, the first
English Parliament at Westminster.

De Montfort's greatest problem was that the king's supporters among the Marcher lords had escaped without great
losses in Lewes. Because he feared the strength of these powerful
nobles, who were old enemies of the Welsh, he made a formal

Harlech Castle

Wales 1267: *the Montgomery Treaty*

from "*A Historical Atlas of Wales*" with permission of Professor William Rees and Faber & F

Carrying the head of Llywelyn II through London

Owain Glyndwr's Parliament House, Machynlleth

Llywelyn II Memorial Stone at Cilmeri

treaty with Llywelyn in order to reinforce him. Edward's escape from prison made the position of de Montfort critical. With his army he found sanctuary in Wales for a while, but they found it hard to survive on the light rations of the native Welsh. They had to confront Edward and his army, and at Evesham de Montfort's career came to an end.

This battle, having disposed of de Montfort, drew the lords of the Marches together with the crown in an united opposition against Llywelyn. In time this would prove too much for him. However, it is clear that this did not bother him unduly at once for he took Penarlag (Hawarden) ten days later and defeated the army that came to fight against him. The fighting continued until 1266, but Llywelyn was the victor finally. Mortimer, the most powerful of the Marcher lords, was defeated with great slaughter when he tried to recapture Brycheiniog (Brecknock). The failure of de Montfort had hardly affected the power of the Welsh prince.

This state of affairs was recognised in the Treaty of Montgomery, which was drawn up between the 1267 Welsh and the government of England in 1267 when Llywelyn's career was at its height. On the one hand he paid formal homage to the king, and on the other the English crown recognised his right, and that of his heir, to the title of Prince of Wales. The crown accepted his political and territorial rights almost as completely as Simon de Monfort had done in 1265. Two hundred years after the first Norman invasion, and twelve centuries after the Romans had invaded Anglesey and destroyed the druids there, Wales had a political order that was strong enough to uphold and defend its national civilisation against the overbearing power of the big state of the Normans and the English.

The type of order that continued to develop over the next ten years in Wales — including a happy relationship between church and state — would have matured further had the nation been left alone to live her own life. Llywelyn paid particular attention to those parts where he was weakest. Concentrating on the east of the country, he built the castle of Dolforwyn

not far from Montgomery, and created the township of
Abermule nearby, where an administrative centre for the
whole of Wales could be established. He tried, but failed to
dethrone the Clare family in the south-east in order to unite
the whole country in freedom. But because his authority did
extend to Senghennydd, six miles north of Cardiff. Earl
Gilbert of Gloucester, lord of Morgannwg, was compelled
to build Caerffili castle in 1268 to defend the lordship
of Morgannwg against him. Gilbert had been in
1268   conflict with him for many years. Llywelyn had the
support of all the local Welsh lords. It was because of his
support for the Prince of Wales that Gruffydd ap Rhys, the
last of the Welsh lords of Senghennydd, was sent as prisoner
to Ireland. About this time Llywelyn defeated the knights of
Morgannwg.

In 1270 he destroyed Caerffili castle, which was then
1270   rebuilt by Gilbert as the biggest castle in Britain after
Windsor. It was the undertaking given by the
bishops of Gloucestèr and Worcester that the castle would
be presented to the king that alone prevented him from
destroying it a second time. The promise was not kept.
Llywelyn was worsted in Carmarthen too: the castle was lost,
and the town, with its 181 English burghers, slid out of his
grasp and returned to its former position as the centre of
royal power.

He maintained a fairly satisfactory relationship with the
Church, although it kept its right to judge and chastise the
prince, as seen in the actions of Anian of Bangor, and Anian
of St. Asaph. The Bishop of Bangor was a scholarly man, a
descendant of the princes, who was to fight for the rights of
his see against Edward with the same determination in the
future as he had shown against Llywelyn. Llywelyn had the
enthusiastic support of the heads of the religious Orders. His
lawyers became increasingly active, and poets and writers
continued to enrich the literature which was, says Trevelyan:

'destined in our own day to save Welsh intellect and idealism from
perishing in the swamp of modern vulgarity.'

He had a good working relationship with the lords of the free Wales, except for Gruffudd ap Gwenwynwyn of Powys and Maredudd ap Rhys of Dinefwr — both of whom had to pay homage for a period — and of course his brother Dafydd who was to succeed him for a short time as Dafydd III.

It was at this time that Llywelyn sent a letter to Edward, who ascended the throne in 1272, outlining the kind of relationship he wished to see between Wales and England, and declaring his faith in a confederal system:

> 'According to every just principle we should enjoy our Welsh laws and customs like the other nations of the king's empire, and in our own language.'

Within Wales an internal system similar to the Swiss order had begun to emerge. In its external relationship with England the order that developed was similar to that recognised in the Statute of Westminster in 1926 between England and her dominions. Inside his country, a federation; outside, a confederation of free and equal states: this was the essence of the Welsh statesman's constitutional vision.

Instead of encouraging a development in that direction, Edward used the huge power of England to destroy the Welsh political framework. He himself was one of the big lords of the Marches; he was indebted to his fellow lords for saving him from Simon de Montfort, and he had been humiliated militarily by Llywelyn. Maurice Powicke says of the 1256 attack:

> 'Edward had been humiliated. Llywelyn had overrun his lands in North Wales and devastated his lordships in the south. Every attempt to organise a Welsh campaign had failed.'

Llywelyn could not therefore expect the friendship of Edward, nor any help against the Marcher Lords. When the coronation ceremony was held in August 1274, after Edward's return from the Crusade, Llywelyn was absent, although he had sent representatives to discuss the situation with Edward. But what led to the war of 1276 was the treachery of Dafydd his brother and Gruffudd ap Gwenwynwyn.

1274

Dafydd was angered by what he considered to be a gross violation of Welsh law. He and Gruffudd plotted together to try and kill Llywelyn. When the conspiracy came to light Gruffudd was given a trial and treated with clemency. Dafydd fled to England to escape trial and was soon followed by Gruffudd. When Edward asked Llywelyn to come and pay him homage, Llywelyn refused on the grounds that the king was giving sanctuary to his enemies, and that it would be dangerous for him to come; and also that Edward was guilty of breaking the Montgomery Agreement about the border lands. Five times he was commanded to come, and five times he refused. He put his case fully before Pope Gregory X, affirming that he would be willing to go and pay homage in a safe place such as Oswestry or Montgomery. English historians, and some Welshmen, say that Edward behaved correctly and even gently, and that Llywelyn was stubborn and rash;

'Puffed up by the panegyrics of bards and ministers who revelled in his bounty.'

Edward's attitude can be interpreted in a different way, as an attempt to provoke Llywelyn to take some action which would be an excuse for attacking him. If it was Edward's ambition to conquer Wales and Scotland, this would be the most reasonable interpretation, and no degree of submission on Llywelyn's part from partial to total would have made any difference.

Two factors aggravated the situation further: Llywelyn's marriage by proxy to Eleanor, the daughter of Simon de Montfort, about Christmas time 1275; and the action of the king in snatching her off a ship near the Scilly Isles when she was on her way from France to Gwynedd. The new king seemed determined on war. At the end of 1275 Edward began to make unusually big preparations to conquer Llywelyn, who now lacked much of the aid that he could have expected in Wales because his political and taxation policy had alienated support. The armies that the king collected at great expense at Chester, Montgomery and Carmarthen, were the largest and best equipped since the Conquest of

1066. In addition he had all the mighty Marcher lords behind him: all this to conquer Gwynedd with its population of hardly more than that of Anglesey today. From 1276 until the summer of 1277 these armies from the north-east occupied Powys Fadog and Powys Wenwynwyn and Ceri, Builth and Gwerthrynion. From the south-west the king's authority was restored in Ystrad Tywi and Ceredigion.

Edward joined personally in the campaign of 1277. A navy from the Cinque Ports attacked Anglesey and 1277 destroyed the harvest there. On November 9 Llywelyn had to yield and agree, in Conwy, to the degrading terms which left him only Gwynedd Uwch Conwy, and the homage of only four of the minor princes in Edeyrnion and Meirionnydd. This conquest brought great fame to Edward. Charles Oman says:

'Edward was a remarkable figure. He was a great soldier and his conquest of Wales forms one of the most notable achievements in medieval history.'

The king took advantage of his victory to strengthen his position throughout Deheubarth where he established his power in the lands which had previously been the property of the sons of the Lord Rhys.

For four years after that Llywelyn, although often provoked to anger, cleverly evaded every opportunity that the king could use as an excuse for attacking him. A. J. Roderick quotes, from a description in one of the Mostyn manuscripts, the attitude of the English of London to him and his noblemen when they visited Edward in London at the end of 1277:

'They were still more offended at the crowds of people who flocked about them when they stirred abroad, staring at them as if they had been monsters and laughing at their uncouth garb and appearance: they were so enraged on this occasion that they engaged privately in an association to rebel at the first opportunity, and resolved to die in their own country rather than ever come again to London, as subjects, to be held in such derision.'

In 1278 Edward decided to release Eleanor de Montfort
from captivity, and she and Llywelyn had an
1278 ostentatious wedding in Worcester Cathedral on the
13th of October in the presence of the king and the
queen. Obviously, Eleanor's connection with the royal family
explained the presence of Edward, as well as his desire to be
reconciled with the last of the supporters of de Montfort.
Apart from being the daughter of de Montfort, Eleanor was
also the niece of Henry III and Edward's cousin.

The peace treaty which Llywelyn made in October 1281
with his old enemy Roger Mortimer, who was perhaps
1281 the strongest of the Marcher lords, suggests that he
did not intend to try and recover his lost lands. On
the other hand his just complaints of harsh mistreatment,
which the king chose to ignore, strongly suggest that Edward
was still following a policy of trying to goad him to act in
a way that would give the crown reason to delete his state.
The most important of Llywelyn's just complaints concerned
his disagreement with Gruffudd ap Gwenwynwyn about
Arwystli. This matter was not finally dealt with for three
years, and Conway Davies's and A. H. Williams's analysis of
the case shows that Edward's decision was completely unjust.
The case centred on the terms of the Aberconwy Agreement,
where it was clear that the king should arrive at a decision
according to Welsh Law. Conway Davies says:

'He, Edward, was untrue to the promise made to Llywelyn ap
Gruffudd. He did not follow his own previous performance. He set at
naught all precedents of his own and his predecessors' time. He
knowingly misinterpreted the evidence collected by his own political
commission. He disregarded all Welsh and Marcher practices. He gave
a perverse and knowingly false interpretation to a vital clause in a
treaty but a little more than three years old. His mind had been made up
before he caused the rolls of his predecessors to be searched, and before
the commission of enquiry was sent on its fruitless errand. For Gruffudd
ap Gwenwynwyn had foretold Edward I's intentions as early as
December, 1279, before the Hopton Commission.'

It was Dafydd his brother and not Llywelyn who kindled
the last fire. He too had supported the king up till now, but

he could not stomach the many injustices which were suffered
at his hands. On Palm Sunday 1282, he captured
1282   Hawarden castle; and then Rhuthun, Hope and
Dinas Brân. A Welsh '*senedd*' which was held in
Dinbych decided in favour of war. Immediately all Wales
blazed into action. The southern lords captured Aberystwyth,
Llandovery and Carreg Cennen. The war spread throughout
most of mid-Wales, although there was scant loyalty for the
Welsh cause in Powys Gwenwynwyn:

> 'The lord of South Powys at Pool,' says Powicke, 'had become a
> baron of the king, more English in sentiment than his neighbours.'

Llywelyn may have had nothing to do with all this, but as
Prince of Wales he could not ignore it. At a time of great
personal grief when his wife Eleanor had just died on the
birth of their baby, Gwenllian, he nevertheless pulled himself
away from Gwynedd and rode into the military storm.

This was a golden opportunity for Edward to destroy
Welsh independence. He acted with great energy, spending
twice as much as he had done on his big forces in 1277, quite
apart from the enormous cost of his magnificent castles. He
assembled ten thousand soldiers around him in Rhuddlan,
including a thousand Welsh archers. He collected a navy of
sixty ships from the Cinque Ports with hundreds of archers on
board on the river Dyfrdwy (Dee). Another navy moved from
Bristol with a great number of men and resources. Other
armies met in the Clwyd and Dyfrdwy valleys. Perfeddwlad
was occupied, and divided between three of the Marcher
lords who were friends of Edward's and who had helped him
to conquer it. Only one Welsh lord was left in authority
there: Gruffudd, lord of Glyndyfrdwy, an ancestor of Owain
Glyndŵr.

Nevertheless, the Norman armies did not get it all their
own way. A host under the leadership of the Earl of Gloucester
was defeated near Llandeilo on the 16th of June, and an
army from Anglesey was destroyed on the banks of the Menai
on the 6th of November forcing Edward to fall back from the
Conwy to the Clwyd line to winter at Rhuddlan. He called

for reinforcements. More men came from the English shires
and fifteen hundred horsemen and professional crossbowmen
from Gascony. In the meantime Archbishop Peckham tried
to make peace between Llywelyn and Edward. Powicke says
of this:

> 'Llywelyn consented to submit himself to the royal will, saving his
> responsibility to his people and his dignity as a Prince. The archbishop
> returned to report to the king. The king replied that he would have no
> treaty with the prince and the Welsh unless they submitted themselves
> entirely to his will.'

The archbishop returned to Llywelyn with the king's proposals.
They were completely unacceptable. They demanded complete
and unconditional surrender from Llywelyn, who would then
be allowed to leave Wales and live in England as Earl on land
that the king would give him in exchange for his yielding
Eryri (Snowdonia) to Edward. The Prince and his council
would have none of this. Powicke says:

> 'Llywelyn in a brief and dignified letter, dismissed the 'form' of
> submission as neither safe nor honourable and said that it had been
> heard with astonishment by all in council. No subjects of his, noble or
> freeman, would allow him, even if he wished, to consent to it. He
> beseeched the archbishop to continue his arduous labours in the cause
> of peace.'

Powicke comments further on the answer given by the Welsh
to the king:

> 'The reply of the Welsh was based on appeal to history and right . . .
> They repudiated the English offer of lands in England, for it came from
> men set on the Prince's disinheritance, so that they might have his
> lands in Wales. They would in no case recognise the exchange of
> Snowdon for land in England, a bargain which would require them to
> do homage to a stranger, of whose speech, manners and laws they were
> entirely ignorant.'

A few weeks after sending this letter, at a time when the Welsh
were getting the best of the war, Llywelyn's life came to an
abrupt and frightening end. He was killed on the banks of the
Irfon, near Llanfair ym Muallt (Builth). What was he doing in
such a dangerous place, so far from Gwynedd which was

surrounded by the armies and navies of Edward, unless he had been enticed there by some clever conspiracy? According to the letters of Archbishop Peckham, a document was found on his body, referring to invitations to go there from the Marcher lords. He was related to the powerful Mortimer family by marriage; perhaps the sons of that family had co-operated in the conspiracy. Very conveniently, the original document disappeared, and also the copy sent to the chancellor by the Archbishop.

However, his enemies were waiting for him when Llywelyn came to Cilmeri on December 12, 1282. The Prince stood with eighteen of his men by the Irfon bridge. These 1282 eighteen could have defended the bridge adequately against horse soldiers, even though they were there in number; but they were confronted by long-bow archers placed among the cavalry — the first time for this type of fighting to be used — and it was these who overcame the eighteen. Llywelyn escaped, but when he was on his way to join his retinue on the land above the river, a horseman, Stephen de Franckton, galloped up to him and ignorant of his identity sent his spear through his body. While Llywelyn lay on the ground fatally wounded, the Norman army attacked his leaderless retinue from the fore and the rear on Llanganten field, and like the eighteen at the bridge, the flower of Wales's freedom army fell under showers from the long bows.

Later on Llywelyn was found still alive. According to Archbishop Peckham he asked many times for a priest, but was not brought one. As T. D. Williams has shown, the Waverley Chronicle records that the wounded Llywelyn was taken prisoner by Edward Mortimer and executed on the spot. Thus, in pain and alone, surrounded by malicious enemies the life of the nation's main hope came to an end, in circumstances which were those of an assassination rather than a battle. For over a quarter of a century this brave cultured man had led his people with extraordinary skill. He was destined to face a Goliath of a country, many times larger than his own, which was finally able to trample him down. We know now that his life was lived to great purpose:

'It was for a far distant generation to see,' says J. E. Lloyd, 'that the last Prince had not lived in vain, but by his life work had helped to build solidly the enduring fabric of Welsh nationality.'

The war continued against Prince Dafydd for another seven months. Despite the vast armaments arrayed against the Welsh, Dafydd's attractive personality and ability as a soldier enabled him to retain the loyalty of his people throughout the winter and spring. The forces which Edward had mobilised were directed against his fortress at Dolwyddelan. Edward took no chances, for he had great respect for Dafydd's military prowess. His forces made no attempt to cross the Conwy estuary but followed the river up to Dolwyddelan, which was captured at the end of January. By then Dafydd had moved elsewhere, probably to Dolbadarn, but in March he and his court surprisingly moved to the beauty of the Dysynni valley in south Merioneth under the glorious slopes of Cader Idris, where for a month they made their headquarters at Castell y Bere, built by Llywelyn Fawr. Before an army of four thousand under William de Valence had reached there, Dafydd had returned to Dolbadarn. Castell y Bere was captured on 25th April. In the meantime an army containing a body of Basque mercenaries had crossed the Lower Conwy valley, and other forces entered Arfon from Anglesey, where they had been inspired by Edward's delivery of Llywelyn's severed head, and made their way down to Harlech, completing the encirclement of Eryri (Snowdonia). At Dolbadarn on 2nd May, Dafydd signed himself on two documents as 'Prince of Wales'. Both concerned the recruitment of men to fight for him, one involving a part of Ceredigion and the other the Builth and Brecon areas. These documents, which were drawn up by the loyal Gronw ap Heulyn, Dafydd's seneschal, were witnessed by a number of his most prominent leaders. In June, however, some of his men surrendered, and as a condition of pardon, they were sent back to take Prince Dafydd prisoner. On 28th June, Edward was able to proclaim his capture. After two hundred years of struggle the French-speaking Normans had completed their last European conquest.

Dafydd was taken to Shrewsbury where a senate met at Michaelmas under the direction of the Chief Justice of England to consider what should be done about Wales. Advantage was taken of the situation to teach the little conquered nation the nature of the higher civilisation it should in future have to bow to. On 3rd October, 1283, in the town of Shrewsbury, in cold blood, Prince Dafydd III was dragged by horses tails' through the streets to the gallows; and there disembowelled before he died, and then hanged, drawn and quartered. The north and the south of England competed for his right shoulder. In four large English towns a quarter of his body was exhibited: the people of London had the pleasure of seeing his head exhibited from the Tower beside that of Llywelyn his brother, which had been sent there from Anglesey. It was a day of great merriment in London when Edward sent the head of the Prince on a pole through the streets of the capital, having set a crown of ivy on it, and accompanied by the sound of horns and trumpets. One can imagine how the crowds laughed at Llywelyn and his brother, 'staring at them as if they had been monsters', as they had done in 1277. Clearly, the people who had conquered the Welsh were men of superior culture and intellect.

> A dacw ben ar bicell, a rhawn meirch
> Yn llusgo yn llwch Amwythig tu ôl i'w seirch
> Gorff anafus yr ôl "eiddila" o'i lin.'
>
> And there's a head on a pike, and the tails of horses
> dragging through Shrewsbury's dust behind their trappings
> the broken body of the "weakest" remnant of his line.

The Welsh realised the enormity of the catastrophe. Gruffydd ap yr Ynad Coch gave moving expression to their feelings in a poem called by Gwyn Williams:

> 'One of the most splendid utterances in Western European literature . . . moving . . . to a tremendous climax in which the Poet's whole world comes to an end, and in which, as in the tragedies of Shakespeare, nature and the order of the universe seems to be imperilled by the disaster.'

Oni welwch chwi hynt y gwynt a'r glaw?
Oni welwch chwi'r deri'n ymdaraw?
Oni welwch chwi'r môr yn merwinaw'r tir?
Oni welwch chwi'r gwir yn ymgyweiriaw?
Oni welwch chwi'r haul yn hwyliaw'r awyr?
Oni welwch chwi'r sŷr wedi syrthiaw?
Oni chredwch i Dduw, ddyniadon ynfyd?
Oni welwch chwi'r byd wedi bydiaw?
Och hyd atad Dduw, na ddaw môr dros dir!
Pa beth y'n gedir i ohiriaw?

See you not the way of the wind and the rain?
See you not the oaks strike each other?
See you not the sea stinging the land?
See you not the truth is preparing?
See you not the sun sailing the sky?
See you not the stars have fallen?
Do you not believe in God, demented men?
See you not the world has ended?
A sigh to you, God, for the sea to come over the land!
What is left to us that we should tarry?

The Centuries of Glyndŵr and the Uchelwyr (Nobility)

I. THE RULE OF THE ENGLISH OFFICIALS

MANY nations, perhaps the majority, have their heroic age, when a large proportion of their people is ready to live and sacrifice and even die for the sake of the whole society. Usually this is a short period, similar to that of Urien's generation among the Men of the Old North, or the age of Alfred in Wessex. Wales saw more than one heroic age, and each stretched over generations; this is the explanation for the almost miraculous continuation of its tradition and language. This is the kind of age that came to an end in 1283.

It is obvious that the death of Llywelyn II and Dafydd III, which ended the 200 year war against the Norman-English, marked the end of a chapter in the history of the nation, but it would be a mistake to see in it any more than that, as a book on British history did when it came to Edward I: 'The history of Wales', it said 'now comes to an end.' The loss which Wales sustained was very serious indeed, but it was far from being fatal. What it lost was its freedom. From now on it would be a nation without a state: that is, a nation that could not shape the conditions of its own life; a nation at the mercy of external events. Of course medieval states are not to be compared in power and importance with the all-powerful modern states. Their powers and functions were very limited. Only in the twentieth century has the state grown so dangerously powerful that it can kill a small nation simply by ignoring it. Nevertheless,

to be without her own government made Wales terribly
vulnerable.

    What Edward did, by means of the Rhuddlan Statute
of 1284, was to turn the whole country into a March.

1284   He kept three parts of the land under his own personal
control, namely, the principalities of the North and
South, and Flintshire, although it was only the lands which
were in Llywelyn's personal possession which came into his
hands. He left the old marcher lordships alone, but added to
their number, — in Perfeddwlad, for example. In the Prince-
dom of the North, the old Gwynedd uwch Conwy, he
established the sort of county control which had already
been in existence for four years in the Carmarthen and
Cardigan areas, by creating the counties of Anglesey,
Caernarfon and Merioneth. These were in reality royal
lordships within a system that was a continuation of Llywelyn's
principality.

    Wales remained, for all this, a country of small states as it
had always been, quite distinct from the civil, county and
legal system of England; and almost completely independent
of London. Goronwy Edwards says of the Norman lordships:

    'Historically the marcher lordships had been erected by their Norman
founders on the basis of Welsh lordships which had previously been
held by Welsh 'princes' of the traditional type . . . if one may adapt a
famous sentence of Thomas Hobbes, the Norman lords of the March
were the ghosts of Welsh princes, sitting crowned upon the graves
thereof.'

Inside the principalities and the counties we got a pattern of
courts, and an administrative system quite similar to that
which had developed under the princes, with the *cantref*
and commote as a unit. The Laws of Hywel were retained in
every civil action but not in criminal cases, and no further
development of them was allowed.

    The great difference in the situation was that all the main
offices were filled by Englishmen. All the lords were Normans,
apart from Gruffudd ap Gwenwynwyn of Powys, and Rhys
ap Maredudd of Dinefwr, who were both allowed to remain

because of their faithfulness to the king. Furthermore, the English had the monopoly of business in the boroughs which now arose around the costly great castles built by Edward to safeguard the order with force. Every town was a little England. David Fraser says:

'More than anything else their job was to defend the king's assets on foreign soil. This is clearly seen by looking at them. In Conwy, Caernarfon and Beaumaris a wall of defence was built around the town, almost entirely at the king's expense. A convenient quay was provided for each of the three towns. And the constable of the castle was, without exception, also mayor of the town and captain of the guard. No Welshman was allowed to live in the English towns nor bear arms in them. This also applied in Flint, Rhuddlan, Conwy, Beaumaris and Caernarfon. No bard was welcome in these towns either. The English suspected that the poets were spies and believed that their poems urged the Welsh to rebel. In the boroughs too, as in the castles, there were porters to take care of the gate and a guard to watch the walls.'

These English were a foreign and inflammatory element in the body of Wales. They quickly became very unpopular and the unpopularity tended to increase rather than diminish. The hatred of the Welsh for them was far more bitter in 1484 than it had been in 1284.

> Lle bu'r Brython Saeson sydd
> A'r boen ar Gymru beunydd.
>
> Where once were Britons, English now
> give the Welsh daily pain.

It is difficult to say which order is the more unbearable: English control within Wales, or, as we have today, English control from faraway London. But by asking this question we are guilty of a Welsh prejudice, which is improper when discussing the history of Wales. An attempt must be made to consider the matter impartially from Edward's point of view. If he were to administer his policy he had no choice but to fill the posts and towns with Englishmen. And his policy? 'At bottom,' says Tout, 'Edward's real policy was to make Welshmen Englishmen as soon as possible.'

II. THE WARS OF MADOG AND
LLYWELYN BREN

Two things became obvious very quickly; first of all, that
Edward's order was unacceptable, and secondly, that the
Welsh were uncowed. The first leaders to rebel were two who
became disillusioned with the system which they themselves
had helped to create. Rhys ap Maredudd had been the only
Welsh prince in the south ro remain subservient, or from the
English standpoint loyal to the king. After a wrong
1287   done to him by the new Justice of the principality of
the south, it was he who rose in rebellion in
the summer of 1287. He captured his old home in Dinefwr,
and then Carreg Cennen on its defiant rock, and Llandovery.
He attacked Carmarthen, and Llanbadarn fifty miles to
the North. Armies from England were called in against him,
as many as twenty thousand soldiers. For six weeks the two
sides fought in Dryslwyn, which was besieged for three
weeks by twelve thousand men, and Newcastle Emlyn
and Cardigan. Rhys was driven to the mountains, caught
four years later, and executed with the same cruelty his
enemies had shown to Dafydd III.

There broke out, three years later, a much more general
rebellion which bore the mark of careful planning. The Welsh
conspired, in different parts of the country, to rise
1294   together while the king was in France. When they
did so however, Edward was still in Portsmouth
with a big army waiting fora fair wind to sail for France.
The great Welsh misfortune in this well-planned rising was
the absence of a wind to take Edward and his army out of
England. Before the wind rose news came that the Welsh had
taken to arms. Madog was their leader in Gwynedd, Maelgwn
in Ceredigion, Cynan in Brycheiniog and Morgan in Morgannwg. It was a national insurrection. In one day there
were attacks on castles as far apart as Caernarfon and Denbigh, Castell y Bere, Cardigan and Builth. Caernarfon was
captured; the sheriff of Anglesey was killed; de Lacy and his

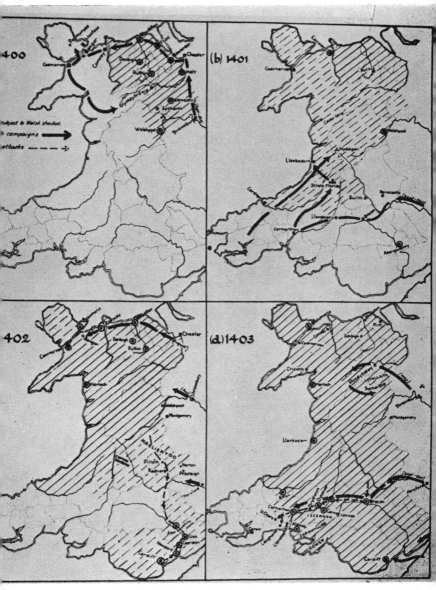

Owain Glyndwr War 1400–1403

from *"A Historical Atlas of Wales"* with permission of Professor William Rees and Faber & Faber

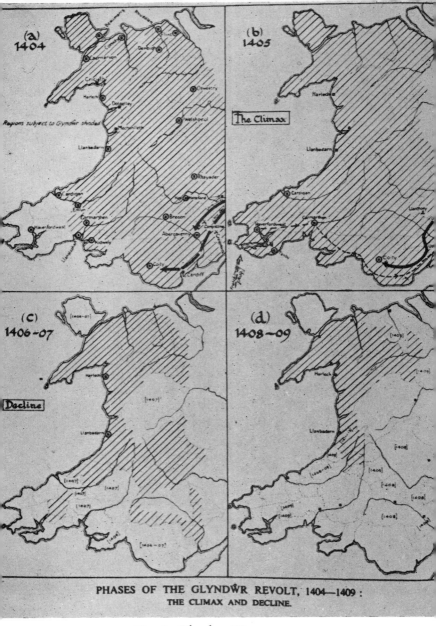

(a) 1404

Regions subject to Glyndwr shaded

(b) 1405 — The Climax

(c) 1406–07 — Decline

(d) 1408–09

PHASES OF THE GLYNDŴR REVOLT, 1404—1409:
THE CLIMAX AND DECLINE.

Owain Glyndwr War 1404-1409
from "A Historical Atlas of Wales" with permission of Professor William Rees and Faber & F

William Wallace

Owain Glyndwr

Copyright Alcwyn Deiniol with permission of City Hall, Cardiff

army were defeated in the vale of Clwyd, and a large part of the countryside was occupied. Madog, who had been in favour with the king's court in the days of Llywelyn II, announced that he was now Prince of Wales. This pattern was repeated in the other provinces. The Welsh of Morgannwg and Brycheiniog attacked castles and destroyed manors; in Ceredigion there was the same type of powerful attacking, and Cardigan was taken. No one can surmise what would have happened had the king reached France before they had taken the field.

Once again the King of England had to lead his forces to Wales to reconquer it. Edward reached Conwy by Christmas, and there he was caught for weeks between the tide of the Conwy and the wrath of the Welsh. Unfortunately for Madog, he could not afford to spend too much time besieging the English army. He had to try to find support in Powys. He was on his way through Montgomery when the Earl of Warwick suddenly attacked him near Caereinion and defeated him with very great losses by using the method of setting long-bow archers among the horse-soldiers which had been deployed against Llywelyn II at Cilmeri and Llanganten. The government of England had great enough reserves of wealth to be able to hire the men of Gwent and Morgannwg in their thousands to break the back of the resistance in their own small country before conquering the French on the battle fields of Crecy, Poitiers and Agincourt. After the Caereinion victory Edward had an easier time on his march through Anglesey, Arfon and Ceredigion, Ystrad Tywi, Brycheiniog and Morgannwg. Cynan and Morgan were caught and executed. The war was over.

Within six years, in order to win the loyalty of the Welsh for the English crown, Edward was supple enough
1301 to recognise the separateness of Wales by giving the most honourable title of Prince of Wales to his eldest son in an investiture in Lincoln in 1301.

Although the next rebellion was confined almost completely to Morgannwg, it showed that the Welsh had not lost their self-respect even in those parts where the Normans were most powerful. We are reminded by the rising of Llywelyn Bren, a cultured, dignified nobleman, that a great deal of the higher lands and valleys of Morgannwg were still under the control of Welsh lords. It was the arrogance of de Turberville, lord of Morgannwg, which inspired Llywelyn and his five sons to rise in rebellion. Thousands of the Welsh of the Blaenau joined him. John Odyn, a burgess and former reeve of Cardiff, brought him corn, wine and foodstuffs through the English lines. He plundered the vale of Glamorgan and attacked Cardiff, Caerleon, Kenfig and Llantrisant but failed to capture the enormous castle of Caerffili, in spite of besieging it for nine weeks. This was his undoing. Edward II sent two armies against him. Llywelyn Bren saw that he could not hope to withstand them. He spoke with great dignity when forced

1318 at Ystradfellte to surrender unconditionally: 'It is better for one man to die than for a whole population to be killed by the sword.' In 1318 he had the same terrible end as Dafydd III had had a quarter of a century earlier, but his followers were treated with clemency because the Welsh were needed to fight against the Scots. .

These powerful rebellions led to the completion of the costly new castle-building programmes on which Edward I and his barons had embarked in the 70's of the previous century. Wales has more castles per thousand square miles than any country in Europe. Always built for strictly utilitarian, military purposes, scores of them are artistic works of great beauty. All of them deepen Welshmen's sense of the long continuity of life in Wales.

III. THE REVIVAL OF SCOTLAND UNDER WILLIAM WALLACE

No DOUBT Madog's war had been of help to the Scots, who rose in rebellion under William Wallace two years later. Wallace, who came from Paisley, was probably descended from the British of the Welsh-speaking kingdom of Ystrad

Clud (Strathclyde). His name, which was sometimes spelt Walays or Walyes, was the term usually used by Englishmen for a Welshman or a Celt. He inspired the Scots, or 1297 succeeded, as an English chronicler put it, in 'reviving the malice of that perfidious race'. The Scots under his leadership overcame the English in Stirling, and sent them out of the country in confusion. Before the 1298 battle two English ambassadors came to Wallace. He sent them away with the words, 'We Scots did not come here to discuss terms, but to fight to set Scotland free.' Edward was compelled to go personally to 1305 Scotland as he had often been to Wales to try to reconquer the country. He succeeded in winning a victory in Falkirk with the help of Welsh long-bow archers — ten thousand Welshmen are said to have taken part in the campaign — but the Scots continued to resist. In 1305 Wallace was betrayed and taken prisoner to London where he was accused of treason. His simple answer was that he could not betray the king of England since he had never been a subject of his. In spite of this he was killed in the same way as Dafydd III.

With Scotland to all appearances subdued by Edward, who took the Stone of Scone to Westminster, the Scots rose again, under the leadership of Robert Bruce this time. 1306 Edward had to face the necessity of reconquering Scotland for the third time, but he died in 1307 near Carlisle (Caerliwelydd), capital of the old kingdom of Rheged. Bruce succeeded in the meantime in winning powerful 1314 support, and at Bannockburn in 1314 he won a sweeping victory in which a considerable number of the Norman aristocracy were killed. The Scots made a noble statement in 1320 which would be just as applicable to Welsh patriots:

> 'We are fighting, not for glory or riches or honour, but completely and only for freedom, which no true man will yield without surrendering his life as well. We wish for no more than that which is ours already, nor any territory beyond our own borders, and we are ready to do everything within our power to secure peace.'

In Switzerland at this time a fairly similar political development may be traced. In 1291 three cantons united in the mountains to free themselves of the overlordship of the Hapsburgs. This is the foundation of the Swiss confederation. By now there are twenty-two cantons there, some of which have less population than Anglesey, but every one enjoying parliamentary self-government. In 1921, the population of Switzerland was only about a million more than that of Wales; yet the Welsh are expected to believe that their rich country cannot maintain one parliament like that which successfully exists in every poor, small canton. With a little more luck at the end of the thirteenth century, or the beginning of the fifteenth, Wales would now be enjoying a system and position similar to that of Switzerland.

IV. THE SPLENDOUR OF THE NOBLEMEN (UCHELWYR)

THE continuation of the Welsh tradition depended on the noblemen after the fall of the princes. These men, who were just below the princes in rank, could command the resources of culture, wealth, knowledge and time to help them fulfill their functions so well. It fell to them to promote the great cause. They knew the history of their nation; they loved its literature; they enhanced its tradition. They were used to defending their country: these noblemen belonged to an essentially military class who held their land according to Welsh law in the traditional manner. Their rights and customs continued undisturbed even after the conquest. Although most of them were debarred from office under the crown they remained the leaders and guardians of national life, which they were determined should flourish. These were no men set apart by their wealth and status. They were a vital and integral part of Welsh society, and outside the boroughs it was thoroughly Welsh in speech and character. They were the upper layer of a community composed mainly of freemen who were close to them in status. 'Nearly the whole population came of old native families', says J. E. Lloyd, 'with the roots of their culture reaching far back into the past'. This is emphasised by D. Myrddin Lloyd, who says that,

'there are only *two* classes really, *bonheddig* (gentle) and common, and throughout . . . the middle ages there is every reason to believe that the majority of our nation belonged to the 'gentle' class, and that the number of commoners decreased from age to age.'

Membership of this big class depended entirely on descent and not in any way on wealth. In three centuries many of this class would be among the *gwerin* (folk), thereby enriching its quality.

When the nobleman was a good and cultured man he was the heart and soul of the neighbourhood; he was its strongest upholder of the values of the national tradition; he gave direction to its life. In other words, the *uchelwr* (nobleman) was the leader. In spite of the strength and number of the Normans and English, and in spite of their wealth, they were foreigners who did not try to integrate themselves at this time with Welsh society. It was members of the Welsh nobility — Llywelyn Bren was a good example — who led all the military efforts to change the system up to the time of Owain Glyndŵr, who was himself an outstanding member of their class. In time more and more of them filled the administrative posts, and by the middle of the fifteenth century the mechanics of government in a large part of the country would be in their hands. Above all else they were the patrons of poetry, *Cerdd Dafod*, and music, *Cerdd Dant*. Their loyalty to their language was splendid. They supported the bards, whose influence continued to grow until the success of the Tudors. Indeed, it was from among the noble families that some of the greatest poets came: Dafydd ap Gwilym, Dafydd ap Edmwnd and Tudur Aled.

After the fall of Llywelyn II some of them, if judged by today's standards when every Welshman is expected to give his first loyalty to Wales, tried to serve two masters. Many of these practical men had been in the service of the Welsh Princes. The best known of them, but certainly not the only examples, came from the family of Ednyfed Fychan, from which the Tudors were descended. Although there was now an English king, where there had previously been a Welsh prince, some of these men kept their positions, serving their new lord with the same loyalty as the old.

Since the noblemen took upon themselves the privileged burden of acting as patrons of our culture in place of the princes, their homes also took the place of the royal courts, where poets, musicians and scholars could flourish. The poets travelled from one home to the other; they became wandering minstrels. The greatest bard to emerge from this able and influential order was Dafydd ap Gwilym.

V. DAFYDD AP GWILYM

A NUMBER of European literatures have their source in the thirteenth and fourteenth centuries. During his wanderings in exile early in the fourteenth century Dante wrote *De Vulgari Eloquentia* with the object of establishing the Italian language as a literary instrument. He argued in this work that although Italy lacked a king she was not without a court. Proclaiming in fact that the greatness of a country depends upon its authors he declared that her language was a kingdom in itself.

However severe the straits to which Wales had been reduced politically the kingdom of the Welsh language had never been as spacious as it was now. For eight centuries great stars had come into the literary firmament, none brighter than Dafydd ap Gwilym. Unlike Dante, the passion of the patriot is absent from his poems, but they do mirror some aspects of the social flexibility that arose in the fourteenth century. His poems do not reflect any of the effects of the terrible Black Plague that struck Wales in 1349, exactly eight centuries after the coming of the Yellow Fever which killed Maelgwn Gwynedd and drove Teilo away to Samson in Brittany, and which returned periodically throughout the century. Nor did his poetry reflect the political situation.

Dafydd was born in Bro Gynin, in the parish of Llanbadarn Fawr, and brought up possibly in Cryngae, Caeo, in the middle of Cantref Mawr by his uncle, Llywelyn ap Gwilym, a nobleman who held the important position of Constable of Newcastle Emlyn. Travelling through Wales he came to know many of the leaders, and in particular the chief bards of his age, such as Madog Benfras of Maelor, and Gruffudd Grŷg of Anglesey, who composed a *cywydd* to the old yew tree above Dafydd's grave after his burial in Strata Florida.

According to Thomas Parry, the authority on his work, Dafydd ap Gwilym stands alone among the bards:

'No one else has the same power, the same unfailing strength, able to convey the same surprise when looking at the world around him, the same faculty for sensing the finer things of life.'

No doubt he owed something to the Mediterranean-centred cultures, especially the troubadours of Provence, but the massive integrity of the great Welsh poetic tradition enabled it to assimilate such influences without changing course. Dafydd loved life profoundly. He celebrated life, with joy and humour. He wrote mainly of women and of nature, and he did this with perfect craftsmanship, using dramatic dialogue and startling images:

'The eternal wonder in the work of Dafydd ap Gwilym is this,' says Thomas Parry, 'however much his poetic energy overflowed — the ideas bubbling out of his head, the images wrestling for expression, each sinew at full stretch, declaring the great excellence of his beloved — he never loosens his hold on his craft, nor forgets the form and pattern of his poems.'

> Minnau, fardd rhiain feinir,
> Yn llawen iawn mewn llwyn ir,
> A'r galon fradw yn cadw cof,
> A'r enaid yn ir ynof.
> Addwyned gweled y gwŷdd,
> Gwaisg nwyf, yn dwyn gwisg newydd,
> Ac egin gwin a gwenith
> Ar ôl glaw araul a gwlith,
> A dail glas ar dâl y glyn,
> A'r draenwydd yn ir drwynwyn.

> I, the poet of a virgin girl,
> most happy in the green grove,
> the languishing heart holding a memory
> and the spirit fresh within me.
> How sweet to see the trees,
> quick vigour in a new garment,
> and the shoots of wine and wheat
> after bright rain and dew,
> and the green leaves on the hill's brow
> and the thorntree freshly tipped with white.

But Saunders Lewis finds in his work a philosophy that is entirely revolutionary to Welsh. In his *Braslun o Hanes Llenyddiaeth Gymraeg* he says:

'The Welsh literary tradition had never before faced the kind of challenge to its principles that it met in this poet.'

These principles were described by Einon Offeiriad in 1322 in his *Gramadeg*. According to these, 'nobility' and hospitality were the particular subjects of *Cerdd Dafod*, and Saunders Lewis says:

'Owen Edwards wrote a charming book on 'Welsh Homes'; did he know that this could have been a suitable title for any really noteworthy anthology of Welsh poetry?'

Many of the *cywyddau* of Dafydd ap Gwilym must be understood as a deliberate reaction against the glorification of nobility. To quote Saunders Lewis again:

'The official compositions in praise of the courts of the noblemen and the traditional poems of the Bardic schools were the greatest influence of all upon his cywyddau. It was in defiance of the glorification of these habitations that he wrote his poems in praise of uninhabited places; in defiance of the cywyddau to houses of wood and stone that he sang to houses of leaf. This clash . . . is the key to his secret . . .'

'He stands among the greatest creative writers in Welsh literature. At a time when the foundations of poetry were being changed or re-assessed, he created, in addition, a new poetic universe, different in its completeness and intentions from anything that had gone before, although he borrowed many elements from it. And this creation was a direct challenge to the gradatory, hierarchic world of Einion Offeiriad and the schools.'

The world which Dafydd created was an innocent, sensuous one, where the happiness of love and the magic of nature reveal his burning passion for life. Like the professional poets for a thousand years before him he revelled in the intricacies of the alliterative systems and internal rhyming of the cynghanedd which are meant for the ear.

> Digrif fu, fun, un ennyd
> Dwyn dan un bedwlwyn ein byd.
> Cydlwynach, difyrrach fu,
> Coed olochwyd, cydlechu,
> Cydfyhwman marian môr,
> Cydaros mewn coed oror,
> Cydblannu bedw, gwaith dedwydd,
> Cydblethu gweddeiddblu gwŷdd.
> Cydadrodd serch â'r ferch fain,
> Cydedrych caeau didrain.
> Crefft ddigerydd fydd i ferch—
> Cydgerdded coed â gordderch,
> Cadw wyneb, cydowenu,
> Cydchwerthin finfin a fu,
> Cyd-ddigwyddaw garllaw'r llwyn,
> Cydochel pobl, cydachwyn,
> Cydfod mwyn, cydyfed medd,
> Cydarwain serch, cydorwedd,
> Cyd-ddaly cariad celadwy
> Cywir, ni menegir mwy.

> O girl, it was pleasant once
> to lead our lives under a birch grove.
> Merrier still the meeting of thighs
> in a woodland retreat, to lie together,
> to wander along the seashore together,
> to stay together on a wooded slope,
> planting birchtrees together, happy work,
> reciting love with the slim girl,
> looking together at thornless garlands.
> It's a blameless craft for a girl—
> to walk the trees together with a lover,
> not to lose face but smile together,
> laugh lip to lip as we did,
> to fall to one another near the grove,

to avoid people, to complain together,
sweet agreement, to drink mead together,
to practise love, to lie together,
to cling together to hidden true
love, never to be told again.

VI. OWAIN LAWGOCH AND THE WAITING FOR A DELIVERER

DAFYDD AP GWILYM was an exception among the poets in his lack of interest in politics and in the future of the nation. Most of the bards gave valiant guidance to the nation. They kept the old ideals in front of the noblemen; they deepened the feeling of national purpose; they announced that the *Mab Darogan* (Son of prophecy) was about to come to save Wales.

After the fall of the princes' order many more Welsh people left the country as pilgrims, students, and most particularly as mercenaries. Many Welshmen found fame in France during the Hundred Years War, using the long-bow described by Giraldus as 'made of wild elm, unpolished and uncouth,' but which had terrible power. Some Welsh captains had their own companies. It is said that Hywel ap Gruffydd and Rhys ap Gruffydd had collected between them about seven thousand Welshmen to fight in the wars. Edward III took about five thousand Welshmen with him to France in 1346. It was Welsh long-bow archers who killed most of the fifteen thousand Frenchmen who fell at Crecy. In this battle the English side lost only a hundred men, and most of those were Welsh. They used the method which destroyed the retinue of Llywelyn II in Llanganten and Madog's army in Caereinion. Dressed in green and white, they were the first troops to appear on a continental battlefield in a national uniform. Even greater success was achieved in the battle of Poitiers, and, in the second part of the war in the battle of Agincourt, where the French had five times as many men as the English.

The long-bow had social repercussions of importance. It

made the *gwerinwr* as important as the knight on the battlefield; it weakened the coats of arms and castles of the lord. It helped to hasten social changes which had already begun in the time of the princes. The returning soldiers too had an influence on the thought, the customs and the literature of Wales. Although ten thousand is a small number in our terms, it meant in a population of only two hundred thousand that a quarter of all the families of the land had a member in the armed forces. These soldiers widened horizons, bringing in influences from other countries, as the saints had done eight hundred years earlier.

There were Welsh soldiers fighting on both sides in France. 'Free companies' fought on the side of the king of France. A. D. Carr says that a company of Compagnons de Galles went to Castile in 1366 to fight Pedro the Cruel. The captain of one of these companies was Owain ap Thomas ap Rhodri, known in Wales as Owain Lawgoch and on the continent as Yevain de Galles, the grandson of Llywelyn II's brother and the sole heir of the princes of Gwynedd. He was described by Edward Owen as 'possibly the greatest
1365   military genius that Wales has produced'. In him the bards saw their *Mab Darogan*. In 1365 he crossed to England, and perhaps to Wales, to claim his inheritance. On his return to France he persuaded a number of able Welshmen to join him, including Ieuan Wyn, who led Owain's company after his death.

Ieuan was somthing of a rake — he won the title Poursuivant d'Amour — but like many of the Welsh in France, popular — and well-known in Paris and in the king's court. In 1369 an Anglesey man was executed for getting into contact with 'Owain Lawgoch, enemy and traitor' with a view to starting a war in Wales. In the same year Owain was given a fleet by Charles V, and he sailed with it for
1369   Wales from Harfleur in 1369, but the ships were forced back to port by storms. In 1372 the king gave
1372   him another navy and an army of four thousand men to win back his land. He made a proclamation announcing he was claiming Wales:

'Through the power of succession, through my lineage, and through my right as the descendant of my fore-fathers, the kings of that country.'

About this Jones-Pierce says:

'(it) shows a sure grasp of his historic claims to the realm of Wales by right and descent from his ancestors, . . . Far less can we ignore the evidence of protracted and widespread official alarm in Wales during those years, and of secret preparations for rebellion if Owain had succeeded in landing on these shores; and of the posthumous appeal of his name for those Welshmen who had rested their hopes on his advent.'

The fleet sailed from Harfleur. It reached the island of Guernsey which it captured from the English; Owain's name remained alive on that island for a long time, in song and story. But while the free Wales navy was at sea, the navy of Spain was defeating the English navy near La Rochelle. Consequently there came a command from the king of France telling Owain to help the Spanish to attack La Rochelle, which was occupied by the English. He had to turn back and he never again had another chance. In 1375 he took his company of four hundred men to Switzerland to fight against the Austrians. There he became a colourful figure in the legends of Berne, but it was now too dangerous for the English government to allow him to stay alive. Before another opportunity came for Owain to complete his Welsh mission he was murdered by an Englishman, John Lamb, who was in the pay of the English government; the assassin received £200 — about £12,000 in our money today — for his atrocious act. So died the last of Rhodri Fawr's line. For years they awaited his coming in Wales, where his name, the most magic name in the consciousness of the Welsh between Llywelyn II and Owain Glyndwr, grew to legend.

VII. THE GREAT EFFORT TO RESTORE FREEDOM

APART from having a direct influence on the Welshmen who participated in them, the wars in France had a great effect on Wales because they changed the character of the imperialism it faced. Up till now it had been Norman imperialism: it was the Normans who had conquered Wales and Ireland, and had come close to conquering Scotland. The English came only in the wake of the Normans as burghers and small officials. French was the language the Normans spoke and the language of their culture. Geoffrey Barraclough says, 'It was not until the fifteenth century that a recognisable English emerged and, when it did, it bore little resemblance to Chaucer's prose'. French was the strongest language and culture that confronted all the Celtic nations in those days, including Brittany of course. But in the heat of the French wars this changed. The Normans became English; they gave a new prestige to the English language. The language of the law in England became English, which thus achieved the status which Welsh had enjoyed in Wales for a thousand years. They turned their backs on French.

'The habits of thought and feeling that were contracted during the Hundred Years war with France,' says Trevelyan, 'sharply defined the new patriotic feeling in the form of racial hatred of the French . . . The feeling against the French outlasted the war, and helped to put an end to the subordination of English to French culture which the Norman Conquest had established.'

It was the English language which made Englishmen of the Normans just as it had made Englishmen of the Welsh of Rheged. By the first half of that century, Bradley says:

'the literary use of the native tongue was no longer a condescension to the needs of the common people. The rapid disuse of French as the medium of intercourse and the consequent substitution of English for French for school instruction, created a demand for vernacular reading.'

During this burdensome period of war, English pride forbade the use of French, in preference to their own language, in the schools. Within two centuries they would be too arrogant to allow anything but English in the official life of Wales.

Edward I's imperialist attitude persisted throughout the cultural change just as Russian imperialism persisted beyond the political change from Tsarist to Communist regime. But it was now English, and not Norman, imperialism. The English language was supported by the power and prestige of a formidable state. The English people had been part of the Roman, the Danish and the Norman empires in their turn; now, however, they had their own English empire. To extend the authority of their state over the lands, the resources and the people of other countries would be the passion which was to possess them for centuries to come — that is the essence of imperialism in every age — and although they were to call the empire British rather than English later on, this changed nothing of its character. The responsibility which the English would be burdened with in little Wales and in the big world outside would be this: to confer on the conquered the blessings of English civilisation, and the English language in particular; to uproot the conquered people from their own language and customs; to turn Celtic people into Englishmen.

But the Welsh were not ardently waiting to enjoy this promotion. They had not yet nursed enough ambition to want to become English. As yet, they clearly could not see where lay the cultural greatness of the people who gave such prominence in their capital to the heads of Llywelyn II and Dafydd III. And, burdened by heavy taxes, they were not so ready either to believe in the economic advantages of English rule as Welshmen, centuries later, in periods of adversity and unemployment, were foolish enough to believe. When the people rose on the side of Glyndŵr, their clear desire was to be allowed to be themselves: they wanted to live as Welshmen, that was all. Since a nation cannot live its own life without freedom, to desire to be a free nation was burning in their breasts. This alone explains the remarkable success of Glyndŵr.

Thanks to the historians, we know now a great deal about the economic suffering and social change of this period. They have drawn attention to the decline of the old close system of the manor and change in land tenure; to the appearance of sub-tenantry and itinerant workers; and to the effects of the many visits of the Black Death on the economy of the society. Without these conditions Owain Glyndŵr would not have had the overall support which he got. But these of themselves would not have caused in Wales more than the temporary disturbance they did in England. It was the patriotism of the Welsh that gave the impetus and the vision to make it possible for Owain to create a national state from scratch and to implement his fine constructive policy. These factors promoted a national solidarity which brought success; not simply local success, as with Jack Cade and his army of forty thousand men in 1450, against whom Mathew Goch defended London and lost his life; not the temporary success of a few months, as in the case of Simon de Montfort; but as a national success which lasted for years. And in the end it was not from lack of vision, nor from fickleness on the part of the leaders, that English imperialism won the day, but such hard facts as fifteen Englishmen to every one Welshman, and the wealth of the English empire, which included Ireland — a hundred times that of Wales.

* * *

On September 16, 1400, the day that an increasing number of Welsh people celebrate as Glyndŵr's Day, a small company of noblemen assembled in Glyndyfrdwy to proclaim Owain Glyndŵr, Prince of Wales: his investiture in fact.

1400

Owain was a nobleman who took his name from Glyndyfrdwy, one part of his lordship: the other part was Cynllaith Owain near the English border, and there, in Sycharth, he was born around 1354. This marcher lord was Powys's greatest gift to Wales. On his father's side he was descended from Madog ap Maredudd, the last prince of all Powys. On his mother's side he was directly descended from Rhys ap Tewdwr, the old royal lineage of Deheubarth, the few remains of whose heritage in Ceredigion came into the possession of the Sycharth family. Marriage connections gave him the right to call himself a descendant of Owain Gwynedd and Gruffudd ap Cynan, and after the death of Owain Lawgoch, he had the prior claim to the heritage of the two Princes Llywelyn. And it was this third Owain who was, in the opinion of the bards, now the *Mab Darogan*.

Owain was therefore a nobleman of royal descent. He represented in his person almost every region of Wales. He received the best education that Wales and England could afford, spending seven years studying law in London, in the Inns of Court which were a sort of university for the aristocracy:

> For I was train'd up in an English court
> Where, being but young, I fram'd to the harp
> Many an English ditty, lovely well,
> And gave the tongue an helpful ornament.

A picture of an English nobleman — 'a worthy gentleman exceedingly well read' is what Shakespeare gives us, and not a Welsh-speaking Welshman happiest in the cultured company of the bards.

He entered the army where he mixed with the thousands of Welshmen in the English forces. In 1384 he was in Berwick in Scotland with his 'prophet', Crach 1385 Ffinnant, in Sir Gregory Sais's company, one of the most able Welsh captains of the day. Again in 1385 he took part in Richard II's attack in Scotland, and won much honour there. Both he, as squire of the Earl of Arundel, and his brother Tudur were present at the naval victory of 1387, when Arundel himself was admiral. 1394 It is likely that he went with the army to Ireland in 1394. In this way he gained plenty of experience which was to be of the greatest value to him later on when he joined many Welsh military leaders who had had similar experience. The one thing which was not in short supply in Wales was military experience.

The bards describe Glyndŵr during these years as an aristocratic soldier. The most prominent of the poets who received his generous patronage, Iolo Goch and Gruffudd Llwyd, both wrote in Sycharth about his achievements in Scotland in 1385. In a famous *cywydd* which gives an excellent picture of the home of a cultured nobleman, Iolo Goch describes the sober Welshness of Owain's court at Sycharth, which is within a few miles of the English border:

Snowdon in Winter by Kyffin Williams

Caernarvon Castle and Town, 1750

> Llys barwn, lle syberwyd
> Lle daw beirdd aml, lle da byd.

> A baron's hall, a place of generosity
> where many poets came and life was good.

There Owain is found with:

> A gwraig orau o'r gwragedd . . .
> A'i blant a ddeuant bob ddau,
> Nythaid teg o benaethau.

> And the best wife of all women
> and children coming in two by two,
> a fair nestful of princes.

Margaret, Owain's wife, was the daughter of Sir David
Hanmer of Maelor, a judge of the King's Bench; he, too,
delighted in the culture of Wales, and was a patron of the
bards, although he came of English stock. They had six sons
and a number of daughters. The *cywydd* describes the tiled
roof and the bell tower of the handsome building which
was their home. It stood on a little hill with a moat around
it: there was an orchard and a vineyard, a dove cot, fish
pool, mill, deer park, meadows and wheat fields; and
inside, gracious hospitality:

Anfynych iawn fu yno	And most unfrequently there
Weled na chlicied na chlo.	did one see latch or lock.

This was the court of the man whom Trevelyan described as
'this wonderful man, an attractive and unique figure in a
period of debased and selfish politics.' This was the home
that Owain left in order to fight for the freedom of his country;
this home, which was a mirror of what the Welsh were
defending, was burnt to the ground together with Glyndyfrdwy by the English in 1403.

* * *

The immediate reason for the meeting on September 16,
1400, was a disagreement between Owain and Reginald
Grey, the Lord of Rhuthun, but the fact that the small

company proclaimed Glyndŵr, Prince of Wales suggests that the proposal had been in their minds for some considerable time. The brave company deserves to be named. It consisted of Gruffudd, Glyndŵr's eldest son; Tudur his brother; Gruffudd and Philip Hanmer, his brothers-in-law; Robert Puleston, his sister's husband; Hywel Cyffin, the dean of St. Asaph, and his two nephews Ieuan Fychan and Gruffudd ap Ieuan; Madog ab Ieuan ap Madog of Eyton; John Astwick; and Crach Ffinnant, a poet and Owain's personal priest. These men remained faithful to Owain — until death in some cases. Owain inspired a wonderful loyalty: up to the end, no one wanted to betray him. Perhaps Prosser Rhys, more than five centuries later, expressed something of the feeling of each of this noble band:

> Ond—glynu'n glos yw 'nhynged
>   Wrth Gymru, fel y mae,
> A dewis er ei blynged,
>   Arddel ei gwarth, a'i gwae.
> Bydd Cymru byth, waeth beth fo'i rhawd,
> Ym mêr fy esgyrn i, a'm cnawd.
>
> A chyda'r cwmni bychan
> A'i câr drwy straen a stŵr,
> Heb hitio yn ing na dychan
>   Cnafaidd nac ynfyd wr,—
> Galwaf am fynnu o'n cenedl ni
> Gymod â'i theg orffennol hi.
>
> Ac os yw'r diwreiddiedig
>   A'r uchelgeisiol griw
> Yn dal mai dirmygedig
>   Yw ple'r cymrodyr gwiw—
> Deued a ddêl, rhaid imi mwy
> Sefyll neu syrthio gyda hwy.
>
> But my fate is to cleave,
>   just as she is, to Wales,
> choosing, though she may grieve,
>   to accept her woes and shames.
> Whatever course Wales yet may follow,
> she's in my flesh and my bone's marrow.

And with that little band
  that love her through strife and strain,
taking no heed of spite
  or knave or fool's disdain,
    I call on our nation to insist
    on oneness with its splendid past.

And if those rootless ones
  and the ambitious crew
hold that a thing to scorn
  is the plea of Welshmen true;
    come what may, perforce I shall
    at their side either stand or fall.

The little army marched through Rhuthun, the town of
Lord Grey, and burnt it down. A thousand years after the
arrival of Cunedda in Wales and fourteen centuries after
Caradog's brave defence, Glyndŵr went to war to restore to
Wales its liberty. He attacked the English boroughs of
Denbigh, Rhuddlan, Flint, Hawarden and Holt; then on to
Oswestry and Welshpool. After this the armies of the nearby
English counties met and defeated them, but not until
Henry IV had commanded the armies of the ten counties to
assemble at Shrewsbury. In Anglesey Gwilym and Rhys, the
sons of Tudur ap Gronw of Penmynydd, had entered the fight,
forcing the king to lead his armies personally through the
northern counties to Anglesey. Rhys Ddu had attacked the
English army there, who then burnt down the Franciscan
monastery of Llanfaes in retaliation for the monks' support of
Glyndŵr. The English then proceeded to Caernarfon, and
back to Shrewsbury through the deep valleys of Dinas
Mawddwy.

Gwilym and Rhys of Penmynydd were Glyndŵr's cousins;
they too had had extensive military experience. Together with
their brother Maredudd, they played a prominent part in this
war from the beginning. They were descended from Ednyfed
Fychan, the family that had been so influential in the time of
the two Llywelyns, and later under the Edwards. This large
family, the ancestors of Henry VII, was the most powerful
of all the aristocratic families of the fourteenth century. They

were typical of the powerful noblemen, experienced in administration and warfare who gave their support to Owain. They were men of consequence in their own community, who held important offices previously held by Englishmen, such as county sheriffs and stewards of castles. In his 'Owain Glyndŵr and the Welsh Squirearchy', R. Rees Davies examined the nature of this support, and the close ties which drew these aristocratic families together.

> ' . . . the pattern of support for Glyn Dwr often dissolves into an infinite network of family relationships extending over several generations and encompassing the whole of Wales in its ambit . . . The support of the Welsh squirearchy brought to Glyn Dwr's revolt the cohesion of an integrated, closely inter-married group of men.'

The Welsh nation had always been a community of communities; now it was like a family of families: the heads of a host of families, with the support of their members, were ready to venture everything — their wealth, their careers and even their lives — for the sake of Wales.

And it was not only the nobles who ventured. Rees Davies shows that the minor officials too were ready with their support:

> 'Lower down the administrative ladder, on the level of commotal officials, the defection to Glyn Dwr's cause was even more total, for those posts were almost exclusively held by Welshmen. To take one example: virtually all the lower officials of Cydweli lordship supported the Welsh revolt at some stage or other; several of them died for the cause, and others paid the price of disloyalty in a long spell of imprisonment.'

This is far from exhausting the support which was given to Glyndŵr. The campaign received important help from the priests, the Brothers of the Orders, and even a pacifist, the Lollard, Walter Brut, a Welsh-speaking Welshman from Herefordshire who preached that Wales had a special mission to dethrone the Papist anti-Christ. The priests were tired of the heavy taxes levied upon them, and the most able amongst them were annoyed that Englishmen were being given the highest positions in the Church as a means of promoting the anglicising of Wales. Of the effect of the war on the Church, Glanmor Williams says:

> 'As one of the most prominent weapons of the English oppression the hierarchy of the Church could not escape hatred, and the ranks of the Welsh higher clerics were quite as opposed to it as the laymen.'

Of the Religious Orders, the Cistercians were always patriots: now the Grey Friars, the Franciscans, also lent their support; as did the Canons of Saint Augustine on Bardsey and in Beddgelert.

Not all the noblemen and the officials and the churchmen came over to Glyndŵr. But very early in the campaign many of the *gwerin* showed their hand, making it a people's war, involving all sections of the population behind Glyndŵr. It was reported to Parliament on February 21, 1401 that the Welsh students were returning from Cambridge and Oxford, where they were quite numerous. Rhys W. Hays has located 390 of them in Oxford during the fifteenth century; that is, although the proportion of the student body who were Welsh was small, it can be compared with the proportion of Welsh students in the national University of Wales in our time. Perhaps it was a fear that the University of Oxford was being Cymricised that was responsible for the disturbances there in 1398 when the English students shouted 'Slay, slay the Welsh dogs.' The Welsh students of the university met in the home of a certain Alice Walsh and there,

> 'with many wicked meetings and counsels . . . Plotted against our Lord the king and the Realm for the destruction of the kingdom and the English language.'

In the same parliamentary report, mention is also made of the return of the Welsh labourers from England to give their support to Glyndŵr. This immediate response to the news that Glyndŵr had been proclaimed Prince of Wales was the first time ever for the *gwerin*, who were to save Wales in later centuries, to play a voluntary part of any importance in a national campaign.

Because it was a people's war it was more cruel than the wars

that had been fought by the small professional armies. Some
historians have referred to its barbarity. Hardly anyone today
has the right to luxuriate in a feeling of superiority over the
followers of Glyndŵr. Their wickedness was innocent enough
compared with the horrors of Belsen and Siberia, Hamburg
and Dresden, Hiroshima and Nagasaki, Viet-nam and Biafra.

While the English parliament legislated severely against the
Welsh, and Henry, the English Prince of Wales settled into
Chester with his council under the directorship of Percy,
Earl of Northumberland (Hotspur), movements were also
afoot in Wales. On April I, Gwilym and Rhys Tudur captured
Conwy castle, and the Welsh of the surrounding area attacked
the town. Percy had to come to terms with them. Glyndŵr
moved to Deheubarth, to the land of Rhys ap Tewdwr,
his grandfather. In May it was reported in parliament
that:

'Owain Glyndwr and other have newly made insurrection and have
gathered together in the marches of Carmarthenshire. They conspire
to invade the realm and destroy the English.'

At this time Owain met Henry Dwn of Cydweli castle, the
biggest man in the county, who had fought beside John of
Gaunt in France and in the retinue of Richard II in Ireland
before becoming steward of Cydweli castle. He was a tower of
strength to Owain, who had previously written him a letter,
which did not reach its destination, claiming that he,
Owain, was the saviour God had chosen to free the Welsh
from captivity. After many years of serfdom, said the letter,
the hour of freedom was at hand, and only cowardice and
laziness could deprive the Welsh of the victory which was
within sight.

In the summer a great host of English were defeated by
Owain with a small army on the banks of the Hyddgen in one
of the valleys of Pumlumon. The king called the levies of
14 counties to meet him in Worcester, but he did not march
until October. He plundered the south and took children
prisoners before returning to England, 'with a great spoil
of cattle'. Among those who were executed in front of

him in Llanymddyfri for his support of Owain was Llywelyn ap Gruffydd Fychan, a nobleman of Caeo. He is described by Adam of Usk in terms that would not recommend him to teetotallers: 'of gentle birth and bountiful, who yearly used sixteen tuns of wine in his household.' The king established his headquarters in the Cistercian monastery of Strata Florida for the same reason as he destroyed Llanfaes the year before, threw out the monks, and filled the church up to the altar with soldiers. But at the same time Owain was gaining control of the counties of Caernarfon and Anglesey; he attacked Welshpool, and also captured some war arms of the English Prince of Wales.

In November Owain wrote letters requesting the help of the leaders in Ireland and Robert III of Scotland, the first in Latin and the second in French. He reminded Robert that they were both suffering under the oppression of their common foe, the English. In April 1402 he saw his greatest success hitherto. He took Reginald de Grey, lord of Rhuthun, prisoner. Then in June, in a sweeping victory at Bryn Glas, Maeliennydd, where Welsh archers of the English army joined their Welsh brethren, he took Edmund Mortimer, head of the greatest of the border families, prisoner. Now, with thousands of soldiers behind him, Glyndŵr was master of Gwynedd and Powys, and enjoyed strong support in Ystrad Tywi.

It was at this time he appeared in Gwent and Morgannwg, where the Welsh of the hills rose up on his side and attacked the English towns of Abergavenny, Usk, Caerleon, Newport and Cardiff. The king came to Wales once again with three armies from Chester, Shrewsbury and Hereford, but did not recover his advantage even though he inflicted severe damage on the country. Glyndŵr profited from his two prisoners; he made a bargain with Reginald Grey, and made an ally of Edmund Mortimer. He received a ransom of ten thousand marks for the release of Grey, and he got a son-in-law when Mortimer married his daughter Catrin. Since Mortimer was Hotspur's brother-in-law, Glyndŵr was now nearer to making an ally of this important man too.

In 1403 the Welsh of Brycheiniog attacked Brecon castle, and the men of Ystrad Tywi recognised Owain as 1403 Prince of Wales and rose with him under the leadership of Rhys ap Gruffydd, the constable of Dryslwyn, and Henry Dwn. Glyndŵr came among them on July 3, and spent the night in Llandeilo. He and his eight thousand men were joined there by Rhys Gethin from the Conwy valley, Rhys Ddu of Ceredigion, and William Gwyn of Cydweli. He captured Castell Newydd Emlyn; Dryslwyn, Carreg Cennen and Llansteffan were delivered into his hands, and on the sixth, the town of Carmarthen surrendered to him. He moved to Saint Clears and Lacharn (Laugharne), but in the campaign seven hundred of his men were ensnared and he suffered heavy losses. The strength of Glyndŵr's cause was shown not only in his victories but also in the fact that he could sustain heavy losses like this and yet remain strong.

On July 10, when Owain was in Lacharn, Hotspur proclaimed war on the king in Chester. Henry, the English Prince of Wales, moved quickly against him to prevent his joining the Welsh Prince of Wales, and on July 21, he was defeated and killed in the Battle of Shrewsbury. Just as Llywelyn II had lost a powerful Norman ally when Simon de Montfort was killed in Evesham in 1266, so Owain now. The king assembled his forces in Worcester to move once again against the Welsh who were such a near threat to the most thickly populated parts of England. His goal was Carmarthen, and there he went and stayed for a while; no sooner had he returned to Hereford in October than Henry Dwn, with Frenchmen and Bretons in his army, arrived in force beside Cydweli castle.

The French gave added strength to the Welsh in Gwynedd too, helping them to gain more than one small victory. Caernarfon was in great danger:

> 'for neither man nor woman dare carry letters on account of the rebels in Wales . . . so that the said castle and town are in imminent danger.'

Aber and Harlech were similarly threatened. The royal council arranged for the supply of reinforcements from Bristol, but in vain; the two castles fell, making Owain master of the country from Caernarfon to Cardigan. He established his court in Harlech and made it the home of his wife and family, and since then this castle had a very warm place in the hearts of the Welsh.

His position was, by now, powerful enough to warrant the convening of his first parliament in Machynlleth. As Adam of Usk remarked in a hostile memorandum:

'Owain and his hill-men . . . usurping the right of conquest and other marks of royalty . . . held or counterfeited or made pretence of holding parliaments.'

Owain would know from the Welsh laws that Hywel Dda had summoned four men from each commote to Whitland, five centuries earlier; and he followed this precedent for his own parliament in Machynlleth, where, in all probability, he was crowned 'Prince of Wales through the Grace of God.'

Now the Welsh independent state was a fact. It had a Prince and a government, armed forces, a civil and diplomatic service, a treasury, a legal system and a parliament. Owain had two immediate objectives: first, to strengthen his position by acquiring powerful and reliable allies; and secondly, to develop a national policy. There was little hope of help from the Irish. He had already appealed to their leaders, and to the Scots, where the king of France too tried to find help in 1401 when he sent a Welsh knight, Dafydd ab Ifan Goch, to the king of Scotland. To the court of France, therefore, Glyndŵr sent his ambassadors, John Hanmer, his brother-in-law, and Gruffudd Young, his chancellor who was probably the main architect of the Welsh state. In a document which is kept in Paris and which was written in Dolgellau in May 1404, Glyndŵr — 'Owynus dei gratia princeps Wallie' — attempted to secure a formal alliance. He succeeded. The agreement was signed in France on July 14.

A second parliament was called in Harlech in August 1405; but it was in the Pennal Parliament, in March 1406, when it was decided to transfer the homage of the Welsh to the Pope in Avignon, that the nature of the policy he developed began to emerge. The policy bore the mark of an orderly mind and detailed knowledge of the political tradition of the Welsh from the period of the two Llywelyns. Like his assumption of the title of Prince of Wales and his diplomacy and political strategy, the fifteenth century Pennal programme showed that Glyndŵr and his counsellors consciously stood in the middle of the traditional policy followed by Gwynedd in the thirteenth century. The two men behind the policy were the Chancellor, Gruffudd Young, a bishop and a lawyer, and John Trevor, who had warned the English government at the end of the previous century, when he was Bishop of St. Asaph that a dangerous situation was developing in Wales. The Welsh state, like others, got its civil servants from the Church. There were two outstanding features of the Pennal policy, which dated from the foundation of the in-dependent Welsh state: in the first place, it was mooted that two universities, one in the North and one in the South, be founded, to educate students in accordance with Welsh ideals; secondly, that the Church of the Welsh, with its archbishopric in St. David's, be independent of England and Canterbury. The rights which the Celtic church of the seventh century championed against the English, and the Princes championed against the Normans — these were the policies of Owain Glyndŵr in the fifteenth century. Only men who knew Welsh were to be appointed bishops and priests in Wales: and the custom of sending money from Wales to support the monasteries and colleges of England was to stop.

> 'In its essence,' says Glanmor Williams, 'the Pennal Policy was a political plan to protect the Church from being used again as a hand-maid of the English state; to close the channels through which the Church's revenue flowed out of Wales; and to turn the influence of the Pope back in the direction of defending the welfare of Wales.'

How different the life and history of Wales would have been, had it been free to operate its own policies. But instead of being served by a Welsh state, in 1536, Wales was swallowed completely by the English regime. Instead of a Welsh church, it got the Church of England — until it was disestablished in

1920 — the English institution called 'yr Estrones' (the foreigner) by the Welsh. Instead of national universities to serve the nation in the way all the universities of Europe did after the Renaissance, it has a collection of big English colleges where hundreds of English teachers teach thousands of English students.

* * *

The agreement with France bore fruit. But in the interim there was bitter fighting in many parts. By the end 1404 of 1404, Glyndŵr was the master of Morgannwg, with Cardiff temporarily in his hands. There had been support for him in the town for some time; among those who were executed in 1402 for supporting him was a citizen of the un-Welsh name of Sperhauke. Because the Earl of Northumberland continued to honour the agreement Glyndŵr had previously concluded with Hotspur, Owain was able to make a tripartite alliance with him and Mortimer, an alliance which would have split England in two, and given Glyndŵr a larger Wales. This remained a dream, for the rebellion of the Earl of Northumberland failed pitifully in May, and he had to flee to Scotland. Glyndŵr also had his failures, and especially in the vicinity of Usk, where the Welsh army was heavily defeated in May of that year. Among those who lost their lives was John ap Hywel, abbot of the Cistercian monastery of Llantarnam, a brave and pious man, whose ascetic life was a good example of the idealism which sustained Owain's cause:

'he was a man of deep piety and fervid eloquence,' says J. E. Lloyd, 'a strenuous preacher of repentance and patriotic self-devotion, whom Bower compares to Jonah, stern reprover of the sins of Nineveh, but who may be more fittingly regarded as a Welsh Savonarola, warning his countrymen that the success which had hitherto followed their arms would be forfeited by a continuance of their evil living. His zeal for the national cause was ardent and sincere; he made it his business to infuse courage into the Welsh troops by going among them before a battle and adjuring them to defend their homes, their wives and their children.'

In Anglesey too the Welsh lost the Battle of Rhosmeirch and forfeited their hold on Beaumaris castle.

On the positive side, a fleet with two thousand five hundred men aboard sailed from France for Wales. When it reached Aberdaugleddau (Milford Haven) at the beginning of August, Glyndŵr was there to receive them with ten thousand of his own men. The fact that he could get as many armed men as this to the field indicates his administrative ability; feeding and arming so many, with such meagre financial resources behind him, was a remarkable feat. That five per cent of the country's total population, most of them unpaid volunteers, should be under arms at one time shows the extent of support for this doughty Prince of Wales. But he was not strong enough. It was superiority in wealth and material resouces that finally gave English imperialism the victory over Welsh nationalism. England could call on more resources from captive Ireland alone, to say nothing of its reserves of wealth in England and France, than Owain Glyndŵr could possibly muster.

With the help of the French reinforcements he attacked Haverfordwest and Dinbych-y-Pysgod (Tenby); Carmarthen and Cardigan were captured. He marched victoriously on through the south of Wales, going thirty miles beyond Offa's Dyke up to the borders of Worcester. No Welsh army had penetrated so deeply into English soil for eight centuries. But Owain could not support his army so far away from home as this, and he had to withdraw in an orderly fashion. The English prince, who had been totally responsible for the conduct of the Welsh wars since January 1404 re-attacked in September. On this occasion, he suffered many losses and had few gains. He would have to wait until the following year for any real gains, and before that, the Pennal Parliament would have met.

Owain called his parliament in Pennal in March 1406 because the King of France was pressing him to give his support to Benedict XIII, the Avignon Pope, rather 1406 than the Rome Pope who had the homage of the English. These were the years of the great schism. It was when he was laying down his conditions about this that Glyndŵr outlined the Pennal policy for Wales.

In the season of Lent 1406 the French soldiers returned to their own country, and although others were sent to replace them, the English succeeded in capturing part of their navy. This was one of a series of misfortunes for Glyndŵr. The power of the English crown was growing; the power of the great barons was waning. Northumberland, who had been hiding in Wales, was defeated. The heir of the King of Scotland was taken prisoner by the English and kept as a hostage, so that Scotland could not give any aid. On April 23 the Welsh lost a battle, in which one of Glyndŵr's sons was killed. Maredudd alone of his six sons survived the war. Then the English recaptured the borderland. But so long as Aberystwyth and Harlech were standing firm there was hope of saving the situation.

But the English concentrated on these two castles. The English armies with their great guns were under the direction of their prince who, bearing the name of Wales, was to lead in a years time a great army of Welshmen to victory on the field of Agincourt. After vainly besieging Aberystwyth for several weeks Henry made a truce with Rhys Ddu, who was defending the castle. He tried to make an agreement that would be acceptable to both sides, but Owain would have none of it. He came down in person to Aberystwyth; he threatened Rhys Ddu and everyone else who surrendered with death; and he entered the castle to hold it as strongly as ever.

In November 1407, Owain lost a friend when Louis of Orleans was murdered in a Paris street; this weakened the French stand against the English. He lost another friend in February 1408 when Northumberland was killed in a battle near Tadcaster, on his way from Wales to Scotland. The English now gathered hungrily around him:

1408

'While Owain was finding it even more difficult to raise troops and keep them together,' says Glanmor Williams, 'there was a rush of heavily armed English nobles and knights to take part in the campaign of 1407. It was widely believed that this would be the end of Glendower and his rebellion and they wanted to be in at the kill.'

After all, for many of them it was a very short journey;

Aberystwyth was only sixty miles from Ludlow, and a little further from Shrewsbury and Hereford. By dint of possessing a host of heavy knights and heavier guns — one weighing two tons exploded in the siege of Harlech — and thousands of mercenaries, Henry succeeded in occupying Aberystwyth by September 1408, and Harlech early in 1409, after Mortimer had starved to death there. But although his family were taken into captivity Owain himself escaped, and the government continued to worry about the situation; a number of Scots and Frenchmen, together with some of his chief captains and counsellors, remained loyal to Glyndŵr, and marcher lords continued to make agreements with him. His last considerable effort was an attack in 1410 on the outskirts

1410 of Shrewsbury from the north of Powys where he remained strong. He lost the battle; Rhys Ddu, Philip Scudamore and Rhys ap Tudur were taken prisoner and executed as traitors. The government continued to station substantial troops in Wales, and even in June 1412 Owain was powerful enough to capture Dafydd Gam of Brycheiniog, a well-known quisling who had fought against him in the Battle of Usk. He was eventually freed by Owain after paying a ransom, and died fighting in Agincourt.

The followers of Glyndŵr remained faithful to the end. In

1415 1415 Gruffudd Young was still working for him in France; it was he who maintained in the Council of Constance, the assembly which ended the scandal of papal schism, that the Welsh were a nation and that they should have a vote there. There was not one attempt to supplant Owain as leader throughout his career, nor one attempt to betray him at the end of his life. Not one Welsh word of criticism of him has survived from that century. It is known that he was not alive in 1417, but no one knows where he died. He disappeared in dignified silence. The poets refused to believe that he was dead; so not one of them composed an elegy to his memory. To them, and to a host of Welsh people, he will never die. His spirit lives on like an unquenchable flame, a symbol of the determination of the Welsh to live as a free nation.

'Throughout Wales,' says J. E. Lloyd, 'his name is the symbol for the vigorous resistance of the Welsh spirit to tyranny and alien rule and the assertion of a national character which finds its fitting expression in the Welsh language . . .

For the Welshman of all subsequent ages, Glyndwr has been a national hero, the first, indeed, in the country's history to command the willing support alike of north and south, east and west, Gwynedd and Powys, Deheubarth and Morgannwg. He may with propriety be called the father of modern Welsh nationalism.'

The Welsh believed he would return when needed by his people. His spirit is needed today. As the nation matures in loyalty towards its own country, it can echo the words used by Dafydd Iwan in his great song:

Myn Duw, mi wn y daw.   By God, I know he will come.

VIII.   WELSH WARFARE BETWEEN ENGLISH PARTIES

IMMEDIATELY after Glyndŵr's war for freedom the people of Wales remained brave and hopeful. If Owain's men had been defeated in battle, their spirit was not defeated despite their great suffering as a result of the war — economically, politically and socially. A quality that was much in evidence among the noblemen of the fifteenth century, was confidence; and the most noteworthy characteristic in the work of the poets of the century, after the initial reaction to the war had passed, was joy. Although Owain had lost the war, the Welsh were once again conscious of their national strength; and they had never been more conscious of the value of their Welsh civilisation, nor more bitterly angry with the English because of the harm that they had done to it. No place had suffered more than the south of Carmarthenshire, but we might consider what R. Rees Davies has to say about Henry Dwn in 1413:

1413

'Dwn had only recently been released from prison for his support of Glyn Dwr, but he had not been in the least chastened by his imprisonment. He was still the lawless swashbuckling squire, coercing and oppressing his tenants and neighbours as before. Accompanied by his plaid he rampaged through the countryside seizing the lands of others, plotting the murder of the steward of the lordship, and — most outrageous of all for a recently pardoned rebel — demanding fines from over two hundred Welshmen who had failed to follow him in his revolt and who had occupied his land during the uprising.'

In the next generation this spirit is seen in Gruffydd ap Nicolas of Dinefwr in the same county, who was married to Mabli, the grand-daughter of Henry Dwn. Gruffydd was not a pleasant character; there was in him too much that was selfish, cruel and arrogant, but the last thing that can be said of him is that he was servile to the English government. He was the effective ruler of great stretches of Carmarthenshire, and his influence reached as far as Pembroke and Cardigan; and although his father-in-law, Maredudd Dwn, was a leader of the Yorkist party in the west, it was Gruffydd who led the Lancastrians until he was supplanted by Jasper Tudor, Earl of Pembroke, the son of Owain Tudur and uncle of Henry VII.

In 1439 for example, Thomas, one of Gruffydd's sons, annoyed the London government by behaving wildly in Ceredigion. This same Thomas was the father of Rhys ap Thomas, the chief victor of the battle of Bosworth, which put Henry Tudor on the throne. When Gruffydd was summoned to Westminster he refused to go. Ralph A. Griffiths tells the story:

'When commissioners were sent to Carmarthen to investigate the situation, they received short shrift. Intimidated by a display of armed retainers, benumbed by judiciously applied liquor and flayed in open court by an indignant Gruffydd, they were arrested and sent back to London humiliated and wearing his livery.'

Gruffydd dared to spend on Carmarthen castle in 1452 the largest sum of royal money that had been spent on any of the king's buildings in southern Wales since the period of the wars of Glyndŵr, and that to his own advantage; and although the king, later on, tried to change the constableship, he and his family kept tight hold of the castles of Aberystwyth, Cardigan, Carmarthen, Cydweli and Carreg Cennen.

The picture which this gives of Wales after Glyndŵr

would not be complete without noting another aspect of Gruffydd's character: his sincere Welshness and his generous patronage of the poets. He was a man of culture and a close friend of Humphrey, Duke of Gloucester, who was one of the chief architects of the Renaissance in these islands; Humphrey collected a magnificent library, studied the works of Dante, Petrarch and Boccaccio and spent much of his time in Wales as Justice of the principalities. Gruffydd was the president and patron of the famous musicians' eisteddfod which was held in Carmarthen in 1453. Apart from the competition that was held there, the council of the Order of Bards met there to discuss, according to Thomas Parry:

'some completely technical points about the work of the poets, and new rules were drawn up for the measures and cynghanedd.'

The most famous of the poets present was Dafydd ab Edmwnd, who won the chair. Cynwrig Bencerdd of Treffynnon (Holywell) won the silver Harp, and Rhys Bwthug of Prestatyn won the tongue for the declamation. The Chair, the Harp and the Tongue went therefore to Tegeingl, over which there had been so much fighting between the Welsh and their enemies — a striking example of the importance of Welsh rule, if the national tradition is to be maintained. Had not Owain Gwynedd won it back, there would hardly have been such a rich Welsh culture there in the fifteenth century. Dafydd ab Edmwnd was an uncle of Tudur Aled — one of the great poets — who died in Cwrt y Brodyr (Court of the Brothers), in Carmarthen, where he had spent his last years as a Franciscan monk. Rhys ap Thomas, grandson of Gruffydd and victor of Bosworth Field, was one of his patrons.

* * *

The Welsh needed all their courageous spirit to meet the grave and unhappy circumstances of their daily life in the years immediately following the war of Glyndŵr. Although the condition of the noblemen shows that too much can be made of the adverse effects of the destruction caused by war,

there was much poverty and social suffering throughout the
country. No doubt this encouraged thousands of Welshmen
to join the English forces in France, where they played a
prominent part, from the battle of Agincourt to the very end
of the war, under the captaincy of many famous Welsh leaders.
Mathau Goch, the best known of them was the subject of
many poems.

Glyndŵr's soldiers did not all go to France of course. Many
of them remained outlaws in the mountains and forests —
'Owain's gwerin' as they were called — adding another
element to the unsettled nature of life in Wales. There is a folk
song still sung about one of them:

Mi a glywais fod yr hedydd	The lark, or so some men maintain
Wedi marw ar y mynydd,	has died upon the mountain;
Pe gwyddwn i mai gwir y geirie	if I knew those word were true
Awn â gyrr o wŷr ac arfe,	a band of armed men would come
I gyrchu corff yr hedydd adre.	with me to fetch the body home.

Some of the outlaws were well known characters. The bards
sang their praises, as Tudur Aled in his *cywydd* to Dafydd
ap Siencyn, a relative of the Tudors.

Dy gastell ydyw'r gelli,	Your castle is the woodland,
Derw dôl yw dy dyrau di.	the meadow oaks your towers.

Rheinallt ap Gruffudd operated on the English border near
Welshpool. Some of the bards themselves were outlaws.
Lewis Glyn Cothi says that he was once protected by Owain
ap Gruffudd ap Nicolas when he was in that situation:

> A mi'n nhiredd Gwynedd gynt
> Yn herwa, yno hirhynt,
> Owain i gadw fy einioes
> Ei aur a'i win im a roes.

> Once when I was in Gwynedd's lands
> a long while with outlaw bands,
> to preserve my life, Owain
> gave me of his gold and wine.

How strange it is that a saga of legends did not gather around these patriotic brigands, comparable to the stories about Robin Hood in England.

The confusion increased when the soldiers came home from France between 1430 and 1440. It must be remembered that there was no kind of central control in Wales, nor anything like the order which the princes and the strong Welsh kings had maintained. Self-government was replaced by bad government. Where there had been six or seven kingdoms under the social and legal discipline of the old order, there were now scores of small independent states, each one under the iron rule of its English lord, who could exercise the right of life and death over his subjects; in addition to these there were the two princedoms. The Welsh were further angered by the fact that English armies were staying on in Wales to keep order although so many soldiers were needed in France:

> 'In the eyes of patriotic Welshmen,' says H. T. Evans in his *Wales and the Wars of the Roses*, 'this military occupation served as a mark of abiding captivity and national subjection.'

A revolt broke out in 1442 under the leadership of Ifan ap Robin in Caernarfonshire and Sir Gruffudd Fychan in Glyn Dyfrdwy. The leaders were forced to become outlaws.

1442

In the princedoms there was a feeling of great bitterness over the continuation of the harsh penal laws passed in 1401-2 which deprived the Welsh of the rights of the ordinary civilians, making them second-class citizens in their own country. No Welshman could own property within a borough, nor near one; he could not hold a position under the crown in Wales or in England; he could not be a juror, nor secure justice in a court under his own oath; no Welshman could marry an Englishwoman, nor a Welshwoman an Englishman. Englishmen administered the law and filled all the high posts. Every magistrate, every castle constable, every sheriff, was English, and there were many complaints of oppression. Although powerful Welshmen managed, later, to resolve the difficulties that this penal code provoked, it was at first the stimulus to violent hatred for the English.

'The Lancastrian penal code,' says Evan D. Jones, 'provoked a violent reaction against everything English for the remainder of the century — against English ways, English laws, English entertainment, English wives, English doctors, and above all English burgesses. "Sais" and "burgess" became synonyms of evil connotation.'

The fifteenth century is the most anti-English century in the whole history of Wales, but it is also characterized by a national pride in Wales and joyous delight and confidence in the national heritage at the highest level. Those Welshmen who tried to win English honours were often despised. Their behaviour saddened Guto'r Glyn:

Ac eraill gynt a gerais   Others, who once were dear to me,
A brŷn swydd a breiniau Sais.   buy English office and dignity.

There was confident hope for the future. When Rhys Goch Eryri asks,

A oes obaith i'n iaith ni,
Faith gof awdl, fyth gyfodi?

Is there any hope for our nation,
Long remembered in song, ever arising?

he gives a triumphant answer,

Oes! Oes! Cwynwn anfoes caith,
Bo iawn gwbl, byw yw'n gobaith.

Ay! Ay! We lament the uncouthness of slaves,
There will be redress, our hope is alive.

The Welsh situation continued to cause some fear in England, as the *Libell of English Policye* which was published about this time, shows:

'Beware of Wales, Christ Jesu must us keep
That it make not our child's child to weep,
Nor us also, if so it go his way
By unwareness; since that many a day
Men have been feared of their rebellion . . .
Look well about, for God wot we have need.'

The nationalism of poets and people is seen in their strong adherence to the Welsh saints. A poem by Lewis Glyn Cothi. 'Cywydd i Saint Cymru', which is infused by the political nationalism of the time, uses the names of the early saints as rallying cries, and closes with the wish that they rule Wales once again.   .

Boed i'r saint bob dri a saith   Let the saints in threes and sevens
Reoli Cymru eilwaith.   Rule Wales once again.

'Certainly it can be claimed', says Keith Williams-Jones, 'that apart from the Virgin Mary, St. Michael and a few of the great Catholic saints, Welshmen were only interested in their own national and, even more so, their own local saints in the late middle ages . . . The Welsh regarded them with great veneration and with a fierce patriotic pride.'

As the century continued, and the soldiers came back from France, the bards looked more and more earnestly for a deliverer. They believed that three men, in their turn, were candidates for this high office: Owain Tudur, William Herbert of Raglan and Henry Tudor. These men were personally involved in events of great significance to Wales, during the half century before Bosworth. This half century laid the foundations of the sad ruin of a nation that we see today. During this period, Welsh nationalism ran aground. When its power was at its peak, it created a situation which led directly to the harmful and restrictive order of the following century. Freedom was the goal: but the tragic mistake of the Welsh when trying to attain it was to aim at government by a Welshman in London instead of a Welsh government in Wales.

Owain ap Maredudd ap Tudur was a member of the great family of Penmynydd, Anglesey, which was descended from Ednyfed Fychan, and which fought for its kinsman, Owain Glyndŵr. It was to this family that the bards looked for the *Mab Darogan* who was to save Wales. Although he had been a successful soldier in France, Owain Tudur did not get the rights of citizenship until 1432, and in spite of the law which prevented a Welshman from marrying an English wife, he married Queen Catherine, the widow of Henry V, clandestinely about 1429. When she met the non-English members of Owain's family she said they were, 'the goodliest dumb creatures she ever knew.' Their two sons, Jasper and Edmund, were proclaimed deputy leaders of the nation. Edmund married the Lady Margaret Beaufort of the Lancaster family, in 1455, when she was thirteen. He died young, in Carmarthen in 1456, and was buried there in the house of the Greyfriars. In Pembroke castle, two months later, Margaret gave birth to his son, Henry, later Henry VII, and it was in Pembrokeshire that Henry Tudor spent most of his youth. Owain, his grandfather, was executed in 1461 in Hereford, after being taken prisoner in the battle of Mortimer's Cross near Llanllieni (Leominster), where Jasper, Earl of Pembroke, was defeated by Edward, Earl March, who became Edward IV as a result of this battle. The armies of both sides were mainly Welsh.

This was one of the battles of the Wars of the Roses. The king of England from 1422 to 1461 had been Henry VI of the Lancastrian family. He suffered long periods of madness, at which times the country would be ruled by Richard, Duke of York. There were several reasons for the war between the Yorkists, the party of the white rose, and the Lancastrians, the party of the red rose who supported Queen Margaret, but in Wales it was looked upon as a struggle for national freedom. Indeed, most of the battles were fought between the Welsh lords. Trevelyan says:

'The wars of the Roses were to a large extent a quarrel between Welsh Lords, who were also great English nobles closely related to the English throne . . . Because medieval England had left half done its task of conquering Wales for civilisation (sic) Welsh tribalism and feudalism revenged themselves by poisoning the Parliamentary life and disturbing the centralised government of its neglectful overlords. But when at length a Welsh army put a Welsh Tudor Prince upon the throne at Bosworth Field, Wales supplied a remedy for those ills in the English body politic which she had helped to create.'

A Welshman views with mixed feelings the part played by Welsh nationalism at this time on the threshold of the modern world. On the one hand, it helped to create those very conditions of debility and poverty in our national life that arose from the political servitude of Wales in the following centuries; and on the other, it contributed to the energy, the strength and the splendid development of the English nation.

At the beginning of the wars Wales was divided between the two great English parties, with the Lancastrians drawing greatest support from the west and the Yorkists from the east, where the lordships of the Mortimers — through whom the York family inherited its right to the crown — ran like a strong chain along the borders.

> 'The propaganda of the bards,' says David Fraser, 'was one of the factors that accounted for the different attitudes of the English and the Welsh to the Wars of the Roses. In England, they deteriorated into meaningless feuds between the different noblemen and their followers. In Wales the wars meant far more to the people. There was more enthusiasm and more idealism behind the fighting, which grew, from being a family row, into a contest for the freedom of the country. In one sense the red rose was supplanted by the red dragon. The cause of the Lancastrians became the cause of Wales. And it was the bards, to a great extent, who induced this new attitude.'

During the first decade of the wars, the Welshman on whom the bards concentrated their attention was William Herbert of Raglan, in Gwent. This cultured nationalist was the son of Gwladys, the daughter of Dafydd Gam. His father had been successful in business in London, a prototype of the modern London Welsh. His own name was Sir William ap Thomas, but Herbert was the name he gave to his children. H. T. Evans says:

> 'A Welsh name had a foreign sound, and was to many suggestive of rebellion . . . It was therefore a stroke of discretion to enter into a wider and more remunerative field of activity than Wales could afford, and to parade an English name.'

Herbert won great fame as a soldier. After the Battle of Towton in 1461 he was made Justice of southern Wales, and it was he who was given the task of winning all Wales over to the Yorkist cause. He was exhorted by Guto'r Glyn and the other bards to concentrate on fighting for the freedom of Wales. Except for Northumberland, Wales was the only place where the Lancastrians were strong at that time, thanks to the efforts of Jasper Tudor. Herbert marched westwards in pursuit of them. The castles of Pembroke and Tenby capitulated easily, but Harlech was effectively defended for another seven years. In defending the castle Dafydd ab Ieuan ab Einion and the fifty men with him won great renown for themselves, and are immortalised in '*Rhyfelgyrch Gwyr Harlech*' ('The War-song of the Men of Harlech').

From now on William Herbert was the chief adviser to the king, a sort of predecessor to Lloyd George. In 1466 his son William married the queen's sister. The following year Herbert was made Chief Justice of Wales, and in 1468 he became Earl of Pembroke. The Welsh bards were delighted. In proclaiming him leader of the nation, Guto'r Glyn calls him to unite all Wales under him, and to free it from the English.

> Na âd arglwydd swydd i Sais
> Na'i bardwn i un bwrdais;
> Barna'n iawn, brenin ein iaith
> Bwrw yn tân eu braint unwaith . . .
> Dwg Forgannwg a Gwynedd,
> Gwna'n un o Gonwy i Nedd;
> O digia Lloegr a'i dugiaid,
> Cymru a dry yn dy raid.

> My lord, don't give the English office
> nor pardon to a burgess;
> king of our language, be aware
> their rights were once thrown in the fire . . .
> Bring Glamorgan and Gwynedd,
> make one from Conwy to Nedd;
> if England and her dukes with anger burn,
> all Wales to your need will turn.

Poor things; they could not see that he was only using Wales for his own purpose in English politics — as the Tudors themselves did:

'For the first time, though not for the last in the history of Wales,' says H. T. Evans, 'Welsh nationalism was used as a lever in the party politics of England.'

But he adds:

> 'Herbert may have been alive to the passionate appeal of the leaders of Welsh public opinion that Wales should not be made the cockpit of contending English factions . . . To the poets there was no dynastic question.'

The glory of this Earl of Pembroke was short-lived, and it was only his fellow Welshmen who remained loyal to him when Warwick rebelled. He fought his last battle 1469 near Banbury on July 26, 1469. In a bloody fight his Welsh army was defeated. One hundred and sixty-eight prominent Welshmen were killed, the cream of the southern nobility. Herbert was taken prisoner and executed. The poets saw his death as a terrible blow for the Welsh nation:

> Ef a'm llas i a'm nassiwn
> Yr awr y llas yr iarll hwn.

> Mine and my nation's blood was spilled
> the hour that this earl was killed.

For

Gwinllan fu Raglan i'r iaith.   Rhaglan was our tongue's vineyard.

Ym Manbri y bu'r dial   At Banbury vengeance was taken
Ar Gymru deg, a mawr dâl.   on fair Wales and repayment done.

IX. THE PYRRHIC VICTORY OF THE WELSH

IN 281 B.C., Pirrus, the Greek king of Epeiros, won a victory against the Romans in Italy itself, but at such a heavy cost that the term 'Pyrrhic victory' still lives on in the languages of Europe.

The Welsh believed that they had won a glorious victory on Bosworth Field by setting a man of Welsh descent on the throne of England. This victory came close to costing the Welsh nation its life. The future would show that this victory was the most catastrophic defeat the Welsh had in all the thousands of years of their history. A military victory: a spiritual defeat. But for this victory the Welsh nation today would probably be living in dignified freedom, making its contribution to world civilization, and living with at least as much economic prosperity and social justice as any one of the countries of Scandinavia.

What is frightening for a Welshman reviewing this period is to see that the Welsh believed that the Wars of the Roses, which came to a close on Bosworth Field, were a continuation of Glyndŵr's campaign. Perverted Welsh nationalism put Henry Tudor on the throne of England. The bards were confused by the legend of Hengist and Horsa and the spurious belief that England had once been the country of the Welsh; this became mixed up in the fifteenth century with the profound desire for a deliverer who would free Wales and restore her old glory.

The Arthurian legend had made the belief in a glorious British past acceptable in England as well as in Wales. In the *Faerie Queen* Spenser sees the Tudor dynasty as a restoration of the Kingdom of the Britons. Whereas the life of England was enriched by the fable, its consequences in Wales were disastrous. It nearly led to the loss of Welsh national identity.

What Edward I had failed to do by defeating Llywelyn II, and what Henry V had failed to do by defeating Glyndŵr was now accomplished by the success of the Tudors. It led to the cynical acceptance of the Act of Union, and in the course of two centuries following that Act it destroyed almost totally the heroic national spirit of the Welsh. The brave, vigorous, confident people of the centuries of the middle ages — people who knew they could stand on their own feet and live their own national life, and who insisted on doing just that — were replaced by servile and undignified people who believed their greatest honour was to die as a nation, and as individuals, so that Britain could be great; people who believed that it was their duty and their privilege to enrich and strengthen England: people who were so lacking in dignity that they could forsake their own language: people so lacking in confidence that they could believe that as a nation they were unable to support even the type of political freedom obtaining in every one of the Swiss cantons. There is nothing despicable about the imperialist rape of the English. What is to be despised is that so many Welsh people themselves help them to ravage their nation.

But this demoralisation was reserved for the future. After the execution of William Herbert the country's hopes were pinned on Jasper and Henry Tudor. Jasper had made his home in Pembrokeshire after the death of his brother Edmund in Carmarthen in 1456, and from then on, until 1485, he spent almost the whole of his time in Wales strengthening the Lancastrian cause. When he did leave Wales for very short periods, he went only to other Celtic countries. Although the bards, who directed the political thought of Wales believed him to be a patriotic Welshman, Jasper's ambitions were wholly English; or, to use the term which became fashionable later on, British. He confined his activities to Wales using Welsh nationalism for his own and his family's ends: and it was because he succeeded in identifying the national cause with his family's ambitions that his nephew ascended the throne of England. After his defeat in the Battle of Mortimer's Cross, he began promoting opposition to William Herbert's campaign, by writing letters from Tenby; but his military headquarters were on the inaccessible shores of Meirionnydd, and Harlech castle in particular, until it fell in 1471. After the death of Prince Edward, the Lancastrian heir, in the Battle of Tewkesbury in 1471, it was Henry Tudor who was the Lancastrian claimant to the English crown. He had been living in Wales since his birth in Pembroke in January 1457, but for safety's sake he was taken to Brittany in 1471. During these Breton years Jasper was his counsellor.

1471

In the same year that Jasper took Henry Tudor from Wales to Brittany a Welsh council was established on the borders, and this council developed into a rather powerful body.

'The Council had come into existence by gradual stages,' says Penry Williams. 'Beginning as a board for running the Prince's estates and a household for his upbringing, it had become by 1476, a recognised

institution for supervising justice in Wales, the Marches, and the English
shires of the border.'

The ascent of Richard III to the throne on the death of
Edward IV was an encouragement to the Lancastrian cause.

      A plot was set afoot to put Henry Tudor on the throne.
1483   The Duke of Buckingham, Lord of Brycheiniog, was
      persuaded to attack England on Henry's behalf. He
was foiled, caught and executed. The bards kept stirring the
people up on Henry's side:

| Y mae hiraeth am Harri, | For Henry there is longing |
| Y mae gobaith i'n hiaith ni. | and there is hope for our tongue. |

So sang Robin Ddu, showing that the language and the
nation were so completely identified that the word 'iaith'
(language) could mean nation.

On August 1, 1485, Jasper and Henry Tudor sailed for
Wales with a small mixed army of two thousand Welshmen,
Bretons and Frenchmen. Henry succeeded here in doing what
Owain Lawgoch had failed to do. He landed in Milford
Haven as the little French army had done which came to help
Glyndŵr eighty years earlier. After they had captured
Pembroke castle, they travelled along the western shores to
Llanbadarn carrying the Red Dragon before them.

'Y ddraig goch ddyry cychwyn.'

The red dragon made the first move.

In his address to the Welsh leaders Henry stressed his faith in
'the nobles and commons of this our principality of Wales', and
his determination to restore 'our said principality of Wales
and the people of the same to their former liberties.' Rhys ap
Thomas marched with a strong army from Deheubarth to
meet Henry in Shrewsbury. There too came the forces of
Gwynedd under the leadership of Richard ap Hywel of
Mostyn, who brought their cattle as food with them. Awaiting
his opportunity was Sir William Stanley, the most powerful
lord in the north-east. On August 22 these forces met the far

larger army of Richard III and defeated it on Bosworth
Field. It is said that Rhys ap Thomas of Abermarlais put
Richard's crown on Henry's head. This victory, by ending
the civil war, enabled England to pursue the policy it had
fitfully followed since the Norman Conquest but which the
French wars had deflected. As H. A. L. Fisher has pointed out,

'Once the forlorn attempt to conquer France was definitely
abandoned, England was able to find her true line of development in the enlargement of her influence over the British
Isles'.

The Welsh did not see things this way. They were excited
by the fact that at last there was a Welshman on the throne
of England. Wales in their eyes had won its national fight for
freedom. They regarded this victory as a glorious climax to
their long heroic campaign. Contemporary opinion in England
and elsewhere was similar:

> 'To the Welsh people,' said Bacon, 'his victory was theirs; they had
> thereby regained their freedom.'

That was the opinion of the Viennese ambassador too:

> 'For the Welsh,' he said, 'it can now be said that they have won back
> their old independence, for Henry VII is a Welshman, a fortunate and
> wise Welshman.'

English historians adopt a slightly different point of view.
When discussing the Battle of Bosworth, Trevelyan says:

> 'Here, indeed, was one of fortune's freaks: on a bare Leicestershire
> upland a few thousand men in close conflict foot to foot . . . sufficed to
> set upon the throne of England the greatest of all her royal lines, that
> should guide her through a century of change down new and larger
> streams of destiny.'

For England, and for the English people, a bright future of
national development opened out under the Tudors. This
big nation had the freedom to realise its possibilities, while
Wales slipped into the position of a submissive province of
England, unprosperous and insignificant.

X. THE GREAT CENTURY

THE hundred years before the Act of Union was the greatest century for Welsh poetry: the result of the national awakening and the heroic attempt to win national liberty. There were more poets of quality than ever before, and in this number were some truly great artists, men of vision and humanity, and masters of their craft — and for them poetry was a craft, a craft ruled strictly by the professional Order of Bards. But they were more than bardic craftsmen; they were public leaders; and just as important, they contributed to education. Formal education remained mainly in the hands of the Church and the Bards, and it was an education given in the Welsh language, but bardic schools continued to have importance.

We learn something of the nature of this education from the manuscripts of the period. Essays in Welsh on theology, astrology, botany and medicine have survived, as well as Welsh translations of Greek and Latin works, and of the Romances which were so popular in France and Italy.

> 'It would not be an exaggeration to say that Wales was partaking of the intellectual life of Western Europe,' wrote Griffith John Williams, 'and remembering this, and realising how the nation could have developed had it been free, the effects of the Tudor policy in Wales can be seen in their proper perspective. For after that, the belief blossomed that English culture was the only culture to be aimed at, and intelligent Welshmen looked upon Welsh as a vulgar dialect, and on Wales before the Tudors as the home of barbarians.'

The language showed great vigour in another way. It won back large areas that had been lost. One example was the Vale of Glamorgan. French had been nowhere more common than here; many of the place-names are French and the Welsh forms are translations or later adaptations which came into use when the Vale became Welsh-speaking again.

Although there were very few rich people among them, the noblemen supported the bards who used to travel from house to house. The number of bards shows that the economic state of the country in the fifteenth century was quite a lot better than the Tudor supporters insisted on believing in the next century, in spite of the sorry effects of the wars of Glyndŵr. An added testimony to this economic prosperity are the beautiful churches which were built in the second half of the century, as those in Wrexham and Gresford, Clynnog and St. John's, Cardiff; and also the screens and lofts and the stained-glass windows which belong to that period. The new organs add their testimony too. Church music throve throughout the centuries as a most important part of Wales's rich musical tradition. There is a poem by Gruffudd Grŷg describing the welcome given the people, Dafydd ap Gwilym among them, when an organ was put in Bangor Cathedral in the previous century.

The national struggle influenced poetry in more than one way. In the years that followed the war it became more serious: the lightness and the humour found in Dafydd ap Gwilym and some of his followers disappeared. The light tone is completely absent in the marvellous work of Sion Cent (1367-1430?). He was a very learned man who maintained that the muse of the Welsh bards was a false one:

'The essential lie in the Welsh literary tradition,' in the words of Saunders Lewis about him, 'was the philosophy that *species* were substances and *ideas* things.'

According to Sion Cent the proper purpose of poetry is the study of man, painting him as he is; its starting point is a scientific observation of the world.

Astudio'dd wyf, was didwyll,
ystad y byd, astud bwyll;
astud boen, ystod benyd,—
ystad bardd astudio byd.

An honest fellow, I study
the world's state, studious care;
studious pain, a swath of penance,
study of the world is the poet's estate.

'Sion Cent is a poet of Christian pessimism . . .' says Saunders Lewis. 'He belonged to the philosophical movement which produced the great change in philosophy which overthrew Scholasticism and which created the modern mind.'

In the generation which followed Sion Cent there is a change of key again:

> 'If we seek words to define the *ethos* or the nature of the poetry of this period,' says Saunders Lewis, 'no doubt the first word in our definition would be: joy. This note is now more definite than in any other century in the history of our literature. It is a social joy and the medium of its expression is praise.'

This praise is real and detailed. In the *'cywyddau gofyn'* the creatures of the field and the products of craft become part of the heritage of poetry. A whole host of things are described and praised:

> 'Their poetry deals with the miracle of being and matter; a world of individual things with a virtue in every one of them. It is a human world: its phenomena teach of the glory of man . . . In a wooded country like Wales carpenters were, of necessity, the chief exponents of art. There is an enormous amount of praise for their work in the *cywyddau moliant* . . . The bards turned in a world of artistic things.'

Those are the words of Saunders Lewis who holds that the consciousness of the value of the Welsh heritage was the true persuasion of all the poetry of the century. Thus although the poets composed their poems (always called 'songs' in Welsh) music for the ear, they had a sustaining intellectual content.

The foremost bardic teacher was Dafydd ab Edmwnd — who stroked a word 'megis fel petai'n ddeilen rhosyn neu'n dant y delyn' (as if it were the leaf of a rose or the string of a harp). The greatest poet was Dafydd Nanmor — 'y gŵr tebycaf i Fyrsil a welodd llenyddiaeth Gymraeg' (the man most like Virgil that Welsh literature ever saw); and, according to Saunders Lewis, Gutun Owain was the finest lyrical poet of the century. Lewis Glyn Cothi, Guto'r Glyn and Tudur Aled are other classical poets. A number of the bards were descended from the noble families; their vocation was a distinguished one, as it had been almost a thousand years earlier when Taliesin composed his poetry.

Some of the pleasantest poems of this wonderfully rich century are anonymous, for example:

The Screen, Llananno Church, Radnorshire

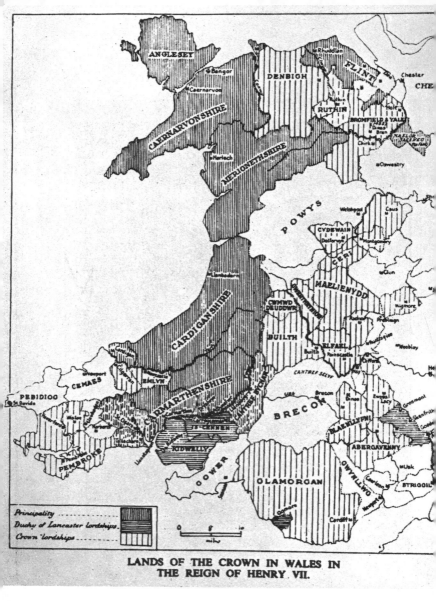

LANDS OF THE CROWN IN WALES IN
THE REIGN OF HENRY VII.

Wales 1500: Crown lands
from *"A Historical Atlas of Wales"* with permission of Professor William Rees and Faber & Fabe

Pan ddêl Mai a'i lifrai las
Ar irddail i roi'r urddas,
Aur a dyf ar edafedd
Ar y llwyn er mwyn a'i medd.
Teg yw'r pren a gwyrennig
Y tyf aur tew o'i frig.
Duw a roes, difai yw'r ail,
Aur gawod ar y gwiail.
Bid llawen gwen bod llwyn gwŷdd
O baradwys i brydydd.
Blodau gorau a garwn,
Barrug haf ydyw brig hwn.

When May comes with its green livery
to give honour to the green leaves,
gold will grow along the threads
of the grove for him who owns it.
Fair is the tree, luxuriant,
with thick gold growing from its boughs.
God gave, the building's faultless,
a shower of gold upon the twigs.
Let the girl be glad there's a green grove,
a poet's paradise.
I've loved the best of flowers;
this sprig is summer's hoarfrost.

Literature flourished in many forms and in many different parts of the country. For example, there is good dramatic poetry in the religious plays which were written for the guilds of Welsh actors in the fifteenth century. Those that remain were composed in Powys. The most famous carols come from Gwent and Morgannwg, all of which were religious poems in free verse; and in Morgannwg too there was a thriving school of prose translators. But it was in Denbighshire that the most productive centres of prose and traditional strict poetry were found.

'For two centuries', says Anthony Conran, 'Wales had enjoyed an outburst of fine poetry unrivalled for its sophistication, it brilliance and poise, by anything the Celts have ever achieved, before or since. Poet after poet, many of them of a standard one must call great, attained to a classical elegance in their art that English poetry can only match in the later years of Elizabeth and the seventeenth century'.

XI. THE COLONIALIST INTERVAL

FOR a thousand years the central theme of the history of Wales had been the resolute struggle of the little nation to keep its identity, to live its own life, to protect its values, and to uphold its tradition. After 1485 there is no further mention of a national campaign; the nation was readier to accept the situation than to fight vigorously against it in order to live its life to the full. It was England that lived purposefully; in Wales all feeling of purpose was finished, apart from that of serving its big neighbour. A host of Welshmen received personal advancement, but their country deteriorated and gradually decayed.

During the half century that followed Bosworth the Welsh were content to be ruled as a colony, with no semblance of self-government. A large part of the land passed into the hands of the king who ruled it personally from London, although he restored the Welsh Council on the borders to help him, and placed Prince Arthur as its president. Unfortunately Arthur died in his court in Ludlow at the age of sixteen, five months after his marriage to Catherine of Aragon, 1502 so that England's chance of having a King Arthur was lost. Henry inherited the principality in the north and the south, as well as Flintshire and the enormous estates of the Mortimers. When Jasper Tudor died in 1495 his great estates too came into the hands of the king, including the lordships of Morgannwg and Pembroke. Although he made Sir William Stanley 'Justice of the North', he found 1521 an excuse in ten years' time to execute him, and took all his great lands in the north-east. In 1521 Henry VIII also executed the Duke of Buckingham, lord of Brycheiniog, and took his lands as well. He bought the lordships of Arwystli and Cyfeiliog. Almost the whole of the marches thus came into the hands of the king. His was, therefore, a very personal rule indeed over Wales.

The deterioration among the Welsh is seen in their response to the way Henry Tudor expressed his Welshness. He is the characteristic modern Welshman, confining his Welshness to sentimentality and personal gain; Henry used Welsh flags, the

Red Dragon and the banner of Cadwaladr. He kept Welsh harpists and poets. He searched his lineage and published it in an attempt to show that he was descended from the Princes. He employed a Welsh retinue. He called his eldest son Arthur, and quickly made him Prince of Wales. The climax of his Welsh patriotism was the celebrating of St. David's Day in London. Although they had none of the substance of national freedom the Welsh were satisfied with symbols. Henry won over the majority of them and bound them in loyalty to the English crown simply by conferring offices and honours on a host of them. William Gruffudd of Penrhyn was made Chamberlain of Gwynedd. Rhys ap Thomas who was made a knight on Bosworth Field, was given one of the highest posts in southern Wales; and to crown his career he was made Knight of the Garter on April 22, 1505. Henry knew exactly how to treat the Welsh — better by far than Sir Rhys 1529 knew how to treat the landowners around him. The relationship of Rhys's grandson with the son of Henry VII was less happy. A quarter of a century after allowing Rhys ap Thomas to wear the Garter, his grandson, Rhys ap Gruffudd, was executed on the charge of conspiring with men from Ireland and Scotland to establish himself as Prince of Wales. The crown alleged that he called himself Fitz Urien — an echo in the sixteenth century of the heroic Urien Rheged of whom Taliesin sang in the sixth. With this last claimant to the title borne by Llywelyn and Glyndŵr the power of the foremost family of Deheubarth came to an end. The centralised English system had won another victory.

Although many believed that the success of Henry Tudor had restored dignity and glory to the Welsh nation, not everyone was satisfied with the king's record; and the bards were not slow to show their disappointment. Llywelyn ap Hywel wrote a *cywydd* to complain about how little Henry VII did for the Welsh, saying:

> Gwell gan Siasbar a Harri
> Yw gwŷr y Nordd na'n gwŷr ni.
>
> Jasper and Harry prefer
> men of the North to our men.

Twenty years passed before he began to rectify the great disadvantages that the Welsh suffered as a result of the Penal Laws. This he did in a series of charters at the end of the reign:

'The charters were granted during the last five years of Henry's reign,' says J. Beverley Smith, 'and their concession has been regarded as a late departure in royal policy, and one designed to fulfil the king's declared intention to deliver the Welsh from the 'miserable servitude' which they had long endured.'

In spite of this, the administration of law was unsatisfactory in Wales; in some parts the old Welsh laws remained, and in others there was hardly any law at all; too often, criminals, even murderers, escaped scot-free. A substantial number of men, many of them inspired by nationalist motives, were still living as outlaws — a state of affairs existing since the end of the Glyndŵr wars: Gwylliaid Cochion Mawddwy (the Red Bandits of Mawddwy) made quite a name for themselves. There was the occasional serious riot, such as the one in Carmarthen which led to the arrest of Sir Rhys ap Gruffudd. There was at least one small rebellion, in Meirionnydd in 1498, when Harlech castle was taken over. But the Welsh situation was scarcely worse than the one pertaining in England or in any other western country; and two generations after the Act of Union the position would not be much better. The situation in England was described at the beginning of the century by a knowledgeable Italian thus:

'There is no country in the world where there are more thieves and despoilers than England; so much so that very few people dare to go out alone in the country, except in the middle of the day when it is light, and fewer still in the towns in the evenings, and fewest of all in London.'

If there was uncontrollable disorder in Wales, the effective answer was surely to entrust the governing of the country to the inhabitants themselves. 'Freedom and not servitude', says Burke in his address on *Reconciliation with America*, 'is the cure of anarchy, the profoundest manual of civil wisdom.' It was not freedom that Wales got, but servitude.

When the situation became more serious in England because of the Protestant reformation — some feared even armed resistance to it in Wales — Thomas Cromwell prepared a number of measures which would strengthen the administration of English law, protect the English government in Wales, and promote a centralist order for the nations of the British islands. The English state was induced, on two heads, to adopt a policy for which there was no justification in Wales itself; a policy of defence in order to protect its own interests; and a policy of aggression in order to swell its own power and enhance English glory to the detriment of the small nations around her, Wales, Ireland and Scotland.

Henry VIII, according to Pollard, is the father of modern imperialism. One of his first moves towards extending the authority of the English state in Wales was to send Bishop Lee to the country as president of the Welsh Council. This man administered law, not grace; his justice was harsh but effective in mid-Wales. He was not admired by everyone; one person who failed to find any virtue in him was the officer who described him thus:

> 'an earthly beast, a mole, and an enemy to all godly learning into the office of his damnation — a papist, an idolator, and fleshly priest.'

Lee persecuted the criminals until his death in 1543; and Parliament passed a number of acts to help him. In spite of this he did not diagnose the cause of the evil, seeing only its symptoms. When the English parliament met in 1536 the first and most important of the measures which included Cromwell's remedy were put before it: the legislation was completed in 1542. And the 'cure' was two-fold: politically and legally, Wales was placed totally under the government of England. Culturally and socially, the intention was to assimilate Wales and to exterminate both the language and the nationality of the Welsh. Although it executed its policy only spasmodically, and although it was not always aware of it, the English government had only one Welsh policy from 1536 until recent times: to abolish the Welsh nation and deny her every liberty to act as a nation. It is the policy embodied in the Act of Union, 1536.

'For Ever and Henceforth Incorporated and Annexed'

In 1536, when action was taken in London to erase Welsh nationhood, England was a powerful, centralised modern state, whereas five generations had passed since her small western neighbour had had experience of statehood. During the years that had passed since Owain Glyndŵr had ruled Wales as its last independent Prince, the nation's leaders had been psychologically prepared for the sacrifice of nationhood. There was no one to stand for national freedom when London now tried to obliterate Welsh nationhood in two ways, one political, the other social and cultural. Politically, the Act probably benefited Wales in tidying its administration. The fractionalisation which had characterised it since The Statute of Wales, 1284, was certainly more offensive to the London civil service than it was to the Welsh people. This was ended by making the 'principality of Wales' co-extensive with the whole country and integrating the whole in England under the control of the central London government. Internally the character of the new order would be much the same as that of the old Principality. A degree of separation from England still persisted, however, for this newly united Wales. This was secured for the purpose of administering law and justice through two institutions. One was the King's Great Sessions in Wales which ensured that Wales (except Monmouthshire) remained a separate jurisdiction until the Court was abolished by an Act of Parliament in 1830. The other was the Council for Wales which had developed from the council of the Principality. This was given statutory recognition by an Act of 1543 under the title of The Council in the Dominion and Principality of Wales and the Marches. Day to day government in the new regime would be in the hands of J.P.'s sheriffs, lords lieutenants and other indigenous officials.

More important to England and more dangerous to Wales

was the other way. This was a positive English effort to assimilate Wales culturally, to destroy the nation's civilisation. Unless this was done there would always be a danger of political resurgence. A process of structural and psychological violence was therefore set in train which has continued to this day. This was the policy accepted by the Welsh leaders and embodied in the measure known as the Act of Union.

Events during the previous generation in Switzerland provide an interesting comparison. Fourteen years after the Battle of Bosworth the Treaty of Basel, 1499, closed the final war of Swiss liberation. The martial people of Switzerland spurned integration in a German empire. They wanted freedom to be themselves. The German aristocracy thought poorly of their democratic ways, and the Emperor Maximilian spoke for them when he referred to the Swiss as 'an ill-conditioned, rough and bad peasant folk in whom there is to be found no virtue, no noble blood and no moderation, but only disloyalty and hatred towards the German nation.' What was disloyalty for the Emperor was self-respect for the Swiss. In Wales, the new loyalty to England meant a new servility among the Welsh who acquiesced spiritlessly in the incorporation and attempted assimilation of 1536.

It was the Act of Union that annexed Wales to England. It must be noted that it was in England, not Britain, that Wales was incorporated, and it was the English language, not a British tongue, which was to replace the Welsh speech. That language of kings and scholars, poets and lawyers was to be demoted to the position of a *patois* without status. From then until the twentieth century, London's policy was to destroy the language and delete the national tradition. The way to annihilate a nation is to obliterate its culture. The way to delete its culture is to destroy its language. This was the policy now followed.

The same policy was followed in Ireland. In his *Traddodiad Llenyddol Iwerddon*, J. E. Caerwyn Williams quotes from a letter which Henry VIII sent to the inhabitants of Galway in 1536, and also the approving words for the policy by the English poet Spenser. Says Henry VIII:

'every inhabitante within the saide towne indever theym selfe to speke Englyshe, and to use theym selffe after the Englyshe facion; and specyally that you, and every one of you, do put forth your childe to scole, to lerne to speke Englyshe.' ..

Spenser explains:

'for it hathe bene ever the vse of the Conqueror to destroy the language of the Conquered, and to force him by all means to learne his . . . the speache beinge Irishe the harte muste nedes be Irishe for out of the abundance of the harte the tonge speakethe.'

Although we should not attribute maliciousness to Thomas Cromwell and the English government, it was the aggrandizement of England that they had in mind. Like all English governments after it, it assumed that what was to the benefit of England was also to the benefit of Wales; and most of the Welsh leaders agreed with this. Centralisation of what would be known as nation-states was the tendency of the age. Four years earlier, Brittany had been swallowed by France through the Vannes Agreement. In accordance with the imperialistic nationalism of the age, England broke free from the European religious establishment. The goal of its government was to build up an imperial power which could be independent of Europe. Paul Johnson wrote, in the *New Statesman:*

'Henry VIII . . . could not accept a hostile supernational ruling on a matter which vitally affected the stability of the English state, and turned to that great repository of English nationalism, the House of Commons . . . The great Reformation statutes state repeatedly and emphatically: "This realm is an Empire" . . . Their architect, Thomas Cromwell . . . believed strongly in the policy of separate English development; he had abounding confidence in English energy, once it was unleashed by breaking the clerical monopoly in knowledge and ideas. He was the first truly English statesman.'

By Thomas Cromwell's Act of Union, Wales was annexed by the English state and merged in the realm which was again an Empire. From now on she was governed as a part of Metropolitan England much as Algeria would later be governed as a part of metropolitan France.

Where before there had been a principality of five counties with Flint and the Marches — where the king's writ had been without power — the Act of Union now established thirteen counties, ruled by sheriffs and justices of the peace, into whose hands most of the local government soon came. The eastern borders of the eastern counties were to form the Welsh border. As David Williams says:

'As the purpose of the acts was to assimilate Wales to England, the question of a frontier between the two countries did not arise, but in fact, the frontier of Wales was thereby determined.'

The administrative system of English law was imposed throughout the land, giving many of the same rights to individual Welshmen as the English had previously enjoyed in Wales. The counties and the boroughs were given representation in Parliament. That is, the legal, administrative and political system of England was extended to include Wales; and the Welsh were to have about one in every eighteen of the seats in that parliament. And it has remained the 'English Parliament' up to our day. If it were at all British it would have granted the freedom to use Welsh, the oldest of Britain's languages, in its deliberations. But if a Member starts to speak in Welsh he is called to order at once by the Speaker. In the only Parliament that Wales has, the Welshman is not even allowed to take the oath in the Welsh language.

In this way the lordships were abolished; but since most of them were already in the hands of the king — only four independent lordships remained — this did not make much difference. What remained of the Welsh law, and particularly the land system, was abolished.

'The Act of Union offered no compromise,' says Hywel Emanuel, 'English law "and none other" was to apply throughout Wales.'

Since the law had not had a chance to develop since 1284, there remained only comparatively little of the old law. An attempt was also made to abolish the different customs of Wales:

> 'utterly to extirp all and singular the sinister Usages and customs differing from (his realm of England).'

And most important of all, the attempt which was made to delete the Welsh language,

> 'a speech nothing like, nor consonant to, the natural Mother tongue used within his realm',

by confining every office to those who spoke English. This is what the seventeenth section of the Act states:

> 'Also be it enacted that all justices, Commissioners, sheriffs, coroners, escheators, stewards and their lieutenants, and all other officers and ministers of the law, shall proclaim and keep the sessions, courts, hundreds, leets, sheriff's courts and all other courts in the English tongue; and all oaths of officers, juries and inquests, and all other affidavits, verdicts and wagers of law to be given and done in the English tongue; and also that from henceforth no person or persons that use the Welsh speech or language shall have or enjoy any manner office or fees within this realm of England, Wales or other the Kings Dominion upon pain of forfeiting the same offices or fees, unless he or they use and excercise the English speech or tongue.'

This is the most deleterious clause in an Act that aimed at the annhilation of Wales as a nation and a country:

> 'Some rude and ignorant people,' it says in the introduction, 'have made distinction and diversity between the King's subjects of his realm and his subjects of the said dominion and Principality of Wales.'

To delete every 'distinction and diversity' between the Welsh and the English was its purpose. In order to ensure this, the First Section of the Act states:

> 'That his said Country or Dominion of Wales shall be, stand and continue for ever from henceforth incorporated, united and annexed to and with this his Realm of England.'

'Incorporated' — Yes. 'Annexed' — Yes. But 'for ever'?

*   *   *

On June 10, 1540, Thomas Cromwell, the author and
architect of the policy of the Act of Union, was
1540   executed. In an anonymous article about him in
the Encyclopaedia Britannica (14th Impression) it
says:

> 'In estimating Cromwell's character it must be remembered that his
> father was a blackguard, and that he himself spent his formative years
> in a vile school of morals. Yet he civilised himself to a certain extent,
> and his atrocious acts were done in no private quarrel, but in what he
> conceived to be the interests of his master and the State. Where these
> interests were concerned, he had no heart and no conscience and no re-
> ligious faith; no man was more completely blighted by the 16th
> century worship of the state.'

Two years after the death of Cromwell another Law
pertaining to Wales was passed. This established four
1542   Chancery and Treasury units, in Denbigh and in
Brecon together with those already established in
Carmarthen and Caernarfon.

These units were organised in circuits for the judges,
bringing into existence a special Welsh arrangement of the
Great Sessions which lasted until 1830. For convenience sake
Monmouthshire was put in the Oxford circuit, and Chester in
the north Welsh circuit. This is the only foundation for the
argument that Gwent is part of England in any different way
from the other Welsh counties. No one ever argued that the
similar arrangement made with Chester made that city part
of Wales.

The 1542 Act gave a statutory basis to the Welsh
Council, which continued in being until 1689. During
the next few years its authority was extended as a court
of law, and especially as an administrative body, but
most of its members were English until the time of the Stuarts.
The Courts of the great Session and the Council, ensured for
Wales a measure of separate treatment from England for the
purposes of administering the law and those state public
services which affected the people's lives most heavily. The
English government and state were weak until the middle
of the nineteenth century; until then the all-important element

in public administration were the justices of the peace and the local officials.

The Protestant Reformation and this political reformation coincided. The one was accepted as quietly as the other, and —that a king of Welsh descent could do no wrong. A. H. Dodd draws attention to other reasons:

> 'Two patriotic *motifs* strengthened the hold of Protestantism on the Welsh people: on the one hand the argument that Rome was responsible, through St. Augustine's mission for impairing the purity of Celtic Christianity and the legendary learning enshrined in its monasteries; on the other hand the identification of the papacy with the despised 'Gwyddelod' (Irish) and the dreaded 'dynion duon' of Spain — both of them standing threats to the long and defenceless Welsh coast.'

Forty monasteries and religious houses were destroyed without a blow; the overlordship of the Pope disappeared without opposition; and the Church of England came into its own without protest from the Welsh side. The sole Church in Wales was now the Church of England. At its head stood the King of England who governed Wales through the English Parliament. Protestantism thus came to Wales with an English name and in an English guise. In England itself it was identified with English nationalism. J. E. Neale says that the marriage of Mary to Philip of Spain, 'aroused the Englishry of everyone . . . to be mere English and to be Protestant began to seem one and the same thing'. The Protestant reformation was not embraced in Wales as a spiritual power; it was forced on a country, where both the patriotism of the people and the leadership of the old Faith were too weak to withstand it effectively. Decades went by before there were any signs of revival in the old Faith. It was not before the end of the fifties that there was a serious struggle between the Catholics and the Protestants of deep conviction for the mind and soul of the Welsh people. When the clash came the opponents had one great bond in common — a burning love for the language and culture of Wales.

Puritanism made hardly any impression on Wales in the

age of Elizabeth, although Breconshire produced the first Welsh Puritan martyr in John Penry, who was
1593 executed in 1593. He had received his education in Cambridge and Oxford, and he did his main work in England; but his second book, which was printed
1588 by a secret press in 1588, was 'An Exhortation unto the Governours and people of hir Maiesties countrie of Wales'. In his appeal to Parliament, which was published as a 'Humble Supplication', he argues fervently for getting a sufficient number of Welsh-speaking preachers in Wales; and this patriotic man was on his way from Scotland to Wales to preach 'in my poor countrie of Wales' when he was arrested and accused of treason. As Tudur Jones says, 'he is sure of a place in the national tradition because of his great concern for Wales'.

The most menacing development was the use made of the English language as a political weapon to kill the
1549 Welsh nation. For a period after 1549, after English had become the language of the church services, which had quite openly become the Church of England in Wales, English was the language of law, administration and religion. Most important of all, from now on, English was the only language of personal advancement. At this time one needed great faith to see any future at all for the Welsh language, and therefore for the national civilisation. It was the English language that had made Englishmen of the Brythons, the Danes, the Vikings and the Normans. From 1536 to our day it has been used to try and make Englishmen of the Welsh. The English language did much more than the government itself to denude the Welsh of their national identity. It was deliberately used to fulfil that function. This policy was described by William Salesbury in 1547 in his address to Henry VIII at the beginning of his *Dictionary in English and Welsh*:

'Your excellent wysdome . . . both caused to be enacted . . . that there shal hereafter be no difference in lawes and language bytwyxte your subjects of your principalyte of Wales and your other subjects of your Royalme of England.'

From the standpoint of Welsh civilisation, language was more important even than 'lawes'. Yet not even so learned a man, and so great an humanitarian as Salesbury had an understanding of the functions of language in society. Anglophiles believed that the sole purpose of language is to convey ideas and feelings. If people could learn to do that in English, why remain faithful to Welsh? They did not see that a language unites the generations; gives deep roots to society and a continuity that makes for healthy development; deepens and enriches its life; mediates between modern and ancient cultures; is able to recreate a culture by its own mysterious power; creates a pattern of values which civilise; enlivens the mental and spiritual life; enriches immeasurably the quality of life of the individual; that her language is in fact the main vehicle of a nation's civilisation. The creation of language is man's greatest feat. In the materialistic age of the Tudors they knew nothing of all this, and if they did, they didn't care. Transmitting a civilisation to the future was not a deep concern of theirs. English was the language of worldly advancement, and this was the most important concern in the life of the great and influential.

In consequence, the governing of Wales was put into the hands of the very small minority who knew English. The monoglot Welsh-speakers — 95% of the nation — became second-class citizens in their own country. The Welsh could enjoy the same rights as the English certainly, but on one condition: that they stopped being Welsh. They could acquire equal rights only if they abandoned their language and learned English. Even in the twentieth century Welshmen would still be persuaded by the combined pressures of law, education and commerce that they could not be fully successful or civilised unless they accepted equality on these terms.

Four centuries after the Act of Union had been passed this atrocious state of affairs would still persist. Until the 1940's for example, if a Welshman wanted to speak Welsh in a court of law in Wales, he had to do so through an interpreter, for English remained the only language of every court of law and the only official language of Wales — even in the completely Welsh-speaking areas. On top of this, the Welsh-speaking witness would have to pay the interpreter for his services; that is, pay for speaking his own language in his own country. Neither a Chinese, nor an Arab, nor a Greek nor anyone else would have to pay for this service when he spoke his own language in a Welsh court of law: only the Welsh had to pay. Even today, in the seventies, when Welsh women prisoners are sent to prison in England they are not allowed to speak Welsh to their visitors. Perhaps they have never before spoken a word of English to their parents, but when the mother or father goes to see their daughter in prison, they may not be allowed to speak Welsh together. The Welsh girl thus receives extra punishment: an insult to personal dignity. She is denied a basic human right, so that the system can keep the Welsh language in its inferior position. The splendid ancient language of the bards and the princes has been the language of second-class citizens ever since the Act of Union was passed.

Facing the British

I. THE ALIENATION OF THE NOBLEMEN

IN THE thirties of this century Jules Benda wrote a book entitled *Le Trahaison des Clercs*. In it, he castigates the intelligentsia, who, by virtue of their position and privileges, should have given France leadership, but had failed to do so. The noblemen, who had been the leaders of Wales in the past, were still the country's natural leaders in the time of the Tudors and afterwards. It was these who betrayed the nation. In contrast with the Irish aristocracy who were in exile or were decimated by death in battle for Ireland, the Welsh aristocracy faded into rootless, anglicised landlords in whom, strive as one may, one can discern little that is admirable. In relation to their native land, its freedom and civilisation, they were as irresponsible as their ancestors had been honourable. It was they who ensured the success of the Tudor policy. It is true that some of the old aristocracy had died out or had been supplanted, and a number of ambitious administrators, merchants and lawyers had risen to take their place, thereby creating a new bourgeoisie with typical bourgeois values. Lawyers were particularly numerous, and, with a few exceptions, rootless. It was claimed that half the lawyers of the kingdom were Welshmen.

> 'This class,' says R. T. Jenkins, 'was chosen by King Henry with the explicit intention of destroying national feeling in Wales. This, in short, was the design of Henry VIII and Elizabeth: to create a new landowning class in Wales, to bind them tightly to the throne and to turn them into Englishmen.'

Thomas Brwynllys, a poet of Elizabeth's reign, complained that these new pseudo-noblemen had no aim beyond profit. They stole the land of the poor, he said, and they did not give hospitality to the poets, and he attributes the situation to the new laws:

An Acte for Lawes and Justice to be ministered in Wales in like fourme as it is in this Realme.

Albeit the Domynyon Principalitie and Countrey of Wales justly and right-uouslye is and ev hath ben incorporated annexed united & subiecte to & under the Imperiall Crowne of this Realme as a verye membre and ioynte of the same. (Wherefore) the Kinges moost Roiall Majestie of mere droite and verye right is verie hedde King Lorde and Ruler, yet notwithstanding bycause that in the same Country Principalitie and dominion dyvers rightes usage lawes and customes be farre discrepant frome the Lawes and Customes of this Realme, And also bycause that the people of the same Dominion have and do daily use a speche nothing like ne consonaunt to the nat-urall mother tonge used within this Realme. sõme rude and ignorant people have made distinccion and divsitie betwene the Kinges Subjectes of this Realme and hys Subjectes of the said Dominion and Principalitie of Wales, whereby grete discorde variaunce debate dyvysion murmur and sedicion hath growen betwene his said subjectes: His Highness therefore of a singuler zele love and favour that he beareth towardes his subjectes of his said Dominion of Wales, mynding and entending to reduce them to the pfecte order notice & knowledge of the lawes of this his Realme, and utterly to extirpe all and singuler the senister usages and customes differinge frome the same, and to bringe his said Subjectes of this his Realme and of his said Dominion of Wales to an amicable concorde and unitie, Hath by the deliberate advise consent and agreement of the Lordes spuall and temporall and the Cõmons in this p̃sent (parliament) assembled and by the auctoritie of the same, ordeyned enacted and established that his said Countrey and Dominion of Wales shal be stonde and contynue for ev fromhensforthe incorporated united and annexed to and with this his Realme of Englande

MDXXXVI

From "The Act of Union" 1536

Y BEIBL CYS-SEGR-LAN, SEF YR HEN DESTA-MENT, A'R NEWYDD.

2. Timoth. 3. 14, 15.

Eithr aros di yn y pethau a ddyscaift, ac a ynddyried-
wydi ti, gan wybod gan bwy y dyfcaift.
Ac i ti er yn fachgen wybod yr fcrythur lân, yr hon
fydd abl i'th wneuthur yn ddoeth i iechydwria-
eth, trwy'r ffydd yr hon fydd yng-Hrift Iefu.

Imprinted at London by the Deputies of
CHRISTOPHER BARKER,
Pfinter to the Queenes moft excel-
lent Maieftie.

1588.

'Mor gaeth yw'r gyfraith a gaid.'

How constraining is the law we were given.

The abundance of poems complaining about the hardness of life during Elizabeth's reign bears testimony to the fact that the Act of Union did not bring about economic stability in Wales. In later centuries the consequences of the Act would be grim indeed: Wales would become a fringe country, governed by a distant London, which would become the distant focus of its life; instead of a balanced economic development, there would be gross imbalance with long periods of poverty and unemployment.

The noblemen were not immediately weaned away from the culture and language of Wales. It was to take three generations even for the highest of the families to lose their Welshness; and the whole class was not anglicised until about the middle of the seventeenth century. Ogwen Williams draws our attention to the Herbert family as an example of this process among the wealthiest people. William Herbert, Earl of Pembroke, who was born in 1501, was more at home in Welsh than in English; it was in Welsh that he spoke to other Welshmen in the royal court. His son (1534-1601) was more English in outlook and language but he too spoke Welsh fluently and was a patron of Welsh scholarship and literature: he intended to establish a college in Wales. His son, William Herbert's grandson, spoke no Welsh, and lived in England. In all probability, the final anglicisation of this class occurred when wives and daughters stopped speaking Welsh in the homes after the Civil War. By this time, the nobles had ceased to identify themselves with their own country and to communicate with it; they gave it no leadership; they felt no responsibility towards it, and, with a few exceptions, acquitted none of their proper duties towards it. A sterile class, they took much out of Wales without putting anything back. They declined into a clique of useless landlords, parasitic and anglicised. As they became richer, the *gwerin* became poorer. These people, who were now the

Englishry, were the all-important justices of the peace. Later on they formed a party — the Tory Party — the party of the Englishry in Wales; the twentieth century struggle between it and the Labour Party — the party of the rootless *gwerin* — would rend Wales on mainly English issues, as had fighting between the two English parties of the War of the Roses. This alienated Welsh upper class, a phenomenon of the last three centuries, is the bitter fruit of the Tudor policy for turning Welshmen into Englishmen: the instrument created to facilitate the implementation of English policy.

> 'The intention of the Tudors,' says J. F. Rees, 'was that Wales should lose separate identity and become completely merged in England.'

The creation of this rootless and sterile and often absentee class was their Welsh masterpiece.

In *Gweledigaethau'r Bardd Cwsg*, written at the beginning of eighteenth century, Elis Wynne gives a description of the fate of the many of the houses in which patrons of Welsh culture had lived.

> 'We descended on an enormous roofless Mansion, whose eyes had been pulled out by the Dogs and the Crows, and whose owners had left for England, or France . . . so instead of the old hospitable family, there is no one here now except stupid old Aunt Owl, or rapacious Crows, or greedy Magpies or the like, to make known the accomplishments of the present owners. We saw a host of such foresaken mansions which could be, but for Pride, the meeting-place of good men, the refuge of servants, schools of Peace and all Good, and a blessing to a thousand small houses around them . . .'

These sentiments echoed in the *englynion* of Ieuan Brydydd Hir, to the Court of Ifor Hael:

> Yno nid oes awenydd,—na beirddion
>   Na byrddau llawenydd,
>   Nac aur yn ei magwyrwydd,
>   Na mael, na gŵr hael a'i rhydd.
>
> Y llwybrau gynt lle bu'r gân
> Yw lleoedd y dylluan.

> There's no more genius there, no bards,
>   no boards of happiness,
>   no gold within its walls,
>   no mail, no generous giver.
>
> The paths where once was singing
> are now the owl's places.

The more Wales's national identity weakened, the more Welsh hospitality which was so fine an aspect of the culture of the noblemen, disappeared likewise. Wales became a lonelier land as it became more English.

Although the nation languished during the reigns of Henry VIII and Elizabeth, many individuals from this class shone in positions of authority as politicians, soldiers, churchmen, scholars and lawyers. William Cecil, Lord Burleigh, was one of the Cecils of Allt yr Ynys on the banks of the Mynwy, and until his death he did not lose contact with his old home. Four Welshmen in succession were bishops on the Isle of Man. One of them, John Phillips, translated the Bible and the Prayer Book into the Manx language. William Thomas, the scholar, was clerk to Edward VI's Privy Council: he was later executed in the reign of Mary for his Protestant zeal. Some succeeded in industry and commerce; Morgan Williams of Morgannwg, for example, built up a prosperous brewery business in Putney. He married the sister of Thomas Cromwell. His son Richard, who owned Neath Abbey and its lands, took the name Cromwell. Oliver Cromwell was his great-grandson. The complete list is long and distinguished, the number of able men who came from this small land of a quarter of a million people is surprising.

Up until the Tudor period most of the *estroniaid* (foreigners) who came to Wales were Cymricised; from then on they became anglicised again; and many of them went to London. A number of the Norman families had become staunch Welshmen and patrons of the Welsh tradition; in the seventeenth century, however, they too turned English, and became London-centred: families such as the Salisburys and Stradlings, Turbervilles and Thelwals, Hollands and Myddletons. It was Sir Hugh Myddleton who brought water

to London. All his family were patrons of Welsh culture —
Sir Thomas Myddleton of Castell y Waun (Chirk Castle) and
William Myddleton who was a poet and a scholar of renown.

Most of the people who went to London stopped serving
Wales; but those who stayed at home too ceased to support
Welsh scholarship and culture. By the middle of the
seventeenth century they had given up patronising the poets
whose position in society had done so much to support the
language even in the half century after the passing of the Act
of Union. The poets remained numerous in the reign of
Elizabeth; the famous Caerwys eisteddfod of 1523 was
followed by another one there, by commission of the Queen,
in 1594. In time the Order of Bards, and their bardic schools
declined and disappeared; and the monastery schools had
stopped being an effective element in the life of the country
long before they were abolished in 1536 and 1539. The boys
who received a formal education went to the new Grammar
Schools, which were established to educate the governing
class. The national language had no place in these schools.
When Latin ceased to be used as the medium it was replaced
not by Welsh but by English. The sons of the wealthiest
families went to Shrewsbury and Westminster and other
schools and universities in England. Wales was left without
indigenous institutions to strengthen its life, and without
leaders to encourage and lead it. The fact that the first book
printed in Welsh was produced in a cave by Catholic fugitives
testifies to this lack of patronage. This great lack necessarily
had a bad influence on the standards of all the arts.
Communication with Europe had helped to maintain standards
in the past; but since England was now the big world to the
ruling class, Wales's connections with the Continent were
cut and as a result standards suffered. Welsh minds became
parochially English, and there was no structure built on the
foundations nobly set by the humanists.

When the noblemen ceased to be Welsh in all but name,
the nation had no one to turn to for national leadership.
One can compare her situation with that of Ireland. The mass
of the Irish population was left leaderless by 'the flight of the

earls' in 1607 and the flight of 'the Wild Geese' in 1690. The
Welsh leaders did not flee but the nation of Wales was left just
as leaderless as the Irish. In Wales the leaders were lost by
anglicisation. They stayed, but as un-Welsh parasites. Wales
had to wait for its *gwerin* to produce its own leaders. The very
idea of a Welsh state was utterly lost; no one mentioned
national freedom now. Already, in the age of Elizabeth,
politics had deteriorated into mere rivalry between the big
families, and for three centuries this is the sum of political
activity. For example, in the struggle between the Earl of
Leicester and the Earl of Essex each had his Welsh faction.
The Earl of Leicester was the brother-in-law of Sir Henry
Sidney, the Chairman of the Welsh Council and an uncle of
the Earl of Pembroke; while the Earl of Essex, Elizabeth's
favourite, came from the Devereux family, of an old Welsh
Norman stock. Typical of this new age is the fact that a number
of Welshmen followed him in his foolish rebellion of 1601 —
to London.

The history of Wales is different from that of England
every step of the way. And one of the main differences between
the two nations over the past four centuries is this: England
had a responsible aristocracy which served it well, whereas
Wales had an irresponsible aristocracy which betrayed it.
For three centuries, the aristocracy was in effect the ruling
class in Wales because they were the justices of the peace.
In their hands was the executive power which affected the
everyday life of the people. The central government's power
was really very confined until about the middle of the nineteenth century. Yet theirs was an English government: it
served England and it strengthened it, while it oppressed and
weakened Wales.

II. THE FAITHFUL REMNANT

ALTHOUGH a new generation arose that did not know much
about the glory of the Welsh tradition, that tradition survived
nevertheless; and the history of Wales, its literature, its

language, the enchanting mother country itself and, although wounded and diminished, the community who had lived there for so many generations also survived. There was still a body of people who knew the value of their heritage, and who were willing to make every effort to preserve and to pass it on. At the heart of the heritage was a pattern of values. The values incorporated in the nation's tradition, enrich the cultural life of its individual members; and the traditions of Europe's nations are basic to (and indeed they compose) European civilisation. Apart from them, European civilisation does not exist. When the life of a nation is destroyed, then a piece of civilisation is destroyed. The first duty of every nation is to remain a nation and to take care of its own corner of the wider civilisation. The people who performed this duty of sustaining Welsh civilisation during the Welsh crisis of the Tudor period, at a time when most of their contemporaries were too busy getting on in the world, were the humanists. One of them at least, Edward Kyffin, who was born within a stone's throw of Sycharth, Glyndwr's home, nearly a century and a half after the death of Glyndŵr, believed that God allowed the nation and the language to survive because he had a purpose for Wales.

> 'How much more should we succour our own language,' he said, 'which Almighty God has defended in the one country in this kingdom . . . among so many quarrelling nations, tumults and destructive troubles which have sought to destroy and ravage our language and our people. No other nation or language in the countries of Christendom say the same.'

If we agree with Edward Kyffin that the life of a nation is in the hands of God, it would follow that the humanists were the agents he used to foster the nation and the language in Wales. During this critical period they are the connecting link in the providential succession which kept Wales a nation. They received the tradition from the bards. William Salesbury, the doyen of the humanists, for example, and also Richard Davies, were friends of Gruffudd Hiraethog, the great poet educated by Tudur Aled, three of them coming from Llansannan in Denbighshire, and Richard Davies from a neighbouring district. 'My chief companion in such things,' Salesbury called Gruffudd Hiraethog, a very influential man who wrote a chronicle on the war of Glyndŵr. Gruffudd Hiraethog was the teacher of Simwnt Fychan, who died in 1606, and a pupil of Tudur Aled who had been in his turn a pupil of Dafydd Nanmor, born early in the fifteenth century. Simwnt Fychan was a poet learned in the bardic traditions, who made his own edition of the bardic rules of grammar, adding a section on *Cynghanedd*. Here we have an example of the advantage that Welsh literature derived from the fact that poetry was a vocation:

> 'For,' says Saunders Lewis, 'in this way a succession of the bardic schools was assured; and since tradition is the essence of all education, there grew and matured in those schools a body of literary criticism and theoretical discussion about literature, that continued from Einion Offeiriad to Simwnt Fychan. And this body of theories is Wales' main contribution to the aesthetic thought of Europe.'

But, from lack of patrons, this great succession came to an end before the middle of the seventeenth century.

It was Salesbury, together with Richard Davies, who had been a fugitive on the Continent at the time of Mary's persecution, who translated the New Testament into Welsh in 1567, and also the Book of Common Prayer: yet another member of this outstanding circle of scholars was Bishop William Morgan who made the magnificent translation of the Bible into Welsh which was published in 1588. When Griffith Jones pioneered the revival of education in the eighteenth century the study of this Bible was the basis of the course. This was followed by the great spiritual revival later on in the century, which shook the nation to its roots. In all of these events Welsh was the medium of communication. And for the next hundred and fifty years, the national tradition was safe in the hands of the alert *gwerin*. It was the *gwerin*, whose better could not be found anywhere, who then fulfilled the functions of the aristocracy; and their mental and spiritual culture was their glory. But had any one of these five links been missing Welsh would not have survived as a spoken language. The bards, the humanists, the translators, the education reformers and the Christian evangelists were all inter-connected. Each one was as completely essential to the continuation of the Welsh tradition as were the heroic efforts of the Welsh of the middle ages down to Owain Glyndŵr.

The main task of the humanists was to try and place Welsh literature on the same footing as the classical literatures as far as purity of forms and wealth of content were concerned:

> 'They evolved a programme for the restoration and development of Welsh letters,' says Geraint Gruffydd. 'This involved the reformation of poetry and the creation of a new prose to be fit vehicles of expression for the New Learning in all its fullness: not only grammar, rhetoric and logic, but also theology, philosophy, mathematics, the sciences, medicine, history, the art of war and so on. It involved the adaptation to the Welsh language of the latest philological techniques, and also the collection and publication of as much as could be salvaged of the ancient learning.'

The continental humanists maintained that a learned language like Latin or Greek had three characteristics: it had been the language of the court and of the prince, it was the language that had been cultivated in schools and, finally, it had been used as a medium to discuss all the arts and sciences. The late G. J. Williams showed that the Welsh humanists maintained that these three characteristics were found in the Welsh language. It was thus equal, in their view, to the languages of Greece and Rome. This belief had a profound, if unconscious, effect on the attitude towards the language in succeeding centuries. Unlike Breton, which was spoken by a larger population, the Welsh language has always been a greatly cherished literary and scholarly tongue.

The work of the humanists, most of them lay graduates of Oxford, show what the attitude of cultured Welshmen would have been towards their language and the tradition of their country but for the anglicising of the educational, religious, legal and political systems. One of their methods was to compose grammars, such as the works of Gruffydd Robert, Sion Dafydd Rhys and John Davies, Mallwyd.

Although most of the humanists were protestants, there were catholics among the. These were particularly strong in the southern marches, and are known to have held services in Welsh in 1605 at Darren, in the woods opposite Ynys Gynwraidd (Skenfrith). Gruffydd Robert was one of the few really great men of this splendid company. He was the elected Bishop of Bangor in Mary's time, but on the accession of Elizabeth he fled to the Continent in the company of Morys Clynnog, the author of *Yr Athrawiaeth Gristnogol* (The Christian Doctrine). Gruffydd Robert lived in Italy for most of his life, as secretary and confessor to the excellent Cardinal Borromeo in Milan. And it was there, in one of the chief courts in Europe, where the Counter-Reformation had its beginnings, that he wrote his famous grammar, a literary piece in the Ciceronian style which reflects the learning and outlook of the Renaissance. 'Here, in the reflections of one of the greatest literary geniuses our nation has ever produced,' says Saunders Lewis, 'we witness the humanism of Renaissance Europe contending with the literary tradition of Wales . . . He (Gruffydd Robert) is the founder of the school of prose writers called by Emrys ap Iwan, the Welsh Classics . . . He is the originator of modern literary Welsh. His style was the pattern for the Welsh humanists. Through him the Ciceronianism of Italy came directly to influence modern Welsh prose, and to create it. Sion Dafydd Rhys, a colourful and erudite member of the second team of humanists, also spent some years in Italy after completing his medical education at Oxford and Siena. He published three remarkable books while he was there, two of which dealt with Greek and Latin grammar and syntax. In the third, which was written in Italian and published in Venice in 1567, and republished later, he compared Italian pronunciation with that of Spanish, Portuguese, German, French, Polish, English and Welsh. On returning to Wales he spent a short period as headmaster of Friars School, Bangor, leaving there to assist his uncle, Bishop Richard Davies, with his translation of the scriptures at Abergwili. Later he practised medicine at Cardiff and Brecon, to which he drew patients from all parts of the country. Of the scholarly works he published after his return to Wales the best known is his splendid Welsh Grammar. The humanists energetically enriched Welsh scholarship by compiling dictionaries and collecting manuscripts. For example, John Gellilyfdy, a lawyer from Flintshire, copied out over a hundred volumes of manuscripts in his own hand. One of the most interesting is *Troelus a Chresyd*, a long dramatic tragedy on a theme used by Shakespeare at about the same time. In 1957 Gwyn Williams drew attention to a feature of particular interest in this play: the dramatist's handling of the character of Calcas:

'In the Welsh play we are given, by means of a long soliloquy, a penetrating analysis of the mind of a Quisling . . . the analysis of Calcas . . . particularly interesting and unique in the history of this love story. Could it be that for sixteenth-century Wales this kind of person, who abandons his own country and its interests for a more profitable existence among his country's enemies, had as much topicality as it had in the Europe of the last twenty years?'

It was Robert Vaughan of Hengwrt, Meirionnydd who made the finest collection of manuscripts. He died in 1666, the same year as Gruffydd Phylip of Ardudwy, the last of the old bards. There were also several historians who strenuously defended the notions about the history of the relationship between the Welsh and the Brythons of England popularized by Geoffrey of Monmouth. The most prominent of these men were Humphrey Llwyd, David Powell, John Davies, and Sir John Price. The last was a typical figure of the Tudor period, the author of *Historiae Britannicae Defensio*, and the publisher of *Yn y Llyvyr hwnn* in 1547; one, though descended on both sides from well known poets, yet profited from the dissolution of the monasteries; a royal placeman, who served at the feast at the wedding of Henry VIII and Anne Boleyn, perhaps because her family, like his, came from Brycheiniog.

But it was in the field of religion that these men did the work which saved the Welsh language and the nation. After 1549 all Church services were in English, adding further to the oppressive pressure of the English on law and the judicial courts and other state bodies. The Prayer Book was translated into Welsh as an aid to salvation and, in less than a generation, it was heard in the churches from Sunday to Sunday. The psalms were set to music by Edmwnd Prys, one of the greatest of the humanists. The New Testament was translated by William Salesbury, Thomas Huet and Richard Davies. This work was completed in the bishop's palace in Abergwili. Richard Davies was a bishop. He followed a fellow Welshman and fellow-exile as bishop of St. David's when Thomas Young was made Archbishop of York. The Bishop's Palace, Abergwili, was the headquarters of the Renaissance in Wales. A picture of it is given by Sir John Wynn of Gwydir, another notable figure, a graduate of Oxford, a landowner, merchant, industrialist, educationalist, patron of literature and himself a writer. He says of the bishop in Abergwili:

> 'he kept an exceeding great post, having in his service younger brothers of most of the best houses in that country, to whom with his own sons he gave good maintenance and education. He called to him William Salesbury, Esquire of Plas Isa, near Llanrwst, and divers others, Welshmen, profound scholars and skilful linguists, and translated the New Testament, the Psalms and Book of Common Prayer into the Welsh tongue.'

The great masterpiece of the period was the translation of the whole Bible; with the help of Edmwnd Prys and Gabriel Goodman this work was done by William Morgan, born in Yr Wybrant, Penmachno, a remote place in the middle of the mountains of Snowdonia. He started this great work in St. John's College, Cambridge, and completed most of it in Llanrhaeadr ym Mochnant before he was elected Bishop of Llandaf.

This splendid work, which was published in 1588, and which was well edited in 1620 by John Davies, one of Wales's greatest scholars, uses the Welsh of the classical poetry in all its powers and purity, its dignity and its refinement. From Sunday to Sunday in the churches of Wales the Word of God would be heard in the language which was spoken in the courts of the princes, the language of the bards of Gwynedd and the bards of Morgannwg; and when 'Y Beibl Bach' (The Little Bible) was published in 1630 with the financial aid of Rowlant Heulyn and Sir Thomas Myddleton, the homes could afford to buy it — a little library of books dealing with the most exalted aspects of life. In this way the Welsh language was restored to its original splendour and identified with what was most important and most dignified. It is impossible to measure the enormous influence of these factors on the character, the mind and the culture of the nation.

III. THE COMING OF BRITISHNESS

IT WAS the highest bourgeois class created by the Tudors, which became less and less homogeneous as time went by, that dominated the seventeenth century in Wales. By the middle of the century it identified itself with England almost entirely; it was English in thought and sympathy, and English in language. As a result this was a century of constant deterioration in Welsh traditional life. But the members of this upper class would not call themselves English: this could hardly have been feasible for persons whose ancestors were Welsh-speaking Welsh people. So they chose to call themselves 'Cambro-British' or just 'British' and their pride was fed by the legend that they were the 'British' who had once possessed England as well as Wales. In two centuries the *gwerin* would be emulating them. When James I became King of England as well as Scotland, he was greeted enthusiastically as 'king of Great Britain'. Later, when Scotland united with England in 1707, many English too would be ready to use the description 'British'; the state was called British, and later still a British nationality was given for passport purposes. The British came into being — 'the form of Englishman created not by God but by lawyers', as Tudur Jones said. Politically and legally, Welsh nationality had come to an end; all the Welsh were British. Later on politicians began to speak boldly about 'the nation' as if there were only one nation on the island. Sometimes, it was called 'the British nation' and sometimes 'the English nation'. English historians and politicians use these terms as though they were synonymous: and in practice both terms do mean the same thing. So the Welsh came to think of themselves as British first and as Welshmen second; while the English were always English first and British second. This is reflected in the political and social loyalty of the two nations. While the English have been splendidly loyal to England and will spare neither blood, nor wealth to defend her, the Welsh consider that the duty of their nation is to serve Britain; the idea of loyalty to Wales disappeared as if it had never existed. For the honour and glory of Britain scores of thousands of them lost their lives in wars: for the sake of the British economy hundreds of thousands suffered poverty and unemployment; for the power and greatness of Britain they sacrificed their national liberty. The Welsh came near to sacrificing their language and their culture and their very existence as a nation on the altar of Britain. The Welsh way of life almost became a British way of death.

The devastating effect of Britishness on the life of Wales is first seen in the seventeenth century. A typical example of this was the Gelli Aur (Golden Grove) family in Carmarthenshire. These used to be called Fychan, but Vaughan was now adopted — the aristocracy had long dropped the old Welsh form of nomenclature; by the middle of the eighteenth century there would hardly be one 'ap' among us. In the Civil War the head of the Fychan family was the ineffective leader of the royalists in the south-west. Lord Carbery was a tyrannical landlord, who was guilty of abusing his tenants in a barbaric fashion. This same man,

'on one occasion, maltreated his tenants in a particularly inhuman fashion,' according to *The History of Carmarthenshire* (editor J. E. Lloyd), 'by cropping their ears, cutting out their tongues, and dispossessing them of their land.'

But whatever his attitude towards his fellow-Welshmen, he was completely and absolutely loyal to the king of England,

and was subsequently rewarded: after the Restoration he became President of the Council of Wales. His brother, William Vaughan of Llangyndeyrn, was a much more humane man than he was: a scholar and a man of culture. His way of helping his fellow-Welshmen was to move them out of the country; in 1617, he established a settlement which proved a failure in less than twenty years in Newfoundland. It was called Cambriol. But William Vaughan too, like all the members of his class, rejoiced in the disappearance of the separateness of the Welsh nation:

'I rejoice,' he said, 'that the memorial of Offa's Dyke is extinguished with love and charity: that our green leeks, sometimes offensive to your dainty nostrils, are now tempered with your fragrant roses.'

When one sees how servile its aristocracy had become one realises how much of a miracle the survival of this nation is.

It was serving England that gave a purpose to the squirearchy of Wales, and which brought wealth and fame to their families. Many continued to serve in the armed forces: Sir Charles Lloyd of Montgomeryshire, for example, a descendant of the princes of Powys, became the general in charge of all the engineers and military installations of Britain; and Sir Thomas Morgan of Llangatwg, Breconshire, who could speak only Welsh when he began his successful military career, ended as the governor of Jersey where the name of Owain Lawgoch still lived. London was the focus of activity for these people. There were, it is true, two other centres that the Welsh made for, not one of them in Wales itself. From Gwynedd in particular they went to Dublin, where there was quite a large Welsh community. Since the Welsh who went to Dublin were so extremely English and Protestant in outlook they had no sympathy with the native and Catholic Irish life. In contrast to the relationship in the middle ages, they looked, upon the Irish as enemies; that too was the attitude of most of the host of Welshmen who settled in Ireland from time to time.

The other centre was Ludlow. This pleasant little town was the nearest the Welsh came to having a capital. It was there that the Council of Wales used to meet, and there that its officers lived. The court there attracted the Welsh nobility away from their own counties to a place where they could come into contact with people from different parts of the country: this fostered in them some small amount of Welsh consciousness that they would not otherwise have had. There, in 1618, with King James, they listened to Ben Johnson's *For the Honour of Wales*, and revelled in such lines as:

'Where hath the crown at all times better servitors.'

In 1634 Milton's *Comus* was played there, and his dignified tribute to Wales was also listened to:

'An old, and haughty nation proud in arms.'

The lawyers of Ludlow presented a plan to incorporate the town in Wales so that it could act as a Welsh metropolis. Had this succeeded Wales would have had a capital with a little more operative power than Cardiff has today; but there is somewhat more Welshness in Cardiff than there was in Ludlow. During the Republican period the Council 1649- was supplanted by other institutions. For three years, 1652 from 1649-1652, the government of Wales as an entity was almost wholly in the hands of General Berry's Commission. David Williams says of this Commission:

'it constitutes the only attempt made throughout the centuries to grant Wales a measure of self-government.'

But this short period of burgeoning political recognition was an unhappy time for the state Church in Wales; three hundred of its clergy lost their livelihood, for good reasons as a rule, such as intoxication and inability to preach in Welsh. When Charles II came to the throne, with a warm welcome from Wales, the Council was restored, and continued in existence until 1689. On its abolition in that year, Wales was left without 1689 any form of national institution except its Court of Great Sessions; and London was to have no further rival in the form of a Welsh capital until Brussels and Strasbourg came into the picture.

London politics were lifeless and unprincipled in Wales throughout the century, being nothing more nor less than a struggle for power between the big families: and the history of the whole of the following century was to be the same. The Bulkeley family represented Anglesey in Parliament for 53 years in succession after the Restoration in 1660, while the borough of Carmarthen returned the Vaughans of Gelli Aur for 62 years. At least, there was something of importance in the balance for England in the Civil War.

IV. ENGLISH PARTY DISSENSIONS AGAIN

WHEN the Parliament party and the King's party went to war against each other, Wales became once again a recruiting ground for the armies of the king, who showed, for as long as he needed the help of the Welsh, some sympathy with Welsh nationhood. This was to be the pattern from now on. The Welsh were destined to be used by England or an English Party. Five centuries earlier, Giraldus Cambrensis had written of the Welsh: 'Their mind is on defending their country and freedom alone: it is for their country that they fight, for freedom they labour!' We have now reached the modern period, when the Welshman defends almost everything except his own country.

Although there were substantial pockets of support for the Parliament party in the south of Pembrokeshire and the small towns of Morgannwg and in Wrexham, it was on the king's side that the majority of the Welsh fought, because Henry Tudor was of Welsh descent: but the situation was totally different from the Wars of the Roses two centuries earlier. At that time the Welsh believed that they were fighting for Wales and freedom: they zealously supported the great Welsh leaders. Now, however, nobody believed the war had anything to do with Wales and freedom, and even the royalist leaders were cool. The war was regarded as a crusade it is true, by a

Griffith Jones

James Davies' School, Grosmont, Gwent, 1815-48

small minority of Puritans such as Vavasor Powell and Walter Cradoc. Tudur Jones tells us that these two recruited over four hundred Welshmen and led them to fight under Cromwell, as captains, in the Battle of Dunbar, in Scotland, in 1651. But, for the most part, the civil war was an English quarrel. Although the battles near Montgomery and Saint Fagans were bloody, this fighting did not affect the course of the history of the Welsh nation at all; and certainly it did nothing to strengthen the Welsh tradition. There had been no enthusiasm when, in 1640, a large army was recruited in Wales to fight in Scotland:

'the largest force ever recruited there since the Act of Union,' says A. H. Dodd, 'and that for a war which served no obvious Welsh interest — to fight the Scottish Covenanters.'

Archbishop John Williams changed sides. He was the most able of the Welshmen who took part in the war, although his native land meant nothing to him except as a subject for sentimental reflection. He had been Lord Keeper of the Great Seal, the only Protestant prelate ever to hold that position. He was a patron of English scholarship and himself a scholar, and it was he who built the beautiful library of St. John's College, Cambridge. He became Archbishop of York. Gardiner, the Civil War historian, maintains that if Charles had trusted John Williams rather than Laud, 'there would have been no civil war and no dethronement.' An exemplar of his class and period, this able man did nothing at all for Wales. He fought well for the king. He repaired and defended Conwy castle at his own cost, but having lost it, he came to terms with Mytton, who led the government army there, and retreated with the king's party.

After England had returned to less violent politics, many Welshmen made a successful political career in a field which was completely English. During that generation, Wales produced one Lord Chancellor, two state secretaries and two Speakers in the House of Commons. Its population by the end of the century was about 350,000, that is, almost 5% of the population of the island. During the reign of Charles II, one Chief Justice was a Welshman; and almost all the chief legal officers of James II were Welshmen. The service given by this generation of politicians to Wales was as meagre as that of the generations which followed it, but it is probable that we have Sir John Vaughan of Trawscoed, Chief Judge of the Court of Common Pleas, to thank for retaining the Welsh courts for another period. Perhaps Sir Leoline Jenkins, who came fron Cowbridge, can be considered as a sort of Welsh benefactor too, since he was the second founder of Jesus College, Oxford. He is said to be the first of the three great judges who served in the Admirality Court. The last of the three, S. T. Evans, was also a Welsh-speaking Welshman from Glamorgan; but while S. T. Evans was a nationalist who supported home rule for Wales, it never occurred to Leoline Jenkins and his prosperous fellow Welshmen to raise their little finger in support of the political liberation of their own nation.

V. THE UPHOLDERS OF THE TRADITION

DURING the troublesome lean period a group of good men continued to strive for what was best in the life of the nation. The one thing common to this group of men, whether secular or ecclesiastic, was their attempt to enlighten the people. With the decline of the older order the bulk of the people became more and more uneducated, though it would be a dire mistake to imagine that a *gwerin* which included a substantial number of descendants of the old freemen was completely illiterate and cultureless. The blood of the noblemen went into the veins of the *gwerin* for a less respectable reason than a mere decline in wealth and status; aristocrats sired numbers of illegitimate children. Take Sir Rhys ap Thomas, for example: although it is not known exactly how many illegitimate children he had, it is certain that he had at least fourteen: ten of them by the sister of the abbot of Talyllychau. Welsh sexual virility was sometimes attributed to the mists. It is impossible to believe that the *gwerin* of Wales, although it had never been a homogeneous class, ever corresponded to 'peasants'. The yokel chewing his straw has been an unknown character in Wales; and he does not exist in Welsh-speaking Wales even today. There, one is continually surprised by the courtesy and the culture which belongs to the simplest and the poorest and the weakest in mind and personality. The education afforded by the Welsh tradition is responsible for this.

Inside the Church, the greatest benefactors were those who could be called Puritans. It was through literature and education most particularly that these people worked. The printed word could be popular and influential although pedestrian, as testified in the verses of Rhys Prichard, vicar of Llandovery, which were publicised by Stephen Hughes under the title *Canwyll y Cymry*. Or it could be excellent in style, and content, as in the work of Charles Edwards, who devoted a substantial part of the second edition of *Y Ffydd Ddiffuant* to a discussion of Welsh history, which he handles with great sympathy. No more splendid prose that this was written in the seventeenth century. It is significant that the author was a native of Llansilin, which is within a few miles of Oswestry near the English border, and close to Sycharth where Owain Glyndŵr was born.

The Puritans were the leaven in the religious bread. They were found inside and outside the Church. Some of them, like Stephen Hughes, who published many valuable Welsh books, remained faithful to the established Church until a hundred and ten clergy were thrown out after the Uniformity Law of 1661. Although the persecution suffered by the nonconformists at this time was not so harsh as that suffered by the Catholics after 1673 (when three were hanged in Wales) it left very bitter feelings. Some of them had been persecuted before this. Vavasor Powell was brought before the law in 1642; in 1653 he was imprisoned for a polemic against Cromwell; and it was in prison that this fiery preacher died in 1670 after spending nine years there. Dozens of Puritans were persecuted in the sixties and scores were heavily fined. Their tough commitment at this time helped to restore a little of its former courage to the Welsh character. They had to suffer the presence of spies because of their stand against the English establishment; these spies were remarkably like the plain clothes detectives who were to become such an unpleasant feature of Welsh political life three centuries later.

About two thousand Welsh Quakers left Wales in the eighties to settle in Pennsylvania because of persecution; an irreparable loss for the nation. For the same reason, the Armenian Baptists of Radnorshire and the Calvinistic Baptists of west Wales emigrated to the same part of America. These groups produced many of America's leaders in the eighteenth century. The names of no less than eighteen men of Welsh descent are found among the fifty-six who signed the Declaration of Independence in 1776. Fourteen generals of Welsh descent fought on the American side in the War of Independence; a number of the state governors and founders of colleges were of Welsh stock; Thomas Jefferson was proud of his Welsh descent.

By now about 5% of the 350,000 population were nonconformist. The first to establish their church outside the state Church were the Independents, whose first chapel was built in Llanfaches in Gwent in 1639. This was the work of three men who had been clergymen of the Church of England: William Wroth, William Erbury and Walter Cradoc. In 1649 John Miles founded the first Welsh Baptist Church in Ilston in Gower; and he also organized other churches, which were founded soon afterwards, in a denominational pattern. These nonconformists had a number of schools and academies which gave an excellent education, such as the academy of Samuel Jones, Brynllywarch, who had been a fellow and don in Jesus College, Oxford. The principal was himself a fine preacher, and the academy produced a number of good preachers, who were also men of great culture, so that it was called the 'University of Nonconformist Prophets'. One of its students was Rees Price, the father of Dr. Richard Price, the philosopher and mathematician, who was educated in a similar academy. Richard Price's *Civil Liberty* had a great influence on the

1639

1649

1628–
1697

American Revolution, and he was invited by Congress in 1778 to regulate the financial affairs and the budget of the States. He received the degree of LL.D. from the University of Yale — an honour awarded only to him and Washington. He welcomed the French Revolution, and it was his *Love of Country* which inspired Edmund Burke to write his *Reflections* in 1790. 'He promoted freedom everywhere,' says his biographer but national freedom was no part of his vision. The author of *Observations on Civil Liberty* was one of the fathers of individualistic radicalism in the countries of Britain.

William Edwards was a nonconformist minister of different inclinations. He was born and bred in Croes-wen near Caerffili, where he remained as a minister all his life. He was both an engineer and an industrial builder. Of all the bridges that he built, the one in Pontypridd is the best known. It is a bow bridge; the largest in the world when built in 1755. This together with its beauty is what made it so famous. E. T. Williams says:

> 'From the start, the bridge excercised a scientific and an aesthetic appeal. Due to its design, which is incomparable, its beauty and its technical secrets, it has generated more argument than any other bridge in Britain.'

Not untypical of the learning nurtured by the nonconformist academies was David Lloyd who spent his life ministering to small congregations in south Cardiganshire. Apart from a mastery of Greek, Latin and Hebrew, he wrote poetry in Welsh, French and Italian, all of which he spoke well.

Although the academies supplied an excellent education in the seventeenth century, neither they nor any other educational institution in Wales, made use of the Welsh language; this applied in the schools of Thomas Gouge, which were founded in the seventies, and later in the schools of S.P.C.K. — a society in which Welshmen gained prominence as leaders, — with the exception of twelve such schools in Gwynedd.

It was not only Rhys Pritchard who used Welsh verses to teach the *gwerin*, but also Richard Gwyn, the Catholic martyr, and Morgan Llwyd, the best known of the Puritans, although it is with fine prose that we associate the name of this mystic, and brilliant thinker from Meirionnydd. His *Llyfr y Tri Aderyn* is the outstanding classic of the seventeenth century, unmatched in its combination of style and intellectual power, until we come to the work of Elis Wynne of Glasynys a generation or more later. An enormous number of Welsh books were published by Catholics, Puritans and Church of England clergymen. Some of the translations are among the classics of the language. In poetry Wales had by now a thousand years of tradition behind her; but 1640-1740, the first century of the second millennium, was a poor one, although it did produce some fine poetry, a few good carols, and many harp lyrics which were a valuable addition to the literary treasury. The greatest weakness of that period, when the power of the Welsh tradition had waned, was the lack of an education in Welsh; but at the end of the century, there was a young shepherd boy looking after his sheep on the slopes of Carmarthenshire who was to transform the situation. Wales has had no greater benefactor than this man, who was known as Griffith Jones Llanddowror.

VI. GRIFFITH JONES AND EDUCATION IN WELSH

GRIFFITH JONES's efforts in this field were not, primarily, to preserve the language; just as the translators of the Bible had not had the preservation of the language as their first concern; and that certainly was not in the mind of Elizabeth's government when passing the 1563 Act. On the contrary, their purpose was to make sure that the Welsh learnt English, so that there would be only one language in England and Wales. This was the policy pursued too in Ireland and Scotland. In both those countries they succeeded in exterminating the Gaelic fairly completely after they had destroyed the old native institutions, and both countries suffered at least as cruelly as Wales from the 'diwreiddiedig a'r uchelgeisiol griw', — the deracinated and ambitious gang. In Wales, ninety per cent of the people were Welsh-speaking in the middle of the nineteenth century. We must thank the translation of the Bible and the Book of Common Prayer, and the schools of Griffith Jones for this. The Welsh language became identified with religion and theological debate. In no other Celtic country did this happen. This is why Welsh did not suffer the fate of Gaelic, Cornish and Breton.

Griffith Jones was an educator and organiser of genius. He was also a great preacher; but it was by following his burning vision as an organiser that he accomplished his miracle. He showed his genius as an educator by ignoring the custom of the schools in the previous century and a half — the grammar schools, the state schools, and the schools of Thomas Gouge and the S.P.C.K. English was the medium of instruction in almost all of those; in the Griffith Jones's schools the medium of instruction was Welsh. That was the secret of the quality of the education which they contributed and their success as a system. Welshmen profit best from an education in Welsh. Acknowledgement of this fact was the key to the success of the Sunday Schools under the talented direction of Thomas Charles, himself a product of the academy in Carmarthen two generations later. To say that Griffith Jones's first concern was not to save the language but rather to save souls does not mean that he had no concern for the language. Tudur Jones has drawn attention to his deep convictions, soundly based on his Calvinistic theology, about language and nationality. In 1739 he declared his belief that to destroy the Welsh language is to defy the dispositions of divine Providence:

'Thus . . . appears the loving-kindness of God, in his confounding the languages, and dispersing the people, by giving them different tongues: and if the goodness and wisdom of God must be acknowledged to run through the whole in general, how can it be denied in any particular branch thereof? May we not therefore justly fear, when we attempt to abolish a language . . . that we fight against the decrees of Heaven, and seek to undermine the disposals of divine providence? . . .'

He interpreted the Genesis story of the Tower of Babel as 'a blast against imperialism'. Humanity stands in such peril of an oppressive world government that God has willed the multiplying of nations and languages over the face of the earth. Therefore it is God's will that the Welsh language shall live; to try to erase it is to defy the wisdom of God.

It was as a preacher that Griffith Jones came into prominence. In 1714, when he was living in Lacharn (Laugharne) as vicar of Llandeilo-Abercywyn, Adam Ottley, bishop of St. David's, complained about his practice of preaching on weekdays in churches, churchyards and sometimes on the mountainside to multitudes of people. They came in their thousands from every corner of south Wales to listen to this passionate preacher, one of the early stars of the great spiritual revival. He satisfied the spiritual hunger of a nation that was tired of laxity and purposelessness. He could not conform strictly to the customs of the church, and often during this period he was called before the bishop and the chancellor. But he had a firm supporter in Sir John Phillips, his brother-in-law, a man of great influence, and a Member of Parliament who was a leading supporter of the humane, educational and religious causes of his day. It was Sir John who gave the living of Llanddowror to Griffith Jones, and who wrote to the S.P.C.K.

1731　　in 1731 suggesting that they establish a 'Welch school' there: today English is the language of the school in Llanddowror, but Griffith Jones's education is not to be blamed for that. His method was to establish circulating schools to teach the people to read; and to read the finest literature, which fed the mind and the soul, namely, the books of the Bible. Most of his pupils were adults; the teachers themselves were peripatetic, staying in different places for a number of months. In the words of Griffith Jones:

> 'most of the masters would instruct for three or four hours in the evening after school time, about twice or thrice as many as they had in their schools by day, who could not attend at other times.'

In similar fashion, the Jews of Israel are taught Hebrew today — which had been dead for two thousand years and more as a spoken language.

By 1737 there were 37 circuit schools, with 2,400 pupils in them. When Griffith Jones died in 1761, it stated in
1761　　*Welch Piety* that 3,495 schools had been established, and over 158,000 pupils had received an education

in them. This accounts for almost half the population of Wales
at that time, and scores of thousands were to follow them in
the future; by now Wales was one of the most literate nations
in the world, and its language was the fine Welsh of the Bible.
Only people of culture could have enjoyed, as the Welsh did
later in the century, the poetic interludes of Twm o'r Nant,
who had learnt to read in one of the schools of Griffith Jones,
in Llanefydd, Denbighshire. Had Wales had a government of
her own, these schools could perhaps have had the same sort
of good influence on the economy as the folk schools had on
the economy of Denmark in the following century; for
although these Danish schools, inspired by Bishop
Gruntvig, taught only two subjects, the history and literature
of Denmark, they were instrumental in creating the strong
economy and political order of that small country which is
destitute of nearly all natural resources except the most
important — human resources.

Despite the malice of the government and the neglect it
suffered at the hands of a rather contemptible gentry, Welsh
civilisation had been saved, by dint of work that was just as
important as the feats of the Princes. But if a voluntary Welsh-
language education saved Wales in the eighteenth century,
compulsory English state education came in the following
century to undermine it. Wales was saved temporarily;
more than that could not be done without national freedom.

It was a tremendous feat of organisation, backed by a clear
vision which brought salvation to Wales. Apart from the
schools themselves, it was also necessary to organize the
teachers, to train them, and to pay them. The hard-earned
pennies of the *gwerin* paid most of the bill. The teachers had a
very small salary, but most were people fired by enthusiasm,
who consecrated their lives to the work; many of them were
men of outstanding intelligence and wide culture. One of
them was Morgan Rhys of Cilycwm, a man of deep spirituality
who wrote some of the finest hymns in the Welsh language,
tens of which are still sung. His salary as a teacher was £4 a
year. It was men and women of his depth of commitment
who restored a sense of purpose and direction to the nation's

life in the 18th century. A house in Llanddowror is still called
Yr Hen Goleg (The Old College). It was there that Griffith
Jones trained the young teachers, to begin with, according to
tradition, in the stable loft, more than a century before
Denmark's first folk college was similarly housed by Christian
Kold. By 1764 the story of his work had reached Russia, and
a detailed report was prepared for Catherine II at her request.

   The schools continued to be successful after the death
1773 of their founder. 1773 was the most successful year of
   all. They continued in existence until 1854, when they
were swallowed up by the English system of the National
Society.

VII. HOWELL HARRIS AND THE
SPIRITUAL REVOLUTION

THE feat of Griffith Jones would hardly have been possible
had it not been for the great spiritual awakening among the
gwerin. To a large extent, this was inspired and channelled by
the leaders who were called Methodists. It is always difficult to
judge to what extent a movement is created by the leaders,
and to what extent the leaders are created by the movement.
There can be no doubt that Daniel Rowland, Howell Harris
and Williams Patycelyn were men of uncommon stature and
that the great revival would not have reached such
revolutionary proportions but for them. It made the eighteenth
century one of the greatest in the history of Wales. The real
hero of the century however was the *gwerin* itself. It crowded
the schools of Griffith Jones thirsting after knowledge; it
swarmed to listen to Rowlands, Harris and Williams in its
longing for the truth. It was completely transformed. It lost
much, no doubt, of its music and dance; but it gained in
dimension and purpose. Much of its vivacity went into the
things of the spirit. The educational revival made the Welsh
literate: the spiritual revival made them articulate.

  The prospects of the Welsh language were transformed too
as the search for eternal life became more and more important

for an increasing number of the *gwerin*. Since truth was more important in the eyes of many of the most able people than getting on in the world, and since Welsh was the language of these spiritual concerns, the Welsh language gained more honour in their minds than English. A century was to go by before material advancement would become the main aim of life among the Welsh — with tragic effect on their values and the place of the Welsh language and tradition in their lives.

Politics contributed nothing at all to the greatness of the century. They were trivial and worthless, completely in the hands of the rich and anglicised who spent large sums of money on bribing the voters. The only cause which evoked the least bit of warmth in their breasts was Jacobitism — a matter wholly unrelated to Welsh interests, of course — and with very few exceptions they were too cowardly to do anything effective even for that. In Carmarthen, politics were so meaningless, that the two parties did not even call themselves Whigs and Tories, but quite appropriately, Blue and Red. Here are examples of the ridiculous character of politics in the eighteenth century: in 1767, a thousand new burgesses were created in Aberystwyth and Cardigan by John Pugh Pryse, Gogerddan (ap Rhys had become Pryse, Pryce, Price and even Rice, long before this); his opponent responded by creating a thousand new burgesses in the town of Lampeter, which belonged to him. The second example is the list of costs of Sir William Paxton when he was an unsuccessful candidate in Carmarthenshire in 1802; this is the bill he faced after a fortnight of voting.

> 11,070 breakfasts
> 36,901 dinners
>   684 suppers
> 25,275 gallons of ale
> 11,068 bottles of spirits
> 8,879 bottles of porter
>   460 bottles of sherry
>   509 bottles of cider
> £18-18-0 for milk punch
> £786 for ribbons

The total was over £15,000. These people hardly meant anything to the nation any more, although it was they, with their loud English, who ruled local government and the courts of law. Between them and English government Wales was humiliated and reached its nadir as a nation. In 1730 the national position appeared bare and hopeless. But in its hour of crisis some who were not of the class called noble took effective hold of the leadership.

*   *   *

Griffith Jones and Daniel Rowland, Howell Harris and Williams Pantycelyn were princes of the nation. We have seen that Griffith Jones was a great preacher. Daniel Rowland of Llangeitho, who. began preaching in 1735, with great authority, when he was only twenty-two, was a convert of his. All these leaders were young. Howell Harris was only twenty-one when he embarked on his tempestuous career — the consequence of a profound spiritual experience, under the ministry of Pryce Davies, the vicar of Talgarth. This also occurred in 1735. He soon came into contact with Daniel Rowland. It was while listening to Howell Harris preaching in the cemetery in Talgarth that William Williams Pantycelyn was converted; he was a medical student of nineteen at the time. Hywel Davies was twenty-two when he was converted by Howell Harris in 1738; and Peter Williams was twenty when he was converted in Carmarthen in 1743. Daniel Rowland and Howell Harris had started on their mission three years before John Wesley felt the heat of the spirit in Aldersgate, and four years before George Whitfield began to evangelise. Although the Welsh evangelists co-operated with George Whitfield, the revival in Wales was wholly independent of the Methodism of England, both in its origins and its history.

The land was harrowed by the old nonconformists who had been a valuable element in the nation for two generations. Centuries later, one aspect of their message was expressed by Elfed:

Nid oes i ni offeiriad	For us there is no priest
Ond Iesu Grist ei Hun;	but Jesus Christ alone;
Nac ordeiniadau eraill	nor other ordinance than
Ond geiriau Mab y Dyn.	words of the Son of Man.

Although their numbers were not large—only about 6% of the population at the beginning of the century — their strength and their influence was growing. They put heart into the moral and intellectual life of the nation. 'Pobl ddeallus' (intelligent people), says R. T. Jenkins of them in his *Hanes Cymru yn y Ddeunawfed Ganrif:*

> 'people of an independent turn of mind, used to thinking for themselves, and relying more on their minds than on their feelings.'

In this they differed from the emotional Methodists, who did not lay the same stress on education or on the things of the mind. Nevertheless, it was the emotional gospel, which they presented with such power, that succeeded in changing the quality of life of the nation, sharpening the mind of its people and making more sensitive their spirit; in effect, a spiritual revival the like of which had not been seen for more than a thousand years. 'Its emphasis was neither morality nor creed,' explains R. T. Jenkins, of the character of the Revival, 'but spirit and power. The Revival took hold of the feelings. The nation was shaken through and through, with fear of judgement in the first place, and, afterwards, with fear of sin and losing God's favour.

As a matter of fact, the chief leaders of the Methodists were drawn from the old nonconformists; Howell Harris and Williams Pantycelyn had been students at the excellent academy of Llwyn-llwyd. And it was the theological arguments about Calvinism and Arminianism that gave an edge to their minds. Because George Whitfield was a Calvinist they co-operated easily with him; John Wesley did not receive the same welcome because he was too much of an Arminian. So although Methodism was a movement within the Church of England, intellectual non-conformity had a great influence on it; and Methodism in its turn influenced the old nonconformists very much, and some of them, such as Lewis Rees of Llanbrynmair and Edmwnd Jones of Pontypwl, co-operated willingly with the revivalists.

It was through the power of their preaching that the revivalists made the deepest impression, and their greatest preacher was Daniel Rowland, who also gave the main theological leadership to the movement. Under the influence of Philip Pugh, a nonconformist minister, he preached the gospel of Christ with a remarkable inspiration and effect. People poured by the thousands from every part of Wales to listen to him in Llangeitho. Large groups walked over the mountains from the counties of the south; some sailed in boats to the nearest harbours, from the north. They listened with rejoicing to Rowland preaching the living and enlivening Word of God.

Daniel Rowland remained a curate all his life; he never rose to a higher position. William Williams, Pantycelyn, too remained a curate; Howell Harris was a deacon. The men who saved Wales were not the prelates but men of vision who remained in humble jobs. These poor people now formed the aristocracy of Wales. They were the spring shoots; the winter was over.

Howell Harris was the son of a carpenter from Llangadog. R. T. Jenkins says of him:

'It is not hard to credit that Howell Harris was the greatest Welshman of the century.'

Although he was called 'Utgorn y Diwygiad' (the Trumpet of the Revival), because of the power of his preaching, he made his greatest contribution through his organising ability. He travelled all over Wales preaching, and suffering much persecution — especially in Gwynedd. In 1736 he and Daniel Rowland started to gather the converts together in 'seiadau' (societies) in order to help them and build them up 1736 in faith. These people met in any convenient centres.

They increased rapidly in number and by 1739 Howell Harris had established almost thirty such 'societies', — and a Welsh presbyterian system was created which ran parallel with the Church of England. It was not until 1811 however that the Methodists finally left the Church of England to form a completely new independent Welsh denomination. As well as the *seiadau*, and later the *Sasiwn* (the national gathering), they also held monthly and quarterly meetings. The organisation of the Methodists as planned by Howell Harris and Pantycelyn was absolutely essential. Without it the effect of the work done by revivalists would have been short lived. In religion, as in politics, causes and communities do not achieve permanent strength or effective influence, unless they are organised into an institution or party. Every effort must be made, though, to prevent the system becoming more important and more powerful than the living thing.

Because of the theological disagreements and for personal reasons, Howell Harris left the brethren in 1750 and Daniel Rowland took over the leadership. They were reconciled in 1762. In the meantime Howell Harris founded a 'family' in Trefecca for his followers, who worked at their different trades and vocations within the institution; there were as many as three hundred and fifty living in this community at one time. He did quite a lot to develop agriculture, establishing in the county the first agricultural society in Wales. He also established a college there to train preachers; for as the movement grew, the need for them increased. The movement matured. The man who was mostly responsible for this was William Williams Pantycelyn.

VIII. PANTYCELYN

IT IS a delightful habit in rural Wales to call a man by the name of his farm or his home, without using either his surname or his Christian name. This aristocratic custom explains why Welsh people know the great William Williams, as Pantycelyn. It was in the farm of Pantycelyn, Pentre Tŷ Gwyn, near Llandovery — his mother's old home — that 1717- he spent most of his life. He was born in Cefn Coed, 1791 Llanfair-ar-y-Bryn nearby; and he was buried in the cemetery of that church in 1791. He was brought up as an

Independent among the old nonconformists; but after his conversion by Howell Harris, he turned his back on them and on his medical career. He joined the established Church, and from 1740 to 1743 he was the curate of Theophilus Evans, the author of *Drych y Prif Oesoedd*, the scintillating history book which is poor history but an excellent book. The Bishop of St. David's refused him ordination. From then on, he dedicated his life to promoting the gospel through the Methodist movement.

Pantycelyn is an important figure in the history of the century for two reasons: in the first place, he was a diligent missionary, travelling thousands of miles on horseback to preach to, to establish and to nurse the *seiadau*; secondly, he was a poet, a hymnist and a writer. It is the second contribution which establishes him among the immortals. There is, however, a close connection between these two aspects of his work: for the remarkable understanding of psychology he showed in his dealings with the *seiadau* is also an outstanding feature of his literary work. He was the real founder of the *seiat*, which, as Saunders Lewis remarks, corresponded fairly closely to the confessional of the Catholic Church — a soul clinic for the mental health of all, although the Methodist confessed not to a priest but to the assembled *seiat*. Pantycelyn is the greatest hymnist of the Welsh language; some believe him to be the greatest poet of Wales in any age. He is a mystical poet, who records the greatest spiritual experiences of the century by expressing his own experience. In the eighteenth century the people of Wales became articulate again. They expressed themselves in the magnificent language of the Bible, and Pantycelyn is their greatest spokesman.

He did not try to express anyone else's experiences except his own, and he did not worry overmuch, nor often enough, about the language. He appeared on the scene when the old social order had disintegrated, and when the professional poets, and the classical poetry whose purpose was to delight and to create beauty, were not even a living memory. 'Pantycelyn', says Saunders Lewis, in his definitive study of him, 'is the first romantic poet in Wales . . . The first Welsh

PARCH. WILLIAM WILLIAMS.
PANT-Y-CELYN.

Williams Pantycelyn

Merthyr Tydfil 1830

Pontypridd Bridge by M. A. Rooker

Penillion Singing near Conway by J. C. Ibbetson

Drawn by W. Howell

W. Gwynt lith. 26 High St. Bartham

Chartist attack on Newport 1839

poet of the modern mind'. He produced an enormous amount of work in verse and prose; he published about ninety books and pamphlets between 1744 and 1791. These included two long poems. His masterpiece, *Bywyd a Marwolaeth Theomemphus*, is a wonderful penetrating study of the progress of soul through a 'period of purification, a period of enlightenment, and a period of synthesis'. All through his life he had an interest in science, and his scientific talent becomes evident in his poetry and other works. According to Saunders Lewis:

'He is the great discoverer of the unconscious, the strong-hold of the passions, and he is the first poet of science and the modern mind in Europe'.

He searched deeply into the secrets of his inmost heart:

Chwilia, f'enaid, gyrrau'th galon,
 Chwilia'r llwybrau maith o'r bron,
Chwilia bob rhyw stafell ddirgel
 Sydd o fewn i gonglau hon.

Search, my soul, to your heart's corners,
 search the long paths thoroughly,
and search all the secret chambers
 that within its limits be.

He knew the inexpressible value of the passions when turned towards God:

Rho fy nwydau fel cantorion
 Oll yn chwarae eu bysedd cun
Ar y delyn sydd yn seinio
 Enw Iesu mawr ei Hun.

Cause my desires to be like singers,
 their fine fingers all to play
on the harp which in its sounding
 has great Jesus' name to say.

Having turned to the object of his adoration, he listened in silence to the voice narrating the unnarratable:

O, distewch gynddeiriog donnau,
  Tra fwy'n gwrando llais y nef;
Swn mwy hoff, a swn mwy nefol
  Glywir yn ei eiriau ef:
    F'enaid, gwrando
Llais tangnefedd pur a hedd.

O, be silent, you wild breakers,
  whilst I listen to heaven's word;
a more heavenly sound and sweeter
  in its language can be heard:
    my soul listen
to the voice of purest peace.

Many of Pantycelyn's hymns are extremely fine lyrical poems which have become a priceless part of the personality of every cultured Welshman:

'Rwy'n edrych dros y bryniau pell
  Amdanat bob yr awr;
Tyrd, fy anwylyd, mae'n hwyrhau,
  A'm haul bron mynd i lawr.

Melysach nag yw'r diliau mêl
  Yw munud o'th fwynhau,
Ac nid oes gennyf bleser sydd
  Ond hynny yn parhau.

A phan y syrthio sêr y nen
  Fel ffigys îr i'r llawr,
Bydd fy niddanwch heb ddim trai
  Oll yn fy Arglwydd mawr.

I look across the distant hills
  each hour for thy coming:
come, my loved one, for it's late
  and my sun's near to setting.

Sweeter than the honey drops
  a minute's joy in thee,
and I've no other pleasure that
  lasts everlastingly.

And when the stars of heaven fall
  like ripe figs to the sward,
there'll be no ebb to the delight
  that's all in my great Lord.

After the providential strengthening ·which it received in
the spiritual revolution, the Welsh Christian tradition
approached the end of the century with the new life of spring
running through its veins.

IX. NEW GROWTH FROM OLD ROOTS.

As the *gwerin* found new roots in their ancient culture they
matured mentally and spiritually. The century saw a renaissance
in literature and scholarship under the direction of
accomplished men who were much more aware of the richness
of the nation's historical and literary background than were
the educators and religious revivalists. The great Revival
itself produced an abundance of literature; and the vigorous
gwerin composed harp verses, ballads and *anterliwtiau* of good
quality. The *anterliwt* was a type of play acted in the open air
with a wagon as a stage. They reached a high standard in the
works of Twm o'r Nant, who expressed his philosophy of
life through them in lively, earthy Welsh. Classical poetry
renewed its prestige through the works of the school of Welsh
Augustans who gathered round the Morris brothers. Lewis,
Richard and William Morris were three carpenter's sons
from Llanfihangel Tre'r Beirdd in Anglesey. Through their
vision, their energy, and their knowledge they became the
centre of a circle of learned men who fulfilled the same sort of
function as the Humanists of the sixteenth century, forging a
link between the old Welsh tradition and the modern period.
The man whose work inspired this revitalisation was Edward
Lhuyd (1660-1709), a botanist, geologist, antiquarian, whom
Griffith John Williams describes as:

> 'the most versatile and able scholar that Wales has ever seen . . .
> It was he who showed the Welsh of the eighteenth century the way.
> His work was a turning-point in the history of Welsh scholarship, and
> this turning-point produced the literary revival of the century.'

The scholars who were inspired by him did not come from
the noble families but from the *gwerin*. The best poet of this
circle was Goronwy Owen; the best scholar Ieuan Fardd, who

was called Ieuan Brydydd Hir; and the most knowledgeable
in the field of Welsh literature, Lewis Morris. Edward Richard
excelled as a scholar and as a poet.

Lewis Morris loved *penillion telyn* (harp lyrics) and made a
good collection of them. Thomas Pennant, travelling through
Meirionnydd around 1780, refers to this form of singing,
where the harp plays the melody and the voice sings the words
in descant:

> 'Some vein of the antient minstrelsie is still to be met in these
> mountainous contries. Numbers of persons, of both sexes, assemble,
> and sit around the harp, singing alternately pennylls or stanzas of
> antients or modern poetry. The young people usually begin the night
> with dancing, and when they are tired, sit down, and assume this
> species of relaxation. Oftentimes, like the modern Improvisitore of
> Italy, they will sing extempore verses. A person conversant in this art,
> will produce a pennyll apposite to the last which was sung: the subjects
> produce a great deal of mirth; for they are sometimes jocular, at others
> satyrical, and many amorous. They will continue singing without
> intermission, and never repeat the same stanza: for that would occasion
> loss of the honour of being held first of the song. Like nightingales,
> they support the contest throughout the night . . . Parishes often
> contend against parishes, and every hill is vocal with the chorus.'

Ieuan Brydydd Hir (1731-1788) was an anglican clergyman
from Lledrod, Ceredigion. He was the life spring of the clerical
school of poets and scholars who formed an intermediary link
between the period of the Morris brothers and the
Gwyneddigion, and the produce of the universities at the end
of the nineteenth century. Saunders Lewis speaks of his
important position in the Welsh tradition:

> 'It was he who brought to Welsh literature the pre-romanticism of
> eighteenth century and also gave it its Welsh characteristics. These
> features became the inheritance of the clerical school. He linked the
> antiquarian studies with the zeal for old Welsh literature, the personal
> and social interest in the world of the harpist, the rural poet and the
> the eighteenth century and also gave it its Welsh characteristics. These
> and social interest in the world of the harpist, the rural poet and the old
> country legends and their reciters. It was he who made Welsh patriot-
> ism, Welsh nationalism even, a part of the heritage of romanticism and
> its learning . . . His own career was a pattern of the life of the typical
> country burning like a lamp in his breast.'

In these devoted men a national consciousness was beginning to germinate anew. Ieuan Brydydd Hir was the first person since the Act of Union to complain strongly of the political oppression suffered by the national language. From the middle of the eighteenth century it continued to develop, although it did not take political expression until the end of the following century: and by then the English — or British — parties had taken tight hold of Wales.

The patriotic clergymen were of course only a very small minority. The Church of England continued to be used as an instrument for the anglicising of Wales. This was in the middle of the period of 150 years during which not one Welsh-speaking bishop was appointed to a Welsh see. It was not only the bishops who were English; sometimes English clergymen were placed in Welsh livings. At least one of these appointments was challenged: and the case of Dr. Bowles, a monoglot Englishman who was appointed vicar of Trefdraeth in Anglesey, was taken to the 'Court of the Arches'. The defence claimed:

'Wales is a conquered country, it is proper to introduce the English language, and it is the duty of the bishops to endeavour to promote the English, in order to introduce the language . . . It has always been the policy of the Legislature to introduce the English language into Wales. We never heard of an act of parliament in Welsh . . . The English language is, by act of Parliament, to be used in all the courts of judicature in Wales, and an English Bible to be kept in all the churches in Wales, that by comparison of that with the Welsh, they may the sooner attain to the knowledge of the English.'

The language policy promoted by the establishment was still that of the Act of Union.

The new patriotism was revealed by the founding of two Welsh societies of influence in London, the Cymmrodorion in 1751, and the Gwyneddigion in 1771. The first is
1751   still active as a scholarly society. The second was associated with the more serious politics started
1771   in the last quarter of the century. It was among the nonconformists, whose congregations were self-governing, that the political radicalism and democracy which

became a main feature of the Welsh political tradition arose; and it was the American War of Independence which awakened a more general interest in politics among them. In 1780 a booklet was published in Wrexham by William Davies Shipley, Dean of St. Asaph, attacking the war and putting forward radical ideas; it led to an important legal case. The author of this pamphlet was Sir William Jones, the greatest authority on the languages and the law of India that the British Isles has produced. He was a son of William Jones, Llanfihangel Tre'r Beirdd, Anglesey, who was a mathematician of great ability and influence. At the end of the century radicalism was further inspired by the French Revolution.

When the Gwyneddigion revived the Eisteddfod in its modern form in 1789, the year of the fall of the Bastille, the subject set for the *awdl* and for the essay competition was 'Freedom': not national freedom, of course — generations were to go by before that idea took hold. In order to discuss the matters which were of interest to the radicals, the Gwyneddigion gave support to *Y Cylchgrawn Cymraeg*. The editor of this periodical, Morgan John Rhys of Llanbradach, was a typical Welsh radical. In his magazine he discussed religious and political freedom; parliamentary and educational changes; he called for the abolition of slavery and class privileges, bribery and the waste of money on wars. Morgan John Rhys was the first to outline a system of Sunday Schools for Wales, and to urge the teaching of English through the medium of Welsh. He once sold Bibles in Paris; and in 1794 he went to America, where he established a Welsh settlement in Pennsylvania; he was made a judge there. He died in 1804, at the age of forty-four; Goronwy Owen had died, when he was about the same age, a generation earlier on his Virginia plantation in the same country. Morgan John Rhys combined in his person the three elements which did most to form the Wales of the nineteenth century: nonconformist Christianity, radicalism, and adherence to the Welsh tradition. Had these been kept together during the last century, by pursuing a Welsh goal great enough to unite them, Wales today would no doubt be a free and Welsh-speaking country;

but by the beginning of the twentieth century each strong stream was already going its own way.

When Rhys crossed the Atlantic in 1797 he was searching for religious and political freedom. The position of the nonconformists and the radicals had worsened even further with the landing of the French forces on February 22 near Fishguard which had a lasting effect on Wales.

1797

Although the French would have had a warm welcome among the Irish, their reception in Wales was wholly hostile. There was nothing in Wales which in any way corresponded to the United Irishmen which, formed by Wolfe Tone in 1795, was dominated by protestant dissenters. Wolfe Tone and his fellows swore in Belfast, 'never to desist in our efforts until we have subverted the authority of England over our country and asserted our independence'. For this purpose they sought to form 'a brotherhood of affection . . . among Irishmen of every religious persuasion, and thereby to obtain a complete reform of the legislature founded on the principles of civil, political and religious liberty'.

The effect of the French invasion at Fishguard was to make conservative Welshmen still more reactionary. After centuries of incorporation in England an eighteenth century Glyndŵr would not have found ten men to greet the French at Fishguard let alone the ten thousand which welcomed the French at Milford Haven in 1404. The Methodists became anti-Radical to a man. There was little support anywhere in Wales for the French Revolution after this. The invasion also magnified the other effect that the war with the French had had on the Welsh: they were Briticised to a large degree: and this has been the effect on them of every subsequent war. Reginald Coupland claims in his *Welsh and Scottish Nationalism* that there is such a nation as the British nation, and that it was at this time that it came into existence:

1797

'The war with Napoleon . . . made the island peoples conscious that they were making history together, and since this historical tradition is the mainspring of nationhood, a British nation may be said to have come into being . . . Though the senior partner's (sic) name may still

be used, especially by foreigners, to cover the whole firm, 'Britain'
and 'British' came into their own. It was the age of the Pax Britannica.
Britannia ruled the waves, British trade followed the British flag. The
British Empire grew to its zenith.'

The Napoleonic war was the first of the popular wars, which
defended nothing of great significance to Welsh civilisation;
but which augmented the power of the British state, centralised
its structure, strengthened its grip on Wales, increased its
psychological integration of Wales in England and diminished
the vitality of the Welsh tradition.

Radicalism expressed itself in a less unpalatable and more
acceptably British fashion by concentrating on the need for
change in Parliament. The cause of parliamentary reform
progressed when the war came to an end. A prominent
1814   leader in the movement was Joseph Harris (Gomer
1773-1825), a Baptist minister, who, in 1814, founded
Seren Gomer, which still appears. The son of a bailiff in
Pembrokeshire, he made a great contribution as a preacher,
hymnist, journalist and political leader. The increasing
industrial population supported the cause of reform — Wales's
population had reached 587,000 by 1801, about the size of
Bristol today — as well as some of the inhabitants of such old
towns as Carmarthen. When the measure was turned down in
1831 there were riots in Carmarthen and Merthyr Tydfil;
but when the Reform Act was passed in 1832 it had little
effect on the political situation in Wales.

Iolo Morgannwg (1747-1826) was a man who combined in
his person all the excitement of his period in its historical,
antiquarian, literary, social and political contexts. In spite of
the perverse streak in his character he was about the most
remarkable genius that Wales ever had — great enough for
the finest Welsh scholar of the twentieth century, Griffith
John Williams, to make him the main subject of his research.
He was born in Llancarfan in the Vale of Glamorgan, near the
site of Cadog's monastery, and died in Trefflemin (Fleminstone)
about two miles away, in the Llanilltud Fawr (Llanwit Major)
direction. He was a stone-mason by trade, and the son of a
stone-mason. He had no formal education, but was educated

by his mother and by the Welsh tradition which was still strong in Morgannwg in the eighteenth century. Through his friendship with the Blaenau (Upland) poets he was inspired to read old manuscripts, and thus began to mature as a scholar. He came into contact with the Gwyneddigion when following his craft in London. This is what awakened his passionate interest in the ideas of the French Revolution; it also fostered in him a burning partisanship for Morgannwg (Glamorgan). The glorifying of Morgannwg became one of the main aims of his life. He insisted that Dafydd ap Gwilym was a Morgannwg man; and Iolo was a fine enough poet to pass off as the great medieval poet's work *cywyddau* which he himself had written. His twofold purpose was to fake Glamorgan origins for Dafydd ap Gwilym and to prove that the greatest of Welsh poets had sung the praises of Glamorgan as well as Gwynedd. These particular *cywyddau* were included in learned lectures in the university on Dafydd ap Gwilym until Griffith John Williams revealed the truth about them. It was he too who revealed that *Gorsedd Beirdd Ynys Prydain* — which Iolo claimed went back to the time of the Druids — was a figment of Iolo's creative imagination. Through Iolo the Gorsedd became an integral part of eisteddfod proceedings, making its debut in that context in the great Carmarthen eisteddfod of 1819. Iolo's deceit was aided by his brilliant scholarship. He was the main collector and editor
1819 of the massive *Myvyrian Archaiology* which has meant so much to Welsh scholars. This man of weak body who left such a mark on the life of Wales had a wide knowledge of archaeology, antiques, architecture, geology, botany, gardening and agriculture, as well as the history of religion and theology.

Wales's religious life continued to develop vigorously until the beginning of the nineteenth century. A number of fine hymnists appeared, among them Dafydd Jones the drover from Caeo; and after him the most exciting of all the hymn-writers, apart from Pantycelyn himself — Ann Griffiths (1776-1805), a farmer's daughter from Llanfihangel yng Ngwynfa, Montgomeryshire, a mystic who was a great theologian as well as a fine poet. One is amazed at the power of her imagination:

Y greadigaeth ynddo'n symud,	The universe moving in him
Ynte'n farw yn y bedd . . .	and he dead in the grave . . .
Rhoi awdur bywyd i farwolaeth,	Putting the author of life to death
A chladdu'r atgyfodiad mawr.	and burying the great resurrection.

and by the craftsmanship of her scriptural images:

Gwna fi fel pren planedig, O fy Nuw,
Yn îr ar lan afonydd dyfroedd byw,
Yn gwreiddio ar led, a'i ddail heb wywo mwy,
Ond ffrwytho dan gawodydd dwyfol glwy.

Make me like a tree planted, o my God,
green on the shore of the living waters' flood,
rooting out wide, its leaves unshrivelling,
but fruiting in the showers of divine blood.

Her great hymns will contine to enrich the spiritual life of Wales as long as the language lives. The following hymn is the fruit of her meditation on the worthiest object of any meditation:

Wele'n sefyll rhwng y myrtwydd
  Wrthych teilwng o fy mryd:
Er mai o ran, yr wy'n adnabod
  Ei fod uwchlaw gwrthrychau'r byd:
    Henffych fore
  Y caf ei weled fel y mae.

Rhosyn Saron yw ei enw,
  Gwyn a gwridog, teg o bryd;
Ar ddeng mil y mae'n rhagori
  O wrthrychau penna'r byd:
    Ffrind pechadur,
  Dyma ei Beilat ar y mor.

Beth sydd imi mwy a wnelwyf
  Ag eilunod gwael y llawr?
Tystio'r wyf nad yw eu cwmni
  I'w gystadlu â Iesu mawr:
    O! am aros
  Yn ei gariad ddyddiau f'oes.

See him stand among the myrtles,
  worthy object of my love,
though as yet I barely know
that he's all earthly things above:
    come, the morning
  he'll be hidden by no veil.

He is called the Rose of Sharon,
  white and blushing, featured fair:
he excels above ten thousand
  earthly things that men count fair:
    friend of sinners,
  he's our pilot on the sea.

What have I to do in future
  with vain idols of this earth?
All their company, I swear it,
  by my Christ is nothing worth.
    O! to linger
  my whole lifetime in his love.

The outstanding development at the beginning of the century had been the provision of a Welsh education through the efforts of Griffith Jones; and it was this which made much of the further developments possible. It is fitting, therefore, that the man who was responsible for another great advance in Welsh education, at the end of the century, should hail from Griffith Jones's own district in Carmarthenshire. The great achievement of Thomas Charles (1755-1814) was his organisation of a system of Welsh-language Sunday schools — completely voluntary schools. The classes were small, adults as well as children were welcomed, no attention whatsoever was paid to the social status of the pupils, and the Welsh language had its rightful place as the medium of instruction. The scholarly Thomas Charles, who received his education in the Carmarthen academy and Oxford, was well-read in Latin, Greek, Hebrew, French and Italian. The essay on Christ in his influential *Geiriadur* (biblical Dictionary) characteristically closed with a quotation from the ancient manuscript, *Llyfr Coch Hergest* (Red Book of Hergest). He has an important place as the main founder of the Welsh Presbyterian denomination in 1811; it was he who inspired the founding of the Bible Society; and it was he who succeeded in securing the wide distribution of a Welsh Bible whose price was within the reach of the poor. But it was through the Sunday School that he made his greatest contribution to the life of Wales.

The Sunday School movement has been described by Jac L. Williams as the most comprehensive educational system ever devised in Britain. It catered for all age groups and for all levels of intellectual ability. It provided motivation by awarding certificates and book prizes for good attendance as well as for attainment. Homework was set and syllabuses were prescribed. Written and oral examinations were arranged and periodicals sold through the Sunday Schools. In some areas even an efficient lending library service was included in this educational provision which affected whole communities . . . it was not unusual for more than 90% of households in Welsh-speaking areas to be associated with a Sunday School. The fruit of this work can be seen in the welcome given to a cart load of Testaments, of which an English traveller in 1810 has left this description:

> 'the Welsh peasants went out in crowds to meet it and welcomed it as the Israelites did the ark of old; drew it into the town and eagerly bore off every copy as rapidly as they could be dispersed. The young people consumed the whole night reading it, and labourers carried it with them to the fields that they might enjoy it during the intervals of their labours.'

In this way the life of the nation was transformed in the course of the nineteenth century. Thus it was that when the population of the towns increased as a result of industrial development, the Welsh tradition was strong enough ro possess them as completely as it had re-possessed the rural areas.

X. THE MERTHYR UPRISING:
THE CHARTISTS:
THE REBECCA RIOTS

IT IS sometimes claimed that it was industrialism and urbanisation which wounded the national language and tradition of Wales most deeply. But a look at the history of the first half of the last century shows how far this is from the truth. Even while the iron industry was developing, and later the coal and steel industries, the towns remained as Welsh in language and culture as the rural districts. A national tradition is a matter of values; it can dominate the life of a town society as completely as that of a rural community. In Wales, its main medium is the Welsh language; where the language is Welsh, the culture will be Welsh; that is, the pattern of values found in the way of life will be Welsh.

The truth of this is illustrated in the history of Merthyr Tydfil, the only large town in Wales in the first half of the nineteenth century. Perhaps it was the biggest industrial town in the world in the 30's. In 1851 it had a population of 63,080, while that of Cardiff was only 18,351. Merthyr was a Welsh town; Wales at that time was a Welsh-speaking country, although it had been industrialised to a great degree. 61% of its workers did work that had nothing to do with agriculture. In 1851 Welsh was the language of 90% of the Welsh people. In his book, *The Character of the Welsh as a Nation*, published in 1841, William Jones estimates that only 100,000 monoglot English speakers lived in Wales at that time. With the exception of south Pembrokeshire and Radnorshire, most of the non-Welsh speakers lived on the borders, and the very mention of that small county reminds one how tenuous the culture of the non-Welsh speakers was, and how small their contribution. It is significant that the rural east of mid-Wales, and the south, were anglicised before the industrial towns, which were completely Welsh in language and culture for generations. There was a higher proportion of people speaking Welsh at this time than there was of Danes speaking Danish. It was not industrialism that killed the Welsh language in the industrial areas, but a combination of factors. Among them was a growth in the power of the central government and the policy of that government, acting particularly through the English educational system; the immigration of hundreds of thousands of English people whom it was impossible to Cymricise in the absence of a Welsh education system and official institutions, and without a higher social and legal status fo the language; and finally the psychological state of the Welsh themselves, who had been so deeply wounded and so thoroughly conditioned by their integration in a state whose dominant nation was fifteen times larger, and a hundred times richer, whose institutions were deciding more and more the Welsh conditions of life.

The language and the culture of Wales did most to safeguard the dignity and humanity of the people of the industrial towns engulfed in the horror of the industrial revolution; although the situation was not seen quite like this in England, where they did not think very highly of the Welsh at this time. Blackwood's Magazine, December 1829 says:

> 'In the west, the Saxon-English are blended with the Welsh; but there is here no gain, because the Welsh cross can add passion chiefly, without higher reasonong powers.'

There can be nc doubt about the wretchedness of everyday life in the second generation of the century. 'Poverty was the keynote to this period,' says David Williams about the decades which followed the end of the war in 1815; and everyone knows about the Hungry Forties. This was as true of the rural as well as the industrial areas; but in the rural areas the people had their roots in a society that was warm, intimate and stable, with a long history, strong customs, and tradition. The harsh circumstances of the industrial town were very different in spite of its quick growth: rapacious and undisciplined capitalism was coarsening the fibre of the workers who came almost entirely from rural Wales into social circumstances which were very different from anything ever seen in Wales before. J. L. and Barbara Hammond write in *The Rise of Modern History*:

> 'South Wales gives perhaps the most complete picture of the worst features of the Industrial Revolution. There the economic man was not a mere nightmare of the textbooks, he was an omnipotent force in a world existing for a single purpose. Where the revolution introduced the new system into a society with a past and a variety of interests, with inhabitants accustomed to the manners and outlook of citizens, its

consequences were less sweeping. This was the case in Birmingham, where the Commissioners on Children's Employment in 1842 reported that there were more customary holidays, and that the hours of labour were shorter and less fatiguing than in any other large manufacturing town. In Manchester the Industrial Revolution was a more powerful force in the life and habits of the town, but Manchester had a history before the revolution, and though its local government was scandalously unrepresentative and inefficient, yet great citizens could find an audience for their warnings and their protests. In Northumberland there were influences outside the great coal and shipping interests that could gradually modify the ruthless atmosphere of the new industry.

'In South Wales, on the other hand, the conditions were more like those of a newly-discovered gold-field or a plantation in tropical Africa. The restraints of tradition, of a common history, of experience in government were all wanting.'

These impartial historians have to turn to central Africa to find comparisons with the deplorable exploitation seen in industrial Wales during the Industrial Revolution. The Welsh had not one political institution to defend them against the rape of capitalism; but they did have a Christian culture to succour their humanity and to inspire them to seek social justice.

Merthyr Tydfil is a mirror of all this. At the beginning of the century Merthyr was the largest centre of the iron industry in Britain. By 1831 it had a population of 26,000, and these were almost wholly Welsh-speaking, the vast majority having moved there from rural Glamorgan and the west. Gwyn Williams — to whom we are indebted for a study of this period — says that only 9% of its 47,000 population in 1840 could not speak Welsh, and only 3% in Aberdare. And these people were quickly Cymricised by the strength of the Welsh life in these towns. Dozens of nonconformist chapels were built in the area: Welsh nonconformity was not something for the middle classes alone, but for the manual working people too; indeed the majority of the working class of the last century were nonconformists. For example in Pontypool in the last century there were twenty-two chapels and two Anglican churches. These chapels were the centres of the intellectual and cultural life of the town, as elsewhere throughout the country. Not all the people were chapel-goers: Zephaniah Williams was a free-thinker who founded a society for people who shared his beliefs in Nant-y-Glo — 'Dynolwyr Nant-y-Glo' (The Humanists of Nant-y-glo). There was also a remarkably rich culture in the taverns — an intellectual, literary and musical culture. The powerful temperance societies also made a contribution to culture, as well as to the improvement of social behaviour. It is primarily through their efforts that choral singing developed and later on the brass bands. Their social work was a boon to the community. Alcohol was the main cause of extreme poverty, as well as a host of other evils. In Dowlais alone there were over two hundred unlicensed public houses. They were exploited by the capitalists then, as in the generations that followed. In their benevolence, the employers built taverns, which they owned outright, above the mine or near an iron works, where the workers could drink beer that had been produced in the employers' breweries; in this way, the men returned to their masters' pockets a good percentage of the pitifully small wages doled out to them.

The *eisteddfod* flourished. In 1831 *eisteddfodau* were held in which the chief subject of the literary competitions was civil liberty. Taliesin ab Iolo, the son of Iolo Morganwg, was an influential school-master in the town. This enlightened man gave the children a Welsh education, and many of them developed into talented and cultured people. It is no surprise therefore that Merthyr produced Joseph Parry, the most prolific Welsh composer of the last century, and the most popular in Wales even today. It is no surprise either that Thomas Stephens, a Merthyr pharmacist, should write *The Literature of the Kymry*, the first critical discussion of the Gogynfeirdd period, which became familiar to European scholars. There was a lively press: the first working-class newspaper in Wales — *Y Gweithiwr* (The Worker) — started publication in 1814. Merthyr Tydfil could claim to be the chief centre of cultural life of Wales.

The town had inherited the remarkable intellectual culture of the Glamorgan hill country. Though this was largely

THE
WELCH CHARTIST MARTYRS!

ZEPHANIAH WILLIAMS.   JOHN FROST.   JONES, THE WATCHMAKER.

Three Chartist leaders

literary and theological in the rural areas in the eighteenth century, it took on a radical political hue in the ferment of urban society where the lively middle class was largely Unitarian. If urban Merthyr was born radical, as Gwyn Williams avers, this was due to the unbroken continuity with eighteenth century Glamorgan radicalism. Thomas Stephens and Taliesin ab Iolo were Unitarians. At the beginning of the century the Unitarians were an influential body in Merthyr. They were the mainstay of the Cyfarthfa Philosophical Society. Although they were mostly drawn from the middle class, they were, even so, staunch radicals. The Independents, though, had the greatest following among the nonconformists, with the Baptists not far behind. The politically aware, who included a number of lawyers, were humanitarian and radical. They discussed issues fervently; but their purpose varied greatly:

'The one issue that united them all was hostility to the truck system,' says Gwyn Williams. 'Here ideals and interest coincided.'

There was a depression at this time in the iron industry, and much suffering and instability as a result. The exciting arguments about the reform of Parliament added to the unrest:

'All the old millenarian ideals of the just society and the moral economy,' says Gwyn Williams, 'came bubbling to the surface.'

William Crawshay, the iron-master, who was a Radical at that time, led a petition for parliamentary reform. After the failure to carry the first Reform Bill in Westminster there were riots in 1831 in Carmarthen, Flintshire and Denbighshire; mounted soldiers were called out to the mining village of Rhosllannerchrugog. The worst riot was in Merthyr. The middle classes joined the workers in protest marches through the town in the evenings. Leaders sprang up among them of the calibre of Lewis Lewis, 'Lewsyn yr Heliwr' who, according to Gwyn Williams, 'had . . . a highly developed sense of natural justice'; and, as a retributive measure against local injustice, 'crowds, in para military formation, directed by Lewis Lewis from a stand in the High Street, scoured the town, raiding over a hundred houses, seizing goods which had been confiscated from the destitute and restoring them to the original owners in a process of reciprocal compensation which was often very complex. Under Reform banners and black flags, they beat off the special constables and finally destroyed the debtors' court itself . . . The Argyll and Sutherland Highlanders marched first, coming from Brecon.'

Notice how often soldiers from one Celtic country are brought in to dispel trouble or rioting in another Celtic country. Until then, there had only been distrurbances in Merthyr; this now developed into open rebellion. The workers attacked the soldiers, who opened fire, and cleared the streets. The soldiers were reinforced by the Glamorgan Yeomanry, yet they had to retreat to Tŷ Pendarren. They were besieged there for three whole days and finally had to leave the town in the hands of the workers.

It is not known how many were killed; at least twenty of the workers lost their lives, and over a hundred were wounded, as well as fifty soldiers. The rebels set up their headquarters on the mountains above the Brecon road. The Swansea Yeomanry were sent out against them; these were defeated and pushed back to Neath. On the Cefn Coed side a company of soldiers were prevented from bringing arms into the town, and a company of one hundred mounted soldiers were driven back. As Gwyn Williams points out:

'These defeats inflicted on regular and militia troops by armed rioters have no parallel in recent British history.'

Work came to a standstill in Cendl, Sirhywi, Tredegar, Ebbw Vale and Nant-y-glo. In Hirwaun a flag was dipped in the blood of a sacrificed calf, and possibly for the first time in these islands the red flag was raised as the symbol of revolt. Thousands of soldiers marched into the town of Merthyr; five thousand of the inhabitants fled. The whole episode came to an end without much more loss of life because the government was in difficulties and it did not want the trouble to attract more attention than necessary. Twelve, including two women, were condemned to penal servitude in Australia. Lewsyn yr Heliwr was first condemned to death, then reprieved and transported. The only one to be hanged was Dic Penderyn (Richard Lewis), a twenty-three year old collier from Pyle. He was popularly thought at the time to be innocent of the crime of which he was accused, and subsequently this was found to be so. He became a legendary name, the first martyr of the workers' movement.

Merthyr Tydfil was occupied by troops for a time, and many who had been thorns in the side of the authorities were victimised. There was widespread fear among the people.

'Bodies were being buried secretly all over north Glamorgan,' says Gwyn Williams, 'widows did not dare claim poor relief.'

At least seven commissions were established by the Government to inquire into the insurrection. A political consequence was that Merthyr and Aberdare were given a parliamentary seat; Henry Guest the ironmaster became the first member. The Guests and Crawshays had come to the district, as the Homfrays had come to Ebbw Vale and the Wilkinsons to Wrexham, because the iron industry in England was depressed. They brought capital and technical knowledge which the Welsh lacked, though an occasional Welsh industrial tycoon did appear. For instance, Thomas Williams of Llanelidan, Anglesey, where he was known as 'Twm Chwarae Teg' (Tom Fair Play), employed twelve hundred miners in Anglesey and hundreds more in his Swansea and English industries. He had a fleet of ore-carrying ships. By 1800 he owned half the resources of the British copper trade and dominated the world market.

In industrial Wales the main consequence of the Merthyr insurrection was to stimulate the growth of the new trade unionism whose leader was Robert Owen, a saddler's son, who was born, and who died in Newtown in the Severn Valley. It was in New Lanark (Llannerch Newydd) that Owen made his name as a humanitarian, educationist and father of co-operation. Although he contributed only indirectly to the life of Wales a strong Welsh strain ran through all his thought, especially in his emphasis on community, co-operation and harmony. Tom Ellis underlined this in a well known speech made in 1892.

'Though Wales in times is largely individualistic', he said, 'we cannot but feel that it has been the land of cyfraith, cyfnawdd, cymorthau and cymanfaoedd, the land of social co-operation, of associative effort. It is significant that the initiator in Britain of the movement for collective and municipal activity in the common effort for the common good was Robert Owen, who embodied in these latter days the spirit of the old Welsh social economy.'

When an independent Welsh national political party arose in the twentieth century it was natural for it to make co-operation a fundamental principle of its social and economic policy.

During Robert Owen's time the towns of the upper Severn Valley were the chief Welsh centres of the woollen industry. There was considerable radical energy in them during the thirties. Voltaire and Tom Paine were discussed, but also Daniel O'Connell, who thought as little of the Irish language as the Welsh squirearchy thought of Welsh. The biggest bone of contention was the Poor Law. This took priority over agitation for constitutional reform despite the workers' bitter disappointment at the effects of the Reform Act of 1832. Chartism took hold there in 1838, particularly in Llanidloes, which was a Welsh-speaking town in those days. Chartism was warmly welcomed by Welsh nonconformity; the *Diwygiwr* proclaimed that it was consistent with Christianity, and *Seren Gomer* gave its support. But none of the nonconformist politicians supported the use of violence. Henry Richard, an Independent minister who became the member of parliament for Merthyr in 1865, arranged for the distribution of ten thousand pamphlets calling upon the Rebecca movement to abstain from the use of violence. The use of violence was discussed in Llanidloes; arms were obtained and there was some training at night. The people were angered when English policemen were sent to the town, and the Trewythen Arms where they were staying was attacked and destroyed. Soldiers were called in and order restored after the workers had occupied the town for a week.

The main field of activity of the Chartist movement was Gwent, where the *Scotch Cattle* also were most active; 1839 and there in 1839 their most famous attack took place.

Their leader was John Frost, the son of an innkeeper from Newport. He had been apprenticed as a shoemaker, but he made his living as a successful draper. He was made a justice of the peace, and became mayor of the town. The language of Newport at this time was Welsh, and the language of the Chartists was Welsh; it was in Welsh that John Frost addressed his followers. Iolo Morganwg had said of Monmouthshire earlier in the century: 'no county of Wales has so large a portion of it wherein the English language is not understood.' Even in the sixties there were numbers of monoglot Welsh speakers near the Herefordshire border. The Welshness of the *gwerin* is an important factor in all the troubles of the period. Reginald Coupland says in his *Welsh and Scottish Nationalism*:

'Like the industrial revolution as a whole, the agitation it provoked in Wales assumed in some respects a Welsh complexion, and it betrayed at times the fact that underneath the cause that the Welsh workers shared with Englishmen lurked a latent sense of national antagonism . . . the owners, the employers, the administrative staff were almost wholly English . . . there was a nationalist flavour to Welsh strikes. Nationalist, too, was the antagonism aroused by 'foreign' labour.'

In contrast to the English reformers who had a knowledge of, and made use of, English history, the Welsh working-class leaders were ignorant of the Welsh past and therefore made no appeal to it. In England the prevailing idea was that royalty and aristocrats were Normans who should be overthrown in order to secure, once again, a free and English England.

As E. P. Thompson points out in his book *The Making of the English Working Class:*

'After the French Revolution, theorists of the popular societies dealt largely in Anglo-Saxon 'tythings', the Witenagemot, and legends of Alfred's reign. 'Pristine purity' and 'our ancestors' became — for many Jacobins — almost any constitutional innovation for which a Saxon precedent could be vamped up . . . From 1771 to the early 1790's the more advanced reformers were marked out by their fondness for Saxon precedent.'

Tom Paine was to speak of 'a French bastard landing with an armed Banditti and establishing himself King of England, against the consent of the natives.'

Today such sentiments are called the 'theory of the Norman yoke'. Knowledge of English history put backbone into the contention that the Englishman had the right to freedom and the vote. Alas there were no such appeals to Welsh history.

If one leader had had any idea of the nationalism of Wales, its history and its tradition, the efforts of the workers would have been immeasurably more effective and purposeful. It was tragic for Wales that the often heroic effort of the workers' movement for social justice was not combined with a Welsh national political programme. Had this happened, Wales with its strong strain of idealism, could have been a social laboratory amongst the most important in the world; and it could have built a strong and balanced economy on the basis of its enormously rich natural resources. In the last century only the countries that had iron and coal were able to create the strongest economies, but Wales continued to be exploited as a British province over the decades, with sad results for the workers and the national tradition.

The Chartists talked about attacking London. But three generations passed before Welsh workers eventually marched on London; by then the capital was safe enough because the marchers were unemployed coal miners whose purpose was to beg for justice.

The Chartists decided to hold a big meeting in Newport on the 5th November, 1839. It is not clear whether an attack upon the town was intended, although the leadership had obviously gone into the hands of the supporters of violence. Three groups were to march into the town: one from Coed Duon (Blackwood) led by John Frost, one from Pontypool, led by William Jones, the eloquent inn-keeper, and one from

Ebbw Vale with Zephaniah Williams at its head — the same Zephaniah who had formed the Humanist Society of Nant-y-glo. He was an inn-keeper from Bedwellte: his son, Llywelyn Williams, known as Pencerdd y De, became famous as a harpist. The plans were ruined by a great rain storm. The authorities were waiting for them; there was an outbreak of violence in front of the Westgate Hotel where some soldiers had been stationed, unknown to the marchers. These soldiers fired into the crowd killing a number of people. The rest fled, but the three leaders were arrested and brought to trial. In the famous trial that ensued the three were sentenced to be hanged and quartered for treason; but the sentence was later commuted and two were sent to Australia. Coupland says of this event:

'Nothing happened in England to match the march of some five thousand Welshmen down from the coal valleys through the darkness and drenching rain of a winter night to Newport . . . nobody remarked that the trouble was suppressed by English soldiers who were paid to do it and shot down twenty Welshmen and wounded several others in the doing.'

No political capital was made of this in and for Wales, and the rise of movements corresponding to Wolfe Tone's United Irishmen of the 1790's or Thomas Davis's Young Ireland of the 1840's was quite unthinkable. Welsh patriotism was still completely cultural in character, lacking any national political consciousness. National consciousness was something that developed in the course of the century. And it must always be remembered that the class that should have been leading the nation had turned its back on its own country generations before. It is true that some of that class objected to the scrapping of the Court of Great Session in 1830; but although they laid great stress on the importance that the Welsh nation attributed to that institution, in their public campaigns, they were nevertheless motivated even in this by self-interest and not zeal for the nationhood of Wales. The leader of the opposition to the abolition of the Court was John Jones of Ystrad (1772–1842), the Tory member of parliament for Carmarthen. He was called 'Jones yr Halen' because of his efforts to get rid of the salt tax. He was a barrister who had been educated at Eton and Christ College, Oxford. Although he himself spoke Welsh, he regretted the survival of the language. The opposition proved ineffective, and in 1830 the last state institution that recognised Wales as an entity disappeared. Before the end of the forties there would be a wide and popular movement in Wales, with Gwilym Hiraethog at its head, supporting the Hungarians in their attempt to secure national freedom from the Habsburg empire. How was it possible to mount such a great national campaign in Hungary? The obvious answer was that the natural leaders of the nation were leading it: aristocrats such as Kossuth, Deak, Szechenyi, Batthyany and Eotvos and their like. Not even one of their privileged class gave a similar lead to the Welsh nation.

Despite this, the consciousness of nationality was developing gradually but surely as a factor in social and cultural life. Take, for example, the Ivorites. This was a friendly society, similar to the Oddfellows, that sought to help its members prepare for burials, ill-health and accidents. It was a completely Welsh order. It was founded in Wrexham in 1836, but its headquarters were moved to Carmarthen in 1838. Within a mere two years, 1838-9, says David Williams, seventy-six lodges were established in the Carmarthen district. It had three aims: to promote the Welsh language, to relieve its members as far as possible from want, and to encourage Welshmen to support each other. This popular support was a real progression away from that apathy towards the language and Welsh identity that had prevailed in the land for over a century; and in this instance too, the Welsh ethos was identified with social justice. The Welsh language was appreciated for its own sake. This was the attitude of the majority of Welsh cultural leaders now: it was the attitude, for example, of a large number of clerics who contributed much to the literature and culture of Wales, and to the *eisteddfod* movement, men such as Gwallter Mechain, Glasynys and Ieuan Glan Geirionnydd — clergymen who were also supporters, incidentally, of Pusey's Oxford Movement.

The Ivorites and their self-respect helped create the mental climate that led to the Rebecca troubles. The rural and industrial areas alike suffered from the way in which the Poor Law was administered. They also suffered from the Englishness of those in authority: the English masters and officials in the industrial towns and the English justices and stewards in the rural areas. David Williams, the chief authority on the history of the Rebecca Movement and Chartism in Wales says:

'Discontent with magistrates was fairly widespread; 'justices' justice,' it was said, was proverbial . . . Difference in language certainly hindered the administration of justice in Wales. Cases were tried in a language which defendants barely understood, and this made the elaborate paraphernalia of the law appear to a bewildered peasantry to be a species of trickery, of chicanery, intended to deprive them of justice.'

The ignorance of this anglicised class, their tyranny and injustice, are described by a correspondent of *The Times*, who said that they were treating the people 'as if they were beasts and not human beings'. In July and August 1843 this correspondent had an opportunity to attend the meetings of the Rebecca followers, where he learnt much about the aims of the movement. In one meeting which was held in a barn in the hills in the parish of Llangadog, Carmarthenshire, their purpose, he said, was to form a farmers' union to demand a lowering of the rents. He gave an account of a meeting in the cemetery of the Baptist chapel in Cwm Ifor, three miles away, which David Williams describes thus:

'All the discussion was in Welsh, but Foster received the assistance of an interpreter, who also translated the resolutions agreed upon These were dated 'the first year of Rebecca's exploits, A.D. 1843,' and the Preamble quoted, in anticipation of John Stuart Mill, the aphorism that the price of liberty was eternal vigilence. An army of principles, said Rebecca, will penetrate where an army of soldiers cannot. The grievances included the toll-gates, the tithe, church rates and high rents. But Rebecca also resolved that no Englishman shall be employed as a steward in Wales.'

Some of the main themes of the century were discussed there: radical idealism; the land and landlord question; the Church of England and the tithes; Welshness and anti-Englishness. In half a century's time much of this was to be the basis of the policy of Cymru Fydd, which added self-government to the list. Small farmers and tenant-farmers made up the body of the meetings; they were the ones responsible for the Rebecca movement.

Behind every question lay the material poverty of an age which witnessed a sudden rise in population. From 1815 onwards the poverty increased. Things improved again from 1850 to 1870, only to slip back once more into a state of financial depression. In spite of its wealth in natural resources, and the talents of its people, Wales has enjoyed very little economic prosperity under the London government. Ap Fychan has left us a document of the real nature o poverty at that time. He was a creative writer and a poet, a theology teacher and one of the princes of the Welsh pulpit in an age of giants such as John Jones, Talsarn and Williams o'r Wern. His father was a man of culture, typical of the *gwerin* at its best; but he and his large family in Llanuwchllyn were very poor. In his autobiography Ap Fychan describes his situation thus:

'We were by now a large family. My father earned only a shilling a day and had to provide his own food in the winter-half of the year; and half a bag of oat flour cost us ten shillings and sixpence: therefore we could hardly afford bread, let alone anything to put on it. For one whole fortnight we were without any bread at all, or cheese, or butter, or meat, or potatoes. We happened to get a few turnips, and my mother boiled these in water giving them to us to eat with the water they had been boiled in; she had nothing better for herself, although she had one child at her breast at the time . . . In the end my mother and father and the whole family became seriously ill. We were like that for a long time, and had to have parish aid. Religious brothers and sisters were very kind to us in these sad circumstances . . . My parents possessed a good feather bed at that time; but since we were receiving parish aid the Overseer of the parish came with his son to our house and pulled the bed away from under my father, who appeared to be on the point of death and very confused by the fever of his disease. They sold the bed to a man from the district who was going to America, and my father was laid down on straw.'

In spite of their poverty these *gwerin* people built hundreds of new chapels all over the country.

But the situation in Wales was not to be compared with the horrors of the Irish situation, where a million people died of starvation under the same English system — as many, if not more, than the whole population of Wales. In one generation the population of Ireland was reduced from eight million to four million. But nevertheless the two countries were compared by the Government:

'I grieve to say,' said Sir James Graham, the Home Secretary of the Peel government, 'that South Wales bids fair to rival Ireland. Poverty and the misconduct of landlords are at the root of crime and of discontent in both countries.'

And although the numbers who went to the United States from Wales at that time were far fewer than the crowds who sailed from Ireland, nevertheless a substantial number of people did go. In the first sixty years of the century about thirty-five thousand Welsh men and women are known to have crossed the Atlantic — almost as many Welshmen as were killed in the first world war; between 1831 and 1860, over five thousand went from Ceredigion (Cardiganshire) alone. But in their new country these people supported a vigorous Welsh way of life, founding scores of Welsh chapels, and publishing at least sixty-one Welsh magazines during the century. The smallness of the population of Wales was not the only reason nor the main one that the number of emigrants was so small compared with Ireland. The chief reason was that the people of the rural areas of Wales were able to move to the new iron and coal fields, taking their culture with them. That was why the industrial areas were so completely Welsh in language in the middle of the century.

At this time the population of the rural counties of Wales started to decrease. The amazing position today is that six of the thirteen counties of Wales are smaller in population than they were in 1851. This is not true of any of the thirty-nine counties of England. But England has its own government. The greatest unrest broke out in Carmarthenshire and its neighbouring areas. It was there, and not in the industrial valleys, that Chartism first appeared in Wales. Its first Welsh

branch was founded by Hugh Williams in the town of
Carmarthen, which had a population of twelve thousand at
that time, and, according to D. J. V. Jones, 'Carmarthen in the
second quarter of the nineteenth century shared with Merthyr
Tydfil the distinction of being a hotbed of Welsh radicalism.'
Hugh Williams came from Derwen Las, near Machynlleth:
he was a lawyer and an Independent who became, at least in
the opinion of the public and the government, the chief
leader of the Rebecca movement. He had received his
education at a local school run by Azariah Shadrach, a famous
Independent minister, who published two dozen books at
the beginning of the century. Hugh Williams was a brother-
in-law of the politician Richard Cobden.

When the poor-house in Narberth was burnt down in
January 1839, a Chartist missionary came into the
1839   area. The Welsh damned the new workhouses for
the same reason that they damned the 'means test' in
the twenties and thirties of our own century: because they
separated families. It is strange how similar were the complaints
against the 'means test' which the Welsh suffered amid the
poverty and unemployment of the first half of the twentieth
century — under the same English (or British) system —
to the complaints of the Rebecca movement and the Chartists,
a hundred years earlier.

On May 13 the gate in Efail Wen above Whitland was
destroyed, as well as the house beside it, by a crowd of people
dressed up as women or in strange clothes, with blackened
faces. It is said that the leader was one Thomas Rees, 'Twm
Carnabwth'. They called themselves 'Becas'. The following
week the toll-gate of Maes-gwyn, Llanboidy was destroyed.
This one belonged to the 'Whitland Trust' which was
responsible for maintaining twenty-three miles of turnpike
roads in the district. No doubt the 'Turnpike Trust' method
of maintaining roads had performed a valuable service during
the previous hundred years but, by now, they were often
ineffective and tyrannical. A way of 'farming' roads was
developed, and the toll-gates increased in number. There were
thirteen of them on the forty-one mile stretch of the Llangadog

and Llandovery company roads. When a farmer took his wagon or cart to fetch a load of lime from the kilns on the Mynydd Du (Black Mountain) he had to pay many times the value of the lime in tolls.

In 1842 the events of 1839 were repeated in many places; by the end of the summer the country was almost 1842 completely free of toll-gates. About a hundred and twenty of them were wrecked, some of them twice and three times over. The custom spread to Morgannwg and the counties of Gwynedd. The men started to rectify all types of unfairness appertaining to tithes, common land, and the injustice of magistrates to name only three. In an attack on the Gwendraeth Iron Works, Shoni Sgubor Fawr (John 1843 Jones), a boxer was arrested with Twm Carnabwth, and Dai'r Cantwr (David Davies), a singer of ballads and a popular versifier. But the event which drew most attention outside Wales was the attack on the Work-house in Carmarthen by about four hundred men in strange clothes on horse-back. They were dispersed by a company of cavalry. Shoni Sgubor Fawr and Dai'r Cantwr and three others were sentenced to penal servitude in Australia.

It can not be said of any particular man that he was the 'Rebecca'. Hugh Williams was named by many; Dafydd Rees, a minister with the Independents and an enthusiastic radical, by others. He adopted the motto of Daniel O'Connell: 'Agitate, agitate, agitate'; 'if you happen to meet a Tory,' he said, 'tell him that you are a Beca.' 'Who is Beca?' asked *Seren Gomer*, and answered, 'Beca is tyranny and poverty'. The government's answer to this question was very different. It said in effect that Beca was the Welsh language, although it did not say this in so many words. It said that the root of the trouble was ignorance, but it held that the cause of the alleged ignorance was that the people were Welsh monoglots who did not know English. The government's way of getting rid of this ignorance was to get rid of the Welsh language.

XI. THE TREACHERY OF THE
BLUE BOOKS

CENTRAL to the story of the century and to the history of the
language and nationality of Wales was the commission
established by the Government in 1846, and the Report
published in 1847. Care was taken that a Welshman should
make the request in Parliament for the investigation; and the
man chosen, William Williams of Llanpumsaint, Carmarthenshire, was an honourable man who was in complete sympathy
with the intention of the Government. The sentence was
decided on before the case was investigated. This was made
clear in William Williams's speech. The intention was the
annihilation of the Welsh language and the assimilation of the
Welsh people. The policy of the Government was still the
policy of the Act of Union; and it now saw a way of realising
that policy effectively. A wholly English formal education
was on the way.

We have now reached a fateful turning point in the history
of the Welsh nation. In the middle of the nineteenth century
almost the whole of industrial Wales as well as rural Wales was
monoglot Welsh, just as a large part of Denmark was monoglot
Danish. The policy of the Act of Union had so far failed,
except with the landlord class and the petit-bourgeois class.
With the development of industry the proportion of Welsh
speakers rose; it was higher in 1850 than in 1800. Thus there
remained — miraculously, considering the geographical
position of Wales and the policy of the English government —
a possibility, as recently as this in our history, of a complete
and full national life, if the country's moral and material
resources were carefully developed together. This was the
position in 1851. That is not very long ago: 1851 was the year
my grandfather was born. He ministered at three new Welsh
chapels with a membership of about five hundred each. In
1883 his eldest son, my father, was born; the same
year a son was born to Eliezer Ben Yehuda, a Polish
Jew who had just gone to live in Palestine. Eliezer's
son was the first child to speak Hebrew at home as

a living tongue for two thousand years. In the early eighties there was only one Hebrew-speaking child in Israel. Today Hebrew is the language of government and law in Israel, the language of the whole of the educational system, including the five universities. Wales did not have to resurrect a language that had been dead for over two thousand years. Already the literature of the monoglot Welshmen of 1851 had an unbroken continuity of almost 1400 years, which is considerably more than the whole history of the Jews from the time of Moses, the father of the nation, to the destruction of Jerusalem.

The ruin of the national language and culture was not the result of the industrial revolution. Industrialisation had strengthened their hold. The havoc was wrought by what may be called the English revolution, which was planned as deliberately as Mao Tse Tung's cultural revolution; and the establishment's powerful weapons were the English schools which all Welsh children were compelled to attend. The sad spectacle of the Wales we see today is the result of the twist given to our history in the middle of the last century. 'A new era has dawned', said Caleb Rees after the Rebecca riots. How red that dawn was can be seen in the words of William Williams's speech in Parliament on March 10, 1846. He was a successful Welshman, a man who had uprooted himself, and thus characteristic of the new middle class:

'If the Welsh had the same advantage for *education* as the Scotch (sic), they would, *instead of appearing as a distinct people, in no respect differ from the English.*'

That was the great aim, and the way to attain it was cruelly clear. The goal was to abolish the Welsh as 'a distinct people', and to secure their assimilation with the English; the method was 'education'. The state had grown enormously in power since Thomas Hobbes wrote of it as *The Leviathan*. It could now arrange things very effectively in every corner of the kingdom, as it proved in the Education Act of 1870. It wielded a weapon that could effectively kill the language, a weapon such as the Tudor state had no conception of a compulsory English

state education — 'the murder machine', as Padraig Pearse
called it. 'Would it not be sound policy,' said William
Williams, 'to send the English schoolmaster among them?'
This was the way to kill the Welsh language; and it had to be
killed — for the sake of the people:

'The people of that country laboured under a peculiar difficulty from
the existence of an ancient language.'

said Williams. Civilising the Welsh — that is, anglicising
them, — would save the state a great deal of money:

'It should be borne in mind,' said Williams, 'that an ill-educated and
undisciplined population, like that existing amongst the mines in South
Wales, is one that may be found most dangerous to the neighbourhood
in which it dwells, and that a band of efficient schoolmasters is kept up
at a much less expense than a body of police or soldiery.'

This, therefore, was the task given to the Commission: to
produce a report, based on testimony which confirmed that
the Welsh must be anglicised, and that the effective way of
doing that was through an English education. As Jane Williams
(Ysgafell) said at the time:

'The commissioners were sent forth with instructions to make out
a case.'

Ieuan Gwynedd insisted that sending three monoglot
Englishmen among the Welsh was like sending three monoglot
Welshmen to inspect the condition of education in the counties
of Norfolk, Bedford and Stafford:

'They came,' said Henry Richard, 'with scornful smiles on
their lips.' They had their helpers among the Welsh, who
were, in the opinion of some of their fellow countrymen,
worse than the three chief commissioners; these assistants
had, according to R. D. Thomas:

'decided to slander their country, and that in accordance with the
purposes and plans of the Council and Parliament.'

But from the government's point of view they all did a
praiseworthy job. In particular the three Anglican Englishmen
on the commission did their work thoroughly. They

Welsh living-room

MERTHYR TYDVIL,
GLAMORGANSHIRE

Merthyr Tydfil about 1840

interviewed a host of upper middle class people and Anglican clergymen who told them exactly what they wanted to hear; in a country where three-quarters of the population were nonconformist, 232 Anglicans and only 79 nonconformists were called to give evidence — and the nonconformists did not include such important leaders as Dr. Lewis Edwards and Dafydd Rees, editor of *Y Diwygiwr*. The evidence presented to them proved not only that the Welsh were wild and ignorant, but that they were also immoral and unchaste. The latter accusation of sexual immorality excited the greatest anger: it was because of this that the episode beame known as *Brad y Llyfrau Gleision* (The Treachery of the Blue Books). The real treachery — the betrayal of the language and the civilisation of Wales — which gives the Blue Books their lasting importance, caused little agitation. Already the commission which had investigated the Rebecca troubles had urged the anglicising of the Welsh, and observed:

'. . . amongst the causes which affect the social condition of the people, is the ignorance of the English which pervades so large a proportion of the country.'

This was like blaming an ignorance of German for rioting in Denmark. Before long *The Times* would be parading the opinion of the landlords and the capitalists by attacking the language as 'the curse of Wales':

'Its prevalence and the ignorance of English have excluded and even now exclude the Welsh people from the civilisation of their English neighbours. An Eisteddfod . . . is simply a foolish interference with the natural progress of civilisation and prosperity.'

The 1847 report was very clear about this. It saw to it that people would associate the national language with ignorance and barbarity, with immorality and material failure:

'The Welsh language,' it said, 'is a vast drawback to Wales and a manifold barrier to the moral progress and commercial prosperity of the people.'

It drew attention to the movement of the population from the rural areas to the industrial towns in an argument which had a lethal effect among the Welsh themselves.

> 'A new field is opened to them, but not a wider. They are never masters . . . *It is still the same people.* Whether in the country or among the furnaces, the Welsh element is never found at the top of the social scale . . . *his language keeps him under the hatches.*'

That was the aim of the Act of Union — to put the Welsh speakers under the 'hatches'. The purpose of the English system was to delete the national identity of the Welsh completely, so that they would, 'in no respect differ from the English'. Yet they had created for themselves a life as full and dignified as that of the common people of any country in the world, and maintained it until it was shattered by a combination of factors beyond their control: the power of a hostile state, capitalist industry, and the schizophrenia that developed among the Welsh themselves as a result of their history from 1485 onwards. It was the combination of structural and psychological violence that overcame them. The commissioners reiterated the policy of the Act of Union in a way which appealed powerfully to the Welsh of the nineteenth century. The Welsh-speaking Welshman was a second-class citizen in his own almost wholly monoglot Welsh land. English was the language of material advancement, the only language of the masters, the law, the government and all official life. This had been the situation since 1536: but it was the circumstances of the nineteenth century that made him conscious of the fact that 'his language keeps him under the hatches'. He was now offered a diabolically attractive new deal. Provided he adopted the language of the English, he could enjoy the same opportunities as the English for getting on in the world. As an individual he was to have an equal chance of succeeding. There was one condition: there would be no Welsh national future. The Welsh people were to become as British as the English, just one of the many tributaries of the mighty British imperial river.

The commissoners quoted the Report of the Royal Commission on the administration of law in Wales:

'The people's ignorance of the English language practically prevents the working of the laws and institutions and impedes the administration of justice.'

The answer proposed was not to Cymricise the law and the institutions of course but to anglicise Wales itself, so that its people could be fitted into the English order imposed on them from London. In accordance with the policy of the Act of Union, the English language was used as a political instrument to assimilate, and so destroy, the Welsh nation.

When stressing how difficult a task it would be to get rid of 'this disastrous barrier to all normal improvement and popular progress in Wales' the commissioners paid an unintentional compliment to the culture of the *gwerin*; for their Report recognised that the Welsh poor had a better grasp of their language than the English poor had of theirs; and they loved their language. Five years later, in a report of 1852, Matthew Arnold, the inspector of schools and a cultured Englishman, praises the superiority of the Welsh children of the 'British Schools' in a remarkably stupid confession:

'The children in them are generally docile and quick in apprehension, to a greater degree than English children; their drawback of course is that they have to acquire the medium of information as well as the information itself, while the English children possess the medium at the outset.'

How therefore were they to succeed in destroying the language completely? English education alone was not enough, said the Commissioners:

'for so long as children are familiar with no other, they must be educated to a considerable extent through the medium of it . . . Still less, out of school, can the language of lessons make head against the language of life.'

Reginald Coupland's comments on this are:

'These were intelligent observations, and if the Commissioners had been able to grasp all that they implied, they might have thought twice before pronouncing their drastic sentence. But they had made up their minds. For the sake of Wales, Welsh must go.'

In attempting to save Wales from its language they did not have to depend entirely on formal English education. The petit-bourgeois in particular were ambitious; their main desire was to get on in the world; and the fact was — since Wales was an unfree country, and incorporated in England — that their world was an English world. This growing group therefore actively furthered the process of anglicisation. Matthew Arnold echoed the thoughts of many of them when he said in 1855:

> 'It must always be the desire of a government to render its dominions, as far as possible, homogeneous . . . Sooner or later the difference of language between Wales and England will probably be effaced . . . an event which is socially and politically desirable.'

In mid-century, the number of people speaking Danish was not much larger than the number of people speaking Welsh, and in proportion to the whole population, they were less. But although there was a higher proportion of German speaking Danes than there was of English speaking Welshmen, the political order in Denmark was Danish; the state worked on the side of the language and culture of Denmark; it created a mental and material environment in which the national tradition of Denmark could flourish. In Wales the political order was entirely English; the state threw its whole weight against the language and culture of Wales; it created a mental and material environment which was completely hostile to the Welsh national tradition. Psychologically it conditioned the Welsh to accept and even to welcome the intensifying structural pressures.

So, in the middle of the nineteenth century, when there was still a possibility that the Welsh nation could live a full national life in a country that was materially far richer than Denmark, circumstances turned against it. The political position and the mental climate proved too much of an obstacle. The endless possibilities of the nation were not realised. In London the will to destroy Wales was strong; in Wales the will to survive as a nation was weak. The upper classes had been on London's side since 1536 and even earlier; it was the *gwerin* who had kept the tradition alive. In mid-century English and anglicism were identified in the minds of the people with the landlords and the capitalist masters. How, then, did so many of the *gwerin*, by the twentieth century, become so attached to the English language and anglicism, as to abandon Welsh and its tradition? The answer centres largely on the state institutions and the political situation; these, however, could never have been allowed to remain so wholly English, had not the lower middle class added their weight to that of the anglicised upper class. The growing new class was as ambitious and was becoming almost as deracinated as the old. They were all British first, and Welsh second; and it was their leadership, and their values, which induced the *gwerin* to accept, and shortly, even desire to be denationalised. In the age of the Tudors it was the upper middle class who performed this function; in the age of Victoria it was the petit-bourgeois. This class took the guts out of both the nationalism and the nonconformity of Wales with its servile and insipid respectability. In addition, the monoglot industrial *gwerin* produced no leader incisive and intelligent enough to appreciate that the Welsh language was the chief enemy of the English capitalist system and that the English language was English capitalism's strongest weapon for keeping the Welsh 'under the hatches', politically, socially and industrially.

Four consequences attended the report of the Commission during this critical period of Welsh history: three of the four were exactly what the Government had envisaged.

First, it revitalised in London the Act of Union policy of the English assimilation of Wales. Secondly, in Wales, although the Welsh language continued to be associated with chapel and *eisteddfod* the 'Blue Books' succeeded in identifying it in the minds of the Welsh, with the disreputable rioting in Merthyr, with the Chartists, and with the Rebecca movement; and, worst still, with ignorance and poverty and the little thatched cottage. English was already the language of government and law and of the upper classes; and now it was even more closely associated with the image of success and wealth, order and civilisation, and not least with Queen Victoria and the British Empire. Thirdly, it led to the completely English education system which was made compulsory for all Welsh children in 1870 and which was avidly received by the parents, if not by the children, as the gateway to the fields of promise. Fourthly, in the strong opposition of a minority to the report we see the seeds of modern Welsh nationalism; it awoke the national political consciousness of the Welsh which was to increase consistently up to 1895.

XII. THE GLORY OF THE GWERIN

SINCE the continuation of the Welsh tradition depended on the *gwerin* after its betrayal by the aristocracy, we must study its quality and its Welshness particularly in the industrial areas, in order to realise what possibilities lay in Wales in the middle of the century. People are aware of the intellectual tradition of the quarrymen in the counties of Caernarfon and Merioneth, and their Welshness is taken for granted. But few people realise how rich and how Welsh life was in the industrial areas nearest the English border in the north-east and the south-east. Mention has already been made of Daniel Owen, the finest novelist in the Welsh language, who was born in Mold in 1836 and who died there in 1895. He was the son of a miner who was killed with two of his sons in the coal mine. His mother came from the family of Twm o'r Nant. He was apprenticed as a tailor at the age of twelve, having received almost no formal education, and although he enjoyed a brief period in Coleg y Bala when he was nearly thirty, he had to return home to his trade owing to the ill-health of his mother and his sister; and from then on until his death he kept a shop in Mold. That is the background of Wales's best novelist. The background of Alun (John Blackwell, 1797-1840) one of the finest lyrical poets of the century, was rather similar. He too came from Mold, but of English descent. He was apprenticed as a shoe-maker at the age of eleven, with William

Kirkham, a literary man. Alun went later to Jesus College, Oxford, after money had been raised to pay for his education upon his winning the *awdl* competition in two *eisteddfodau*. He edited *Y Cylchgrawn*, printed in the famous press of Rees y Ton, Llandovery. This was the press which reprinted, in 1848-9, the three fine volumes of the *Mabinogion* of Lady Charlotte Guest, and the productions of the Welsh MSS. Lloyd (1815-70), the musician, was another who came from Mold. His father was a cabinet maker, who was later ordained as a Baptist minister. Ambrose Lloyd was a commercial traveller who composed hymn tunes which are sung in every chapel in Wales, and in many other places too including pubs and rugby grounds.

Thomas Gee (1815-98), the son of a Denbigh printer, was apprenticed to his father. He was one of the century's main leaders, if not the foremost. He preached with the Calvinistic Methodists; he worked for the Sunday Schools, with the temperance movement, and his work with many social and political causes indicated the great change among Methodists since the days of the conservative John Elias, who frowned on social and political commitment. It was as a publisher and editor that Gee made his greatest contribution. In 1845 he started to publish *Y Traethodydd*, a theological and literary review of distinction, which still appears regularly. Its editor was Dr. Lewis Edwards, Bala, who wielded great influence through it. It was the means of educating and cultivating a wide readership and particularly among the Methodist ministry. Lewis Edwards was born and bred on a farm in Penllwyn, Ceredigion; but it is with Bala, where he was principal of the college, that his name is always associated. Like so many of the leading men of the century he combined the talents of pulpit, stage and press. For about two hundred years clergymen and nonconformist ministers were the national leaders; but in contrast with the great saints of the fifth and sixth centuries who belonged to princely families, these men were the product of the *gwerin*. The cream of the nation, both in intellect and character, entered the ministry; the hundreds of memoirs written about the ministers constitute an important part of the literature of the century.

In 1857 Thomas Gee founded *Baner Cymru* which amalgamated with the *Amserau* in 1859, to form the praiseworthy paper which is still published in Denbigh today. The *Amserau* was founded in 1843 by Gwilym Hiraethog (William Rees, 1802-83) in Liverpool; he was another of the most versatile men of his generation. As a young man he had been a shepherd on the slopes of Mynydd Hiraethog; he only spent a few winters at school. He was taught *cynghanedd* (the intricate closed metres of Welsh poetry) by an old bachelor farmer, a neighbour of the family. He published an enormous amount of poetry; he wrote for the press all his life. This Independent minister became one of the main political thinkers of his age in Wales, and he propagated his beliefs assiduously on the platform as well as in the press. He is considered to be one of the fathers of the popular lecture which became such an important feature of the *gwerin* culture. It was he who agitated for freedom for Hungary; he had met Mazzini and corresponded with him; he worked vigorously for the abolition of slavery in America. By now there was such a thing in existence as a Welsh public and political life — a development of the utmost importance — and Welsh was its language. Very few contributed more to it than Gwilym Hiraethog.

The press developed enormous importance in the middle of the century, second only to the pulpit and the platform: and the most influential of the newspapers were very nearly all Welsh language publications. They were papers of culture and vision. *Baner ac amersau Cymru* was the most important. This radical paper was the creation of Thomas Gee, its editor. He built up a circulation of 50,000 extending over the whole of Wales; but it had far more readers than that: and listeners too, for it was the custom to read it out aloud in the cobbler's shop or in the smithy for people who could not afford to buy a copy themselves.

Perhaps the most remarkable man who worked with

Thomas Gee in Denbigh was Gweirydd ap Rhys (Robert John Pryse, 1807-89). In character and outlook he resembled Thomas Stephens, the pharmacist from Merthyr, and Charles Ashton the scholarly policeman from Dinas Mawddwy. Gweirydd was born in the parish of Llanbadrig in Anglesey. By 1818 both his parents were dead, and he was kept by the parish. He became a skilful weaver, and in time opened a shop to sell his product. He had only four days formal schooling; yet he mastered English, Latin and Greek. He compiled five dictionaries; he was editor of *Papur y Cymry* and an indefatigable contributor to the press, and he also wrote a great many pamphlets. When Thomas Gee published *Y Gwyddionadur* in ten volumes of over 700 pages each, at a cost of £20,000, it was Gweirydd ap Rhys who contributed most of the articles. His chief works were *Hanes y Brytaniaid a'r Cymry* (The History of the Britons and the Welsh) and *Hanes Llenyddiaeth Gymreig* (1130-1650) (History of Welsh Literature). His work is characterised by a scholarly thoroughness which sent him to the original sources in manuscript. He and Carnhuanawc performed the enormous service of rescuing the history of Wales from oblivion. According to Thomas Parry, 'Gweirydd ap Rhys should be considered one of the chief heroes of the nation.' His children were also talented. 'O na byddai'n haf o hyd', which was composed by his daughter Buddug is still a popular song; an exhaustive study has recently been made by Tecwyn Lloyd of the work of his son Golyddan (1840-62) who was apprenticed to a doctor when he was only thirteen years old. He came head of the list in the first examination for M.D. in Edinburgh University. He was well read in the literatures of France, England, Greece and Rome. Like other Welsh poets, his ambition was to write a great epic in the style of Milton : and he came nearer to succeeding than anyone else in the century. His most worthy work is the seven thousand line *pryddest* on 'Angau' (Death) which he composed at the age of nineteen.

In Llanarmon Dyffryn Ceiriog, eight miles from the English border, Ceiriog (John Ceiriog Hughes, 1832-97), the best lyric poet of the century was born. As a youth he went to work as a clerk in Manchester, where he associated with many literary, musical and bohemian Welshmen whose influence on him was great. In 1865 he returned to Wales to work as a station master for the Cambrian Railway. Some of the best lyrics of the language are found in his masterpiece, *Alun Mabon*. His poems were immensely popular and are still often heard.

Alun Mabon won the prize for the pastoral in the national eisteddfod of Aberdare in 1861. The adjudicator who awarded him the prize was Aneurin Fardd or Aneurin ab Brydydd Gwent (Aneurin Jones, 1822-1904). The son of Shôn Fardd (John Jones), a miller, Aneurin Fardd was a civil engineer who later became a printer — he printed *Y Bedyddiwr* in Pontllan-ffraith. By now the tide of the eisteddfod movement was rising, and Aneurin Fardd was known throughout Wales as an adjudicator; but he was also a poet. With Elis Wyn of Gwyrfai he won the chair for his *awdl* 'Arthur' in the Ivorite Eisteddfod in Rhymni in 1859. This man was a close friend of Aneurin Bevan's father, and his Christian name was given to that great but deracinated politician. Aneurin Fardd was one of the two bardic teachers of Islwyn (William Thomas, 1832-78), a philosophical and mystic poet, who is considered by many to be the greatest Welsh poet of the century; *Yr Ystorm* was his attempt to compose an epic. Lewis Edwards had a great influence on him and on many others in the 'Bardd Newydd' (New Poet) school of poets. They suffered from a basic weakness which is seen in nearly all the poets and writers, politicians and public leaders of the century: a lack of knowledge and understanding of the Welsh past. Islwyn's other teacher was Gwilym Ilid of Machen, the official poet of *Cymdeithas Cymreigyddion y Fenni* (The Abergavenny Cymreigyddion Society).

Cymreigyddion y Fenni were a society of national importance centred on Abergavenny. It was only in the Abergavenny area that members of the aristocratic class took an interest in things Welsh and threw in their lot with the middle class and the *gwerin* in favour of the Welsh tradition.

Gwenynen Gwent (Lady Llanofer, 1802-96) and her husband, Sir Benjamin Hall (builder of Big Ben), who by his marriage united two great neighbouring estates, were brilliant exceptions to the Englishness of their class. These two learnt Welsh and became distinguished patrons of Welsh culture. Gwenynen Gwent co-operated in the work of collecting Welsh folk songs with Maria Jane Williams, Aberpergwm (1795-1873), a fine musician and singer, and the best guitar-player in Wales; and Brinley Richards (1819-95), the son of a shop-keeper in Carmarthen; and Bardd Alaw (John Parry, 1776-1851), the son of a stone mason in Denbigh. The original founder of the society was Carnhuanawc (Thomas Price, 1787-1847), who is a fine example of the cultural animation of the century bred. He was the son of the Vicar of Llanfihangel Bryn Pabuan, Breconshire. Much about the life of that part of Wales is described in his biography, written by Jane Williams (Ysgafell, 1806-85), an able woman who had opposed the Blue Books in 1847. Carnhuanawc attended three schools in the village before going to Christ College, Brecon — the very English school that had moved from Abergwili to Brecon in the time of Henry VIII. At home he heard the songs and the traditions of the *gwerin*, the *cywyddau* of Dafydd ap Gwilym and melodies on the harp. That was the nature of life in Breconshire. In the twentieth century the government destroyed a substantial part of the Welshness which remained by throwing hundreds of the native Welsh-speaking people out of their farms on Mynydd Epynt, where families had lived for four and five hundred years on the same farm, and planting a large military camp there. Carnhuanawc became an excellent Welsh historian. His special interest in the literature, history and archaeology of the Celtic countries reflected the Celtic awakening which was afoot; he travelled in Ireland and Scotland, Cornwall and Brittany. This fine Welsh scholar was an important link between Wales and Brittany. He encouraged Welsh education. He built a Welsh school at his own cost in Gelli Felen near Crucywel (Crickhowell); and when Llandovery College was founded as a Welsh-language boarding school in 1848, he, like Lady Llanofer, was one of its patrons.

The statement of intent which he formulated for *Cymreigyddion Y Fenni* placed Welsh education first.

> 'In the first place,' he said, 'to foster the language . . . The necessity to arrange the means for Welsh children to have their education in the Welsh language in the daily schools as well as in the Sunday schools.'

Carnhuanawc's speeches in the great *eisteddfodau* are a testimony to the cultural condition of Wales before the Betrayal of the Blue Books. In Mold in 1824 he said:

> '. . . perhaps it would be difficult to point out any other country in the world in which the peasantry and lower classes feel such an interest in literary and intellectual pursuits as the people of Wales do.'

And in the Brecon eisteddfod in 1826, he said:

> 'I have no hesitation in asserting that the Welsh language at the present day to the Welsh peasant is a much more cultivated and literary medium of knowledge than the English is to the Englishman of the same class . . . Show me another language in the world in which such a body of knowledge is found in the hands of the common people! Show me another race of men on the face of the earth among whom the labouring classes are the entire patrons of the press.'

Among the first members of the Society were Lady Charlotte Guest and her husband, and when writing to Carnhuanawc asking to join, she mentioned the 'glorious old language of the line of Gomer' immortalised through Welshmen's 'defence of their country and of their freedom'. For almost twenty years, between 1834 and 1853, the Abergavenny Eisteddfod was an important event in this heartening period of patriotic awakening. As a matter of fact, throughout the whole of Wales, the institution which did most to nurture the national consciousness was the *eisteddfod*. The Abergavenny Eisteddfod gave valuable prizes — £70 for an essay, for example; this would be worth many times as much today. Thousands thronged there from Gwent, Morgannwg and Brycheiniog. They lined the streets of the town, whose colourful flags were flying everywhere, watching the long processions. In these processions there were wagons carrying harpists, *penillion* singers and poets; men and women in colourful Welsh costumes; the schoolgirls of Llanwenarth; a press printing the president's greeting; beautifully decorated horses pulling carriages carrying eminent people from other countries, Celtic scholars, and the best Welsh writers; followed by the aristocracy from neighbouring counties, in gaily decorated horse-drawn vehicles; and many bands to keep the procession in step. The activities of this society in Gwent did much to nurture the consciousness of dignified Welsh nationality.

Carnhuanawc became vicar of Llanfihangel Cwm-du in 1825, and was buried there in 1848. In *Crwydro Brycheiniog* Alun Llywelyn Williams recounts a sad experience he had when visiting Cwm-du which was remarkably like the imaginary scene in Bala in which Islwyn Ffowc Elis describes the death of the Welsh language in *Wythnos yng Nghymru Fydd*:

'and since the smith was at his work there I could do no less than have a chat with him and ask about the Welsh language in the district. "There's an old man living in that house across the road," he said, "who speaks Welsh I believe." He went to the house to fetch him, and returned shortly bringing with him an old man of about eighty years of age who appeared to be almost blind, and who walked slowly, leaning on his stick. I greeted him in Welsh, but it was in English that he replied at first. I do not know when he had last heard a word of his mother tongue, but it was as if he could not, for some minutes, persuade his tongue to pronounce the sounds which were now so strange to him. At last, he started to speak slowly and hesitantly in the language of his mother. And then the dam burst, and I listened to the flood of the sweetest Welsh words that I have ever heard. There were tears in the eyes of the old man when we had to say good-bye.'

The System had done its work well. The language of the princes and the poets was dead in Cwm-du. The people were educated.

The poet Islwyn was typical of his period in his love of *eisteddfodau* and of competing in them. The country was studded with preacher-poets like him; but Islwyn spent much of his time as an editor and a regular correspondent for the press. He was responsible for the poetry column of *Y*

Gwladgarwr and *Y Glorian*. Many Welsh newspapers existed to promote the welfare of the workers. Both *Y Gwladgarwr* and *Y Gweithiwr Cymreig*, which was founded in 1859, were published in Aberdare and the first paper published for the working-class, *Y Gweithiwr*, was published in 1814 in Merthyr, and later *Utgorn Cymru* was also published there to support Chartism. (*Y Diwygiwr* and *Seren Gomer* also supported the Chartists of course). In 1875 *Tarian y Gweithiwr* was founded in Aberdare, and this paper continued in existence until the thirties of this present century; and *Llais Llafur* was started in Ystalyfera in the Swansea valley as late as 1898.

There were many periodicals as well as these newspapers of course. Some of them were mainly devoted to religious and denominational matters: *Y Tyst*, *Y Goleuad*, *Y Llan* and *Yr Ymofynnydd* have been in continuous publication since this period. *Y Gymraes* which was founded in Cardiff in 1850 under the patronage of Lady Llanofer and edited by Ieuan Gwynedd (Evan Jones, 1820-52) — one of the most gifted journalists of the century — was different from the others in being specifically for women readers. Ieuan Gwynedd was reared in poverty near Dolgellau; he went to Tredegar as a minister with the Independents; and before his premature death he made a great name for himself defending Wales and its moral and national character against the calumny of the Blue Books. Particularly influential in the northern areas were *Y Genedl* and *Yr Herald Gymraeg*, which still appears.

The rich cultural content of the majority of these papers reflected the values of their readers. Ieuan Gwyllt (John Roberts 1822-77) who was a tireless contributor to them on musical subjects moved to Aberdare, in 1858, to edit *Y Gwladgarwr*. He was the son of musical parents from Penllwyn near Aberystwyth, and was educated in the school kept by Dr. Lewis Edwards in Penllwyn before it moved to Bala. He began life as a solicitor's clerk before going to help Gwilym Hiraethog as assistant editor of *Yr Amserau*. He was ordained a minister with the Calvinistic Methodists. He lectured extensively throughout the country and wrote knowledgeably about music. He was one of the pioneers of tonic sol-fa in

Wales. In 1861, when he was a minister in Merthyr Tydfil, he founded *Y Cerddor* (The Musician), which he edited until 1873. In 1859 he published his *Llyfr Tonau Cynulleidfaol*, a volume of the best hymn tunes of many countries, to which he added an appendix in 1870. 17,000 copies were sold in four years. Germany and Austria were the countries from which many of the tunes were drawn. The German chorale has had an especially heavy influence on Welsh hymnology, including Ieuan Gwyllt's own work. Some of his hymn tunes, such as 'Moab', will live for ever. Ieuan Gwyllt contributed a great deal to the enriching of musical culture in Wales, especially in the field of vocal music. The composer, Tanymarian (Edward Stephens, 1822-85), of Maentwrog, was born in the same year as Ieuan Gwyllt. He too became a minister of religion with the Independents. He was well-known as a writer and poet, preacher and lecturer, critic and leader of *Cymanfaoedd Canu* (Singing Festivals). His oratorio 'Tiberius' is still sung. Choral singing developed throughout the country, and the *Cymanfa Ganu* became an important institution. The most popular composer of tha period was Gwilym Gwent (William Aubrey Williams, 1838-91), who was born in Tredegar. By calling, he was a blacksmith. He led a brass band, a musical institution which grew more and more audible and visible in the industrial areas. A large number of the *gwerin* became musically literate; they read not only books, but music too — usually tonic sol-fa, rather than the old notation. An institution which did a great deal to encourage this, and which has been jeered at by knowing snobs, was the *Gobeithlu* (Band of Hope).

The vigour of the newspapers and such activities as these suggest the strong Welshness of the industrial areas of the south-east in the middle of the century: it is confirmed too by the mass of Welsh books published by the presses of Gwent and Glamorgan. This came to light in the report made by Tremenheere for the government in 1839 on the language question in the districts of Newport and Merthyr. He showed that English was taught in only 18 of the 47 schools in these areas: and of the pupils who went to night schools, almost all

of those who could read at all, read only Welsh. As late as
1852 Matthew Arnold reported of the infants' school of
Blaenau Gwent,

'the lower part of this school might with advantage have more done
to anglicise them.'

The life of 'Blaina, Mon' testifies to the thoroughness of the
work done before the end of the century. But in mid-century
the majority of its inhabitants had a Welsh education in the
Sunday schools, which were praised by the Commission of
1847; and they also had a Welsh education in the chapels —
each one an 'island of hope' in the industrial desert around
them — and in the myriad meetings held in them and their
schoolrooms during the week. The Welshness and Welsh
culture of some of the inns should not be forgotten while
stressing that it was the chapels which became the social foci.
There was a rich literary and musical pub-culture in the
industrial towns. Around the chapels and their Sunday schools,
where the adults as well as the children heard the sound of
Welsh for hours every Sunday, there grew a maze of cultural
and literary societies and of special meetings for young people
and children. Later in the century they were also to have their
dramatic societies and their choirs which, after spending
three or four nights a week for months in rehearsal, brought
large audiences as well as the choristers themselves into the
sound of magnificent music when one of their wide repertoire
of oratorios was performed. Their concerts were held, as their
eisteddfodau, *cymanfaoedd canu*, public meetings and, later, even
dramatic performances were held, in the chapel, which was
called a *tŷ cwrdd* (meeting house) rather than a temple. The
chapel was the social centre.

In consequence, a tightly-knit community evolved, rich in
intellectual culture in the unpromising circumstances of
the industrial towns. In the coal valleys rich communities were
created, many members of which delighted in the things of
the mind and spirit — *Y Pethe* as they were called by Llwyd
o'r Bryn: the essence of the national civilisation. Of course,
only some of the people lived like this, but the proportion

Composer's ms. of National Anthem of Wales

Welsh Not

Nantgarw Porcelain Plate

Salmon Leap on the Rhondda c. 1815

Wattstown, Rhondda in the 1920's

was high enough to leave the stamp of its character on the whole society. One is astonished at the numbers of those who, after long and laborious hours in industry or on the land would master the difficult twenty-four strict metres of Welsh poetry, often in informal evening classes. This is the culture which is called the Welsh way of life. For hosts of humble men and women this humane manner of living was a cause. There were hundreds of thousands of people in Wales whose lives were governed by a cause much greater than they themselves; people who lived purposeful and disciplined lives; people who read widely and thought for themselves; people who had something to say and who knew how to say it; people who were proud to support good causes with their time and energy and money. It was these people who, in 1872, gave money which they could ill-afford to found the university college in Aberystwyth and later at Bangor; it was they who bought the Welsh newspapers and periodicals and books — often expensive — which flowed from the presses. It was they who built, against a background of material poverty, thousands of chapels (at the rate of one a fortnight throughout Wales between 1800 and 1850) and schools throughout the land, without a halfpenny's help from the government. And it was they who paid the ministers' salaries. In 1860 in Merthyr Tydfil for example, £8,600 was paid to maintain the ministers of the several chapels; this amount would have to be multiplied many times to estimate its value in terms of today's pound. G. T. Clark says:

> 'the Welsh people are very remarkable for their power of combining; and their power of self-government . . . (is) something marvellous. In our Schools, nine-tenths of the people are Dissenters: they go to their own chapels, they pay their own ministers, and they manage the matter entirely themselves.'

These were the Welsh of the mid-century before the System got hold of them and submerged their civilisation in a flood of English. It was they who made it a great century in the history of Wales. There were no 'yokels' or 'rustics' in rural Wales; nor a rootless proletariat in industrial Wales; but

people of education, cultivated and civilised by their nation's
traditional way of life which was certainly limited but rarely
trivial. Among them were many who never saw the inside
of a day school; without exception, they all received the most
valuable education that society can give, an education in
the values of their national tradition. A great part of the hidden
strength of their nonconformity was the use it made of the
essential elements of the Welsh intellectual tradition: its
sermons and hymns and anthems, its appeal to the mind and
the emotions, and its use of the Welsh language. Without
the help of either a government or a privileged class, the
gwerin created a civilised pattern of social life. How would
Wales look today, and what contribution could it be
making to the world if it had a government to support
and nurture this way of life rather than to ravage and destroy it?

One night, sometime in 1856, a man who was a weaver
and wool merchant was walking along the banks of the
River Rhondda in Pontypridd. His name was Evan James.
He had been an inn-keeper in Bedwellte and was something
of a poet. That evening he wrote some verses which were to
become important in the history of Wales. In these verses he
wrote simply about his country: he celebrated its mountainous
beauty, every valley and crag, every river *and stream,
and the sea which forms a rampart around this ancient land.
He sang of the great men in its history, the poets and musicians,
the heroes and patriotic soldiers who had given their lives
defending its freedom. He wrote of its enslavement under the
foot of the enemy. He gloried particularly in the language,
for whose continued existence he longed passionately, and
stated emphatically his eternal loyalty to his national heritage.
He had a son, James, who was working at the time with his
father in the woollen factory in Mill Street, but later went to
keep a public-house in Mountain Ash. James James composed
a melody, to his father's words, and called it 'Glanrhondda'.
How suitable, and yet how ironical it is, that two of the
gwerin of East Glamorgan, who lived at the time of the great
convulsion, when Wales was still Welsh in language, should

have composed the words and the music of the national anthem of Wales:

> 'Mae hen wlad fy nhadau yn annwyl imi'
>
> 'The old land of my fathers is dear to me'.

XIII. THE VICTORY OF THE BOURGEOIS

IT IS a truism to say that the Welsh civilisation would not have declined among so great a part of the people after the middle of the century had Wales had its own government. Had it been an autonomous country, creating the conditions of its own life, with a government to support it, Wales in 1971 would probably be as strongly Welsh as Denmark is Danish. The problem is to understand why its people did not demand their national freedom and why they did not oppose despoliation by the British state. Why did they welcome so spinelessly the system which denationalised them? Most of the answers to this question have already been supplied. Conditioned by a history of four centuries as an integral part of England and having lost the leadership of the privileged classes, they no longer thought as a nation and they did not reason politically. When a national consciousness developed it was a cultural one; and when eventually they began to think politically it was social radicalism which inspired them. This political radicalism was not fused with national consciousness. The Welsh civilisation had been saved by the great spiritual revolution which gave birth to a splendid network of religious institutions; but for this the nation would have been dead in the first half of the nineteenth century, and the Welsh today would be no more than an odd sort of English or British. Even so, a spiritual revival which expressed itself in and through a political order was not experienced. The Welsh political awakening coincided with the tremendous growth in the power of the state, the British empire and the British parties. It is true that there was a national awakening, but the Britishness proved too strong for it. From the beginning Welsh political nationalism expressed itself through a British medium, within a British party; it readily accepted the British environment, and the most that it sought was recognition for Wales within the British political system. In the end, the strength of Briticism proved too much even for this, and no measure of national autonomy was achieved, let alone that degree of self-government enjoyed by the Swiss cantons. Tom Ellis and Lloyd George never dreamed for even that much. When considering this, we should remember, how small, and therefore how vulnerable, the population of Wales was: 5% of the population of the island in the beginning of the century and in mid-century; 4.9% today.

In the second half of the century the middle-class grew in number and influence. This was a period of fantastic industrial development and economic growth. David Thomson in *Europe Since Napoleon* says, 'The outstanding developments in Europe during the two decades between 1851 and 1871 were the industrial and commercial supremacy of the United Kingdom in the world . . . The United Kingdom was the only industrial and commercial power of great importance. She produced fifty-seven million tons of coal when France produced only four and a half million and the whole of the German *Bund* only six million; more than two million tons of pig-iron when France, her only rival, produced less than half a million tons; and she commanded more than half the whole world's tonnage of ocean-going shipping . . . Until the 1860's Belgium was the only European country to keep pace with Britain in industrial growth. In her resources of iron, coal and zinc she was particularly fortunate . . . By 1870 her own mineral resources of iron and zinc were becoming exhausted, but she remained a manufacturing and exporting country because she had the technicians and skilled workers, the industrial plant, enterprising management and business organisation and good communications.'

Wales also had coal, iron, zinc and other mineral resources. By 1913 she was producing over sixty million tons of coal annually. More than half of it was exported through her fine ports. She produced nearly all the anthracite found in these islands, a high proportion of the steel, and virtually all the tinplate which was basic to so many secondary industries, which were found not in Wales but in the English Midlands. Despite her great natural wealth Wales has not had a strong economy because, unlike the far poorer countries of Scandinavia, there was no correlation between the structure of her political and economic life and the structure of the historic national community. She suffered the usual fate of peripheral provinces which lack indigenous political institutions. Little difference could be discerned between her economy and that of a colony. It has been said that the chief economic functions of colonies were to supply raw materials for use in the manufactures of the governing country, to provide markets for its manufactured goods, and to secure places of investment for its commercial enterprise and its surplus capital. These functions Wales fulfilled for England. The bourgeoisie were content that this should be so and the workers were willing to be taught by them. Those who did not think of Wales as a political entity would never consider her as an economic entity requiring balanced economic development in the interests of the national entity rather than simply the exploitation of her raw materials. They could not know that in the future their Britishness would lead to massive unemployment, poverty, depopulation and migration. This was an exciting time to be British, and British they were determined to be.

It was not only that the state was British; it was a huge imperial power. From month to month the British Empire grew in size, power and glory. Its language was English. English was also the language of America, outside the Empire. English was the language of Canada and Australia too. Under the influence of Macaulay who died in 1859 English became the language of government and law in India, where the princes and the nobles behaved in a way that recalls the aristocracy of Wales two and a half centuries earlier. In an atmosphere such as this, the gradual ascendancy of English as the language of Wales came to be regarded almost as a divine ordination in the minds of the Welsh middle classes, especially as this was the only path to material success. The British government honestly believed that it was civilising the Welsh by anglicising them:

> 'Nor is to be wondered at', said Reginald Coupland, one of the most enlightened of the Empire's servants, 'that they so unmistakeably identified the "march of progress" with material advance, and so complacently assumed that the best service that could be rendered to Welshmen was to make them more like Englishmen. For they were living in the intellectual climate of Macaulay's England. The reign of the "Philistines" was at hand.'

Yr Artist yn Philistia (the Artist in Philistia) is the title given by Saunders Lewis to a series of studies which he made of writers in the second half of the century. The effect of the state on Welsh national life was philistine. The state and the government have no more important function than to maintain and nurture the nation's civilisation. Yet the British state crushed and ruined the Welsh civilisation. The grace of our national life was inundated by an ugly spreading Englishness. At the same time the countryside, whose incomparable beauty can bring tears to the eyes, was disfigured by a plague of ugly towns and villages, ugly public buildings, ugly houses and ugly furniture. Ugliness, injustice and materialism were vital elements in the Britishness of the period, in its social and political manifestations at home as well as overseas. This was the 'march of progress' which the Welsh took pride in. Industry did not compare with this in ugliness; industry could be remarkably beautiful for that matter, and, in any case, one could escape from the physical manifestations of ugliness as the poet Williams Parry did:

> O olwg hagrwch Cynnydd
>   Ar wyneb trist y gwaith
> Mae bro rhwng môr a mynydd
>   Heb arni staen na chraith,
> Ond lle bu'r arad' ar y ffridd
> Yn rhwygo'r gwanwyn pêr o'r pridd.

> Remote from ugly Progress
>   on the factory's sad face
> there's a region between sea and hill
>   without a stain or trace,
> save where the plough from mountain earth
> ripped the sweet spring to birth.

But it was impossible to escape from the ugliness which was woven into the texture of life. The Welsh did not see it as ugly; as with the people of their period generally, the ugliness was beauty to them. An increasing number of them extolled the exciting imperial achievements of Britain, and basked in the reflected glory of the victories which the British armies won against the Maharattas and the Sikhs, the Zulus and the Matabele. They rejoiced when the Basutos and the Ashantis were conquered, and when Langalibalili was defeated and his people dispersed. They swelled up with pride when Abyssinia was overcome by the Indian army; when opium was forced on China; and when General Roberts attested the expert craftsmanship of the Birmingham guns which killed thousands of Afghans and set a puppet to rule their country. When the Welsh won military glory by defeating the Zulus in Rorke's Drift, not one of them doubted their right to be there, thousands of miles from the shores of his own oppressed country, facing the spears of the natives of the dark continent for the good of the British Empire.

Naturally a large and important part of the nation did not find this at all admirable. Radicals such as S.R. (Samuel Roberts, 1800-85) opposed all war. 'The Christian has not the right to be a soldier' — was the basic principle of S.R. on this point, and he promoted it through the influential *Cronicl*. He bitterly attacked the Crimean War and Disraeli's imperialism, and also the American Civil War, in spite of his strong opposition to slavery, because he believed that war was as bad as slavery. Henry Richard was another opposed to military imperialism; for forty years he was secretary of the Peace Society — founded in London through the hard work of Joseph Tregelles Price (1784-1854), the master of Neath Abbey Iron Works, a Quaker and humanitarian who made a

doughty effort to save Dic Penderyn. Evan Rees of Montgomeryshire, the author of *Sketches of the Horrors of War*, was
the first secretary of this society which had Welshmen as
secretaries for almost a hundred years. With Elihu Burritt,
Henry Richard arranged a series of peace conferences in
Europe. The last of these was held in Frankfurt in 1850.
S.R. was a member of the British or English deputation.
In his biography of Henry Richard, Charles S. Miall quotes
this press report:

> 'Mr. Richard, at the first sitting, moved a vote of thanks to the
> Senate of Frankfort . . . and in doing so he asked his countrymen to
> give emphatic contradiction to the suspicion that they were the enemies
> of Germany — (prolonged cheers) — and to indicate that they desired
> to see Germany powerful, united and free. (The entire English
> delegation rose and vehemently cheered this sentiment.)'

Notice that there is no nonsense here about the Britishness of
Henry Richard's fellow-countrymen: they were English.
And the Huns of 1914 were still respected as Germans.

But although only a few Welshmen were imperialists, as
yet, the fame of the British Empire and its promotion of the
British way of thinking, intensified by Victoria's two Jubilees,
did much to wean them from their *Cymreictod* (Welshness).
They were all the more easily uprooted because they lacked
knowledge of their own history and of a philosophy which
attributed great value to national community. Had they been
aware of their national history they would not have been
driven like chaff before the imperial wind; but they knew
little of *y glendid a fu* (the beauty that was); they had been
suffering from amnesia for centuries. They knew much more
about the history of Israel than the history of Wales, but
although the religion of the Jews of the Old Testament was
inseparable from politics and nationalism, it was only with
Jewish 'religion' that the Welsh identified themselves, and not
at all with the nationalism through which it was often
expressed. If they had given any thought to their own
society, they would have known the priceless value of the
human community we call the Welsh nation, and they would
have tended their roots in its history and tradition. Griffith

Jones's vision of the place of the nation in God's world had been lost completely. They were individualists. They did not know that in reality there is no such thing as an individual; they had no true understanding of the nature of man: that we are all human persons, social creatures woven into the warp and woof of society; created by society; that our social nature is the very essence of our humanity. Lacking any conception of this, they felt free to leave their national community to fare for itself while they got on in the world as 'individuals'.

This lies behind their blindness about the value of the Welsh language, which is the heart and the blood of Welsh civilisation. This is a pattern of values, and the chief function of a nation is to transmit these values from generation to generation. The chief function of the state is to create the conditions which allow the nation to live its life fully, and thus make it possible for its members to live a full life as individual persons. In the end, the purpose of it all is to enable every human being to live his own life as fully as possible. The national awakening in several European countries led from an emphasis on culture to effective political action, and this led to the establishment of independent nation states. They felt the need to create their own state which would safeguard their nation's life. As Lewis Namier says:

'The politically minded cannot feel truly free except in a state which they acknowledge as their own, and in which they are acknowledged as indigenous: that is, their own national state.'

In Wales this did not happen. That which lies behind the failure of the Welsh of the nineteenth century to do this helps to explain the deterioration in the quality of the religious life of many. Pietism, as ugly as anything else in this life, is what is too often found in the respectability which is so far away from the spirit and social concern of the thousands of chapel members and deacons who stood up to the soldiers in Merthyr Tydfil, who marched with the Chartists, and who destroyed the tollgates with Beca.

Five examples will clarify the prevailing attitude to language. In the introduction to his six hundred page volume

Heroines of Welsh History published in 1854, the author, T. J. Llewelyn Prichard discusses:

> 'The merits or mischief of reviving in literature an antiquated and degenerated (sic) language . . . It is already the misfortune of modern Europe to possess too many cultivated dialects . . . In order to do full justice to their national literature, and to make it an object of interest to others they should divest it of its native garb (the Welsh language) and present it to the world in a form more qualified to allure the general reader; namely an English costume.'

Lewis Edwards, the most influential mentor of the century, corresponded with his wife and friends in English. When his son, Thomas Charles, was appointed principal of the University College of Wales in Aberystwyth in 1872, his father wrote to him thus:

> 'But of course you would belong to the English chapel, and preach there, though not often.'

The third example is Beriah Gwynfe Evans (1842-1927); this versatile and energetic man from Nant-y-glo, Monmouthshire, was secretary of the nationalist movement, 'Cymru Fydd', in 1895, and also secretary of Cymdeithas yr Iaith Gymraeg (Welsh Language Society) in his time. He was editor of many Welsh papers, and a pioneer of drama; his first play was 'Owain Glyndwr'. He was an eisteddfod man all his life, and became Recorder of the Gorsedd of the Bards. Despite all this, when he was headmaster of Gwynfe school, Llangadog, he used the 'Welsh Not' zealously to punish children for speaking Welsh in school. The fourth example is Sir John Morris-Jones, a great scholar and patriot, who was one of the chief benefactors of Wales and its language. When he went up to Oxford as student he thought in the same way as the majority of his class, and in a debate he supported the proposition, 'that the extinction of the Welsh language would be beneficial to Wales.' His lectures on Welsh literature were given in English. The last example typifies much of the controversy that surrounds the language and nationality of the Welsh. The following words belong

to Eben Fardd (1802-63), the finest poet of the century in
the strict metres:

> 'By a seeming immutable destiny, the sceptre has departed from
> out of Wales, the power and dominion have passed to other people,
> whose political and lingual empire seems to assume a paramount
> influence over all the ancient dynasties, peoples and tongues of bygone
> ages. So that we cannot do better, at the present time, than to mark
> well the significant beck of allwise Providence, and fall in with the
> mighty tide of national mutations, which no human policy can avert,
> or human power withstand.'

The will to die had firm hold of the Welsh. The fact that the
language and the tradition of Wales have remained alive in
face of this shows their amazing resilience.

XIV.   THE ESTABLISHING OF THE
ENGLISH SYSTEM

WHAT made 1870 a blacker year than 1282, and even 1536, was
the imposing of the English educational system on all the
children of the country. Perhaps the nationalism of Wales
would have been too strong to allow such an act of barbarism
a quarter of a century later; but in 1870 this was only starting
to sprout. The most striking manifestation of the death-wish
in Wales was its willing acceptance of this hideous system.
But for the servility of the Welsh people, the English
government could not have shattered the Welsh tradition in
such a large part of the country. It is the spiritual factor that
decides the course of history. More dangerous than a powerful
external enemy is internal weakness. How different were the
experiences of Wales and 'the windy peninsula' of Denmark!
This was a very difficult period for the Danes too. The German
language had penetrated deeply into the country, and in 1864
Denmark lost its richest area, Schleswig Holstein, to Prussia.
It answered this defeat by setting up, with the help of the
government, the famous residential Folk High schools — a
magnificent contribution to education. About a third of the
country's population passed through these schools. Only two

subjects were taught — through Danish of course — the history of Denmark, and its language and literature. Nevertheless, Richard Livingstone could say of this education in *The Future of Education*:

> 'It has transformed the country economically, given it spiritual unity, and produced perhaps the one educated democracy in the world.'

Even in economics the spiritual factor is all important. Despite a dearth of natural resources — a problem unknown to Wales — Denmark proved that a determined nation can create a healthy economy. It depends on what Livingstone calls 'spiritual unity' in the nation, that is, a healthy nationalism. This was ensured by rooting the people firmly in their own history and literature:

> 'The individual becomes part of a larger pattern, and a spirit grows up which checks selfishness, encourages men to feel themselves members of a community, and makes cooperation not only possible but natural . . . The schools have done much more than educate individuals. They have turned Denmark from a depressed country into the most successful farming community in Europe.'

This completely national education was the basis of their industrial success; today only 7% of Denmark's population works on the land. Denmark became industrialised without undue injury to its language and culture.

In the system imposed on Wales, the language of the country was not used as the medium of instruction. A foreign language was used to teach the children of monoglot Welsh people. Since the most thorough way of teaching a language is to use it as the medium for teaching other subjects, the Welsh language suffered terribly. Worst of all, it excommunicated the Welsh language completely from the schools. It was not even taught as a subject. And when a child was heard speaking it, the 'Welsh Not' was put around his neck; and when that child heard another speaking it, in turn, put it around *his* neck: the one wearing it at the end of the day was punished. In his autobiography *Clych Atgof*, Sir O. M. Edwards looks at his experiences in Llanuwchllyn under an English schoolmistress:

'Every day the Not, under its own weight as it were, would find its way from every corner of the school, to my neck. This is a comfort to me even today: I never tried to get rid of the Not by passing it on to someone else . . . Damnable system, I am grateful when I remember that there is hope that I shall see the time when I can dance on your grave. It was not the school-mistress's fault, but the system's . . . I spoke one language, and the school-mistress another — and I learnt nothing. But for the Welsh Sunday School, I should be illiterate today.'

The language which in the Middle Ages had been more extensively used for educational purposes than any modern European language was wholly excluded from the state schools, and when in the 90's secondary schools were established following the Intermediate Education Act of 1889, they too, followed the same philistine pattern, which for the most part they still retain. The use of the mother-tongue as the language of instruction was completely ignored. This was essential in order to implement the Act of Union policy of ensuring that the Welsh 'shall instead of appearing a distinct people, in no respect differ from the English.' The Welsh themselves tolerated it in the belief that it gave their children the only way of getting on in the world.

In England the intellectuals understood the importance of the mother tongue in education. This is how it was put in *The Teaching of English in England*, a report published by the government in 1921:

'We state what appears to us to be an incontrovertible fact, that for English children no form of knowledge can take precedence of a knowledge of English, no form of literature can take precedence of English literature, and that the two are so inextricably connected as to form the only basis for a national education.'

Every day school in Wales kept from its pupils a knowledge of the Welsh language and Welsh literature which should 'form the only basis for a national education'.

At this time England was following in Ireland too a policy of cultural genocide which was even more destructive of Irish civilisation than military slaughter and political plantations had been. Cromwell had been active there in 1652. In imposing his 'settlement' following the seige of Drogheda and the massacre of the townsfolk, Cromwell had said, "It has pleased God to bless our endeavours at Drogheda . . . The enemy were about 3,000 strong in the town. I believe we put to the sword the whole number . . . I wish that all honest hearts may give the glory of this to God alone, to Whom, indeed, the praise of this mercy belongs'. Two centuries later, with the help of starvation and emigration, the National Education Board of Ireland, founded in 1831, succeeded in getting rid of thousands of Irish speakers, and the purpose was the same: to eliminate the nationalism of the people. The teaching of Scott's lines in the schools was forbidden:

> 'Breathes there a man, with soul so dead
> Who never to himself has said,
> This is my own, my native land!'

In their place, these words written for the purpose by Archbishop Whately were urged:

> 'I thank the goodness and the grace
> Which on my birth have smiled,
> And made me in these Christian days
> A happy English child.'

For well over three centuries English had been the sole language of law in Wales. This is illustrated by an event in 1871 when a number of persons led by Osborne Morgan, Q.C., the Liberal M.P., petitioned the Lord Chancellor to appoint a Welsh-speaking judge. The Lord Chancellor reminded them in his reply, that:

'there is a statute of Henry VIII (27 Hen. 8, c. 26) which absolutely requires that legal proceedings in Wales shall be conducted in English, legal proceedings had been in English for 300 years, and, moreover, the Welsh language is dying out . . . probably the best thing that can happen for Wales is that the Welsh tongue should follow the Cornish into the limbo of dead languages.'

On this ground the Chancellor's aversion to doing anything which might tend to keep alive the dying language is intelligible. He appointed a Mr. Homersham Cox.

The Welsh situation in 1870 was thus: the only language of the law was English; the only language of government and official life was English; the only language of the privileged upper classes was English; the only language for getting on in the world was English; and the only language of the education given to each and every child in every daily school in the land was English. In no time at all a large number of attractive school books were published — in English. The daily papers came into Wales — in English. Films came — in English. Soon radio was to come into every home — in English. English officials came by the hundred, and English immigrants, who could not be assimilated, by the thousand. The towns and the villages were dotted with announcements and directions and advertisements of every kind — in English. When television arrived, it too ensured that the Welsh homes were filled with the sound of English. And the people were conditioned to think that this was good for them. The remarkable thing is, in spite of the fact that three quarters of the people of Wales have been deprived of their heritage, that the language has lived at all on the lips of so many.

XV. MICHAEL D. JONES AND THE NATIONAL AWAKENING

In order to survive as a nation, it was necessary for Wales to have political freedom to create its own conditions of life; a government and state to serve Wales. The democratic way to win national freedom this required was by creating an independent Welsh party which could win elections. This was not realised at the time. But what gives unity to the political history of the second half of the century is the gradual movement towards self-government as an aim, and towards creating a Welsh party as the effective way of serving Wales and attaining that goal. By 1895 quite big steps had been taken in the direction of these two aims; then the movement declined suddenly, and the nation stood still, at the mercy of new powers.

In the main, there were three subjects which angered the Welsh: the ecclesiastical issue, that is, the privileged position of the Church of England in a country of Nonconformists; the land question, that is, justice for tenants from their English-speaking and Anglican landlords; and the many-faceted subject of education, which included the question of the church schools. These issues produced a radical programme which was completely Welsh in spirit and which the Liberal Party attempted to realize. They brought the Welsh noncon-formists into conflict with the anglicised landlords who, to all intents and purposes, had ruled Wales for three centuries and more, when the central government was weak. With the growth in the power of the state, the landlords were supplanted by its even more dangerous anglicism.

The struggle against the English-speaking landlords and masters helped to rouse the political consciousness of the *gwerin*; and after Disraeli's measure had given the vote to a substantial number of them in 1867, the fruit of this was seen in the important election of 1868. That election is a milestone in the history of Wales, although Lloyd George exaggerated when he said, forty years later:

'it woke the spirit of mountains, the genius of freedom that fought the might of the Normans.'

The radicals were inspired by its revelation of their strength; and a new confidence arose in Nonconformity, which had already received spiritual reinforcement from the revival of 1859. Welshness became articulate in politics. Twenty-one Liberals and twelve Tories were returned. In Denbigh, George Osborne Morgan was returned for the Noncon-formists, through the powerful support of Thomas Gee; and in Merthyr, where the number of electors had risen after the 1867 Act from 1,387 to 14,577, Henry Richard, who was significantly called the Apostle of Peace and the Member for Wales, was elected. He was the first member of Parliament to reflect the Welsh mind in parliament, where he said in 1869:

'no question relating to Wales has occupied the attention of Parliament in the memory of man.'

Yr eiddox yn wladgar,
Michael D. Jones.

Michael D. Jones

Thomas Gee

With two exceptions, this was true of the first two generations of the century.

More important than the election itself were the events that took place afterwards. Some of the landlords were so angry that they committed acts of reprisal against those tenants who had voted against the Tory candidates. Seventy-one tenants were turned out of their farms in Ceredigion and Carmarthenshire; and, it was claimed, Lord Penrhyn sacked eighty workers for the same reason. This atrocious behaviour strengthened the Liberal cause by giving it martyrs; and it is true to say that the Liberals remained longest in those counties where the people suffered either on this score or from their refusal to pay the *degwm* (tithe). The Liberal Party continued to grow; it was Welsh, radical and Nonconformist; in the 1880 election it won every seat in Wales except four. During the hundred years 1870-1970 the Tory party has been without very substantial support in Wales; it has not won more than nine seats in any election, and those only in the most anglicised areas. In spite of this, Wales has had for most of that hundred years been subjected to arrogant Tory government. The nation has never experienced a democratic order which gave it the right to choose its own government. England has always decided the colour of Wales's government. A self-governing Wales would be as tenaciously radical as Norway or Sweden; for radicalism has been the Welsh political way of life, just as conservatism has been England's.

The Liberals' hold on Wales was strengthened by Gladstone. He won the hearts of the people, less because he married a Welshwoman and came to live in Hawarden, than because he went to the National Eisteddfod in Mold in 1873, and called the Welsh language 'a venerable relic of the past'. The fact that the people loved this patronising reassurance from the Grand Old Man speaks volumes about their psychological state. In 1881, through Gladstone's government, and for the first time ever, a Welsh Act was passed: the Sunday Closing Act. It was a day of rejoicing when the Parliament of Wales — for that is what the English parliament is — passed an Act appertaining to Welsh life.

1881

L F—Z

Only the London government could change the conditions of life in Wales through an Act of Parliament; but in the meantime the Welsh had been acting independently, under the leadership of Sir Hugh Owen, to establish in Aberystwyth in 1872 a college awarding degrees, and calling itself the University College of Wales. The financial support which they gave to the college is something the *gwerin* can be proud of. This was a national action, as was the establishing of the University of Wales in 1893. The first sentence of the University Charter announced:

'There shall be and there is hereby constituted and founded a University in and for Wales . . . with the name of the University of Wales . . .'

In other words, the University of Wales was to be like the universities of Europe since the days of the Renaissance, a national institution serving the nation though welcoming students from other countries. From the time of the founding of the colleges in Aberystwyth onwards, there has been an organic relationship between the University and the society outside.

What weighed most heavily on the mind of the Welsh in the seventies and eighties — and also after the turn of the century — was the economic position of agriculture. With the close of the civil war in America it returned to its usual position of depression. It had only enjoyed real prosperity during war-time; for the policy of governments has been to import cheap foodstuffs to keep wages down. There has never been a government that thought of agriculture in social terms; the considerations have always been exclusively economic. If the greed of the landlords is added to this, the land problem grows enormously. A generation earlier it had led to the direct action of the Rebecca riots; now that political action was possible, the Liberal Party was the one to profit by it. As the only political medium of the *gwerin* at that time it became the Welsh national party: a party for the industrial as well as the rural Welsh. The land problem 1886 played a prominent part in the 1886 election when, once again, thirty Liberals were returned, and only four Tories. 1886 was a seminal year for Welsh nationalism. The influential Dafydd ap Gwilym Society was established in Oxford, and the first branch of the Cymru Fydd movement in London. But the most significant happening of the year was the election on 14 July (the anniversary of the fall of the Bastille) of Tom Ellis (1859-99) as Liberal M.P. for Merioneth.

Tom Ellis was the son of a small-holder from near Bala. After attending the British School in Llandderfel, and the Grammar School in Bala (where he was the contemporary of such notable men as O. M. Edwards, D. R. Daniel, and J. Puleston Jones) he went to University College, Aberystwyth, and later to New College, Oxford. To judge from his remarks in later life, it was Aberystwyth that benefited him most. There his companions included nationalists who were to become prominent in the life of the nation later on: J. E. Lloyd, the great historian; T. F. Roberts, the son of a police-sergeant, who was to become Principal of the college in 1891; Ellis Jones Griffith, one of the most brilliant Liberal members of Parliament at the end of the century; Samuel T. Evans, the son of a grocer from Sgiwen, another of the parliamentary company, who became President of the Probate, Divorce and Admiralty division in the High Court in 1910. Kenneth O. Morgan says, in his fine book *Wales in British Politics*, 1868-1922:

> 'The young patriots who were associated with the University College at Aberystwyth in the early 1880's were profoundly influenced by the idea of nationalism and more intuitively sympathetic to the ideals of Young Ireland.'

During this generation Irish nationalism proved a strong influence on Wales; it was an inspiration to the young, but an obstacle to the older generation, who identified it with Papism and violence. But it was the positive influence that was most important; this is what inspired *Young Wales* and later *Cymru Fydd*. Not only Ireland, but the nationalism of Hungary and Italy before it, left its mark on Wales. Tom Ellis read the works of Mazzini avidly; and the great Italian continued to influence the course of Welsh nationalism until the middle of the twentieth century, because his idealism was so in tune with the Welsh mind:

> 'Once man says to himself in the true seriousness of mind and soul,' said Mazzini, 'I believe in freedom, in a country, in humanity, it is essential for him to fight for freedom, for his country, and for humanity, to fight daily, nightly, as long as life remains in his body.'

Mazzini stressed the obligations of men and nations just as much as their rights; he gave priority to the rights of humanity as well as the rights of nations. Some Welsh nationalist ideas sprang from the radical nationalism of the 1848 revolution on the Continent.

This was true of the ideas of the Welshman who had the greatest influence on the young nationalists, Michael D. Jones (1822-98), the most complete Welshman of the century, an Independent minister, and principal of the Independents' College at Bala. He was a classical scholar who wrote a Welsh grammar, and also took a keen interest in scientific subjects. His point of view is seen in a statement that he made in 1856:

> 'Because the Welsh are a conquered people in their own country . . . they have lost their self confidence; they do not believe that they can do much, and for that reason they attempt very little. They believe, like all serfs, that it is their master alone who has the power . . .'

In a generation whose deference to everything and everybody English was not free from servility, Michael D. Jones corrected the balance by drawing attention to imperfections in English character and behaviour. 'Their aim,' he said, 'was to be the ruling race wherever they may be . . . They subdued the Welsh in Wales, the Scots and the Irish. Since then their rapacity has led them to steal two continents, North America and Australia, from the natives who they are craftily annihilating in order to possess their land'.

Writing in 1885, at the peak of imperial prestige he found the attitude of the Empire-builders to the native peoples lacking in humanity:

> 'The armies which are depriving them of their independence are but licensed murderers. The war in the Sudan, in which aristocrats are prominent, will remain through the ages a stain on English history.'

In the Christmas issue of *Y Celt*, 1886, he returned to the theme:

'The Irish kill an occasional landlord illegally. But the English have for centuries been passing laws to enable them to shed the blood of some nation or other, one after another, and these are the people of whom Mr. Rendel says that their hearts are right!'

Stuart Rendel, a boon friend of W. E. Gladstone, was the Liberal M.P. for Montgomeryshire and chairman of the Welsh Parliamentary party. Michael D. Jones developed a body of social and economic radical and anti-capitalist thought, springing from Christian beliefs. He believed the Welshman's lack of confidence in his language and nationality to be inseparable from his lack of economic initiative; and both stemmed, as he thought, from a profound moral failure. Here is Gwenallt Jones's opinion of him:

'Michael D. Jones was a saint; the greatest Welshman of the nineteenth century; the greatest nationalist after Owain Glyndwr.'

Like Emrys ap Iwan (Robert Ambrose Jones, 1851-1906) he was a man of immense natural talent: he was a powerful debater and fighter for the things he believed in, and he despised England-worship. But unlike Emrys ap Iwan, Michael D. Jones influenced his own generation largely through his own activities. On the other hand, Emrys ap Iwan, who also saw the defence of the Welsh language as a political matter which demanded the rejection of the idea of Empire, contributed to national thought through the medium of creative writing; but it was not until T. Gwynn Jones had published his biography in 1912 that the influence was mostly felt. With his penetrating mind and his fine style he taught the Welsh to respect themselves; the theme of his message was that they had to remain a nation:

'Remember that you are a nation through God's ordination. If you are unfaithful to your country and your language and your nation, how can you expect to be faithful to God and to mankind?'

These two were ministers of religion, as were all the main political leaders of Wales until the middle eighties, and the great majority, to the end of the century.

Michael D. Jones's great creation was *Y Wladfa* (the Welsh settlement in Patagonia). His purpose in this great venture was to establish a free Wales on Patagonian soil. He tried to get the thousands who were already leaving Wales to settle in a colony in Patagonia, and he made it clear in his brochure on the venture that if Wales were self-governing the Welsh would not be compelled to emigrate. In this new Wales the farmers would own their own land, and the workers would control their own industries: for Michael D. Jones hated capitalism as much as landlordism. He faced many critics, including the British government which was dissatisfied because he was unwilling to accept its patronage for his overseas venture. One of his critics was the Breton, Charles de Gaulle, a great-uncle of the late President of France, who met him in his capacity as secretary of the Breton Movement *In Brenuez Breuz*. A heroic effort was demanded of all those emigrants who wanted to make a new home in the harsh environment of a rather desolate and inaccessible corner of South America. But the results there were indicative of what the Welsh could have done had their own country been free. For ten years after 1865 the Welsh in Patagonia were completely self-governing. They established a little state and drew up a constitution for it — in Welsh of course. It was a very remarkable one. Every youth and girl of eighteen had the vote; it took over a century to secure the same thing in Britain. The voting was by secret ballot. Welsh was the language of the parliament and the law and the courts of justice. School books were printed for the children — in Welsh of course: the Education Act of 1870 did not stretch its claw into Patagonia. Bryn Williams, the historian of *Y Wladfa*, says that this is 'the first example of practical democracy in South America.' It can be added that it is the only example the world has ever seen of Welsh democracy and it was created by the Welsh *gwerin*. As Saunders Lewis says:

> 'this is the first independent political action of the Welsh *gwerin* since Wales lost her independence and her aristocracy in the Tudor period.'

1865 (margin)

Behind this venture was the radical nationalism of Michael D. Jones. He based his ideas firmly on the Bible. He summarised one aspect of it all in this sentence:

'There is no consistency in defending personal freedom, and simultaneously attacking independence and national freedom.'

But it was not only national freedom that he sought, but also national economic development for the sake of the common people; he severely attacked the 'rape of the capitalists'. His understanding of the history of Wales fostered his ideas of co-operative action and his zeal for a Celtic Alliance between the Irish, the Scots and the Welsh. In order to promote a Welsh policy he believed that a Nationalist Party in parliament was essential; but he claimed that neither this, nor self-government for Wales was feasible, without first of all building up a nationalist party in the country. He brought his influence to bear directly on some of the leaders of what can now be called a national awakening. On his way to a *cyhoeddiad* (preaching engagement), when passing Cynlas, the home of Tom Ellis, he always took care to go in plenty of time to have a long talk with him. Michael D. Jones was the strongest influence in making a nationalist of Tom Ellis, who was able to write enthusiastically to his friend D. R. Daniel in June, 1885: 'Wales will have like Scotland and Ireland a national council, which is the acquisition of Home Rule, sooner than the most ardent Welsh nationalist ever anticipated'. Even before he was elected to Parliament at twenty-six years of age he was insisting that Wales would, 'never have due attention in an English Parliament till its representatives have capability, unity and courage enough to act independently of the other two parties.' They would not want to frustrate the aims of Mr. Gladstone, 'yet our duty is towards Wales'. Michael D. Jones's note of self-respect was struck by him time and again. 'You believe as I do', he wrote to Lloyd George in 1890, 'that Wales may and should live her own life, boldly, honestly and without cringing to anybody. By respecting her own life Wales will respect her neighbours.'

O. M. Edwards, too, said many times that he had felt

himself influenced by the man whom he called the 'vanguard of Welsh awakening in all its aspects.' He described, in *Clych Atgof*, a morning he spent in his home, Bodiwan:

'When leaving Bodiwan,' he said, 'one had decided to do what one could to serve one's country and its people.'

Through Tom Ellis, and also directly, he influenced Lloyd George. In a meeting in Blaenau Ffestiniog in 1886, which was to become well known, the speakers were Michael D. Jones, Lloyd George and Michael Davitt, the founder of the Land League in Ireland.

Through his gifted disciples Michael D. Jones had a great influence on the politics of the decade 1885-95, a period of greater political turmoil in Welsh affairs than ever before or after. In 1886 the Welsh members of Parliament met to form a Welsh parliamentary group. The most pressing item of all was the dissociation of the Church of England in Wales from the state, and it was a subject that excited the most heated emotions. The defenders of the privileged position of the Church prophesied every calamity were it to become self-governing; the nonconformists attacked, with righteous anger, the connection of the Church of England — *Yr Estrones* as Thomas Gee called it — with the state. Today we know that its freedom has been of immense benefit to it and to the nation. The matter was discussed in Parliament in May 1889, but Gladstone kept away — Welsh Liberalism did not have enough power in British political terms to force him to take any steps. Kenneth Morgan says that it was William Abraham (Mabon, 1843-1922), who made the most valuable contribution to the debate:

'the pathos of his speech being heightened by his apparent unfamiliarity with the English tongue.'

Mabon, as he was generally known, typified the culture of the mining communities. Son of a collier of Cwmafan, a district noted for musical talent, he started working in the mines at ten years of age. At fourteen, when his mother had

long been widowed, he was the leader of the Band of Hope
in his chapel, and was the conductor of the chapel choir at
sixteen, and a teacher in the Sunday School. When he moved
to the Rhondda he was made the precentor of his chapel, and
he became a lay-preacher. He was a powerful public speaker,
a popular conductor of *eisteddfodau* and a member of the
Gorsedd of the Bards. His early practice of poetry and his
singing talent became overlayed by his public and professional
work, though he often made social use of these talents. 'What
I am today, whatever that may be', he said later in his life,
'I owe to the Sunday School, Band of Hope and to the
Eisteddfod'. This was the testimony of a man of whom his
biographer, Eric Evans writes,

> 'for nearly two generations the policy of the miners' organisations
> was moulded almost entirely by his outlook on industrial questions.
> Conciliation and arbitration, which were his solution to the problem of
> relationships between employers and men, became the official policy of
> the South Wales miners' unions in the years of his supremacy. Under
> the influence of his ideals the mining district of South Wales enjoyed
> a period of nearly two decades during which no stoppage occurrred . . .
> it was mainly by his untiring efforts that the workmen did, in fact,
> become organised.'

The monthly miners' holiday which he secured, was known as
Mabon's Day. He laboured hard for the Eight Hour Day and
for the Workmen's Compensation Act. He was the main
author of the sliding scale agreement which governed miners'
wages. But his biggest work was to build up a strong trade
union organisation which led to the creation of the South
Wales Miners' Federation, of which he became the first
president in 1898. Since 1885 he had been an M.P. — the first
Welsh miner to be elected to Parliament — and in 1911 he
was made a Privy Counsellor. Mabon's death in 1922, when
the devastating economic depression had already begun,
marked the end of an epoch in the Welsh coalfield.

In some of the rural districts the burning issue of the tithe
fired the land question. Hardship was as much at the root
of this as it had been of the Rebecca movement. David
Williams calls the 'tithe war' the 'Rebecca riots of North

Wales'. This, again, was an echo of the situation in Ireland, where the land issue, under Michael Davitt's direction, was one source of power to the elbow of the nationalist party. Tom Ellis and others rejoiced that the farmers were ready to use unconstitutional methods:

'The tithe war,' he said, 'is kept up very well, and the farmers of Wales are winning golden opinions in England for sturdiness and backbone. It is a form of awakening in Wales.'

When the farmers refused to pay their tithes, the auctioneers came with a troop of policemen, as many as fifty sometimes, to sell the property. The farmers arranged for horns to be sounded when the group appeared near a farm, 1887 whereupon the neighbours would hasten to defend the farmer. In May 1887, in Llangwm in Denbighshire, many people were wounded in a scuffle; in Mochdre, fifty farmers and thirty-four policemen were hurt, and the military were called in. These disturbances continued throughout the following two years. Lloyd George was delighted:

'Do you not think,' he said to Tom Ellis, 'this tithe business is an excellent lever wherewith to raise the spirit of the people.'

Thomas Gee offended the English by urging the Nonconformists of Wales to decline to give welcome to the Queen when she came to Wales in August 1889. In 1890 there were long debates in Parliament over the tithe measures, 1890 and Wales was the focus of attention in almost all of them. Once again, as in the time of Rebecca and the Chartists, Wales got attention because there had been violent demonstrations. This was more than acceptable to Lloyd George:

'It was a glorious struggle for Wales', he said. 'Wales practically monopolised the attention of the House for fully three weeks. To my mind, that is the great fact of the Tithe Bill opposition.'

This combination of direct, even violent, action and political action led to the establishment of the Land Commission in May, 1893, which took the land question out of the political arena. Wales had some measure of success in education too; in 1889, the year which saw the establishing of the County Councils, the Secondary Education Act was passed, and in 1893 the University of Wales was founded: in short, it received the kind of English institutions which were desired at the time. Wales was maturing politically, and, as a result, beginning to move. It moved in the teeth of persistent opposition from the Conservatives who fought hard, and with characteristic arrogance, to make the thirteen counties safe for unionism. Their standpoint was clear — 'there is no such place as Wales'.

In the 1890 election Lloyd George (1863-1945) was returned to Parliament. Welsh nationalism was the most prominent feature of the election address of this talented radical, who had been brought up by a cultured uncle, a shoe-maker by trade, in Llanystumdwy. For ten years he was the leader of vigorous Welsh radicalism and nationalism. He brought to the political field an unequalled combination of gifts — more, perhaps, than anyone else who came after him in Britain. For five years, 1890-95, his brilliance as a politician made the establishment of the nationalist party, both in the country and in Parliament, seem a real possibility. For five years it was a race between radical nationalism and Briticism. The latter won. The national effort was doomed to failure, and Wales never recovered from it. It would be foolish to blame Lloyd George alone for this failure and for the deterioration witnessed in the years that followed; but some of the blame must rest on his shoulders and despite his admirable service to England — or Britain — he probably did more harm than good to Wales. In this he recalls Henry VII, four centuries earlier. Their effect on Wales was strikingly similar. Lloyd George tightened the hold of Briticism on Wales at the cost of its Welshness; it led to a long line of young Welsh politicians who saw themselves as second Lloyd Georges, walking the great stage of London and winning personal glory in 'a wider circle of service', as he used to say.

In these years, the main link between Lloyd George and Welsh nationalism was *Cymru Fydd*. This was of course a

Liberal movement. It began, like the Cymmrodorion and the Gwyneddigion a century earlier, in London, where it was founded in 1886; it published a short-lived magazine bearing its name. The first branch in Wales was established in Barry in 1890 by Llywelyn Williams (1867-1922), who was a farmer's son from Llansadwrn in Carmarthenshire; he was a barrister and a journalist and also a writer and a Welsh historian. He became the Member of Parliament for Carmarthen: one of the sincerest of the brilliant company in parliament at that time. He was the only one to make a consistent stand against military conscription and to defend the conscientious objectors during the first world war. He believed that the Welsh should be nonconformist in politics as well as in religion.

Cymru Fydd laid great stress on history and culture, as did continental nationalism. J. E. Lloyd and O. M. Edwards were among its most active members. But during the next five years it grew more and more political. Lloyd George placed self-government at the head of the list:

'I am sure,' he said, 'that Wales would be an example to the nations of the world if it were given self-government — an example of a nation which chased oppression out of the hills, and of a nation which gave birth to a glorious period of liberty and justice and truth.'

Tom Ellis spoke more soberly, but with the same conviction. In an address in Bala in September 1890 he outlined his programme and his philosophy clearly. He spoke in detail of developing the economy of Wales, of its history and culture, of a National University, Library and Museum, and of the use that should be made of the county councils. He then went on to say:

'for these things we work, but most important of all, we work for a Legislative council, elected by the men *and women* of Wales, and responsible to them. It will be a symbol and an emblem of our national unity, a weapon with which to work out social ideals and industrial welfare, a pledge of our inheritance in the British Empire, an ambassador to our message and an example to mankind, a central point for our nationhood, an embodiment and fulfilment of our hopes as a people.'

Eighty years ago, the main aim of the recognised leaders in Wales was a parliament answerable to the people of Wales.

In 1892, the nationalists had their great opportunity. A Liberal government was again returned. It achieved a landslide victory in Wales, where the young leaders had been canvassing their national programme with a militancy unequalled by any Liberal or Labour leader since.

The Tories retained only three seats. At once the Member for Flint, Herbert Lewis (1858-1933) — one of the most sincere Welsh members of parliament — pressed the Welsh members to sit together as a 'solid phalanx' so that they could be as militant for the national cause in Parliament as they had been in the country. But the enthusiastic advance was checked when one of the chief leaders, Tom Ellis, accepted office. It was only a minor office — junior whip — but he was prevented from fighting for Wales in Parliament and in the country. This was the one act which did most to impede the movement for self-government. It is easy to blame Tom Ellis now, but it should be remembered that Welsh nationalism was in its infancy at the time, and that it was reasonable for him to believe that Wales would gain immeasurably from working within the system; as a Fabian, this was the most congenial way; and of course he did not act with knowledge of the bitter experience of these last eighty years. His biographer, Neville Masterman, describes his predicament:

'He had to ask himself how far such administration (Gladstone's) was likely to produce legislation in conformity with his own ideals, especially those for Wales; or whether, on the other hand, with a few of his young friends willing to follow such a policy, he should try to form an independent Welsh nationalist party. Could better results be produced by working through the Gladstonian party . . . or would he be more effective in exerting pressure from without.'

Wales has paid heavily for Tom Ellis's fateful decision. He opened the path that Lloyd George made into a main highway for the Welsh to advance in the English political world. He slowed down the surge of nationalism; thus, this appointment was a victory for the English establishment. One of his companions, Arthur Price, recognised this, and wrote, years later:

> 'he himself did not see that if a genuine Welsh Home Rule Party was to be constituted, it must be as independent of English Liberalism as of English Toryism . . . and . . . all other questions should be subordinated to it alike on platform and in the Press . . . The idea of a Welsh national Party was new to (the Welsh people). The conception of a Welsh national parliament was also strange. New ideas spread in so far as the world sees that men are prepared to make sacrifices for them.'

Welshmen were not ready to make sacrifices for their country. Since the nationalism of the period lacked either a historical or philosophical basis, it also lacked toughness. The idealism and loyalty to Wales of even the best patriots was sickly. Strong Briticism and personal ambition were the hallmarks of that generation.

Not surprising, Wales had little place in that Parliament and many members were angered when Ireland monopolised the attention of the House. The Irish won their position by acting independently. The point was taken in Wales. In August 1893, the Liberal Federation of South Wales decided, in a meeting in Aberdare, that Welsh members should form an independent parliamentary party unless the government presented a measure to disestablish the Church of England at the beginning of the 1894 session. In February 1894 the Federation of the North met in Newtown:

> 'It was definitely agreed there', says William George in his book on the history of *Cymru Fydd*, 'to stand behind the Members of Parliament if they decided to form an independent parliamentary party.'

The measure for disestablishment was brought, but because it was not given priority by the government four Welsh members refused to accept the Liberal whip. This rebellion in Westminster under the leadership of Lloyd George was only a small one, but it was new and daring, and of a piece with what was happening in Wales, where the press stood almost unanimously behind the four. Had the government refused to present the disestablishment measure, the rebellion could have led to greater things.

In Wales, *Cymru Fydd* was quickly growing into a big national movement in which self-government played the most prominent part. In a congress in Llandrindod in August 1894 a constitution was drawn up for it; and in June 1895, Alfred Thomas (later Lord Rhondda) was elected its president, and Beriah Gwynfe Evans its full-time secretary. At the same time the Liberals of Wales united for the first time to form a national Federation. But because Lloyd George and his colleagues had campaigned so vigorously and successfully, it now appeared that *Cymru Fydd* could oust the Liberal Party and become, as Michael D. Jones desired, an independent national party. In his biography, Vyrnwy Morgan claims that it was the intention of Lloyd George and the leaders of *Cymru Fydd* to create an independent party that would win Welsh national support, in much the same way as the Irish National Party had done in Ireland.

> 'More powerful and decisive,' says Kenneth Morgan of the disagreement about disestablishment, 'was the pressure being exerted by the Cymru Fydd movement which now threatened to submerge all Welsh Liberalism beneath the call for Welsh home rule.'

It was undoubtedly in response to this independent action that Lord Rosebery, now the Prime Minister, came to Cardiff in January 1895, to address the 'National Liberal League' and make there a surprising statement in favour of self-government for Wales as for Ireland and Scotland. This remarkable success was followed by another in the House of Commons. In April 1895 a motion was passed confirming 'Home rule all round' in principle. Here is the motion:

> 'That this House is of the opinion . . . that it would be appropriate to transfer to legislatures in Ireland, Scotland and Wales and England the control and government of their own domestic circumstances.'

The swift progress made in the quarter of a century that had elapsed since the notable election of 1868 was a tribute to the effectiveness of even minimal independent political action. The policy of the Act of Union was on the defensive.

XVI. THE COLLAPSE

THE national political consciousness which sprang into being after the Treason of the Blue Books was now a tree bearing fruit in its season; but its leaf withered. Since the Prime Minister had just made a statement in favour of self-government for Wales, a Welshman in 1895 would have every reason to believe that it was only a matter of time before a parliament would be seen on Welsh soil. Why did it not come? How is one to explain that Wales in 1971 has less control over the political and economic conditions of its national life than it had in 1895? The answer lies inside Wales itself; an internal moral failure is the explanation. Especially was there a failure to create an independent Welsh political party. This failure condemned Wales to three generations of moribund existence, without purpose or sense of direction.

After choosing its national officers, the organisation of *Cymru Fydd* grew rapidly. Hundreds of branches were formed. Lloyd George, Herbert Lewis, Frank Edwards, and Llywelyn Williams worked especially hard. But there was also quite a lot of disagreement between some members, such as D. A. Thomas (afterwards Lord Rhondda) and Lloyd George, who was accused of trying to be a dictator: and the most ardent 'Britishers' among them lifted their voices in criticism of Welsh nationalism. The explosion came in a meeting in Newport in January 1896 of the South Wales Liberal Alliance, which continued to act independently of the North. Lloyd George went there as a representative of one of the southern branches A motion was proposed to delete the division in Wales, as a preparatory step towards the establishing of one Council for Wales. The proposer was Elfed (the Rev. Elvet Lewis, 1860-1953), the hymnist and national poet from Cynwil Elfed. The temperature of the meeting began to rise. It went red hot when Alderman Robert Bird of Cardiff shouted:

'Throughout South Wales there are thousands upon thousands of Englishmen . . . a cosmopolitan population who will not tolerate the predomination of Welsh ideals.'

David Lloyd George by Augustus John

Wales 1916: *recruiting cartoon*

When Lloyd George attempted to answer the personal
references to himself he was shouted down, and he had to
address the crowd outside in the open air. Next day the
headings of the *Western Mail* were:

'A Welsh radical Bear Garden' —
'Outbreak of anti-Welsh feeling' —
'Will not tolerate Welsh domination' —

It was clear that it would not be easy to form a national
movement; and if it did not come easily, it would not come
at all in that particular generation, which did not have the
moral fibre to labour selflessly to build a national party
capable of winning any measure of political freedom. After all,
getting on in the world was the important thing. And it was
not personal ambition alone that weakened the Welsh; they
also suffered from a sort of national schizophrenia. They did
not know properly who they were; they did not see clearly
where their political allegiance lay. Were they Welsh, or were
they British? Of the two, was it Wales, or was it Britain that
claimed their first loyalty? This dilemma is reflected in the
person of Elfed himself, the man who proposed the resolution
which led led to the fiasco in Newport. Elfed loved Wales.
There is no doubt about that; his life and his poetry show it
clearly. In *Caniadau Elfed*, on the page facing the poem *Arthur
Gyda Ni* (Arthur with us) which abounds with Welsh emotion,
is his poem 'O Navis':

'Brydain, fy ngwlad, a'th glôd ar y moroedd,
Ple mae dy rwyfwyr am fyned a thi.'

Britain, my country, with your fame on the seas,
where do your oarsmen wish to take you?

He loved Britain too. Britain was his country, Wales was his
nation. He was an English nationalist but a Welsh patriot. We
have seen a main objective of English nationalism had been to
create one nation in these islands. It was called the British
nation. English nationalism, by calling itself British could
more easily persuade the Welsh, Scots and Irish to acquiesce

and even to co-operate in their assimilation. The Lloyd George and Tom Ellis nationalists sought a compromise whereby the identity of Wales could be preserved and a measure of self-government secured, while at the same time accepting as Britishers the rest of the programme of English nationalism. The number who took this attitude shrank quickly. By 1919 they were a very small minority. The majority by then identified themselves wholeheartedly with British (English) nationalism. They accepted the political incorporation and the cultural assimilation of Wales as inevitable if not desirable. Their main concern was that Welshmen as individual persons should have every opportunity of getting on in the Empire and the world; or, as they would put it, 'winning distinction for themselves', and 'amicably associating with England in her high destinies'. They regarded the nation's duty to transmit her civilisation to the future as so much 'poetry', remote from the reality of life.

Elfed's position is the ambiguous position of most of the best of his generation. Only Michael D. Jones, Emrys ap Iwan and their close followers stood for an uncompromising loyalty to Wales. The national movement was like a house divided against itself. With its confusion of identity and its belief that it could serve two masters, it was doomed to failure from the beginning.

That is why such a tiny puff of wind from a few arrogant Englishmen was enough to blow the house down. *Cymru Fydd* dragged on for a while, but before the end of the century it had sunk into the ground. It is a mistake to suppose that *Cymru Fydd* was destroyed by strife between nationalism and radicalism; they were synonymous. Both, however, were destroyed by the same thing: Briticism and the ethos of 'getting on in the world.' In consequence, Welshmen have still to know what it is to have a government which integrates them in their total human environment instead of alienating them from it, and whose political and economic policies are governed by a social vision in which the development of the national tradition is given high priority.

One after the other the heroes who had borne the heat of

the day died. Both Michael D. Jones and Thomas Gee died in
1898; and Tom Ellis, the best of the members of parliament,
died in 1899. Then came the war with South Africa to fan the
flame of Britishness into a bonfire. By now a whole generation
of English education had left its mark, perhaps most heavily
in the failure to assimilate scores of thousands of the children

of immigrants. As well as the economic depression
1900   in the rural areas, there was poverty in the industrial
          districts which were crowded with English and Irish
immigrants; in another twenty years there would be twenty
thousand Irishmen in Glamorgan alone, strengthening the
Labour Party which began to rise towards the end of the
century. For six months, in 1898, the miners were on strike,
and lost cruelly in the end. In 1896 three thousand quarrymen
in Penrhyn started a strike which lasted for over a year; and
in 1900 another three-year long strike began. These grave
troubles diverted people's attention from political matters
to industrial matters. When the 1900 election came, only
fifteen Liberal candidates mentioned Welsh matters; and only
ten opposed the war with South Africa. For the future, the
most important event in that election was the victory of Keir
Hardie as Independent Socialist for Merthyr Tydfil.

In 1904 the last of the great religious revivals took place
          under the leadership of an ex-miner, Evan Roberts.
1904   Although he shook many churches out of their
          lethargy, and although many of the converts remained
sincere Christians, his work was soon destroyed by the First
World War. The sole spark in Welsh political life was the
mutiny led by Lloyd George against the Education Act of 1902.

Then came the 1906 election. The Liberal Party swept
1902–   Britain; the only victory of a radical party to compare
1906   with it was that of the Labour Party in 1945. In Wales
          not one Tory was elected, but the Liberal Party was
no longer a Welsh national party, if we understand by that
a party that fought seriously for the welfare of Wales. Keir
Hardie was again returned in Merthyr Tydfil, and four
miners' representatives in co-operation with the Liberals were
also elected. With the support of the Liberals like this, the

Labour Party had a total of 29 seats from the four countries. The Conservatives had 111,093 votes, that is, 36% of the total Welsh vote; the Liberals and Labour between them had 200,063.

In an article in the *Llenor*, Ben Bowen Thomas describes the situation thus:

> 'The heart of the Liberal Party in Wales was weakened, and in spite of the sweeping public victories the Members of Parliament won on many platforms, the old radical spirit receded. Its organisation was perfected, but the living thing disappeared. The period of the fine old idealism was coming to an end. By the 1910 election the Welsh National Party had lost its chance to win for Welsh matters their undeniable and recognised place in the politics of Britain. It is true that the country was involved in every measure and reform which was adopted, and that those years were not without their individual benefactors to the life of Wales — the National Library, the National Museum, and the Welsh Board of Health are sufficient evidence for that — but, from now on, Wales' special politics tended to turn into disconnected quarrels about small injustices . . . When E. T. John rose on March 11, 1914, to bring the self-government measure for Wales before the House, the few who were present listened to his voice as to the sound of one risen "from the dead".

Only a dozen members supported E. T. John's measure. For a generation until the end of the century, nationalism and radicalism had been one in the Liberal Party. They both parted company with it at the same time. It is true that Lloyd George's golden age of radicalism was opening out before him; Michael D. Jones's teaching continued to inspire him to shatter the rule of the upper classes in England; but among the Welsh wing of his party, radicalism had withered almost as completely as it withered sixty years later in the British Labour Party. The retreat from militant Welshness affected many aspects of life, including religion — the Nonconformist churches became more pietistic — and university education. Writing in 1906 of Tom Ellis, Arthur Price asks:

> 'Would he have kept all his old enthusiasm for education, when confronted with the painful fact that the Welsh university colleges are no longer as they were in the early eighties, the nurseries of nationalist leaders?'

The function of the Welsh M.P. now was to support Lloyd George — 'our Mordecai', as one of them called him. The *Welsh Review* summarised the position thus:

> 'We believe that this is the right outlook. Let us make the most of our opportunity. Let us reinforce Mr. Lloyd George's hands so that Wales may profit substantially by his position. When Mr. Lloyd George became a member of the Cabinet, it signified the death blow to the impractical dream of an independent Party for Wales. There was to be no Parnell for Wales now. A splendid ideal perhaps, but not politics. The new minister is admired by the whole of Wales, and no one would accuse him of treachery or deceit. He remains a leader for Wales and the hero that the other members were elected to support.'

When the idea of an independent Welsh party was lost, political nationalism was buried; and Welsh political talent was buried too — in the British Empire. But it was given a very respectable funeral, by able Welshmen who advanced their own interests admirably. Between 1906 and 1918 about three dozen members of parliament from Wales held office, or were given a worthwhile honour.

It is proper to ask what sort of country Wales would be today if *Cymru Fydd* had grown into a strong enough Party to win national freedom: would it have developed in a manner comparable to the five Scandinavian countries? Or would the life of Wales have deteriorated even more than it has? Would its national tradition be stronger, or weaker? Would it be more anglicised than it is, or more Welsh? Would there be more unemployment, poverty, depopulation and emigration, or less? Would there be less social justice, or more? Would there be less freedom? Would European civilisation be the poorer? Would there be less peace in the World? ould the international order be weaker, or stronger?

Although the Liberal politicians had turned their backs on the national cause, the position at the beginning of the century was by no means hopeless. Quite a lot of Welsh culture remained; the poet-miner was still teaching the *cynganeddion* to his butty underground, by chalking on the back of his big shovel. In 1901, in spite of all the havoc caused by the educational system and immigration, 929,828 of the people, which was 49.9% of the population, still spoke Welsh, though the percentage of Welsh speakers under twenty years of age would be far lower. They had failed to kill the language in the valleys of Glamorgan and Gwent at a time when their population was considerably higher that it was to be in 1971. Here are the proportions of Welsh speakers in 1901:

Merthyr Tydfil	..	..	57.5%
Margam	..	..	62%
Rhondda	..	..	64.5%
Rhymni	..	..	69%
Maesteg	..	..	72%
Aberdâr	..	..	72%
Neath Valley	..	..	75%

Further west, the situation was better and the proportion higher; in Cydweli, where the tin industry was prospering, 93% of tha people spoke Welsh. It was rural east Wales and the coastal towns that had turned almost completely English speaking. Some light is thrown on the situation in Monmouthshire at that time by the home circumstances of a little boy who started to attend Sirhywi school with his sisters Myfanwy and Blodwen; Arianwen and Iorwerth would be joining him there later. In his biography of Aneurin Bevan, Michael Foot records:

'The family background was that of Welsh nonconformity in its heyday, with its self-reliance, pride, resource, music . . . (his father) managed to lead a full life in the home and community. A fine craftsman . . . he installed . . . an organ around which the family assembled to to sing hymns and Welsh folk songs every Sunday night. Every Sunday morning and evening he walked to the Carmel Baptist Church and walked back with the deacons and the other mighty arguers, six or seven abreast across the road, debating the sermon and invoking his deep knowledge of the Bible . . . He belonged to the Cymrodorion and won prizes at the inter-chapel eisteddfodau, one for a love poem . .'

In a few years' time the System would have completely killed the language and culture of Aneurin Bevan's father's generation in that area. In this period the Vale of Glamorgan lost its Welsh for the second time. I remember an old man in the thirties, of the name of William Beer, living in Pentyrch, at the foot of Mynydd y Garth on the northern border of the Vale; he was the secretary of Bronllwyn chapel. William Beer was a Cornishman; he had come to Pentyrch as a young boy to work in a quarry, and so Welsh was the area that he was forced, along with everyone else who came there, to learn the language. When I came to know him, Welsh was his first language. But by that time a Welsh service was held only once a month in Bronllwyn chapel. In the lifetime of that old man the System had done its work with sweeping success in Pentyrch. English civilisation had arrived.

The national effort of the last quarter of the century left a priceless legacy of literature and scholarship to the nation. It was patriotism which inspired the greatest men of that period. Patriotism was the inspiration of Sir John Williams (1840-1926), who can be regarded as the founder of the National Library, to which he donated his fine private library which included the Peniarth manuscripts. He was the son of an Independent minister who farmed in Gwynfe, Llangadog; he became a famous doctor in the academic world; he was the royal family's doctor for a long period. In the first quarter of the twentieth century, the spirit of the poets and the writers woke up and, as a result, Wales experienced a literary renaissance which produced some of the finest poetry of the centuries. It was not university education alone which inspired the renaissance, but education fired by patriotism; and leaders came not only from the University of Wales itself, but also from Oxford where generation after generation of talented men were inspired to serve Wales by the Dafydd ap Gwilym Society. Sir O. M. Edwards was a student at both universities, and Glasgow as well; it was he who exerted the profoundest influence of his time because of the vision and passion which sustained him through decades of able and unstinting work as historian and creative writer, journalist and educationist. His work was infused by a passionate vision in which, as he wrote:

> 'All is sacred — every hill and valley. Our country is something alive, not a dead grave, under our feet. Every hill has its history, every neighbourhood its romance . . . And for a Welshman, no other country can be like this. The Welshman feels that the efforts of the fathers have consecrated every field, and that his country's muse has sanctified every mountain. And it is the fact that he feels this way that makes him a true citizen.'

He was a historian by vocation, a writer by instinct. It was he who divined the basic weakness in the national movement: it was ignorant of the history of its own country. He tried to make good the deficiency; and he was joined in this work by the greatest historian of the century, Sir J. E. Lloyd; the masterpieces which he produced more than sixty years ago remain standard works. Sir O. M. Edwards founded and edited a number of periodicals including *Cymru'r Plant* for children, and one *Wales*, in English. The most influential of them was *Cymru*, and old men today are heard speaking of their debt to it: through these he nurtured a generation of young Welsh writers. He wrote readable books, and edited and published scores of volumes of the works of others. But it was his efforts in bringing Welsh to the schools, after he had been appointed Chief Inspector of Schools in Wales that constitute perhaps his most important work.

Another scholar who enriched the literature of Wales is Sit John Morris-Jones, who made a magnificent contribution towards purifying and enriching the language and setting higher standards in literature. The poems of his which remain in the memory of the *gwerin* are the ones that praise the land of Wales, the nation and its past, and which long for freedom and a national future — a very new note in Welsh poetry. Every Welshman knows of his lyric poem *Cymru Rydd* (Free Wales), but few realise how completely novel this political nationalism was in poetry. For that matter, has any Welsh leader in a British party today mentioned a national future for Wales?

Er hyn i'm gwlad y canaf	And yet I sing my country,
Oherwydd Cymru fydd	for Wales shall one day be
Ddedwyddaf gwlad a glanaf	the happiest and loveliest land,
A dyfod y mae'r dydd	a time when we will see
Pan na bydd trais i'w nychu,	no violent hand to waste her,
Nac anwr i'w bradychu,	no coward to betray her,
Na chweryl i'w gwanychu,	no quarreling to weaken her
A phan fydd Cymru'n rhydd.	and when Wales shall be free.

In the world of scholarship we must not forget the great and varied contribution of Sir John Rhys (1840–1915), who was born in a small one-storey cottage near Ponterwyd at the foot of Pumlumon; a farmer's son, who made his name as a leading Celtic scholar in Oxford, where he spent twenty years at Jesus College. There he influenced O. M. Edwards, John Morris-Jones and W. J. Gruffydd and many another of that brilliant generation.

T. Gwynn Jones, too, was a committed patriot. His *awdl*, *Ymadawiad Arthur*, which was published in 1902, was a turning point in the history of Welsh poetry. In it, this political nationalist treats of Wales's past and, through it, he presents his exalted vision of the ideal Wales. Wales had, in him, a poet with a profound understanding of the nature of patriotism. W. J. Gruffydd was also a political nationalist, but in his poetry he celebrates man's life in its other intensities. He is also a master of Welsh prose. It must be remembered that two of Wales's foremost poets, both nationalists, had written some fine poems before the First World War; they were R. Williams Parry, who was early recognised as a poet of European stature, and T. H. Parry Williams, who continues to subscribe to the literature and life of Wales. The national movement also had a strong influence on popular lyrical poets like Eifion Wyn, Wil Ifan and Crwys. The national stirring provided a healthy spur to all the arts. The collection of fine buildings in Cathays Park, Cardiff and the National Museum in particular, are a manifestation of this in architecture. Inside the City Hall there are sculptures of some of the chief historical figures of Wales. Drama too showed great vigour; music developed, especially in the instrumental field. The movement therefore left a permanent legacy in scholarship, prose and verse, and the rest of the arts as well as in cultural and educational institutions such as the University Press, the Board of Celtic Studies, and, of course, the National Museum, the Folk Museum and the National Library.

*   *   *

At its outset the Labour Party appeared to be developing along Welsh lines. It is true that Keir Hardie was a Scot, but he declared, from the beginning, his sympathy with Welsh aspirations. He had supported Home Rule in Scotland long before he came to Wales. In 1888 he said:

> 'I am strongly in favour of Home Rule, being convinced that until we have a Parliament of our own, we cannot have the many and great reforms on which the people have set their hearts.'

In his opinion a Welsh Party was also essential.

> 'It seems to me,' he said in 1906, 'that the Irish Parliamentary Party's way of working should be the way for any national party.'

He said that he believed that a national party should incorporate the thought and feelings, language and national aspirations of the people it represented. But his life's great passion was the pursuit of social justice: a strong challenge to the individualist ethos of the Welsh of the time, when getting on in the world was the main goal of the majority. It is important to realise that Keir Hardie was the leader of the industrial workers of Wales right up until the war. He was an honest man of high principle. And although he was a socialist, it was the language of Welsh radicalism which he unwittingly used to present most of his policies. This is perhaps not surprising, for he constantly tried to adapt social conditions to Christian standards. The new representatives elected to Parliament to represent the miners in 1906 also accepted the old radical viewpoint. William Brace, the best-known of them, said that he was a 'whole hearted Welsh nationalist'. The Labour movement produced its own poets and writers, such as R. J. Derfel, Silyn Roberts and T. E. Nicholas, Y Glais, an

Independent minister who became the main Welsh exponent of the Communist cause in the next generation. Under the leadership of Keir Hardie, the Labour Party identified itself with every national cause and institution in Wales. Kenneth Morgan says:

> 'The success of Labour spokesmen in harmonising their programme with the national self-consciousness of Wales goes far towards explaining their success in the subsequent general election.'

There was hope at this time that the Labour Party too would grow into a Welsh national party.

But anti-Welsh and British elements were rearing their heads. Mabon lost his influence with the new unions and Keir Hardie, too, eventually lost the day to a combination of Marxism and Briticism which fostered values different from his own. To the Marxists the class war was given priority: with them, the proletariat and not the nation came first. The thorough-going Marxists, however, did not exert the strongest influence over the new mind of the industrial valleys; it was the syndicalists, under the leadership of Noah Ablett (1883-1935), a former student at the Central Labour College, who did so much to wean the Welsh workers away from their Welshness. He and William Brace and their colleagues had already defeated Mabon. They now turned their sharp weapons against the masters, aiming at more than an improvement in wages; their goal was to do away with ownership entirely. A little committee which included A. J. Cook who had been a lay-preacher with the Baptists, was formed and the policy of the Syndicalists was published in a booklet, *The Miner's Next Step*, which tried to combine Syndicalism with Marxism. It differed basically from the later policy of the Labour Party in pleading decentralisation and workers' control.

These men promoted the great Cambrian strike in 1910-11. Winston Churchill was the Home Secretary at the time, and he caused great anger by sending soldiers, both cavalry and infantry, to help the police. Keir Hardie wrote:

> 'The Rhondda and Aberdare valleys are thronged with police, mounted and otherwise; detachments of soldiers are billeted . . . The entire district looks like a besieged area in war time. Men, women and

> children have been mauled by police batons and the Press of the
> country have been practically unanimous in describing the people as
> ·riotous rowdies of the hooligan type.'

The military did not cow the men of the Rhondda, and they
did less physical injury there than later in a Llanelli riot where
six men were killed in what has been called 'a little massacre'.
The Rhondda miners were starved into accepting the mine-
owners' terms after the Miners' Federation of Great Britain
withdrew the pittance of £3,000 a week which it had grudginly
granted them. However, their strike was not in vain; it led
to the ultimate acceptance of the minimum wage policy in all
the coalfields of the countries of Britain.

But the government did not only send soldiers to attack
Welsh people; if the Rhondda had its steel bullets, Caernarfon
had its circus. Soldiers were sent there to dazzle the people
with their disciplined marching. In 1911, Prince Edward, later
to become Edward VIII, was invested Prince of Wales, to the
great advantage of Lloyd George and the government. The
Welsh loved the show: but not so Keir Hardie, who wrote in
the *Merthyr Pioneer*:

> 'Wales is to have an 'Investiture' as a reminder that an English king
> and his robber barons strove for ages to destroy the Welsh people and
> finally succeeded in robbing them of their lands . . . and then had the
> insolence to have his son 'invested' in their midst.'   •

Keir Hardie, the Scot, was now the voice of Welsh radicalism.
He said, in a May day rally held by the Labour Party in
Tonypandy:

> 'the ceremony ought to make every Welshman who was patriotic
> blush with shame. Every flunkey in Wales, Liberal and Tory alike was
> grovelling on his hands and knees to take part in the ceremony. Funds
> could be raised for that purpose with ease, but when there was money
> wanted to help workers to gain even a living wage it could only be
> found with difficulty.'

A Labour government was to be responsible for the next show
of this kind; but by then its radicalism too would have disappeared.

With the sky darkening over Europe, Haldane, the minister
of war, was calling for conscription. Against this background

very little excitement was caused by the arguments in Parliament about the disestablishment of the state church. Industrial troubles received the most attention in a country whose population had now passed the two and a half million mark, almost as much as the population of Denmark. When the Great War broke out in August 1914 it was warmly welcomed by the enthusiastic British Welsh. Of the nations of Britain, it was Wales that sent the highest proportion of men into the armed forces to fight in a war which was to prove the end of a period in its history. Over 280,000 men went into the forces. The war years saw the deepest cleft in the history of the nation; the Wales of 1919 was very different from that of 1914.

This war was fought between great military powers for position on the continent of Europe: it exemplified the truth of H. C. Simmons's words: 'There can be no real peace or solid world order in a world of a few great centralised powers.'

But Great Britain and its Empire assumed a new guise in the world as the defender of the freedom of small nations. Tens of thousands of Welshmen left their own fettered country to die in a ditch in Flanders or fall in the mud in Paschendaele for the freedom of Belgium and Serbia and Montenegro. The miners who had preached the brotherhood of man left their pits to go and kill their brother-workers on the continent of Europe. Nonconformists, who listened every Sunday to the gospel of love and peace, went almost mad with fury and hatred when they thought of Germans. For years the Christians who were safe at home were fed with lies and possessed by a spirit of vengeance, while over in France and Flanders:

> 'A gwaedd y bechgyn lond y gwynt,
> A'u gwaed yn gymysg efo'r glaw,'

> The wind was full of the shrieks of boys,
> their blood was mingled with the rain.

The nonconformity of Wales was never to recover from this apostasy. The soldiers came back to predominantly empty chapels, if they continued to attend chapel at all after the horrific experiences which had shaken their faith to its very roots. The miners returned to find that Englishmen had taken their places in the pits in their absence. Those who survived the battles came back to a land whose Briticism was stronger and fiercer than ever. And in the middle of the barbaric tempest there was Wales, like God himself, according to Hedd Wyn, 'ar drai ar orwel pell' — ebbing on the distant horizon. Its fate was movingly symbolised by the overwhelming silence which prevailed when the name of the winning bard was called in the Birkenhead National Eisteddfod. No one rose, for the poet had been killed in the Battle of Pilkem Ridge a few weeks earlier.

In spite of the adverse effect of the war on the spiritual and cultural life of Wales, it had, if possible, an even worse effect on the political environment. The greatest harm was done to the national tradition·by the enormous increase in the state's power. A. J. P. Taylor says:

'Until August 1914 a sensible, law-abiding Englishman could pass through life and hardly notice the existence of the state, beyond the post office and policemen . . . The Englishman paid taxes on a modest scale . . . All this was changed by the impact of the Great War. The mass of the people became for the first time, active citizens. Their lives were shaped by orders from above; they were required to serve the state instead of pursuing exclusively their own affairs . . . The Englishman's food was limited . . . His freedom of movement was restricted . . . *The history of the English state and of the English people merged for the first time.*' (*my italics*).

And among the English people who merged with the English state were the Welsh. The war, which required massive centralisation, took English nationalism a great step forward in its aim of creating one British nation with one English mind. The harm which it did to the life of Wales was immeasurable and permanent; the Welsh pattern of values and culture was shaken to its foundations; A. J. P. Taylor is able to claim that 'the war left few permanent marks on British life,' because, for him the terms 'British' and 'English' are synonymous.

The effect on the Labour Party in Wales was soon apparent in its enhanced imperialism. The war dealt a death blow to radical Liberalism, and wounded the radicalism of the

Labour Party almost to death. It is no exaggeration to say that it killed Keir Hardie. This principled man clung to his Christian and socialist values. He opposed the war. A few days after it had been declared, he addressed his constituents in Aberdare at a big meeting. He was hardly allowed to speak; he was shouted down. As soon as he rose to his feet, according to the *Aberdare Leader* he was 'welcomed',

> 'with loud hooting . . . A large section of the crowd began singing 'God save our gracious King'. Then most of the crowd got up on chairs etc. and it was impossible to proceed. A few minutes elapsed and then a section of the audience again struck up "Rule Britannia".'

Keir Hardie continued to try to speak. He was heard saying 'that the proper attitude for this country ought to have been one of neutrality (loud hooting, followed by the singing of 'Rule Britannia'). He was silenced, and then he was followed to his lodgings by a hostile crowd who shouted, 'Turn the German out!' Emrys Hughes, his son-in-law, said:

> 'we could see that he was deeply distressed. He had not expected this in Aberdare, among the mining folk. "I know what Gethsemane was like," he said . . . It seemed that all his life-work had been in vain.'

He returned to London, and Ramsay Macdonald said of him on his return:

> 'he was a crushed man . . The war struck Hardie like a physical blow and a spiritual blight. He had had such faith that the international forces of the working class would resist it — and now in every country the Socialist leaders were voting war credits and urging their fellowmen to fight. Hardie was utterly crushed by the tragedy of it.'

Within a year he was dead, at the age of 59. Wales would not again see a Labour leader who clung so tightly to his Christian principles. One cannot imagine *him* manufacturing atom bombs as the Attlee government did, nor consenting to the building of Polaris and adding £450,000,000 a year to the expenditure on arms, as the Labour government of 1964-70 did; nor can we imagine him supporting imperialistic America in Vietnam and helping to promote the horrible war in Biafra. It is possible that Aneurin Bevan would have had more affection for the Welsh language and nationality had Hardie lived; and perhaps for the culture of his father. In the by-election in Merthyr which followed Hardie's death, C. B. Stanton was returned and it is claimed that he was elected 'on the straight war ticket', to fight 'against the Huns for our homeland'. He was a miners' agent; like most of his colleagues he spent a great deal of time on recruiting campaigns. They were remarkably successful ones; thousands of miners went to the front, leaving their jobs to be taken over to a great degree by Englishmen.

This shameful meeting in Aberdare has an importance second only to the Newport meeting of 1895, when Lloyd George was shouted down. It shows how the war destroyed the political idealism of Wales. It bruised its Welshness beyond measure, although Lloyd George's success added to the self-confidence of the Welsh people as individuals:

'the most inspired and creative British statesman of the twentieth century,'

is A. J. P. Taylor's opinion in his *English History* 1914-45. Taylor could not call the old leader of Welsh nationalism an 'English statesman'; but Lloyd George himself was not always so sure. For example, when discussing the 'freedom of the seas' in Versailles after the war, he stated:

'The English people will not look at it. On this point the nation (sic) is absolutely solid.'

It was extreme British patriotism which characterised the election after the war.

'The so-called coupon election of December 1918,' says Kenneth Morgan, 'was marked in Wales as elsewhere by intense patriotic frenzy.'

Ten members of the Labour Party were elected; each one a supporter of the war. Already the Labour Party was almost as British in thought and character in Wales as were the Liberals, who succeeded in returning twenty-two members.

SYR OWEN M. EDWARDS

[Darlun gan Swain

O. M. Edwards

Wales 1927: unemployed miners marching to London

Aneurin Bevan

Saunders Lewis   Copyright Welsh Arts Cou

This was perhaps the most 'British' election ever witnessed in Wales:

'The coupon election' says Kenneth Morgan, 'marks a further stage in the erosion of the Welsh national movement as a political force.'

Power in Wales after the war lay in the Labour Party and the Trade Unions. The war had given them a huge impetus as the 1939-45 war was again to do in twenty years time. The more thoughtful among them supported the idea of 'guild' socialism; it was the natural complement of the thinking that lay behind *The Miners Next Step* and the old Welsh tradition of decentralisation and co-operation, presented by Michael D. Jones and Tom Ellis. These ideas were widely discussed when the Sankey Commission's report on the future of the coal industry was published. But as the influence of Ruskin College and the Central Labour College grew, more English conceptions occupied the field, and by the beginning of the twenties the policies of the Webbs — Beatrice and her husband, Lord Passfield — were extensively accepted. Since then, the aim of the Labour Party has been bureaucratic Whitehall control in industry and money as well as in politics. It opposed decentralisation; it argued for large units in every field, the bigger the better. It believed that this was more efficient, and efficiency was its main aim. Since this was also the goal of the conservative politicians of the right, and since they too were firm believers in centralisation and large units, their attitude to Welsh nationhood was the same; Britain was the large political unit. No one thought in terms of Wales; no one worked for Wales; Wales was never taken into consideration when policies were being framed. And since the British state was growing so powerful — and was to continue to increase in power throughout the next generation — it could destroy Wales, simply by ignoring it. The development of this process, and the growing resistance to it in Wales itself, was to be the most meaningful part of the history of the nation during the next half century.

In 1920, the Church of England was disestablished, to its own great good, though this was not so obvious then as it became later. A few of the Liberal leaders continued to support self-government, and a conference was arranged in Llandrindod in 1919. But they did not have enough power even to secure a debate in parliament in 1920 when a very favourable Speaker's Conference report was published on home rule. Although Lloyd George was Prime Minister, he did not go out of his way to help. Every time a debate was requested in the House of Commons, he would find a way of pushing the matter to one side. In spite of this, when a deputation went to him to press for a Secretary for Wales, his advice to them was, 'Go for the big thing'. It was the same with the Labour Party. Its more enlightened members, such as Will John of the Rhondda, Morgan Jones, Caerffili, and D. R. Grenfell, Gower, voiced their support for Home Rule. It became an official part of the Party's programme as a result of the support of its annual conference, and it was confirmed more than once. In 1918 conference had stated:

> 'Labour believes in self-government. The Labour Party is pledged to a scheme of statutory legislatures for Scotland, Wales and even England, as well as of Ireland.'

In 1929 it announced in its election manifesto:

> 'Labour would support the creation of separate legislative assemblies in Scotland and Wales.'

Its chief British leaders made strong statements in favour of self-government. Ramsay Macdonald insisted that it would be one of the most important measures of a Labour government, adding: 'All my life I have supported self-government for Scotland, Wales and Ireland.' Arthur Henderson, who did more than anyone else, apart from Keir Hardie, to build up the Labour Party, and who became Foriegn Secretary in the Labour Government of 1924, believed:

> 'One could not imagine a country where federal self-government has a better chance of success than Wales . . . Given self-government Wales could become a modern Utopia.'

He stressed that the smallness of the country was a great advantage from the standpoint of good government. There was no doubt about it: these leaders believed that self-government would be the best possible thing for Wales; but nothing was done about it. It was decided that it would not be to the advantage of the Labour Party.

Wales had no form of national movement now to help get things done. It had been very different in Ireland, and in 1921 Lloyd George signed an agreement with the government of De Valera. A chief architect there of the Easter Rebellion of 1916 was the Marxist and Labour leader, James Connolly. Before he was shot in Kilmainham prison he said:

> 'We succeeded in proving that Irishmen are ready to die endeavouring to win for Ireland those national rights which the British Government has been asking them to die to win for Belgium.'

He referred to the Socialists on the other side of the Irish Sea, claiming that they would never understand why he was there; they all forgot, he said, that he was an Irishman. Wales did not produce one socialist leader who was ready to put Wales first, let alone die for her. Wales bred British Imperialists, although some of them called their Briticism, Internationalism. The last thing they wanted was for Wales to contribute as a country to the international order. Had it been otherwise, perhaps U Thant would have visited Cardiff in 1970, as he did Dublin where he paid high tribute to Ireland's fine record of leadership in international affairs through the United Nations.

Welsh life continued to deteriorate politically and culturally, socially and economically. As a province on the fringe of England with no control over its own life, without a national party to make good the wrongs done to it, and the policy of the Act of Union still dominating the mind of London, nothing but deterioration could be expected. But the gravity of the situation it experienced was far beyond the expectation of any man. When Aneurin Bevan returned to Tredegar in 1921, at the age of twenty-three, after two years in the Labour College in London, he could not find any work. Apart from six weeks digging ditches at the side of the road, he was on the dole for three years. For unemployment was already a plague in Wales. Tens of thousands came out of the forces in 1919 to discover that there was no work for them. Moreover, there would not be enough work in Wales until the next war. Only in wartime did Wales enjoy full employment.

The history of Wales between 1914 and 1945 is a catalogue of war and depression. These are the factors that ruled its life. But its servile people continued to believe that it was a fine thing to be ruled from London. They kept asking how a poor self-governing Wales would be able to pay out dole to the unemployed, without waiting to consider that neither the degree of poverty nor unemployment would exist, if Wales were self-governing, any more than they exist in other small countries in the north of Europe.

'Only the Labour and Socialist parties of Scandinavia and New Zealand responded to the challenge of great economic depression,' said Franz Borkenau. 'These were all small countries, with strong trade unions and they were not burdened by the pressures of international politics.'

He could have added that 1920-40 were the only years of freedom in their whole history that Latvia, Lithuania and Estonia enjoyed, and that they experienced in these two decades a remarkable renaissance in their economic and cultural life. In Wales unemployment was not just a local tribulation but a national one. Although thousands left the country every week, unemployment rose to a staggering 33% at the beginning of the thirties, continuing at this level from 1930 to 1934; in Anglesey and Ceredigion this figure rose to 50% of the registered workers. The figure would have been much higher had more women registered; in 1923 there were only 83 insured women workers in the South Wales area, for every thousand men, while there were 348 in the United Kingdom as a whole. The number of unemployed was further reduced by the emigrants who left

Wales. People left by the thousand, indeed by the hundred thousand: for the only remedy the government offered was redeployment of labour. Moving the people out of Wales to industry in England was its answer, thus shattering Welsh communities. Half a million had to leave their country between 1921 and 1939. They were forced to leave rural counties and towns alike; 259,000 had to quit the industrial valleys leaving behind them thousands rotting on the dole. They were given soup by charitable people in the soup kitchens; they were sent old clothes from affluent families; groups of them went to sing for alms on the streets of London, and others marched all the way to the capital — which was comparatively untouched by the depression — in pitiful protest. They continued to praise enthusiastically the system of government, which was uprooting energetic and intelligent young people, destroying the life of the older generation, and making a wilderness of the valleys and their community life. The policy of the Act of Union was realized through economic mismanagement the like of which could not be found in the whole of Europe.

The economic failure of the British political order did almost as much harm to the language and culture as the educational policy. Between 1911 and 1921 the number of Welsh speakers fel from 977,000 to 929,000, and the proportion from 43% to 37%. Whereas the great majority of the people in the third quarter of the previous century were monoglot Welsh-speakers, now, two generations later, the great majority were English-speaking monoglots. Thanks mainly to O. M. Edwards there were signs of improvement in the system; but this fine man died in 1920. Like Michael D. Jones and Tom Ellis before him he was buried in Penllyn. His son, Ifan ab Owen Edwards, who founded *Urdd Gobaith Cymru* (Welsh League of Youth) in 1922, was buried there half a century later; and in the same year, J. E. Jones, another great patriot, who gave his whole life to the building up of Plaid Cymru and who had also gone to school in Bala, was buried nearby. There is no area

in the whole of Wales which did so much to enrich
the life of the nation as Penllyn, through which Tryweryn
flows.

In 1923 an institution was established in London which was,
in the form it took within a few years, to affect Welsh life
profoundly and which would rival the educational system
as an anglicising force. This was the B.B.C., the most powerful
weapon to come into the hands of the cultural imperialists.
Like the schools and colleges, at first it simply ignored the
existence of a Welsh culture. 'London was thought of,
almost without discussion,' says its official historian, 'as
the cultural metropolis, the place from which the best was
likely to come'. Crumbs would later be thrown to Wales to
alleviate slightly the devastation caused by the Welsh famine
in the mass media. The injury done to Wales was known but
complacently dismissed. 'The local cultural loss' said Sir
John Reith, 'should be to a considerable extent offset by the
quality of London programmes.' This 'local cultural loss'
was to be magnified tenfold by London-centred television,
which would fill Welsh-speaking homes with the sound of
scores of hours of English programmes each week, so that
more English would be heard from the box than Welsh on
the hearth.

This development was but one aspect, if the most perilous,
of the immense growth brought by the war in centralised
control which was to make the U.K. perhaps the most highly
centralized country in the world. Civil servants and local
government officials multiplied, so that there were scores of
thousands of them in Wales alone. The Welsh language was
excluded from the work of this vast bureaucracy which
affected Welsh life more intimately as each year passed.
For the most part, government simply ignored the existence of
a Welsh national community. In fact, no London government has ever made the health of Welsh civilisation, and the
language which is its main medium, a chief objective in
organising Welsh life in education, law, broadcasting, the
economy or the land and its use.

The only flash of hope in national politics was the election

of G. M. Ll. Davies as member of Parliament for the University
of Wales. He stood as a Christian Pacifist, and accepted
1923   the Labour Whip in Parliament. The election of this
saintly man in 1923 proved that there was still some
backbone left in the graduates of the University of Wales.
A congress which met in Shrewsbury in 1922 was a complete
failure. Called to promote self-government, only fifty
attended, and these did not speak with one voice. There was
a series of general elections in 1922, 1923 and 1924, and with
each one the candidates paid less attention to Wales.
1922   In England, Wales did not get any attention at all,
1924   of course. The editor of *The Welsh Outlook* wrote,
after the 1924 election:

> 'We cannot remember any election giving so little attention to
> Welsh affairs.'

The Liberal Party in Wales had lost all its vigour and passion;
it could not even persuade anyone to chair its parliamentary
party:

> 'Welsh Liberalism,' says Kenneth Morgan, 'once inspired by a
> passionate, radical idealism, now seemed corrupted and decadent.'

By now there was no pretence of doing anything for Wales
in the Labour Party either, although it continued to reaffirm
until 1929 its policy of self-government for Wales. Labour
formed the government at the end of that year and by
1925   1925 it was clear that it intended to do nothing.
Despite its weakness, had it been determined to do
something for Wales, it could have enlisted the co-operation of
the Liberal Party, but it made no effort. Its leaders were ready
enough to pay tribute to the language and cultural heritage of
Wales but even that disappeared in time; 'land is land' as
one of its Welsh members of parliament said, expressed its
attitude. National idealism was supplanted for some by the
conception of class warfare, without any attempt to unite it
with the national struggle, as Connolly had done. In half a
century there is no record of any one of them campaigning for
Wales, as Lloyd George had done in the nineties, to awaken

and uphold the national spirit; on the contrary, they cooled
and suffocated it. That Lloyd George did not wholly lose
his nationalist sympathies is shown by his attitude in 1936
towards the removal of the trial of Saunders Lewis, D. J.
Williams and Lewis Valentine from Caernarfon to the Old
Bailey because a Welsh jury had failed to agree to finding them
guilty of arson at the R.A.F. bombing school in the Llŷn
peninsula. Lloyd George wrote at that time to his daughter,
Lady Megan:

> 'They yield when faced by Hitler and Mussolini, but they attack the
> smallest country in the kingdom which they misgovern. This is a
> cowardly way of showing their strength through violence . . This is
> the first government that has tried to put Wales on trial in the Old
> Bailey . . . I should like to be there, and I should like to be forty years
> younger.'

But no accepted political leader spoke publicly in this way
in the twenties and thirties. Wales was leaderless and lacking
in all sense of purpose and direction. This was the position in
1925. Between 1895 and 1925 the deterioration in the national
position was as apparent as the improvement earlier between
1865 and 1895.

In England in 1925 a new attitude to the countries of the
British Empire was beginning to crystallize. In that year
Balfour drew up the definition of dominion status which was
to be incorporated in the Westminster Statute of 1930. He used
the word 'Commonwealth' to define the community of the
countries of Britain, which along with Canada, Australia,
New Zealand and South Africa would form the British
Commonwealth:

> 'free and equal nations in no way subordinate one to the other in
> any aspect of their domestic and external affairs.'

In twenty years it would be the policy of the English government to transmute the Empire into a Commonwealth of
free and equal nations. But the policy was never applied to
Wales. No one dreamed of the Welsh nation in the context of
this development in 1925: there was less reason for thinking

about it then than there had been for almost fifty years. When the first Labour Government was formed, Wales had no form of national party in the country or in parliament: no effective voice was raised in favour of its rights; the worst depression in Welsh history was under way; her few nationalists were scattered in two British parties; nonconformity was finished as a political force; two-thirds of the people did not possess the national language. Now at last the final success of the policy of the Act of Union was in sight. The national life of Wales seemed to be coming to an end.

In that year two history books appeared in the *Home University Library* series: *Wales* by W. Watkin Davies and *Irish Nationality* by Alice Stopford Green. The outlook and the values of the two authors which become apparent in the peroration of each, help us to understand the recent history of these two Celtic nations. The one employs a dignified and heroic rhetoric: the other exhibits a sickening pride in the personal success of the Welsh who got on in the world, showing a self-satisfied and sentimental servility and talking bogus nonsense about freedom and justice and equality and the prominent place given in the Commonwealth to a nation which was dying a squalid death in political captivity. This is how Mrs. Green finishes her book:

'In memory of the long, the hospitable roll of their patriots, in memory of their long fidelities, in memory of their national faith, and of their story of honour and of suffering, the people of Ireland once more claim a government of their own in their native land, that shall bind together the whole nation of all that live on Irish soil, and create for all a common obligation and a common prosperity. An Irish nation of a double race will not fear to look on Irish history. The tradition of that soil, so steeped in human passion, in joy and sorrow, still rises from the earth. It lives in the hearts of the men who see in Ireland a ground made sacred by the rare intensity of human life over every inch of it, one of the richest possessions that has ever been bequeathed by the people of any land whatever to the successors and inheritors of their name. The tradition of national life created by the Irish has ever been a link of fellowship between classes, races, and religions. The natural union approaches of the Irish Nation — the union of all her children that are born under the breadth of her skies, fed by the fatness of her fields, and nourished by the civilisation of her dead.'

Here is Watkin Davies's peroration at the end of a chapter called 'The Dawn':

'Thus from being the last refuge of hunted tribesmen, a land swept time after time by the tide of invasion, Wales has come to be actively and amicably associated with England in her high destinies. Everywhere Welshmen are participating to the uttermost in the wider life of the Empire. In all the professions, in literature, in the arts, in trade, in the Civil Service, in the Army, in the Navy, and in the Diplomatic Corps they are winning distinction for themselves.

The outlook in Wales is full of promise. The old period of antagonism between the Welshmen and Englishmen seems, happily to have come to an end. The democracy has won the day; and all obstacles in the way of the development of what genius lies hidden in the people have been removed. Home Rule is sometimes spoken of, but it is generally by the theorists and doctrinaire pedants. Most patriotic Welshmen would be content with a slightly increased measure of local autonomy. The vast majority of the nation are satisfied that equality of opportunity for all the inhabitants of the British Isles, irrespective of race, has been achieved, and that in literature, in art, in music, in scholarship, in the professions, in politics and in commerce there is nothing to hinder a Welshman from winning any distinction he may merit. The discordant cry of the extreme nationalist is occasionally heard, with its glorification of all that is vulgar and unworthy of preservation in the Welsh tradition. But this wins little sympathy. As a whole the people have seen a fairer vision than that of an independent Wales: the vision of a Commonwealth living a life of ordered prosperity; upholding and illustrating the great principles of justice, equality and freedom, to secure which so many eyes have been dimmed with tears and so many fields sodden with blood; a Commonwealth in which Wales, in virtue of its splendid tradition of passionate idealism and tireless spiritual effort, shall enjoy a foremost place.'

In this dark hour, a small company of six men met in a little room above a café in Pwllheli during the week of the National Eisteddfod there. They founded an independent national party. They seemed a pathetically small company to undertake the huge task of building up an independent political party in Wales, for the first time in its history. The candle they lit was a small one, but because of the blackness of the night around them it gave out quite a light. Although the party only received 609 votes when it stood in the 1929 parliamentary election, it was there that the hope of Wales lay.

Wales Endures

I WRITE these words on 26 April, 1971. Tonight the census forms which will tell the government how many Welsh people can speak and read and write Welsh are being completed; that is, how successful its policies have been in Wales during the last few centuries. But, for Wales, this Sunday is notable for a more important reason than the census. While I sit here in comfort, over fifty young Welsh people are in prisons in England and in Wales — twenty-five of them girls — because of their attachment to their country and language. The girls have been taken to prison in England where their parents, if they visit them, will not be allowed to speak to them in Welsh. They are a small number from a splendid host of the nation's youth who have suffered imprisonment for its sake during the last few years. There is a new spirit afoot in the land. When before was there a generation of Welsh people ready and willing to suffer for their country? We have to go back to the time of Owain Glyndŵr for comparison. These young men and women are not individualists whose main aim in life is self-advancement. They are people who are so passionately conscious of their responsibility that they put the good of their national society before their own; people who put their fellow-countrymen's right to live a full life before their personal careers, men and women who let a great cause direct their lives.

The national movement to which these young people belong has a world-wide significance. By striving to hand on to future generations the civilisation they have inherited they are fighting man's battle for human dignity and humane living everywhere they may be. It is a mistake to under-estimate the significance of the Welsh struggle. Through-out the world, the inhuman machinery of the huge and rootless systems in politics, commerce and industry, is

443

trampling on man's humanity and shattering his personal life. A continual decline in people's ability to create the conditions of their local and national environment, and a continuous increase in bureaucratic power, which is becoming more and more impersonal, is seen everywhere. The technological mass-society and personal freedom become more and more incompatible. In every field, including university education and local government, the huge impersonal unit rules the day. In enormous units, people tend to lose dignity and significance. They become footloose and deracinated, without roots in a warm neighbourhood or a national community. The human person becomes the abstract man. The workers become more proletarian, and the middle classes more vainly suburban. And the logic of the dominating centralism is totalitarianism.

Voices everywhere are raised against the grey and mechanical ugliness of modern society, but men feel like helpless prisoners. Thousands reject this type of society, but cannot break out of a regime that is able to use people for its own purposes. Throughout the world there is a dire need for a more humane and civilised political system and economy. In scores of countries there is hunger for an order which respects the identity of each human person which gives priority to quality of life in community. There is a thirst for a government which will ensure for every single person and every nation the opportunity to be what they are: to realize their potential to the full; for an order which fully respects man's humanity; an order which perceives that man is essentially a social creature, closely woven into the texture of his own society; an order which recognises generously in all its policies that man has a soul and a mind as well as a body; an order that takes good care of his roots in society, and of the roots of society in history and in national traditions, the fruit of a slow growth, which is so fundamental to his own personal good and to the health of his civilisation. The successful establishment of such an order in Wales in which her civilisation could develop along the lines of its own genius, would be a help to those who are fighting the battle for the dignity of man everywhere.

The crisis of Welsh identity becomes more acute with every passing month. The Welsh-speaking Wales of the rural areas has ceased to exist. Unemployment has depopulated the two-thirds of the land which were the bastions of the language, and the influx of thousands of English people has disrupted traditional community life. These incomers have usually expected the natives to defer to them in matters of language and culture, and without being consciously arrogant, they have insisted on an English medium education for their children even in Welsh-speaking districts. One English person usually expects the language of the company or the public meeting to become English for his sake. The Welsh normally defer to this out of courtesy or from the more servile feeling that everything English excels anything Welsh. No one complains of 'ramming English down people's throats' whereas there are frequent complaints against 'ramming Welsh down people's throats' when its use is insisted on in education or broadcasting. Public life and primary schools in Welsh-speaking areas have too often been allowed in these circumstances to become as English as their commerce, law courts, university colleges and secondary schools. Local councils on which all but two or three members were Welsh speaking, have conducted their affairs wholly in English, which has been of course the only language used in most council offices. Parish meetings and even farmers' union business and agricultural shows have by the same token been conducted in most Welsh areas wholly in English.

Nevertheless, despite this profound moral weakness, it remains still possible to create in Wales a humane, civilised and thoroughly Welsh order. Our country possesses all the necessary resources in its people and in its tradition. Wales is still a national community. Her language and culture are still powerful bulwarks against the rising tide of rootless proletarianism and suburbanism. In spite of the cruel loss from emigration and depopulation, the talent

of the Welsh still remains, and also many of their
ideals. The natural ability which often stems to the surface
even yet in the most thinly populated areas is a source of
constant wonder. It manifests itself in industry and commerce,
in politics and all the professions. There has never been a
shortage of talent in the nation; and there is no shortage
today. I used to dote on the society on Mynydd Epynt,
where John Morris-Jones's *Cerdd Dafod*, the classic work on
the closed metres of the *cynghanedd*, was an important book
in many a home; and I loved the wonderful vigour of the
society in the Tryweryn valley where there was a fine company
of *englynwyr* and harpists. Like Thomas Pennant in the
eighteenth century I too heard *penillion* singing that continued
for hours in farmhouses. 'They (would) continue singing
without intermission, and never repeat the same stanza; for
that would occasion the loss of honour of being held first of
the song.' The War Office destroyed the Epynt community;
and Cwm Tryweryn lies under the water; for these are the
years of the deliberate destruction of Welsh-speaking rural
communities. Gwenallt sang of the havoc wrought by the
Forestry Commission to the land where his roots were in
Rhydcymerau.

Ac erbyn hyn nid oes yno ond coed,
A'u gwreiddiau haerllug yn sugno'r hen bridd:
Coed lle y bu cymdogaeth,
Fforest lle bu ffermydd,
Bratiaith Saeson y De lle bu barddoni a diwinydda,
Cyfarth cadnoid lle bu cri plant ac ŵyn.
Ac yn y tywyllwch yn ei chanol hi
Y mae ffau'r Minotawros Seisnig;
Ac ar golfenni, fel ar groesau,
Ysgerbydau beirdd, blaenoriaid, gweinidogion ac athrawon
    Ysgol Sul
Yn gwynnu yn yr haul,
Ac yn cael eu golchi gan y glaw a'u sychu gan y gwynt.

And by this time there are only trees,
their impudent roots sucking the old earth;
trees where once there was neighbourhood,
a forest where there were farms,

the lingo of the English-speakers of the South
where once was poetry and divinity,
the barking of foxes where once was the cry of children and
   lambs,
and in the darkness in the middle of it
the lair of the English Minotaur;
and on the branches, as though on crosses,
skeletons of poets, deacons, ministers and Sunday school
teachers
whiteneing in the sun,
washed by the rain and dried by the wind.

But poetry and the harp remain important with the guitar now a ready help in scores of neighbourhoods. As Anthony Conran has pointed out, 'The Welsh poet is still a leader in his community, a national figure who appears at public functions and is constantly called upon to give his opinions on questions of the day. He is therefore able to talk, in his poetry, of political matters (and even of international affairs) with the certainty that a lot of influential people are going to listen. No English poet has been able to do this since Tennyson.'

Only a short time ago we lost the 'Three Bobs' of Merioneth — warm, immortal men: Bob Owen of Croesor, the ex-quarryman turned lecturer and scholar; Bob Tai'r Felin, the cultured old farmer and ballad-singer, whose tenor voice rang out like a bell, even at eighty years of age; and Bob Lloyd — Llwyd o'r Bryn — famous throughout Wales as a story-teller, lecturer and compère of *Nosweithiau Llawen* and *Eisteddfodau*: a farmer, a poet, and a man of letters. These three lived all their lives in Meirionnydd, two of them in Penllyn. We have only just lost Ifan Gruffydd, the 'man from Paradwys', an ex-soldier, and a County Hall caretaker; a remarkably eloquent lecturer who wrote two volumes of autobiography which will remain among the treasures of the language. Another of the same ilk who died in the same year was the beloved and versatile Huw T. Edwards, a trade union leader who published volumes of prose and verse in Welsh — in the strict metres as well as in free verse — and who was a generous patron of the weekly newspaper *Baner ac Amserau Cymru*.

A month ago, a local poet was looking for a patron in this area to help him to publish a book of poems. He sought the aid of an old farmer, himself a country poet. 'How much will it cost?' asked the old man. The poet mentioned a substantial sum of money and the farmer wrote out a cheque for the required amount immediately. Seven miles away is the border of the anthracite coal field. There, some years ago, six miners published a volume of their own poetry, giving the profits to help one of their fellow-miners receive a higher education. This ex-miner has now become one of our best historians. In this same county of Carmarthenshire a volume of poetry published in a series of county poetry included the works of eight farmers, four miners, three grocers, two carpenters, a policeman, a dentist, a commercial traveller, an insurance man, a bank manager and steel, tin plate, railway and forest workers, as well as a number of teachers and clergymen. The two poets from my own parish were a cobbler and a road-worker. We pride ourselves in this parish on our successful *eisteddfodau* and our cultural societies. We have a fine choir which sings all the great oratorios: the leader of the choir and of the orchestra is an ex-railway signalman. He plays a number of instruments himself, and also teaches others to play them. Three years ago in the National Eisteddfod both the Chair and the Crown were won by farmers of neighbouring Cardiganshire. Last year, a Pembrokeshire quarryman won the Chair, the learned adjudicators taking it for granted that the poem was the work of an academic. Wales's tradition therefore still endures. This tradition continues to give character and wealth to the life of the anglicised industrial valleys — only 2% of the children in the Rhondda valleys now speak Welsh, and even less, only 0.5% in Merthyr Tydfil — but it is in the Welsh-speaking areas naturally that its values count most. It is there that the insipid material uniformity of today has done the least harm: the language is a bulwark against it.

Although the language has retreated in so many areas, it yet remains of immeasurable importance in the life of Wales, and it continues to develop and to be enriched. The language is the heart and soul of the national civilisation, the most creative and hopeful element in the life of the nation. At last it is beginning to resume its place in official and public life. It has made important advances in college and primary education; in the secondary schools too the position is very slowly improving; and even in the university it is tentatively beginning to win its place as the medium of teaching. Thus, the language endures; and it could yet be used by the whole nation in every aspect of its life. The literature remains too, enriched beyond measure by the contributions of the brilliant men and women of this present century who have refused wealth and conventional success in order to serve Wales. Its music has been enriched in the same way; the folk songs remain, not only as a source of entertainment, but as a basis upon which to build. The land of Wales, too, endures. Every Welshman from Anglesey to Gwent is aware of the landscape, which remains as strikingly beautiful as it was when our first Celtic ancestors reached its shores. And the history of the people who dwelt here remains. This mountainous peninsula has been inhabited, since the time that the Romans built Carmarthen and Caerwent 1900 years ago, by people who have lived together and worshipped together, striven together and prayed together, suffered together and rejoiced together. What made them a nation was living so long together in this land through the medium of the Welsh language. Nothing can take the past away from us.

When Britishness was on the point of destroying Wales, its glory departed. The British Empire joined the Roman and other empires in the limbo of dead things, but the Welsh nation survives. It is true that it is cruelly eroded, but Wales endures as a nation of vast potentialities. The most exciting things about Wales today are her possibilities. If Wales is to realise its potential, it must win its freedom — the freedom to supplant an order of government which finds a low level of unemployment and emigration in England unacceptable, but acceptable, on a far higher level, in Wales; an order where the establishment allows the media to destroy the language and culture, and even uses them to stifle Welsh national aspirations and policies; and an order where the united opinion of the Welsh people is ignored on matters, such as the drowning of the Tryweryn valley, when English welfare is affected. Freedom is essential in order to replace a system which has ravaged the rich traditional life of Wales by a more civilised and humane form of government.

Our generation has seen scores of nations throughout the world achieving freedom. When in 1945 the San Francisco Conference was held to create the United Nations there were still about six hundred million people in the world who were not fully self-governing. By 1970 only a small number had failed to attain full national equality. In extending freedom to the new nations of the old empire, England has prepared the way for Wales, if it has the will, to join a Britannic confederation of free and equal nations. For confederative union of the nations of these islands is a practical proposition. It would secure unity in diversity; it would create a mosaic of free nations instead of the present state monolith.

But liberty is something that has to be won, and won through hard work and sacrifice, and unyielding determination. In Wales the first step is to supplant the present 'diwreiddiedig ac uchelgeisiol griw' (the deracinated and ambitious crowd); and to resist the unbearable arrogance of London civil servants and politicians who always know what is best for Wales.

Support for the bureaucratic British system must be withdrawn in favour of a Welsh democracy. With will and vision this nation can create her own environment. There are no economic and political powers in existence which her will cannot subdue. In the confident spirit of the young generation there is enough moral strength to ensure a free and just Wales which can transmit her civilisation to the future and make her worthy contribution to inter-national order.

When thousands of Indians stood firm in 1930 in the face of the guns and truncheons of British soldiers and policemen — Indian by nationality perhaps, but British by loyalty — something revolutionary happened in the history of their great country. Gandhi had led a huge pilgrimage to the sea shore to break British law by making salt from sea water. The patriots were met by hundreds of policemen and soldiers. They were cruelly maltreated, although the pilgrims themselves committed no violence at all. Louis Fischer says, when describing what happened:

'The British beat the Indians with batons and rifle butts. The Indians neither cringed or complained nor retreated. That made England powerless and India invincible . . . after that, it was inevitable that Britain should some day refuse to rule India and that some day India should refuse to be ruled . . . Technically, legally, nothing had changed. India was still a British colony. India was now free.'

Constitutionally, India was still in servitude. In the minds of her finest men and women she was already free. They walked the Indian earth with heads held high as free people.

In the same way the cream of Welsh youth behave today like free people. When the police are doing their utmost to provoke them, when they maltreat them — young women and men alike — they remain disciplined, leaving the violence to the agents of the British state. In these young people and their supporters Wales is already free. They are only a small minority, it is true, but as a proportion of the population of the country they are more numerous than Gandhi's heroic marchers. And they are the creative minority: it is they who have the cause, the conviction and the internal resource. It is they who respond to Wales's call. And the call today is not for people to *die* for their country, as so many chose to do in the heroic past, but to *live* for her. They are the new shepherds on the old hills. Because of their splendid commitment to the land of their fathers, Wales has a future as a nation.

When the Czechs were part of the Austro-Hungarian Empire during the last century, with no more freedom than Wales has today, and the life of the nation and the language in the balance, Palacky, their national historian, wrote his five great volumes on the history of his nation up to the time it lost its liberty in 1526. It was this achievement, more than anything else, which revived the spirit of his people. He concluded his masterpiece with these defiant words: 'We were here before Austria: we shall be here after her too.' He spoke the truth. The Austrian Empire disappeared, but the Czech nation lives on. We too can say 'We were here before Great Britain'. And the spirit now rising in our land gives us the confidence to predict, 'We shall be here after her too.' For the day is coming when Wales and Scotland, Ireland and England will arise out of the ashes of Great Britain to associate in harmony with each other in a partnership of free and equal nations.

Vol. 34.   No. 4

PICTURE POST

January 25, 1947

Welsh Nationalists Climb into the Black Mountains to Demonstrate Against the Army's Demands
They have organised their pilgrimage to Llyn-y-Fan, a lake famous in Welsh history and folk-lore, lying under the highest peak in Carmarthenshire. Local authorities have been told by the War Office that it is to be taken over.

WAR OFFICE LAND GRAB: WALES PROTESTS

500,950 Welsh acres held

There are complaints from many parts of Britain about the amount of land the War Office is holding. At a Welsh mountainside meeting, speakers protest that the demands on Wales are three times as heavy as those on the rest of Britain.

Photographed by HAYWOOD MAGEE

ptember, 1936, three Welsh Nationalists, ders Lewis, distinguished Welsh scholar and letters, the Reverend Lewis Valentine and Williams, one of the foremost short-story in Wales, set fire to a bombing-school, which twin Government was erecting on a beauty-Caernarvonshire. They did so after their nt had made verbal protests to the Govern-d had failed to have any effect. The only f the fire-raising was that they were each d, at the Old Bailey, to nine months'

imprisonment. They found that very few people in Britain, and that includes Wales, had any sympathy for them. A fortnight ago D. J. Williams led a pilgrimage to Llyn-y-Fan, a lake in the Black Mountains, to protest against the War Office's plans to take over more Welsh beauty-spots as battle-training grounds. This time the Nationalists have the sympathy of most people in Britain who, after they have seen the way war has wiped out cities, and have grown accustomed to the idea of a bomb which makes tanks as obsolete as the famous Home Guard

pikes, want the countryside, at least, to rem intact and undespoiled.

Four hundred people travelled up the mounta side through mist and rain, some on horseback, m of them on foot, to the lake where in the twel century a shepherd-boy saw a vision of a girl w walked on the water with a herd of fairy cattle. E their pilgrimage had nothing to do with clou legend. Dan Thomas, a Cardiff bank-manager, charge of the ceremony at the top, shouted into t wind, "Our procession is like a funeral. But it

Wales 1947: Protest against War Office seizure of land in Welsh-speaking Wales

Wales 1971: incident in language campaign

Part of Cardiff civic centre

Copyright Alcwyn Deiniol

Capel Garmon fire-dog from first century

20th century scene on Carmarthenshire
Black Mountain — Mynydd Du
'Rhyddid' –– Freedom

Aros mae'r mynyddau mawr,
 Rhuo trostynt mae y gwynt;
Clywir eto gyda'r wawr
 Gân bugeiliaid megis cynt.
Eto tyf y llygad dydd
Ogylch traed y graig a'r bryn,
Ond bugeiliaid newydd sydd
 Ar yr hen fynyddoedd hyn.

Ar arferion Cymru gynt
 Newid ddaeth o rod i rod;
Mae cenhedlaeth wedi mynd
 A chenhedlaeth wedi dod.
Wedi oes dymhestlog hir
 Alun Mabon mwy nid yw,
Ond mae'r heniaith yn y tir
 A'r alawon hen yn fyw.

The mighty mountains still remain,
 over them still the wind is strong,
and you still hear with the dawn
 as of yore the shepherd's song;
and the daisies still, still grow
 round the foot of rock and hill,
but the ancient mountains know
 new shepherd after shepherd still.

And the customs of old Wales
 are changing as the years go past;
as one generation fades
 a new one follows on the last.
After a life stormy and long
 Alun Mabon is no more,
but we still speak the old tongue,
 sing the old songs as before.

INDEX

(to main topics)

Aberdâr, 351, 355, 378, 382, 431, 432.

Aberffro, 74, 182.

Abergwili, 153.

Aberhonddu, 177 see also Brecon.

Aber-miwl, 226.

Aberteifi, 167, 169, 177, 180, 192, 210, 223, 240 see also Cardigan.

Aberystwyth, 174, 177, 210, 212, 231, 269, 270, 272, 331, 384, 402.

Ablett, Noah, 427.

Abraham, William (Mabon), 408-9, 427.

Act of Union, The, 282, 286, 292, 293, 294-303, 305, 341, 366, 370, 371, 373, 415, 435, 437, 441.

Adam of Usk, 263, 265.

Aethelfrith of Mercia, 30.

Agricola, 30, 34.

Alfred, 70, 136, 137, 138, 139, 140, 141, 237.

Amserau, Yr, 376, 382.

Anarawd s. of Rhodri Mawr, 132, 137, 138-140, 141.

Aneirin, 33, 51, 53, 54, 76, 77, 78.

Anglesey (Sir Fôn),19, 22, 28, 29, 32, 35, 54, 59, 72, 82, 96, 113, 119, 132, 148, 167, 171, 172, 181, 193, 209, 217, 219, 225, 229, 231, 235, 238, 241, 259, 262, 267, 355, 377, 436.

Anian bishop of Bangor, 226.

Annales Cambriae, 134.

Arfon, 75, 96, 97, 126, 209, 220.

Arllechwedd, 209.

Armes Prydein, 96, 98, 119, 142, 143.

Arnold, Matthew, 371, 372, 384.

Arthur, 19, 47, 64, 68-9, 72, 76, 97, 100, 142, 200, 202.

Arwystli, 163, 223, 290.

Asaph, St., 97, 134.

Ashton, Charles, 146, 377.

Asser, 138, 139.

Athravaeth Gristnogavl, 313.

Athrwys, 120.

Augustine, St., 97, 110-113, 121, 122, 152.

Badon, Mount, 68.

Bala, Y, 375, 381, 404, 437.

Baldwin, Archbishop, 194, 205.

Banbury, battle of, 281.

Baner ac Amserau Cymru, 376, 447.

Baner Cymru, 376.

Bangor, 97, 134, 205, 217, 385.

Bangor Isgoed, 30, 97, 111, 112, 124.

Bannockburn, 243.

Bardsey Island see Enlli.

Bede, 60, 63, 64, 97, 110-113, 122, 124, 142.

"Beibl Bach, Y," 316.

Bere, Castell y, 234, 240.

Bernicia see Bryneich.

Berwyn, St., 83.

Bevan, Aneurin, 378, 422, 423, 432, 435.

Beuno, St., 98, 114.

Blackwell, John (Alun), 374, 375.

Bleddyn ap Cynfyn, 166.

Blegywryd, 144.

Book of Kells, 123.

Bosworth, battle of, 143, 277, 281, 282, 285, 290, 291, 295.

Brace, William, 426, 427.

Brecon, 43, 50, 214, 224, 234, 313, 379, 380.

Breconshire, 301 see also Brycheiniog.

Bretons, 16.

Brigantes, 27.

Brittany, 15, 16, 18, 19, 48, 49, 50, 51, 69, 81, 283.

Brochwel Ysgythrog, 72, 98, 126.

Bruce, Robert, 243.

Brut y Tywysogion, 119, 125, 126, 136, 137, 147, 153, 154, 158, 166, 177, 184, 200, 210, 213.

Brychan Brycheiniog, 44, 50, 82, 83, 84, 86, 90, 127, 138,

Brycheiniog, 44, 83, 109, 127, 138, 140, 150, 161, 165, 167, 171, 172, 176, 191, 197, 225, 241, 264, 314, 380.

Brynach, 50, 84.

Bryneich (Bernicia), 76, 99, 116.

Brythonic (language), 26, 33, 39, 46, 51, 52, 53, 64, 66.

Brythons, 36, 39, 43, 46, 49, 51, 55, 60, 61, 62, 63, 64, 65, 75-77, 87, 111-113, 131, 143, 150, 301.

Buallt (Builth), 167, 218, 224, 229 see also Llanfair ym Muallt.

Buchedd Dewi, 95.

Buddug (Boadicea), 30.

Builth see Buallt.

Byrnach, 72.

Cadafael, 117, 118.

Cadell f. of Hywel Dda, 137, 138, 141.

Cadfan, 114, 115, 119.

Cadog, 58, 71, 72, 73, 83, 84, 85, 86, 88, 91, 97, 101.

Cadwaladr ap Gruffydd ap Cynan, 176, 177, 178, 180, 184, 185, 210.

Cadwaladr Fendigaid, 118, 119, 291.

Cadwallon, 115, 116, 117, 129.

Cadwallon ap Ifor Bach, 212.

Cadwallon Lawhir, 59, 72.

Cadwgan ap Bleddyn, 170, 171, 172.

Caeo, 188.

Caereinion, 241, 250.

Caerffili, 184, 226, 242.

Caerhun, 28.

Caerleon, 27, 30, 31, 34, 35, 38, 40, 162, 214, 242.

Caernarfon, 28, 31, 34, 35, 62, 82, 146, 238, 240, 259, 262, 264, 265, 374, 428, 440.

Caernarfon(shire), 98.

Caersws, 34.

Caer-went, 27, 32, 33, 38, 58, 66, 84, 86, 449.

Caerwys (eisteddfodau), 308.

Cain, St., 83.

Caldey Island (Ynys Bŷr), 99.

Cambrian Strike, the, 427.

Camlan, 68.

Cantref Bychan, 178, 183, 196, 221.

Cantref Mawr, 31, 83, 97, 174, 183, 184, 188, 196, 221.

Canwyll y Cymru, 323.

Caradog, 26, 27, 30, 52, 58, 59, 68, 84, 259.

Cardiff, 19, 35, 85, 148, 167, 184, 242, 267, 287, 313, 319, 349, 415, 435.

Cardigan, 184, 186, 191, 213, 214, 218, 238, 241, 265, 268, 272, 331, see also Aberteifi.

Cardiganshire, 448, see also Ceredigion.

Carmarthen (Caerfyrddin), 31, 32, 33, 34, 35, 71, 155, 169, 173, 178, 183, 184, 196, 213, 214, 218, 221, 226, 238, 240, 268, 272, 293, 320, 327, 344, 345, 353, 364, 365, 401, 409.

Carmarthenshire (Sir Gaerfyrddin), 24, 43, 44, 84, 317, 326, 347, 360, 363, 432, 448.

Carnwyllion, 196, 221.

Carreg Cennen, 221, 240, 264, 272.

Castell Newydd Emlyn, 240, 264.

Catraeth (Catterick), 78; 117.

Cecil, William (Lord Burleigh), 307.

Ceingar, St., 83.

Celts, 16, 17, 18, 19, 20, 21, 28, 29, 35, 38, 39, 54, 69, 71, 88, 96, 104-6, 142.

Ceredigion, 90, 97, 98, 109, 127, 134, 137, 138, 140, 141, 155, 167, 170, 171, 172, 174, 177, 178, 180, 184, 185, 186, 200, 210, 211, 213, 219, 221, 229, 234, 241, 255, 272, 363, 401, 436, 448 see also Cardiganshire.

Ceri, 229.

Cerrig y Gwyddel, 59.

Charles, Thomas, 327, 347-8.

Chartism & Chartists, 356-359, 361, 363, 373, 393, 410.

Chester, 30, 31, 33, 38, 40, 140, 148, 161, 167, 175.

Chester, battle of, 97, 98, 112, 113, 124, 126, 163, 228.

Chester, synod of, 97.

Cilmeri, 233, 241.

Cistercians, 217.

Claudius, 23, 27.

Clud, 197.

Clydog, St., 83.

Clynnog, 98, 287.

Conwy, 25, 137, 169, 170, 229, 214, 262, 321.

Cook, A. J., 427.

Cornish, 16, 49.

Cornovicians, 66.

Cornwall, 18, 35, 48, 50, 51, 54, 54, 62, 63, 69, 75, 79.

Corwen, 167.

Council of Wales and the Marches, 299, 309, 319.

Cradoc, Walter, 320, 324.

Crawshay, William, 353.

Cromwell, Oliver, 124, 307, 321, 323, 397.

Cromwell, Thomas, 293, 296, 299, 307.

Culhwch ac Olwen, 69.

Cunedda, 44-7, 50, 51, 53, 54, 59, 62, 72, 82, 83, 87, 90, 96, 97, 114, 132, 153, 259.

Cybi, St., 72, 73, 96, 97, 101.

Cydewain, 163.

Cydweli, 176, 183, 213, 218, 221, 223, 264, 272, 422.

Cyfeiliog, 290.

Cyngen of Powys, 126, 132, 135, 136.

Cymmrodorion Society, The, 342, 412.

Cymreigyddion y Fenni, 378.

Cymru Fydd, 362, 395, 403, 411, 412, 415, 416, 418, 421.

Cynan Garwyn, 54, 75, 98, 109, 112.

Cynddelw Brydydd Mawr, 98, 181, 189.

Cynllaith, 163.

Cynog, St., 83.

Cynwyl Gaeo, 83, 174.

Cystennin, 82.

Dafydd, prince, 45, 227, 230, 234, 237, 240, 242, 254.

Dafydd ab Edmwnd, 245, 273, 288.

Dafydd ab Owain Gwynedd, 193-4, 209, 218.

Dafydd ap Gwilym, 74, 189, 245, 246-50, 287, 345, 379.

Dafydd ap Gwilym Society, The, 403, 423.

Dafydd ap Llywelyn Fawr, 215, 218, 219.

Dafydd Benfras, 199, 216.

Dafydd Nanmor, 288, 311.

Danes, the, 127, 132, 136, 137, 139, 140, 147, 148, 150, 152, 154, 155, 167, 171, 182, 190, 301.

Daniel, D. R., 403, 407.

David, St., 43, 82, 83, 85, 86, 90-96, 98, 101, 109, 165.

Davies, David (Dai'r Cantwr), 365.

Davies, George M. Ll., 439.

Davies, Hywel, 332.

Davies, Dr. John (Mallwyd), 312, 314, 315.

Davies, Richard, 310, 311, 313, 315.

Davies, Walter (Gwallter Mechain), 360.

de Breos, William, 210, 211.

De Exidio Brittanniae, 63, 71.

Deceangles, 25.

Deheubarth, 127, 137, 141, 143, 149, 153, 156, 157, 173, 174, 176, 183, 183, 185, 188, 191, 192, 196, 208, 210, 229, 255, 284.

Deifr (Deira), 76, 99, 116.

Demetians, 25.

de Montford, Eleanor, 228, 230.

de Montford, Simon, 224, 225, 227, 230.

de Montgomery, Roger, 161, 163.

Denbigh (Dinbych), 231, 240, 375.

Denbighshire (Sir Ddinbych), 119, 163, 353.

Derfel, R. J., 426.

Descriptio Kambriae, 157, 195, 205.

Dinas Basing, 181, 186.

Dinas Brân, 231.

Dinas Emrys, 59.

Dinas Mawddwy, 146, 377.

Dinefwr, 32, 92, 127, 182, 184, 192, 196, 210, 221, 240.

Diwygiwr, Y, 356, 369, 382.

Dolau Cothi, 31.

Dolbadarn, 234.

Dolforwyn, 225.

Dolgellau, 382.

Dolwyddelan, 209, 234.

Dowlais, 352.

Dream of Macsen Wledig, The, 33.

Dream of Rhonabwy, The, 69, 75, 181, 200.

Druids, the, 28-30, 113.

Drych y Prif Oesoedd, 202, 336.

Dryslwyn, 32, 264.

Dublin, 100, 132, 166, 318.

Dwn, Henry, 262, 264, 271, 272.

Dwynwen, St., 83.

Dyfed, 37, 42, 44, 54, 59, 62, 71, 89, 93, 109, 127, 134, 138, 139, 167, 168, 172, 181, 183, 184, 186, 189, 190, 200, 212.

Dyfrig, St., 84, 85, 92, 100.

Degannwy, 74, 126, 163, 169, 212, 218, 219, 222.

Ebbw Vale, 354, 355.

Edeirnion, 163, 229.

Edmund Tudor, 278, 283.

Ednyfed Fychan, 216, 219, 246, 259, 277.

Edward the Confessor, 70, 156, 158.

Edwards, Charles, 323.

Edwards, Frank, 416.

Edwards, Huw T., 447.

Edwards, Lewis, 369, 375, 378, 382, 394.

Edwards, O. M., 396, 403, 407, 412, 423, 424, 425, 437.

Edwards, Thomas (Twm o'r Nant), 329, 339, 374.

Edwards, Thomas Charles, 394.

Edwards, William (Pontypridd), 325.

Edwin of Deira, 76, 114, 115, 116.

Efail-wen, 364.

Eifionydd, 221.

Einion Offeiriad, 248.

Eisteddfod, Cardigan, 1176, 192.

Elen, 33, 37, 59, 82, 96.

Elfael, 191, 197, 224.

Elfed, 53, 115, 117.

Elfodd, 122, 134.

Elias, John, 375.

Eliseg, column of, 37, 125, 126.

Ellis, Thomas Edward, 356, 388, 402, 407, 408, 410, 412, 413, 419, 420, 433, 437.

Emlyn, 190, 210, 214, 223.

Emrys Wledig, 62, 93.

England, 22, 24, 35, 36, 37, 38, 43, 45, 46, 47, 49, 51, 52, 53, 54, 55 passim.

English, the, 23, 37, 39, 42, 43, 49, 54, 60 passim.

Englynion y Beddau, 133.

Enlli (Bardsey), 84, 85, 120, 132.

Epynt, Mynydd, 379, 446.

Erbury, William, 324.

Erging, 124.

Eryri, 158.

Eulo, 181.

Europe, 19, 86, 87, 189, 191, 200, 201, 203.

Evans, Beriah Gwynfe, 394, 415.

Evans, Elis Humphrey (Hedd Wyn), 430.

Evans, Evan (Ieuan Brydydd Hir), 306, 339, 340, 341.

Evans, Evan (Ieuan Glan Geirionydd), 360.

Evans, Samuel T., 322, 403.

Evans, Theophilus, 336.

Ffydd Ddiffuant, Y, 323.

Fishguard (Abergwaun), 132.

Flemings of Dyfed, 42, 173, 183.

Flintshire (Sir Fflint), 163, 353.

French landing at Fishguard, 1797, 343.

Frontinus, 30.

Frost, John, 357, 358.

Gaer, Y (Brecon), 34.

Garmon, St., 62, 64, 83, 87, 100, 113.

Garn Boduan, 25.

Gee, Thomas, 375, 376, 377, 400, 408, 410.

Gelli-wig, 69, 97.

Geoffrey of Monmouth, 62, 69, 202, 314.

George, David Lloyd, 280, 388, 400-408, 410-421, 428, 432, 434, 435, 439, 440.

Gerald of Windsor, 171, 204.

Gildas, 60, 63, 71, 72, 73, 74, 75, 87, 88, 89, 93.

Giraldus Cambrensis, 15, 17, 18, 23, 128, 129, 146, 157, 172, 179, 186, 191, 192, 193, 194, 195, 196, 204-8, 212, 320.

Glamorgan, 22, 197, 322, 351, 352, 353, 419, 422, see also Morgannwg.

Glyn Rhosin, 91.

Glywys, 58.

Glywysing, 58.

Gododdin, 76, 78, 79, 117, 119.

Gododdin, Y, 53, 68, 179.

Goodman, Gabriel, 315.

Gospels of Chad, 128.

Gouge, Thomas, 325, 327.

Gower, 149, 173, 176, 183, 196, 221.

Great Session, The, 299, 359.

Grenfell, D. R., 434.

Gresford, 287.

Grey, Reginald, 257, 263.

Griffith, Ellis Jones, 403.

Griffiths, Ann, 345.

Gruffudd ab yr Ynad Coch, 235.

Gruffudd ap Cynan, 163, 164, 165, 166-175, 176, 179, 188, 193, 197, 255.

Gruffudd ap Gwenwynwyn, 218, 221, 222, 224, 227, 230, 238.

Gruffudd ap Llywelyn, 132, 152-9, 161, 166.

Gruffudd ap Llywelyn Fawr, 218.

Gruffudd ap Nicolas, 272.

Gruffudd ap Rhys ap Tewdwr, 173, 174, 176, 177, 180, 183, 211.

Gruffudd Gryg, 287.

Gruffudd Hiraethog, 310, 311.

Gruffudd Llwyd, 256.

Gruffydd, Ifan, 447.

Gruffydd, W. J., 425.

Guest, Charlotte, 375, 380.

Guto'r Glyn, 276, 279, 280, 288.

Gutun Owain, 288.

Gwallter Map, 153.

Gweledigaethau'r Bardd Cwsg, 306.

Gwenllian m. of Lord Rhys, 174, 176, 188.

Gwent, 58, 71, 82, 84, 86, 109, 120, 138, 139, 140, 144, 150, 155, 157, 161, 162, 163, 171, 172, 178, 191, 197, 200, 202, 220, 224, 263, 289, 324, 357, 380, 422.

Gwenwynwyn, 208-213.

Gwerthrynion, 229

Gwrtheyrn (Vortigern), 37, 59, 60, 61, 62, 73, 83, 143.

Gwrtheyrnion, 59, 62.

Gwyddoniadur, Y, 377.

Gwyn, Richard, 325.

Gwynedd, 28, 44, 45, 59, 71, 72, 73, 75, 87, 96, 98, 109, 114, 126, 131, 134, 137, 138, 143, 148, 149, 153, 154, 155, *passim,* 263, 264, 284, 316, 318, 334, 345, 365.

Gwynedd uwch Conwy, 171, 219, 229, 238.

Gwyneddigion Society, The, 341, 342, 345, 412.

Gwynfardd Brycheiniog, 91.

Gwylliaid Cochion Mawddwy, 292.

Gwynllŵg (Wentloog), 58, 167, 191, 219.

Hanmer, Dafydd, 257.

Hardie, Keir, 419, 426, 427, 428, 431, 434.

Harlech, 234, 264, 265, 268, 283, 292.

Harris, Howell, 165, 330, 332, 333, 334-5.

Harris, Joseph (Gomer), 344.

Haverfordwest, 173, 213, 222.

Henfynyw, 90.

Hengerdd, 54.

Hengist and Horsa, 60, 63, 143, 282.

Henry II, 181, 183, 185, 196.

Henry VII, 259, 272, 277, 278, 282.

Herbert, William, 277, 279-281, 283, 305.

Heulyn, Rowlant, 316.

Hirlas Owain, 179.

Historia Brittonum, 131, 134.

Historiae Brittannicae Defensio, 314.

Holyhead (Caergybi), 35, 73, 97, 122.

Hotspur, 262, 264, 267.

Huet, Thomas, 315.

Hugh, Earl of Chester, 171.

Hughes, John Ceiriog, 377.

Hughes, Stephen, 323.

Hyddgen, 262.

Hywel ab Owain Gwynedd, 178, 183, 185, 187, 189, 193.

Hywel Dda, 75, 98, 132, 141-7, 148, 149, 150, 153, 154, 157, 164, 182, laws of, 144-6, 166, 194, 200, 216, 265.

Iago s. of Idwal Foel, 148, 154.

Idwal Foel, 141, 142, 143, 148, 149.

Ieuan ap Sulien, 152.

Ifan ab Owen Edwards, 437.

Ifor Bach, 184.

Illtud, 38, 49, 73, 83-89, 91, 97, 100, 101.

Intinerarium Kambriae, 195, 205.

Iolo Goch, 256.

Iolo Morganwg, 21, 28, 86, 344, 357.

Ireland, 15, 18, 19, 22, 43, 44, 48, 50, 51, 54 *passim.*

Irfon, river, 232.

Irish, the, 16, 23, 35, 36, 39, 41, 44, 45, 46, 49, 50, 59, 63, 65, 66, 72.

Ivorites, 360, 361.

James, Evan, 386.

James, James, 386.

Jasper Tudor, 272, 278, 280, 283, 284, 290.

Jenkins, Leoline, 322.

Joan d. of K. John, 209, 217, 218.

John, E. T., 420.

John, Will, 434.
Jones, Aneurin (Aneurin Fardd), 378.
Jones, Dafydd (Caeo), 345.
Jones, Edmund, 334.
Jones, Evan (Ieuan Gwynedd), 368, 382.
Jones, Griffith (Llanddowror), 311, 326–330, 332, 347.
Jones, J. E., 437.
Jones, J. Puleston, 403.
Jones, John (Gellilyfdy), 314.
Jones, John (Shoni Sgubor-fawr), 365.
Jones, John (Talsarn), 362.
Jones, Michael D., 399, 404–8, 415, 418, 419, 420, 433, 437.
Jones, Morgan, 434.
Jones, Owen Wynne (Glasynys), 360.
Jones, Robert Ambrose (Emrys ap Iwan), 405, 418.
Jones, Samuel (Brynllywarch), 324.
Jones, T. Gwynn, 425.
Jones, William (the Chartist), 358.
Jones, Sir William, 342.
Julius Caesar, 16, 23, 26, 28, 29, 131.

Kentigern (Cyndeyrn), 77.
Kidwelly, see Cydweli.
Kyffin, Edward, 310.

Labour Party, the, 306, 419, 420, 426, 427, 428, 431, 432, 433, 434, 435, 439.
Lee, Rowland, 293.
Lewis Glyn Cothi, 274, 277.
Lewis, Elvet (Elfed), 416, 417, 418.
Lewis, J. Herbert, 413, 416.
Lewis, Lewis (Lewsyn yr Heliwr), 353, 355.
Lewis, Richard (Dic Penderyn), 355, 392.
Lewis, Saunders, 440.
Lewis, Titus, 92.

Lhuyd, Edward, 126, 339.
Liber Landavensis, 120.
Liberal Party, the, 401, 402, 415, 419, 420, 439.
London, 148, 161, 182, 185, 239, 345, 358, 431, 435, 436.
Ludlow, 270, 290, 318, 319.
Llanbadarn-fawr, 91, 134, 148, 152, 155, 177, 240.
Llanbedr Pont Steffan, 178.
Llancarfan, 71, 86, 87, 101, 120, 148, 344.
Llandâf, 84, 85, 205.
Llandeilo, 92, 231.
Llandochau, 120.
Llandovery (Llanymddyfri), 83, 84, 173, 178, 184, 196, 210, 231, 240, 335, 365, 375.
Llandudno, 136, 167.
Llandudoch, 148, 177.
Llanddewi Brefi, 91.
Llanfaches, 324.
Llanfair ym Muallt, 214, 224, 234, see also Builth.
Llanfyllin, 221.
Llangadog, 44, 199, 210, 334, 361, 364.
Llangadwaladr, 114, 119.
Llangeitho, 334.
Llangollen, 132, 163.
Llanidloes, 356.
Llanilltud-fawr (Llantwit Major), 32, 49, 87, 89, 99, 100, 120, 148, 344.
Llanofer, Lady, 379, 382.
Llansteffan, 178, 183, 190, 213, 264.
Llantrisant, 241.
Llanuwchllyn, 396.
Lloyd, Charles, 318.
Lloyd, J. E., 403, 412, 424.
Lloyd, John Ambrose, 375.
Lloyd, Robert (Llwyd o'r Bryn), 384, 447.
Llwyd, Humphrey, 314.
Llwyd, Morgan, 326.

Llwyn-llwyd, 333.
Llyfr Coch Hergest, 133, 347.
Llŷn, 19, 44, 209.
Llyn Cerrig Bach, 22.
Llyn Safaddan, 44, 140.
Llyn-y-fan, 21, 44.
Llywarch Hen, 67, 77, 124, 129, 133, 136.
Llywelyn ap Iorwerth (Llywelyn Fawr, Llywelyn I), 136, 153, 179, 193, 205, 208-217, 219, 224.
Llywelyn ap Gruffudd (Llywelyn II), 162, 179, 205, 214, 218-35, 237, 241, 245, 250, 251, 252, 254, 264, 282, 291.
Llywelyn ap Gruffudd Fychan o Gaeo, 84, 162, 263.
Llywelyn ap Seisyll, 153, 154, 166.
Llywelyn Bren, 242, 245.

Mabinogion, 43, 127, 131, 134, 168, 200, 375.
Macsen Wledig, 33, 36, 37-8, 40, 45, 46, 47, 51, 58, 59, 62, 81, 82, 83, 96, 98, 116.
Machynlleth, 265, 364.
Madog ab Owain Gwynedd, 194.
Madog ap Maredudd, 180, 181, 185, 193, 255.
Madog o Wynedd, 240, 241, 242, 250.
Maelgwn ap (Lord) Rhys, 210, 211.
Maelgwn Gwynedd, 45, 49, 54, 72-4, 75, 78, 87, 96, 97, 100, 115, 126, 132.
Maeliennydd, 178, 213, 224, 263.
Maelor Saesneg, 180.
Maesyfed, 197, 214, see also Radnorshire.
Maldwyn, 163, 345.
Manaw Gododdin, 44, 53, 77, 78.
Maredudd ab Owain, 149, 152, 153, 157, 164, 221.
Maredudd ap Rhys, 221, 223, 227.
Mathrafal, 182.

Meidrim, 35.
Meilyr, 175.
Meirionnydd (Meirioneth), 174, 177, 209, 219, 221, 229, 238, 283, 292, 374, 447.
Mercia, 78, 115, 116, 118, 124, 125, 136, 137, 139, 150, 155, 161, 162.
Merfyn Frych, 131-35, 137.
Merthyr Tudful, 344, 349-357, 364, 373, 385, 419, 448.
Miles, John, 324.
Milford Haven, 268, 284, 343.
Mold (Yr Wyddgrug), 163, 181, 218, 374, 401.
Môn, see Anglesey.
Monmouthshire (Sir Fynwy), 43, 97, 119, 357.
Montgomery (Trefaldwyn), 163, 169, 170, 214, 224, 225, 228, 321, treaty of, 225.
Morgan Mwynfawr, 58, 120.
Morgan, George Osborne, 398, 400.
Morgan, William, 311, 315.
Morgannwg, 58, 71, 86, 109, 120, 127, 134, 138, 140, 149, 150, 155, 157, 161, 167, 172, 191, 200, 212, 220, 221, 222, 241, 263, 267, 289, 290, 316, 320, 345, 365, 380, see also Glamorgan.
Morris, Lewis, 339, 340.
Morris-Jones, John, 394, 424, 425, 446.
Morris, Richard, 339.
Morris, William, 339.
Morys Clynnog, 313.
Myddleton, Hugh, 307.
Myddleton, Thomas, 316.
Myddleton, William, 308.
Mynydd Carn, battle of, 164, 165, 167.
Mynydd Parys, 32.
Mynyddog Mwynfawr, 53, 78.
Myvyrian Archaiology, 345.

Nant Carno, battle of, 148.

Nant-y-glo, 354.

Narberth, 43, 364.

National Eisteddfod, the, 448.

National Library of Wales, the, 423, 426.

National Museum of Wales, the, 425, 426.

Neath (Castell Nedd), 169, 354.

Nennius, 45, 59, 60, 62, 63, 68, 78, 122, 131, 134, 142.

Nest, wife of Gerald of Windsor, 172, 181, 189, 204.

Newport (Casnewydd), 162, 191, 357, 358, 416, 417, 432.

Newtown (Y Drefnewydd), 355, 414.

Nicholas, T. E., 426.

Normans, the, 23, 42, 95, 147, 156, 158, 160-236, 301, 357.

Norsemen, the, 126, 132, 134, 150.

Northumbria, 78, 79, 113, 115, 116, 117, 118, 125, 161.

Offa, 125, Offa's Dyke, 25, 79, 125, 154, 156.

Ordovicians, 25, 26.

Ostorius, 25, 27, 31, 147, 159, 222.

Oswald, 116, 117, 124.

Oswestry (Croesoswallt), 116, 124, 163, 181, 185, 228, 323.

Oswy, 117-118.

Owain ap Cadwgan, 172.

Owain ap Gruffudd ap Cynan, 176, 177.

Owain ap Hywel Dda, 148-9.

Owain Cyfeiliog, 179, 185, 193, 194, 209, 213.

Owain Glyndŵr, 26, 69, 84, 95, 117, 217, 231, 245, 257-271, 277, 282, 284, 287, 291, 292, 310, 311, 312, 323, 443.

Owain Gwynedd, 125, 175, 176, 179-187, 188, 193, 197, 205, 209, 210, 218, 255, 273.

Owain Lawgoch, 250-252, 255, 284, 318.

Owain Tudur, 272, 277, 278.

Owen, Bob (Croesor), 447.

Owen, Daniel, 41, 163, 374.

Owen, Edward, 146.

Owen, Goronwy, 339, 342.

Owen, Syr Hugh, 402.

Owen, Robert, 199, 355-6.

Padarn, St., 72, 91.

Patagonia, 100, 406.

Parry, John (Bardd Alaw), 379.

Parry, Joseph, 352.

Parry, R. Williams, 425.

Parry-Williams, T. H., 425.

Patrick, St., 43, 47, 64, 77, 85, 87.

Paulinus (Peulin), 83, 84, 90, 91, 92, 174.

Peblig, St., 82.

Pelagius, 61, 87, 104-5.

Pembroke (Penfro), 167, 169, 170, 171, 172, 173, 177, 189, 191, 196, 283, 290.

Pembrokeshire (Sir Benfro), 19, 21, 36, 42, 50, 59, 84, 92, 98, 100, 148, 152, 173, 178, 213, 320, 448.

Pencader, 155, 183, 192.

Penda, 116, 117, 118, 124.

Pengwern, 66, 98, 114.

Pennal, 35, 265, 266, 268.

Penmachno, 114.

Penmaen-mawr, 20.

Penrhyn Quarry Strike, 419.

Penry, John, 301.

Pentyrch, 423.

Perfeddwlad, 209, 211, 212, 221, 231, 238.

Phillips, Sir John, 328.

Phylip, Gruffudd, 314.

Picts, 35, 37, 63, 64, 65, 66, 69, 71, 85.

Pontypool, 358.

Pontypridd, 226, 325, 386.

Powell, David, 314.

Powell, Thomas, 146.

Powell, Vavasor, 321, 323.

Powys, 37, 53, 54, 59, 66, 71, 72, 96, 98, 109, 112, 114, 115, 124, 126, 132, 136, 138, 143, 149, *passim*, 263, 270, 287.

Powys Fadog, 193, 209, 229.

Powys Wenwynwyn, 209, 210, 229, 231.

Prestatyn, 181.

Price, Sir John, 314.

Price, Joseph Tregelles, 391.

Price, Richard, 324.

Price, Thomas (Carnhuanawc), 377, 379, 380, 381.

Prichard, Rhys, 323, 325.

Prys, Edmwnd, 315.

Pryse, Robert John (Gweirydd ap Rhys), 60, 146, 376.

Pugh, Philip, 334.

Pwllheli, 442.

Radnorshire (Sir Faesyfed), 119, 324, 349, see also Maesyfed.

Rebecca Riots, the, 356, 361, 363-5, 369, 373, 393, 409, 410.

Red Bandits of Mawddwy, see Gwylliaid.

Red Book of Hergest, see Llyfr Coch Hergest.

Rees, Dafydd (Llanelli), 365, 369.

Rees, Lewis (Llanbryn-mair), 334.

Rees, Thomas (Twm Carnabwth), 364, 365.

Rees, William (Gwilym Hiraethog), 105, 360, 376, 382.

Rendel, Stuart, 405.

Rheged, 117, 118, 119.

Rheinwg, 127.

Rhodri Mawr, 132, 133, 134, 135, 136-8, 140, 141, 149, 150, 153, 154, 157, 164, 252.

Rhodri Molwynog, 119, 125.

Rhondda, 22, 428, 448.

Rhos, 222.

Rhos & Rhufoniog, 163, 209.

Rhosllannerchrugog, 353.

Rhuddlan, 163, 169, 181, 186, 193, 212, 218, 231; Statute of, 238.

Rhun s. of Maelgwn Gwynedd, 75, 76.

Rhun s. of Urien Rheged, 76.

Rhuthun, 231, 259.

Rhydcymerau, 84.

Rhigyfarch, 91, 95, 152.

Rhys, the Lord (Rhys ap Gruffudd), 174, 176, 179, 180, 182, 183, 184, 185, 186, 187-97, 208, 210, 213, 216, 217, 220, 229.

Rhys ab Owain, 164, 166.

Rhys ap Gruffudd, 291, 292.

Rhys ap Maredudd, 239, 240.

Rhys ap Tewdwr, 164-5, 167, 172, 175, 177, 184, 188, 189, 200, 204, 255, 262.

Rhys ap Thomas, 272, 273, 284, 285, 291, 322.

Rhys Goch Eryri, 276.

Rhys Gryg, 212.

Rhŷs, John, 425.

Rhys, Morgan, 329.

Rhys, Morgan John, 342, 343.

Richard, Henry, 356, 368, 391, 392, 400.

Richards, Brinley, 379.

Robert of Rhuddlan, 163, 166, 167.

Robert, Gruffydd, 312.

Roberts, Bob (Tai'r Felin), 447.

Roberts, Ellis (Elis Wyn o Wyrfai), 378.

Roberts, John (Ieuan Gwyllt), 382, 383.

Roberts, R. Silyn, 426.

Roberts, Samuel (S. R.), 391, 392.

Roberts, T. F., 403.

Romans, 23, 24, 26, 27, 28, 30, 31, 34, 35, 36, 38, 39, 52, 53, 61, 63, 74, 76, 86, 108, 112, 130, 147, 161, 167, 169, 449.

Rowland, Daniel, 330, 332, 334, 335.

St. Asaph, 97, 181.
St. David's (Tyddewi), 138, 139, 152, 164, 165, 205, 217.
St. Fagan, 321, 416 (Folk Museum).
Salesbury, William, 301, 310, 311, 315.
Samson, St., 87, 89, 99, 100, 101.
Saxons, 36.
Scotch Cattle, 357.
Scotland, 15, 18, 34, 35, 44, 45, 46, 48, 50, 51, 53, 54, 68, 69, 75, 79, 82, passim, 242-4.
Scots, 16, 50.
Seisyllwg, 127, 137, 138, 141.
Senghennydd, 184.
Seren Gomer, 344, 356, 365, 382.
Shadrach, Azariah, 364.
Shrewsbury, 45, 161, 171.
Silurians, 25, 26, 58.
Simwnt Fychan, 311.
Siôn Cent, 287.
Siôn Dafydd Rhys, 312.
Sirhywi, 354, 422.
Stephens, Edward (Tanymarian), 383.
Stephens, Thomas, 352, 353, 377.
Strata Florida, 189, 197, 200, 216, 217, 218.
Strathclyde (Ystrad Clud), 47, 77, 79, 118, 122, 141, 143, 170, 242-3.
Suetonius Paulinus, 28, 29, 30.
Sulien, 152, 155, 164, 165.
Swansea (Abertawe), 132, 148, 169, 173, 176, 196, 212, 355.
Sycharth, 116, 255, 310.

Taliesin, 33, 47, 51, 53, 54, 55, 75, 76, 77, 288, 291.
Tal-y-llyn, 22.
Tathan, St., 84, 86, 91.
Tegeingl, 163, 174, 180, 181, 182, 185, 186, 209, 219, 273.

Teilo, 49, 83, 91, 92, 100, 120, 127.
Tenby (Dinbych y Pysgod), 152, 183, 268, 283.
Thomas, Alfred (Lord Pontypridd), 415.
Thomas, D. A. (Lord Rhondda), 416.
Thomas, Ebenezer (Eben Fardd), 395.
Thomas, Robert (Ap Vychan), 362.
Thomas, William (Islwyn), 41, 163, 378, 381.
Traethodydd, Y, 375.
Trahaearn, k. of Gwynedd, 1654-5, 167.
Trawsfynydd, 174.
Treachery of the Blue Books, 366-74, 416.
Tredegar, 354, 435.
Trefeca, 335.
Tryweryn, 446, 450.
Tudors, the, 143, 216, 373.
Tudur Aled, 245, 273, 274, 288, 310, 311.
Tysilio, St., 98, 114.

University of Wales, 402, 411.
Urien Rheged, 53, 54, 76, 77, 79, 97, 98, 109, 117, 133, 134, 237, 291.
Usk, 178.
Uthr Pendragon, 69

Vale of Clwyd (Dyffryn Clwyd), 163, 209.
Vale of Glamorgan (Bro Morgannwg), 73, 86, 87, 148, 184, 242, 236, 344, 423.
Valentine, Lewis, 440.
Vaughan, Sir John, 322.
Vaughan, Robert, Hengwrt, 314.
Venodotians, 25.
Vikings, 126-7, 301; see also Norsemen.

Vortigern (Gwrtheyrn), 37, 59, 60, 61, 62, 73, 83, 143.
Voteporix, 43, 47, 71, 93, 127.

Wallace, William, 242.
Welch Piety, 328.
Welsh Church, the, 120-23.
Welsh language, the, 42, 46, 49, 51, 52, 53, 55, 71, 88, 170, 192, 197, 198, 203, 356, 357, 360, 371, 373, 394.
'Welsh Not', 394, 396.
Welshpool, 263.
Wesley, John, 332, 333.
Wessex, 70, 136, 137, 138, 139, 141, 142, 148, 161.
Whitefield, George, 332, 333.
Whitland (Hendygwyn ar Daf), 144, 197, 364.
William the Conqueror, 45, 159, 162, 165.
Williams, D. J., 84, 440.
Williams, Griffith John, 344.
Williams, Hugh, 364, 365.
Williams, Jane (Ysgafell), 368, 379.
Williams, Archbishop John, 321.

Williams, Sir John, 423.
Williams, Llewelyn, 412, 416.
Williams, Maria Jane, 379.
Williams, Waldo, 168, 169.
Williams, Taliesin (Taliesin ab Iolo), 352, 353.
Williams, William (M.P.), 366, 367, 368.
Williams, William (o'r Wern), 362.
Williams, William (Pantycelyn), 92, 330, 332, 333, 334, 335-8, 345.
Williams, Zephaniah, 352, 359.
Winwaed Field, battle of, 117, 119.
Woodstock, 184, 219, 222.
Wrexham, 156, 163, 287, 320, 355, 360.
Wroth, William, 324.
Wynn, Sir John (Gwedir), 315.
Wynne, Elis, 306, 326.

Yale (Iâl), 126, 180, 181.
Yn y Llyvyr hwnn, 314.
Ystrad Marchell, 179.
Ystrad Tywi, 127, 137, 138, 139, 141, 155, 156, 166, 171, 172, 186, 210, 213, 221, 229, 241, 264.